Thinking Riding

Thinking Riding

BOOK 1
Training Student Instructors

by

MOLLY SIVEWRIGHT
F.I.H., F.B.H.S., F.A.B.R.S.

Illustrations by Christine Bousfield

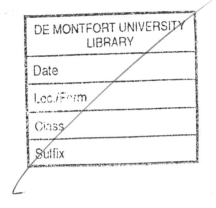
J. A. Allen
LONDON

British Library Cataloguing in Publication Data

Sivewright, Molly
   Thinking riding.
   1. Horsemanship – Study and teaching
   I. Title
   798′.2   SF310.5
   ISBN 0–85131–321–3

First published in 1979 by
J.A. Allen & Company Limited
1 Lower Grosvenor Place
London SW1W 0EL

Reprinted
1982
1986
1989
1992
1994

Printed in Hong Kong by
Dah Hua Printing Press Co. Ltd.

Foreword

Molly Sivewright's book *Thinking Riding* is more or less an image of the author herself. It reflects with an unwonted explicitness her idealism, enthusiasm and personal engagement in everything that concerns riding and teaching riding, in a world where the number of riders interested to learn and improve is perpetually increasing, while the number of instructors, 'who really know what it's all about', is getting relatively more and more scant.

For that reason her book, based on the wisdom of both past and present Masters of Equitation as well as on her own years of practical experience, is addressed mainly to the present teachers and instructors, in order to improve and widen their knowledge and capability to put riders of all ages, who seek for the truth, on the right – although not always the shortest – way as far as the basic riding, training and developing of horses are concerned.

The author's firm and courageous determination to include everything of permanent value when guiding riders and instructors, not the least as far as dressage is concerned, to keep to that right way, has brought her to the – in some circles probably quite provoking – unsealing and reinstatement of some movements and actions of great empirical value.

Thinking Riding is a book well deserving of an unreserved recommendation. But a solely superficial perusal would not be of much help. In order to draw the right conclusions the book must be read with due consideration, in other words the reader must be a 'thinking reader'.

GUSTAF NYBLÆUS
President of the F.E.I. Dressage Committee

To Charles

Contents

Introduction

Purposely the title of this book can convey two different meanings, dependent on which word is given emphasis; how it is read or said:

'Thinking *riding*' – conveys an informal flippancy whereas '*Thinking* riding' provokes a more profound approach to the whole subject.

If the former 'sporty' approach is transformed to the latter more thoughtful version, then this book will have served its purpose well.

Horses and the riding of them is becoming increasingly popular on a world-wide scale, and as a result there is a great need for good, well-trained and qualified riding instructors and staff capable of teaching new riders, of improving the present standard of the more experienced horsemen and of training and looking after horses and ponies.

The popular sport of riding can have wide and adventurous horizons, and may well have a profound effect on the participant's character, personality and, in fact his whole mental attitude to life in general. Riding horses, especially as a member of a class, or out of doors in the open countryside, teaches the pupil to look and plan ahead, it widens his views, and shows him, in the nicest possible way how to think of, for and with another living creature, after putting the horse's needs before his own. Already countries who regard riding as a rich capitalists' sport have had to change their views entirely and are recognizing that riding develops many human qualities which go towards the making of better citizens. Thus a policy of resentment has changed to one of encouragement, and instead of taxing riding schools out of business they are actually resuscitating and subsidizing them.

'A school is only as good as its instructors' is a true saying, but there is an acute shortage of trained and qualified instructors. Many of the world's famous cavalry schools have either closed down, lost their most experienced instructors, or their direction has changed to training competition horses and riders rather than to producing instructors.

So on one hand we have more people of all ages wanting to learn to ride, and on the other hand the list of good instructors which is diminishing at an alarming rate – the supply does not begin to meet the increasing demand, and this can be a dangerous situation for horses and riders alike.

To add to the problem, in this modern age of mechanical and scientific wonders, the majority of new riders have no background knowledge of horses.

9

Few of them have any idea of the ways and traditional practises of the countryside; the majority will have been born and raised in a town.

A present day riding instructor has additional responsibilities for he must teach his pupils a wide range of subjects, far beyond the obvious one of 'how to ride a horse'. Unless he learns to appreciate this need, his pupils will receive only meagre and superficial education, a mere scratching of the subject's surface. They will learn only how to stay on their horses' backs with a modicum of safety and comfort to themselves, remaining ignorant of the feelings, ways and well-being of the horses on whom they sit. It would be far better for the horses if these pupils were taught to ride bicycles instead. One obscure advantage to the present trend of rising prices and costs for horses is that it provides an economic and fairly secure safeguard against the exploitation and misuse of horses.

The British Horse Society has evolved an excellent scheme by means of which it encourages high standards of horsemastership and of equitation throughout the country. The first part is the BHS Approvals Scheme, whereby all member riding schools are inspected; their general standards of instruction and of horse and human care are assessed, and approved or not, according to their merits. The second and equally important part of the scheme is the BHS Examinations System which tests and raises the standards of stable management, riding, the training of horses and of the various grades of instructor, from the assistant instructor up to the more advanced general level required for the BHS Fellowship. The candidates attend the schools in order to learn how to look after horses and how to ride them. The schools prepare their riders for the tests which have been set by the Society's senior and most experienced and qualified equestrian experts who also lay out the guide lines for all examiners officiating on the official panel, and run courses and study and discussion days for instructors, examiners, and judges (of dressage, showing and even of legal matters too). Fortunately most British people have a strong competitive, creative streak in their natures, they like to take tests, the challenge excites their ambition, so they join the Society, take its tests and add to its strength. The British Horse Society also works in close cooperation with the Association of British Riding Schools whose main objective, as its title suggests, is to look after the interests of all its member schools. In these ways the British system of horsemanship is preserved and its doctrine and teaching is kept alive and in a flourishing state in a similar manner to the best-kept English garden. Its original plan is laid out on classical lines adapted to suit the national environment, climate, temperament and needs, it is then carefully tilled, weeded and re-stocked at each season of every year.

The British system of horsemanship has been in existence for many hundreds of years. It is based on a proud history of countless generations of British families who have worked with horses – on the fields, in the mines, carting, carrying, ploughing, jousting, hunting, racing. The labours, sports, pursuits, work and play in which British people have had a horse as a willing, vital partner are legion.

The thinking horsemen who worked horses developed a craft: the thinking riders developed an art – and the term 'classical equitation' evolved in this latter group.

'Classical equitation' is a term often loosely applied by writers or instructors in an effort to add weight to their own personal ideas or methods. However, used in its correct context it could be a useful term and for that reason it is worthy of consideration.

For any art form to qualify as 'classical' it must have passed the test of time; in most cases quality and elegance are also necessary and certainly these must apply to training methods and riding styles both on the flat and over fences – 'Does it work? and does it look right and good?'.

Classical equitation was founded by famous equestrian masters of the past and the same threads can be traced through to this day. The methods are based on a love of horses and the highest moral code of behaviour, of kindness, correction and reward, of communication leading to mental and physical harmony, and combined with a thoughtful building and development of confidence, strength and ability until perfect performance is achieved with no visible effort yet obvious mutual enjoyment.

Classical equitation goes with and even enhances Nature – it never goes against it. It is kept alive and vigorous by constant use and proof and continued earnest research, testing and proving, retaining only the best which is true, and rejecting that which is false or forced.

In order to safeguard classical equitation throughout the world, to prevent it from being misguided, misunderstood, misinterpreted, or from suffering from any similar negative downhill misdemeanours, the FEI, the only official international equestrian body, has appointed and elected the finest exponents of the art to write the rules and design competitions to keep the sport or art true, alive and of the very best quality. These officials set the dressage tests, design the jumping courses, train the judges and evaluate and advise the competitors, from whose ranks will be chosen future members of the FEI. Thus is classical equitation kept on a level and even an ascendant plane.

The British system of horsemanship has a long and interesting history. William Cavendish, the Duke of Newcastle, is our greatest claim to fame. As a scholar he studied on the continent and wrote his famous book 'A General System of Horsemanship' whilst in exile in 1665. It is a fascinating book written in an era of much strife, thought and change and was referred to and quoted and mis-quoted by subsequent masters up to the present day.

The various editions of the British Cavalry Manual of Horsemanship provide further intriguing fields for research and reveal the effect that wars, particularly the First World War, had on the methods of training British riders and horses, for, almost overnight our aim changed. From training on long-recognized classical lines for a classical end-product, we turned to quick-result methods to produce an unmatchable fighting force. Raw recruits and green remounts were transformed into efficient, disciplined and drilled cavalry squadrons, capable of swift manoeuvres and of charging and wheeling as one, using revolutionary training aids to overbalance the horses into canter so that they were bound to canter off with the chosen legs leading, and many other quick and forceful tactics were invented.

Field Marshal Haig's observation on the success of our changed war-time training methods, written at the British General Headquarters in 1918 explains the situation all too clearly. He wrote:

'The power of an army as a striking weapon depends on its mobility.

11

Mobility is largely dependant on the suitability and fitness of animals for army work.'

Unfortunately the later editions of the Cavalry Manuals were reprinted in their changed, unclassical form. They contained many strange, illogical and almost unnatural directives which were followed or even elaborated upon by other civilian authors during the post-war years.

When I was judging at Australia's International Equestrian Expo in 1975, in Adelaide, I was most impressed on three counts:

1 The quality of the horses and riders of the South Australian Mounted Police, and their musical ride which was the best, the most thrilling, I had ever seen, for the riders' aids were invisible and the horses' basic gaits were all so good. The grey horses were ridden in snaffles, with one hand (a lance was in the other hand), and they all went *forward*, calmly yet eagerly, working perfectly as a team, yet without a trace of dullness.

2 The square-dance performed by a hundred and sixty pony club riders, collected together for the first time ever for the opening ceremony. Ten riders to each chalk-marked circle, all weaving identical intricate patterns at the same time. A wonderful team yet each group's homes were literally thousands of miles apart.

3 Colonel Mike Ansell's almost uncanny ability to 'see' with other senses despite his total blindness. This was revealed by his summing-up of the Pony Clubs' performance. 'That was *wonderful* – and only one of those children made one small mistake.'

When I returned to Adelaide in 1977 I was delighted to find two of the South Australian Police Instructors were amongst the riders assembled on the lovely city parkland at the beginning of the course. I told them how impressed I had been by their musical-ride 2 years before, and asked whether they had any special training textbook. The next day I was given a small, carefully wrapped parcel – it was their equitation 'Bible'; it had 'never been allowed out of the barracks before, would I therefore take great care of it?' When, eventually, at the end of a hot sunny November day I reached the peace and quiet of my hotel suite, I unwrapped the precious package and there was a brass-bound British Cavalry Manual, of 1885. *This* was the foundation of such excellent training of horses and riders. With a mixture of pride, joy and exploration I read that little book – through to the small hours of the next morning. All its instructions were right up to date – and were so very much better and more classically correct than the later editions re-edited and reprinted in the 1930s. This confirmed the conclusion I had reached years before concerning the deflection of our classical equitation to military transport and manoeuvres.

In the late 1940s and the 1950s Colonel and Mrs V. D. S. Williams studied and sought and collected advice from British and international experts. This work was carried out while a course for selected riders and instructors was running at St George's School, the new National Equestrian Centre. At the end of the two 3-week courses they produced a British Manual for civilian riders and members of the Pony Club. The value of this little book has been unrivalled for many years and its worth has been recognized all over the world; certainly it has been translated into many different languages. It is written in a simple and direct form, its purpose being to provide a reminder and reference book for experienced horsemen and to introduce the subject to new 'equitators'. I was fortunate enough to work with the team which compiled this first basic British Manual, and found the research, arguments, discussions and final agreements fascinating. It really fired my interest and I have been on the working party of the official text books ever since – for over 30 years!

Now, nearly three decades later, three changes have come about. First, standards have risen, secondly there is a great demand for and interest in a wider and deeper knowledge of equitation, thirdly the demand for good and informed instruction exceeds the supply.

Riding schools and clubs are springing up all over the world in an endeavour to meet this demand, many in countries with little or no equitation background or training. I hope this book may bridge the gap, and prove to be of help to new schools of equitation, as well as to instructors and riders of all standards and ages – and their horses too – perhaps most of all.

General Notes for Instructors

1 Planning a school of equitation

First, the long-term objective must be selected and once this has been resolved it should be adhered to in all subsequent planning, in order that the school's work may be as progressive and productive as possible, with a positive goal.

Before embarking on such a project many factors must be considered such as the location, local amenities and attractions, existing buildings and facilities, and above all – does it appeal? Does it feel right?

I must confess, at this point, that when our respective parents first saw our 'nap selection' – Church Farm, Siddington, just outside Cirencester in Gloucestershire, they thought we had taken leave of our senses. That we should be leaving the security of a life with the British Army for a very uncertain future in an almost derelict farm seemed quite incomprehensible. But then they had seen it on a damp, foggy November day, when there were two workmen in woolly hats 'patching up' the farmhouse roof, and had noted the Victorian wallpaper hanging off the interior walls in shrouds, and the one and only tap below the hand-pump in the scullery, which together with two 'places' back-to-back in the garden, formed the sum total of the plumbing system. They failed to find the exterior any more inspiring for that comprised sodden laurel over-growing vigorously, as were nettles and brambles, and a sea of mud lay under foot.

My husband and I have always loved the Cotswold countryside and although the farm itself was 'nearly derelict' it had great charm and the ancient tithe barns gave it a wonderful feel of history, permanency, and of the close proximity of the church; to us it seemed absolutely right. We donned our denims and set to work to put it in order – the sketch-maps on pp. 16 and 17 give an outline of how Talland has been built up over the past 20 years.

WHERE TO START

Apart from the obvious requirements of size, structure, security, light, ventilation and drainage, the main guide lines concerning the buildings required for a School of Equitation may be summarized as follows:

Select and keep the eventual objective clearly in mind.

Make the best of the buildings which already exist – if they are old or even

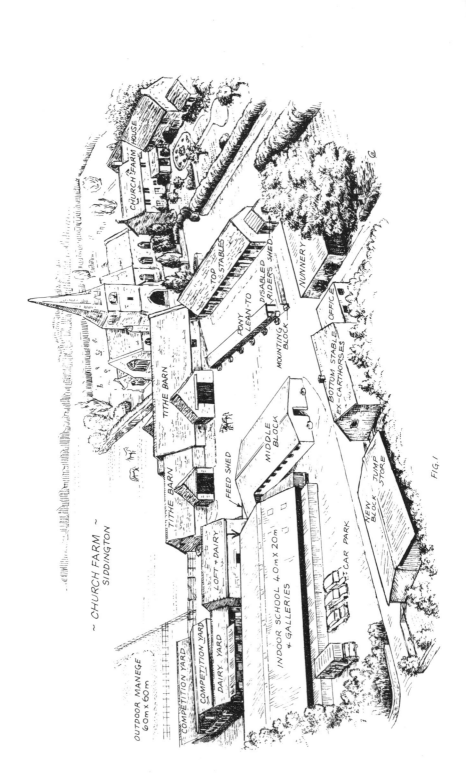

~ CHURCH FARM ~
SIDDINGTON

OUTDOOR MANEGE 60m x 60m
COMPETITION YARD
COMPETITION YARD
DAIRY YARD
LOFT + DAIRY
FEED SHED
TITHE BARN
TITHE BARN
CHURCH FARM HOUSE
TOP STABLES
PONY LEAN-TO
DISABLED RIDER'S SHED
MOUNTING BLOCK
MIDDLE BLOCK
INDOOR SCHOOL 40m x 20m + GALLERIES
CAR PARK
NUNNERY
BOTTOM STABLE OFFICE EX-CARTHORSES
NEW BLOCK
JUMP STORE

FIG.1

16

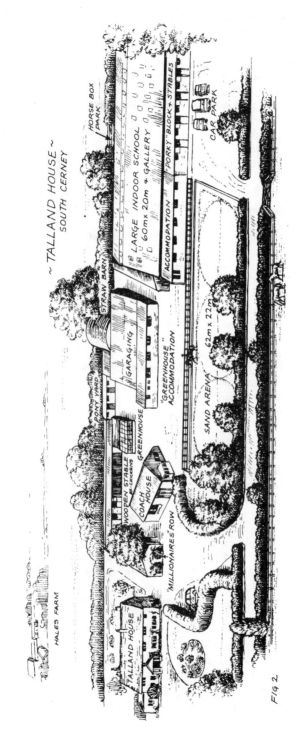

~ TALLAND HOUSE ~
SOUTH CERNEY

HALES FARM

HORSE BOX PARK

STRAW BARN

PONY YARD

GARAGING

"GREENHOUSE" ACCOMMODATION

LARGE INDOOR SCHOOL
60m x 20m + GALLERY

ACCOMMODATION

"PORKY" BLOCK + STABLES

CAR PARK

WOODEN STABLE & CHICKENS

GREENHOUSE

COACH HOUSE

"MILLIONAIRES' ROW"

SAND ARENA
62m x 22m

TALLAND HOUSE

FIG 2

17

ancient they will give the whole establishment a precious sense of history and of belonging, they will contribute much to its 'soul'.

Always envisage the whole concept before making any alteration or addition.

Think very carefully before erecting new buildings.

Think big enough – cost and space wise.

Weigh up all possible ways, means, permutations and purposes.

Leave adjacent ground-space for further extension or additional buildings.

Draw the plan, walk it, ponder it – and sleep on it, before going ahead.

Do not be greedy; quality should be the goal rather than quantity; Student instructors need care, guidance and personal attention, they cannot be mass-produced – this maxim also applies to the school's horses and all pupils, young and old.

Start in a small way – *little and good* – and then keep the standards *high*.

Besides the basic necessities of:

A house – a home, including living accommodation for instructors and students.

All main services – water, electricity, drains, buses, shops and so on.

Stabling – in buildings which are sound, warm and airy.

Land – well fenced, watered, sheltered and kept in good heart.

Enclosed schooling areas with good footing and safe fencing. A small enclosed area is essential for children, beginners and young horses for SAFETY.

An office – which is central, pleasant to work in, secure, efficiently equipped including a first-aid box and directives.

A lecture room – warm, well-lit, containing useful samples of bits, shoes, bones, etc. diagrams and a blackboard.

Appropriate, secure, dry and well-lit storage-space for: saddlery, rugs and equipment, fodder, including hay and straw, poles, cavalletti and fence-building material.

One or more manure heaps – strategically placed, for storage, near enough but not too near stables (flies); and for carting. These should always be squared-off, and tidily kept.

Rubbish disposal – all rubbish should have suitable containers which are regularly emptied and cleaned.

Lavatories for yard workers and non-residents.

A car and lorry-park – near to the entrance, so that motor cars are not moving around in the stable-yard amongst horses and children.

A loading place for horseboxes – with non-slippery footing.

Fire extinguishers, and fire precautions and rules clearly displayed.

Mounting-block(s).

An implement shed – containing the vital tractor and its various, invaluable attachments.

A workshop.

Extra water reserve in case of fire. We found one of these quite by chance at Church Farm when the off hind wheel of the corn-merchant's lorry quietly sank through the top of the cindered-incline we use for loading young horses into a trailer – it had found us a wide, deep underground water-tank which now has a metal cover – it is always full even in drought-conditions.

The following should be added as circumstances and finance permit:

An indoor school.

Outdoor manèges.

A jumping lane.

Further human comfort and convenience rooms.

THE HORSES

The horses and their equipment must be as good as money can buy. It is only possible to teach potential instructors and to improve riders on good quality horses. The horses must be sound, they must move well, having three good basic gaits, they must be well trained and they should have no major defects in their conformation. In fact, ideally, every horse a school possesses should be capable of being in the ribbons, or of winning a rosette at a local show, in a dressage test, and in a riding horse class, as well as having a clear round over show jumping or hunter trial fences.

To purchase a sizeable number of these equine paragons would need the backing of a millionaire – and although a principal of a school of equitation is usually a dedicated idealist, he rarely has a bottomless bank account, so what is he to do? There are three courses open to him:

1 He buys 'ready-made' horses of inferior quality – with the obvious disadvantage that a common horse is rarely a good mover and often has a sluggish if not unwilling disposition.

2 He buys some young mares who are thoroughbred or nearly so, with good bone and substance, and who display an easy co-operation, and breeds from them using the HIS stallion scheme. This is a good back-up plan but is probably too lengthy a procedure to provide the main source of supply.

3 He buys young, untrained, spoilt or problem horses who can be trained or retrained by the school's instructors. This is surely the best plan, for the price is usually realistic and all parties benefit to the maximum. The vendors have the purchase price rather than the problem, the school has a horse and a challenge, and the horse may well benefit most of all, providing that the school's training is correct.

Regardless of how picturesque or modern, salubrious and well-maintained is the stable-yard, or how extensive the acreage, it is the instruction provided that gives a school of equitation its reputation. 'A school can only be as good as the quality of its teaching.'

The school's principals and the chief instructor must select their team of instructors with great care. Ideally they should all have trained at the school so that they are thoroughly conversant with each and every facet and stage of the system taught – they will then not only understand the methods but they will believe in them, and thus their teaching will have the full impact of sincerity. A school which produces all its own instructors can be assured of a high standard of loyalty as well as first-class instruction and a vital team-spirit pervading the whole school.

However qualified, experienced and senior his instructors may be the chief instructor must always continue to have their welfare at heart; if he fails them in this, they may well fail him by becoming stale and uninspiring in their teaching.

19

The school's tuition must be carefully considered from every aspect whilst retaining the main objective.

The plan – This must be clearly set out and must explore and cover every aspect including:

The farming programme, housing, stabling, fodder, facilities, improvements and maintenance.

The type of pupil to be trained and for what purpose; this will depend largely on the chosen interest of the school's principals and/or its chief instructor.

The type of horse required. External, novice riders will need reliable, hardy types; residential career-students will need horses with more quality to give them a correct feel for the required gaits and form. (Unfortunately the cost of the upkeep of the latter is far greater.)

The syllabus – outlines the content and scope of instruction within the school. The syllabus should combine correct basic principles with qualified specialization, and flexibility combined with efficiency. Differing course-purposes require tailor-made syllabii.

The programme – termly, monthly or weekly programmes, listing important events, lectures and lessons in chronological order. It will give a general picture of the pattern of each rider's work, indoor, outdoor, theory carefully measured in proportion to the respective requirement. The yearly wall-chart must be referred to and be meticulously kept up to date.

The timetable – gives a clear picture of each day's activity, lesson or lecture, its time and place, and horse and instructor details. There should be several copies of this timetable, displayed on the various notice-boards and in the office. Any revisions must be entered on all lists, otherwise – 'Order, and counter-order equals *dis*-order'.

No instructor can afford to be jealous, narrow-minded or restrictive; neither must he be complacent or indolent. The chief instructor should encourage his instructors and pupils to attend outside lectures, and to take notes at visiting instructors' courses. Naturally all consequent discussions must be constructive and never destructive; that is a basic moral code. He must suggest books to read and diagrams to draw – even if the latter efforts do not exactly resemble the original, at least the students will have gained a better understanding due to their personal industry.

All this extra-curriculum work is vitally important to the breadth and depth of every instructor's career; be he young, old, novice or experienced, if the chief instructor does not lead him into exploration of wider fields, no one else will.

The chief instructor has an urgent responsibility to keep himself up to date so that, having directed his instructors' researches, he may then give them thoroughly sound advice and leadership during the ensuing discussions. He must also delegate responsibility and then check periodically that those with delegated duties are carrying them out satisfactorily.

The instructors in their turn must set simple homework for their pupils, and they will reap great rewards themselves when, for instance, a group of small children proudly produce their 'master pieces' at their next riding lesson. The drawn horses on which the points are indicated may not win prizes in a conformation class but each one is a heart-warming proof of endeavour.

20

Instructors, and especially the chief instructor, must not allow themselves to be harassed by the pressure of modern life whose tempo becomes more hectic every day. He must guard against becoming a veritable pressure cooker, he must communicate, be seen to communicate and be appreciated as someone with whom his pupils can communicate. A little flexibility will often relieve the pressure, or even extra work or concentration on some other creative project – preferably one which helps someone else's lot, will prove to be a constructive safety valve.

Time for relaxation, days off, and periodical holidays are essential for the recharging of every instructor's batteries. There is much truth in the saying that 'a change is as good as a rest', and going away to another area or even abroad to give Courses can prove to be refreshing, invigorating and stimulating.

Most instructors are notoriously bad at asking for time off; they become too involved in the school's work, its pupils and horses, to want to leave it even for a short spell. The chief instructor must be fair and firm, insisting that they take the holiday due to them, and explaining that everyone will benefit from the revitalization provided by the enforced rest.

THE PUPILS

This section is difficult to start and quite impossible to finish – the range, scope and horizons are limitless. That last word could be a key word, for a school of equitation should have almost no limits to the pupils it accepts – the only exceptions should be those who cannot accept and abide by the school's rules and code of behaviour, but even these should be warned and given a second chance, even if only a short one!

Beginners, would-be riders with physical handicaps, nervous riders, aggressive riders, humble riders or haughty riders, all have a place in a school of equitation and will in their turn make a contribution to it. Whereas keen enthusiasm is a heart-warming quality, the less-keen can also present an interesting challenge. All pupils have potential, it is up to the school's instructors to develop it by encouragement, example and tuition. Sometimes the more nervous, diffident child who comes from a family with no experience of horses or even country life can develop into the brightest of stars.

Perhaps a word here about parents would not come amiss. For our purpose I would divide them into two main categories, i.e.

1 *The helpful* – they encourage, and lead or give support when it is needed; they teach their children how to behave with thought, consideration and respect for others; and above all they are young at heart and can feel how their offspring feel, and appreciate and respect their reactions.

2 *The harmful* – interfering, overbearing, overambitious parents sometimes even selfishly hoping for personal glorification through their children's successes in the form of rosettes, prizes and certificates. They may even be supercilious concerning their child's *need* to learn – a strong force in children of all ages, unless it is quashed at an early age. Unfortunately some hunting parents hold the opinion that their children can ride – they have been hunting since they were 6 years old – they don't need *lessons*! That is very sad, for often this is yet another potential rider lost on the scrapheap of waste material.

21

I remember well the words of a famous West Country pony club district commissioner – 'Parents – they're a menace! At camp all parents should be put in the horse-trough!' I think she must have had some particularly difficult characters to cope with. Personally I prefer the maxim, 'parents have their uses' – a typically British understatement! Most parents are wonderfully helpful, giving invaluable guidance and support, just when it is most needed. One of the finest horsemasters I have encountered was a parent of a member of our pony club team; his *care* of and for his son's horse was a joy to watch – he also happened to be a master of foxhounds. He had bred and trained the horse himself, and thanks to his loving care and attention, that same horse was still as sound as a bell and looking superb when at 20 years old, he was being hunted for short days by the master's daughter.

2 The chief instructor, his leadership and team

LEADERSHIP

'It is almost a truism to say that he who would control others must control himself. He must have a quieter and more impartial mind than those whom he would restore. He must not either command or reprove until he is fully acquainted with all the circumstances of the case. He must convey the impression that he will listen to the voice of reason only, and not be moved by entreaties, that he remembers and does not forget, and that he observes more than he says. He must know the characters of those with whom he deals; he must show that he has a regard for their feelings when he is correcting or reproving them. The great art is to mingle authority with kindness; there are a few, but a very few, who by some happy tact have contrived so to rebuke another as to make him their friend for life.

Thus in the exercise of authority there must be a basis of kindness and good-will but many other qualities are also required in those who would influence or control others. Perhaps there must be a degree of reserve, for the world is governed, not by many words, but by a few; and nothing is more inconsistent with the real exercise of power than rash and inconsiderate talking. We are not right in communicating to others every chance thought that may arise in our minds about ourselves or about them. There is a noble reserve which prevents us from intruding on the feelings of others, and sometimes refrain from asking for their sympathy or approbation. Dignity and self-respect are the natural accompaniments of authority, and the essence of dignity is simplicity. We must banish the thought of self, how we look, what effect we produce, what is the opinion of others about our sayings and doings; these only paralyse us at the time of action. We want to be, and not to seem, to think only of the duty which we have in hand to be indifferent to the world around. We want to see things in their proper proportions; not to be fidgety or uneasy about trifles, not to be greatly disturbed about any of those evils which lightly pass away and are cured by time.'

From a sermon

BENJAMIN JOWETT, 1817–1893
Master of Balliol College
Regius Professor of Greek at Oxford University

That human beings will all have a correct mental approach when they embark on the responsible task of training others for a successful future career is often taken for granted or totally overlooked. In fact, the mind requires just as much training and self-discipline as does the body.

Whether instructors are aspiring to train humans or horses, they must first develop a correct mental attitude themselves; this is even more important than developing a correct physical attitude, position, on or off a horse – and heaven knows that is important enough!

The Spanish Riding School has a good directive which says, 'Every rider must not only ride but must also think, as only a thinking rider will be able to attain his goal in a relatively short time without spoiling his horse.'

'*Calm, forward* and *straight*' is General L'Holte's famous motto and excellent it is. All three of these qualities have much value in their own right, but it is in the combination of all three together that their true worth lies; and this in turn is doubled to its full strength only if both the mental and physical aspects of the motto are given due consideration:

Calm: a calmness of mind removes excess tension from the body and enables the owner of the calm mind to transmit and to receive ideas and influences with ease, to sort them for his own use.

Under difficulties or duress much self-restraint and discipline is needed to retain a calm mind; this is equally important when communicating with a highly strung pupil or a sensitive horse. It is quite possible to transmit calm providing the main supply is staunch enough.

Good equestrian work can never result from a tense mind nor excess physical tension.

Patience, logic and confidence often provide vital supports when calm is being sorely tried. For example, if a horse baulks at a new exercise in his training, it is always far better to stop rather than to join battle. During the ensuing pause the trainer should ask himself 'How can I re-present the exercise so that the horse will understand it better and so that it will be easy and comfortable for him to perform it?' and he will call on his own past training and his feel to provide the solution. Thus the all important calm is restored and with the next attempt the required movement will inevitably 'happen' with incredible ease.

Many riders produce work in a competition which is far below the standard of their work at home. Naturally this is very disappointing for them. Of course the tense atmosphere of the show or event itself may be a contributory factor, but quite often the cause may be found within the rider himself, and it may be quite simply that he forgets to breathe. Excess tension, trying too hard to do one's best, or worse, anticipation of meeting every disaster in the book, will make free, deep breathing impossible for the rider. This constraint will be transmitted instantly to the horse whose performance and gaits will deteriorate at once. Therefore to any rider who encounters unexpected difficulties every time he competes I would say, 'remember to breathe deeply and well through-out your round in the show-jumping or dressage arena.' In the latter case, humming a melody (quietly!) while entering the arena can be a help, and if your smile saying 'Good morning, Thank you for your time and trouble' to the judge, meets with a friendly acknowledgement then it is so much easier to 'Proceed in trot' (working or collected) and to ride the remainder of the test feeling that 'God's in His Heaven, all's right with the world,' breathing freely – and with a calm mind. If the brain and heart are starved of oxygen they cannot remain calm! This is a basic fact which is well worth remembering and passing on to pupils.

Forward and straight: these speak for themselves, from the mental and physical aspects – both must be foremost in our minds, and both qualities must be carried out in all our work.

Think forward and straight; go forward and straight, always with a lively impulsion contained by a confident calm.

Tact, kindness, and humour sensibly mixed form an essential lubricant to life; of these qualities tact is the most obscure. The source of the word is the Latin – *tactus* – to touch, and it is used as a measure of the special ability to 'touch' people, mentally rather than physically; a perceptive sensibility to their feelings and probable reactions. Tact provides the knowledge of what to say when difficult human problems or situations arise whereby they may be solved with immediate effect or turned to good account without causing affront or offence.

Although some people are more gifted naturally, and others may be guaranteed to 'put their foot in it', and rub people up the wrong way, tact may be developed, in the latter cases tactfully!

There is a risk that instructors, most of whom are perfectionists at heart, may give orders or commands which are unnecessarily harsh, loud or abrupt; they are so absorbed, and intent on the end result that they forget their pupils' sensibilities and override them rough-shod. There is no need for a continual stream of commands in a riding school, in fact, a shout should be reserved for the occasional emergency. Often a hint or suggestion will have a far better result, especially if it follows a clear, quietly spoken explanation.

Tact will also provide an essential measure to the amount and type of correction to be of maximum benefit to the pupil at that moment. For example, it would be tactless folly to try to change riders' style and method a month or so before a major competition, for to do so could easily destroy their flair and confidence, whereas helpful suggestions of improvement to their present method will prove both beneficial and to their performance and ego.

The discipline of the mind must contain *tenacious concentration*, elastically woven from kind, patient thoughts, not from overbearing, aggressive drives. This power of concentration – mind to mind with the pupil or horse, is not born overnight but may be developed during the years. Its effect and strength is easily demonstrated by any good trainer when he is working his horse in hand in an utterly quiet indoor school. Of horse and rider, the horse is the most readily receptive and therefore provides a better demonstration because his mind is acutely sensitive, and it is straightforward – his 'receiver' is not jammed with the complex mental hang-ups which often confuse the rider's mind and impede direct transmission through the lines of communication.

Young riders should be taught to think of and with their ponies as soon as they start to ride; they must be taught to concentrate, not only on where but also how their pony-companion is feeling, mentally and physically. Certainly an emphasis of this form of communication will do more than any other

24

training guide line to ensure happy, forward-going school horses. A horse has incredible sensitivity which is so often abused by lack of appreciation, when he is regarded as a rider's machine rather than an ever-willing partner with an undauntable desire to please.

Instructors must be careful that their strength of will is used in a correct way with regard to the students and pupils they teach and the horses they train. It is all too easy for a strong-willed person to dictate and dominate but this is no way to train humans nor animals. A truly great instructor will lead, guide, inspire and influence by sincere and subtle means which allow his pupils the opportunity to imitate, think, question, reason and judge, and eventually to follow their instructors' example because they believe in his ways and methods implicitly, and have been given the freedom, encouragement and responsibility to develop their own personality and confidence in their own judgment and ability. For example, if a pupil is riding in a competition, although the presence of his instructor will be of undoubted psychological assistance, he should be able to compete just as well and put up an equally good performance without assistance. All riders should have been taught how to ride-in, to prepare themselves and their horses for a competition to the best possible advantage, effectively, stylishly, with careful consideration of and for their horses and courtesy to the event's organizers and their fellow competitors.

Thus all pupils, human and equine should reflect their training in their way of thinking and going – 'Calm, *forward* and *straight*'.

3 Planning the courses

The efficiency and value of a course will depend a great deal on the amount of thought, expertise and planning put into the designing of the syllabus and its day to day programme.

A course may be of any length from two or three days to a lifetime. Each course must be compiled and tailored to suit its ultimate aim, e.g. an examination or a competition, overcoming horse or rider problems, or general education and improvement. All the different time-periods within the course must be worked out with equal care, consideration and balance.

The four seasons of the year, each month, each week and each day must all be considered and blended, so that they complement each other. The general work of the school, or each ride, and of individual horses and riders must all be weighed up separately and together as a whole before the best plan can be resolved and the syllabii set.

Pupils should be divided into rides, each ride having its own instructor who is responsible for ensuring that all his pupils cover the syllabus and attain the standard set. Each instructor should work with his ride as often as possible so that he may teach them the skill of their craft in the stables, their handling of horses and people as well as in equitation. He must watch that the horses allotted to his pupils are suitable for the advancement of both the rider and the horse and must make suitable exchanges if any are incompatible. He must report any such change to the chief instructor.

The chief instructor must have regular meetings with his instructors to check progress, to see if his support is needed in an advisory or disciplinary capacity, to organize an interchange of instructors for individual lectures, demonstrations or practical sessions, to arrange informal competitions and assessments. He will allot lesson times, schooling areas, lecture-rooms and other facilities. The chief instructor will relate and discuss the principals' farming, grazing, worming and maintenance plans. He will invite, receive and discuss any suggestions his instructing-team may have to offer, and should make detailed enquiries into the welfare of each and every horse and pupil in the school's care. These instructors' meetings are an integral part of every school of equitation; all such meetings should advance the instructors' education as well as strengthen the bonds of purpose and unity throughout the whole school.

Courses, the syllabii, and their daily programmes should be adhered to but must also be flexible – readily adapted to suit special circumstances and to accept unexpected opportunities.

When the chief instructor is working out his syllabii he must plan a gradual increase in the demands of the work so that there is a constructive and progressive build-up, specially tailored to accommodate all individual requirements. Visits to studs, competitions or places of equestrian or general cultural interest broaden and freshen-up the pupils' minds as well as providing an ease in the horses' work-schedule; the variety provided by these occasions is of inestimable value to all concerned.

Lessons missed due to absence at competitions, hunting, illness or some other reason, must be made up by an extra lesson or by condensed repetition at the beginning of the next lesson.

The equitation training programmes of riding pupils, student-instructors, and horses should always consist of three parts:

   i Riding in an indoor school or enclosed manège.
   ii Riding over fences.
   iii Independent confirming work, riding in the open, across country, etc.

Of these, the first basic training takes place in an enclosed school, and over small fences; the third component, the independent work to confirm lessons previously learnt, are best carried out in the open, so that even a simple instructional hack is of inestimable value, giving time for thought and feel and extra guidance or help if required. Every week's programme should include riding out of doors, not only to provide variety but also the opportunity for practical application in relaxed surroundings and at a slow tempo. Thus there must always be a sensible balance and combination between school-riding, jumping and riding in the open; all three are essential to the production of a good horseman and a well-trained horse which is a pleasant ride.

In whichever of the three phases the instructors are working their classes, even on a short, concentrated course, the emphasis must always be on teaching simply, the correct techniques and encouraging a feel for balance and rhythm rather than relying on an increase of demand and pace, thrills and spills to fill up the lesson period. Instructors must also have the preservation of the horses' mental and physical form, of their basic gaits, their mouths and their schooling high on their list of priorities throughout every lesson of every course.

During the inclement weather of the winter months, the instructor must remember to include work out of doors, and similarly in the warm summer months, school-work must not be neglected.

26

Where an equitation school has one or more indoor schools, the chief instructor must be sure to include work out of doors at least twice a week for all horses, and to use both schools for all rides. This exchanging has another more subtle advantage, if the two schools are well separated – at Talland they are over a mile apart – an interchange of indoor schools provides added variety of surroundings, it also ensures a unity rather than a separation and an unpleasant rivalry between the instructors and their rides. On the other hand team competitions will always stimulate interest, progress and even rivalry of the right sort.

4 Student-instructors

A career or a life with horses? Usually they are one and the same, for the equine species tends to be extraordinarily time and interest consuming. Although there is an endless list of specialist and non-specialist jobs available, the scope of a riding instructor's career is boundless for he should be a jack-of-all-trades and a master of them all! Besides being a skilled rider he must be dexterous in his work with horses both in the stable and outside. Pupils and horses must thrive in his care. All this proficiency will only come about with *training*, *practice* and *experience*.

Before any young person decides to embark on a course of training to qualify as an equitation instructor he or she must embark on some serious heart and soul searching. A career with horses will not necessarily be a glamorous one – far from it, invariably it involves a great deal of very hard work, providing a never-ending test of mental and physical strength and stamina. Besides enthusiasm and all the other necessary qualities listed later, a student-instructor will need a bottomless supply of energy and resilience.

When the arduous training is completed, the hard work continues and the responsibilities increase. Although instructing can be deeply and richly rewarding – to the heart more than the pocket! – it can also be severely demanding.

The instructor's tasks and responsibilities and the difficulties of the judgments and corrections are multiplied and magnified automatically by the fact that the pupils are human as well as equine, and many varieties of temperament within all age-groups will have to be coaxed and cajoled into improvement in both species. That 'instructing is an art and not an exact science' is a very true statement.

The chief instructor and his team are responsible for the training of all the junior instructors whose potential must be developed at every possible opportunity. As with a beginner rider the young instructor needs encouragement and careful training from the start.

Many student-instructors are young people, coming straight from school, in which case the transition from a school pupil to an assistant instructor is often a far greater step than they or their parents envisage.

The formal lessons in the classroom and organized school-homework are replaced by a teacher–college aspect where the student is expected to carry out much research for himself.

In some ways a teacher college has a less complex structure than a school of

27

equitation which trains instructors, for at the latter in addition to the study periods or lessons there are many and varied practical sessions in the stables, the tack-rooms, the yard, and out on the farm, or whatever land the school may have, and also there are real, live pupils to be met and helped.

Owing to sharply rising costs, and matching fees, the preparatory courses are necessarily very short in comparison with any other career-courses, therefore they are also very concentrated. As well as acquiring a wide field of basic knowledge and compiling their notebooks, the students also have to learn to become members of an adult world, and to develop the ability to impart their knowledge to others. They have to learn to be responsible citizens and to think about and acquire the qualities mentioned in a later chapter – certainly the mere contemplation of such a great transition, if not transformation, in so limited a time would be an overwhelming Herculean task if there were not, from the very first day, a tremendous bond of willing co-operation between the instructors and the students.

It is imperative that the chief instructor makes out a sound syllabus with a work-programme for each course which ensures that all the important, fundamental principles of equitation and stable management are covered in lessons and lectures, practical demonstrations, and supervised application within the first month.

During this time, the student-instructors should be encouraged to ask questions, to phrase and project them clearly, and to give 2–5 minute lecturettes and simple demonstrations on the work they have been taught; this confirms that they have understood and learned the lessons and triggers off a build-up of confidence in talking in front of a group of people. They should also practise school-commands and figures, and will soon overcome their natural self-consciousness if their first efforts at instructing practice are given by individuals in turn, the whole ride being on foot in a quarter of the arena with the markers rearranged appropriately.

The students should be given lectures on training young horses and should be taught how to handle and use lungeing equipment. If the school possesses some ponies these are excellent for the purpose of teaching students how to lunge, for they are quick-witted, usually need extra work before being ridden by young or disabled children and will not be damaged by small circles as will a big horse. As soon as the students are sufficently proficient they may learn to lunge each other.

Although, at first each student is allotted a horse or a share of a horse whose ways and movements he will get to know and understand and who will help him during riding lessons to improve his riding, later in the course, and over a period of time, pupils should be given the opportunity to learn from many different horses, each one of whom will teach some new and extra facet, of temperament or of his way of moving. For example:

A sluggish horse will help to develop positive, effective forward-driving aids, combined with tact, and reward for improved responsiveness.

A 'hot', impatient, or nervous horse will improve the rider's feel, anticipation and his patience, as well as the harmony of his aids, the speed of his thinking and trained reactions, and how to mete out firm but fair control.

An independent, inattentive horse will need a rider who has a cool but well-tuned perception to instil calm concentration into the horse's mind as well as a strong seat and effective influences.

A young horse will need a good, patient and sensitive rider who will give him confidence as he learns new work, and whose horsemanship is correct and easy for the young horse to understand, follow and enjoy.

A school's horses should not all be paragons of virtue; pupils must be given the opportunity to ride badly trained horses, i.e. those who are nappy, who are timid, stubborn, or even malicious; those who buck, rear or refuse to jump. When riders are sufficiently experienced, secure and correct in their riding, they must be taught how to manage these difficult horses and how to retrain them by patient research, intelligent correction and reward, so that ultimately a better future is assured for all these horses.

All great instructors agree that the horse is the best schoolmaster. The late Brigadier Friedberger used to tell the following Irish tale to illustrate this point.

'Mickey was an Irishman who had a great way with horses. They came to hand and prospered under his guidance; In the terms of sixty years ago he was a great nagsman. At schooling horses he was a craftsman; they went well for him and were always beautifully balanced. Active they were, and graceful, but never "busy" – nor fussy, neither he nor his horse. "What is your system, Mickey?" asked an owner, "How do you *know* so well what to do next?" "Sure, your honour," said Mickey, "the horse tells me."' This tale has a good moral for riders, trainers and instructors alike.

Children's classes of all standards, and beginners' lessons are extremely important subjects on their own, and students should be taken to watch and later to help at as many of these as possible; they cannot have too much practical experience in this field.

Instructors should also grasp every opportunity to take their students to listen to and watch more advanced lessons to aid their understanding and to illustrate further the aims which they are striving to achieve.

As often as possible groups of students should be taken to assist at Pony Club rallies, horse shows, and competitions to widen their practical knowledge. Also they should be taught how to assist as jump-stewards, when they will learn how to build jumps correctly: giving due regard to the track at approach and on landing and rules of construction, with particular regard to safety. Later they will find this work in the arena with the instructor to be of great value, giving them a first hand insight into the building of a course of jumps, teaching them to appreciate the track between the fences, how the terrain, footing and pace affect related fences, and how rider and horse problems may be solved and their performance improved. Students should also be taught how to teach juniors to re-erect jumps accurately, safely and quickly when the jumps have been knocked down, without disturbing horses, riders or the instructor as they do so. All these things should be explained and shown in a patiently helpful way, rather than by shouting reprimands to correct a mistake. These jump-stewards soon come to take a pride in forming a quick, quiet and efficient ring-party.

Gradually, as their knowledge and confidence develop, student-instructors should be led to an increase in demand, through a logical progression, until they may be entrusted to teach short but complete parts of any one of the beginner-rider lessons with supervision but without aid or interruption. Later, as their confidence, ability and experience improve, they will be allowed to give complete lessons, then to run a course for a group of pupils – after which 'rundle by rundle,' and . . . the world is their oyster!

5 Qualities of an instructor

Although it is a common belief that 'a good instructor is born and not made', and that a person has to have 'a gift for instructing', this is not true. Sometimes this viewpoint may be offered as a convenient excuse for not taking a ride, but that is another matter!

There are many horse-people or enthusiasts who have quaked in their boots when it was first suggested that they give one or two basic commands to a group of riders, and who, as their confidence increased, made really *good* teachers.

From the first the following points should be explained and discussed, not so that they can become a paragon overnight, but so that little by little and steadfastly they can climb the instructing ladder . . .

Besides the obvious practicalities of excellent health, above-average physical strength and dauntless tenacity and reserves of endurance, an aspiring instructor must contemplate, develop and amass the following qualities:

1 *Sincerity* and *integrity.*

2 *A love and understanding* of humans and horses – imparting CONFIDENCE to both.

3 *Responsibility* – a conscience – CARING – a need to HELP.

4 *Observation* – keen and trained; noting the overall picture as well as minute details – open eyes backed by an open mind.

5 An intense *interest* in all aspects of equitation, the driving force, or . . . *dedication.* A genuine interest in every individual.

6 *Self-control* – enabling the instructor to discipline others as well as himself.

7 *Reliability* – stemming from conscientiousness and common sense.

8 A helpful *manner,* and courteous manners.

9 *Humanity* – sympathy, tolerance, tact; the ability to feel exactly what others are feeling and to communicate. An understanding of the psychology of horses and riders.

10 *Leadership with authority and diplomacy* – a strong personality, which inspires confidence and commands *respect* and control without noisy disturbance (shouting), yet being open-minded, without obstinacy or vanity. Certainly give a 'rocket' if it is deserved, but wipe the slate clean immediately afterwards; do not 'go on' about it and never allow a black mood to develop.

Although the instructor must never lose his temper, there are occasions when a dull and unresponsive class may have to be shaken up and 'galvanized' by a display of temperament (fire and brimstone!) by the instructor in order to show the depth of his need for the ride to attend, to liven up and to produce results. If he has to put more pressure on to any one pupil he must never overdo this, and must be generous with praise as soon as the pupil makes the desired endeavour.

11 An unquenchable *thirst for knowledge* of all aspects of the subject; knowledge to impart and knowledge to support his teaching. His own learning never ceases. He should have an unbiased curiosity, and a spirit of adventure.

12 *A sense of timing* – a complex and vital quality which enables the instructor to know exactly when to help, interrupt or intercept; when to sympathize, to listen or forcibly to propel. A good sense of timing is essential in all matters pertaining to the horse and particularly for the instructor, riding or training horses, or when he is teaching a rider how and when to apply his aids both on the flat and when riding over a course of fences. Some instructors are born with a highly sensitive and competent sense of timing, some are not so fortunate, but with realization, thought, training and practical application it can become a finely tuned instructing quality which will add much to the joys of communication, and to the efficiency of actions even beyond the confines of the horse world.

13 *Patience* – endless! With horses and riders.

14 *Enthusiasm* – putting 110 per cent of himself into his teaching of equitation or stable management, and inspiring similar enthusiasm within his pupils.

15 *Determination* – in the wider sense; tenacity of purpose and principles.

16 *Loyalty* – to the National Federation and its associate societies, committees and clubs; to the school, its chief instructor, its staff, and to all pupils.

17 *Duty* – to do a good job, putting pupils and horses first.

18 *Calmness* – ensuring a 'cool head' in a crisis, and imparting calm to others.

19 *Generosity* – to give praise for work well done, especially to children, beginners and to horses; to encourage the slower pupils and more nervous pupils.

20 *Optimism* – but not to let it mislead sound judgment!

21 *Courage* – of many parts; of convictions, over what is right; to impart to pupils who doubt their own or their horse's ability – not to be confused with bald-headed 'nerve'.

22 *Intelligence combined with thoughtful concentration and thoroughness* – attention to detail; leading to simple efficiency rather than to petty confusions!

23 The ability to be *natural* – giving honest opinions and appraisals without causing hurt or affront.

24 *Humility* – facilitating a continued assimilation of knowledge, thankfully accepting correction and admitting to mistakes when made.

25 *A sense of justice* – be FAIR – taking the trouble to collect all the facts of the case and to analyse them carefully before deciding judgment or sentence.

26 *Pride* – in the school's and in the personal appearance and output. Of the right sort – the wrong sort can obliterate humility – without humility learning ceases, and so does improvement. 'A place for everything and everything in its place.' 'Clean, tidy and efficient, ready for inspection!' All being well and happy, and receiving the best-possible tuition.

27 *Punctuality* – this includes an early appreciation of delay and delegation of a substitute in time, to ensure the instructor's work is being carried out even while he is detained.

28 *A sense of humour and a lively imagination* – remember we ride for *FUN* – Instructors should provide strong incentives to encourage learning and improvement, tempering their instruction with variety – sugar the pill!

29 *Clarity of thought* and speech.

30 *The voice* – is an integral factor in *communication*. The manner in which the chief instructor uses his voice when teaching will invariably be reflected in his instructing staff and his students, he must bear in mind that: His voice must convey *confidence*, authoritative control, calm, clarity of instruction, and it should attract and maintain interest and attention. His commands should be carefully selected and clear, with preparatory phrases or words whenever they may be necessary for better understanding and smoother execution of the required movements and exercises. His explanations and corrections must be brief and exactly timed for the pupil to have the quiet and occasional prompting to enable him to get the FEEL of the work. Riders switch off – not listening – if there is a barrage of continual chatter.

31 *A lightning perception* – a kind of seventh sense, to 'feel' the mood of the establishment, class, pupil or horse, and thus to turn it to best advantage, or to arrest trouble – even an accident before it occurs. To know how far a pupil can be 'stretched' without being over-faced.

32 A SPARK – a vital yet undefinable quality which inspires interest, confidence and maximum efforts and therefore ensures top performance, result and enjoyment from each lesson and every minute of the day!

33 *Turnout* – should always be neat, clean and practical, from the top of a tidy head to well-polished boots on the feet. Instructors should never overdress in clothes which are ostentatious or of an unsuitable style, and they should encourage similar dress-sense in their pupils, e.g. over-waisted, or too short jackets (unbuttoned!) tight breeches, lanyards or cords (with or without embellishments), yards of veiling, bulkily tied hunting-ties or stocks and outsize 'button-holes' with foil-enwrapped stalks and accompanying greenery are not correct and should *not* be worn. Although a horseman should always look inconspicuously well-dressed, this need not be dependent on the depth of his pocket.

INCORRECT & SLOVENLY   NEAT & PRACTICAL

FIG.3   TURNOUT

Jewellery – I would not wear it because I have always been brought up to believe it is 'not done' – however, young students are realists and it has a far greater effect if the instructor forewarns of the disaster which could occur from an ear-ring caught in a mane, a necklace caught on a branch, or a pin driven into the chest; obviously the gorier the details the better the effect!

34 *Personal example* – the most difficult quality – instructors must practice what they preach.

A useful test for all instructors is: 'Think before you speak: Is it *true*? Is it *necessary*? Is it *kind?* – if not – don't say it!'

6 Voice production and control for instructing and lecturing

When an instructor teaches, issues commands, or lectures to his pupils, it is equally important that:

he is heard,

he is understood,

he arouses interest – he may even inspire.

Public-speaking, the stage, elocution, teaching and lecturing are all variations on a similar theme; of these, the first three call for specialist training which is to an unnecessarily high standard for an equitation instructor. However, the subject of voice production is too important to be ignored.

The chief instructor and his team must appreciate that although some students may have had a good start in this respect, at home and at school from playing in charades, participating in amateur dramatics or operatic performances, or from elocution or singing lessons, many will not have had this advantage and may well need some help.

Sadly the art of conversation has waned pathetically in the last decade due to the accelerated tempo of life and the lure of the effortless pastime of gazing at the television set. As TV increases in size, quality of output, and attraction, so it replaces the desire for communication, contact and home-made entertainment within the family-circle. At schools and colleges the supersedence of written work over that which is given orally must also play a contributory factor in the modern difficulty, if not failure, to communicate.

Time must be made available and students must be given the opportunity to practice discussing speaking to an audience; they must be advised and encouraged to develop the use of their voices for instructional purposes.

Instructors must teach their students the basic rules:

(a) To utilize all the component parts of *the voice,*

  i The vocal chords – the strings of the instrument (some more musical than others!).

  ii The resonant chambers – of the skull, chest and even of the stomach (e.g. a belly-laugh!).

  iii The lungs – the fuel-supply; to be of full value these must be well filled, particularly at the bottom of the lungs.

(b) *Good posture* – if standing, the feet should be slightly apart and the weight distributed equally on the outsides of both feet. If sitting, the body's weight should be borne equally and squarely by both seat bones. In both cases the pelvis should be upright, straight, and level, the stomach pulled in, the diaphragm and rib-cage well lifted and the shoulders straight and level with the neck and head poised gracefully above them. The back should be well stretched, up to the top of the back of the head.

(c) *Breath-control* – deep breathing should be developed as a natural habit, commencing from the lower rather than the upper ribs; the mind must measure the utilization of the exhalations and 'season' it with spice and variety of tone, pitch and volume. Shyness usually impedes breathing, the positive thinking must over-ride "nerves".

(d) *A natural manner* – combining ease, confidence, sincerity and a degree of urgency.

The above directives coupled with the following points will form a useful foundation from which to commence the voice and confidence building process:

Find the aim of the talk or lecture – also any local background or problems, if applicable.

Audience assessment

Size – approximate numbers.

Who are they? Old, young – horsey, non-horsey – mixed?

What do they want and need to know?

How much can they absorb?

What form of enlivening variety will be best to maintain maximum interest, e.g. props (saddlery), drawings, slides, films, jokes.

Audience accommodation and arrangement – in the most advantageous position.

Prepare – make a plan. For example, introduction, content – the message, and concluding summary – all within the given time limit.

Think – and take a deep breath, before speaking – make a half halt to refuel before each phrase – but avoid sounding stilted or un-natural.

Organize the *mental attitude* – positive thinking is 'a must'. (*You* want to do this, practice makes perfect or at least it brings about improvement.) Feel the audience's mental pulse – be acutely aware of the mood and reactions you are creating.

Control – Fill the lungs with air to the maximum – the brain needs the oxygen – the voice needs the fuel. Ration the output – do not over feed the throat with air or words – speak slowly and clearly but *not* in a monotone – produce some sparks! Resist the temptation to fidget or over-gesticulate.

Keep it simple – audience interest can only be maintained if understanding is total.

Be aware – of the audience's need, appreciation and reception.

Be flexible – lectures must always suit the audience – be ready to adapt, in mid-stream if necessary.

Keep up the *interest* – right to the end of each sentence – the last word must be clearly spoken. The final summary must be well-projected, a tiring audience may need extra stimulation, but 'punch-lines' should be kept to a minimum, and in proportion. Imagine the head as an instrument – and speaking to be the skilful playing of that instrument.

Keep *calm*.

Relax – especially in the throat, as well as mentally. (There is always

someone else who will need more help than you – if not – be glad for them!)
Excess tension is just as detrimental to speaking as it is to riding, especially if it is located in the neck or the nerves.

Put your *heart* into your speaking – mean it!

Be prepared to *work* – inconspicuously but indefatigably; never deteriorate into monotony of content or tone.

'Lift up your voice' – not to the hills but to reach a friend sitting in the back row, or riding just beyond the farthest member of your ride.

There are several *exercises* which improve a speaker's ability and range. They are described in detail in most textbooks on the subject so I will give but a brief summary of the six exercises which I have found useful.

1 Practice correct, *deep* breathing – this is also excellent for general health. Start with a big, expansive yawn, and lift the diaphragm well in order to inflate the lungs from the lower ribs and stomach area. Inhale for as long as possible; hold it, and then count slowly while exhaling. Gradually deepen and lengthen the inhalation, the pause and the exhalation. Repeat for 2 or 3 minutes, before a rest and further repetition.

This is also a good exercise to help overcome nerves, stage-fright, and for cross-country riders.

2 Mouth-opening – to allow the sound to come out! Use the words, 'Why' and 'Loud', several times each, quite quietly but really working and stretching the lips and lower jaw. Say 'why' five times, then stick out the tongue and stretch it up, down and about, before returning to say 'loud' five times. Repeat the exercise several times. This is helpful for mumblers or those who speak through gritted teeth.

3 (a) Using the bone structure of the skull to develop a resonant quality to the voice, hum, with the lips just touching. Choose an easy note and work on it. Think about and listen to the sound; hold the palm of the hand in front of the mouth and turn up the volume of the humming. Stretch the hand away – crescendo; bring it near – diminuendo; play with the volume and feel the resonance. Eventually, the hum can be 'thrown' against a wall, three or four metres away – but never risk straining the voice.

(b) Singing quietly, thinking of resonance and opening the throat, and increasing the voice's note-range. Use the letter 'H' in front of all the vowel sounds, and practice scales – up and down (for this purpose 'Hah' is better than 'Hay').

4 Reading aloud slowly, with exaggerated, overemphasis of enunciation and articulation.

5 Preparing and giving short lectures on simple, practical subjects.

6 Using a tape-recorder – often constructive criticism of a student's teaching voice is received with frank disbelief – a tape-recorder is most useful for it proves the point. The first impact provides the severest shock; thereafter a resistant immunity sets in.

Self-consciousness is the worst obstacle to be overcome. Few students will either take the trouble, or risk making fools of themselves if left to their own devices, they need to be organized, led and taught by their instructors. Students need to be given *confidence*, composure, practice and encouragement in this subject.

7 Basic principles for giving riding lessons

Instructors are responsible for the SAFETY of their pupils as well as for their IMPROVEMENT: they must always remember that lessons are only fully assimilated if they are INTERESTING, SIMPLE, and FUN.

THE RULE OF AUTHORITY AND CONTROL

It is absolutely imperative that all pupils are taught that although they must be self-reliant and even adventurous as they ride together, in company, they must remember and apply the rules of safety and courtesy. See Chapters 10 and 12. In the majority of cases at a school of equitation, someone is designated to be in charge of the ride. During the time allotted that person is given and must exert absolute control; the riders must always obey any command given, without pause or question, even though the commander-of-the-movement may be comparatively junior to the remainder of the ride.

Accidents occur most usually when riders fail to pay attention, when they ride figures carelessly, are distracted by or participate in idle gossip and fail to keep correct distances between their horses, or to keep them under judicious control. They must always remember the horse's potential to be 'dangerous at both ends'.

FIG.4 FAILING TO KEEP...........DISTANCE OR CONTROL

1 *Preparation*

The aim of the course or of the individual lesson must be established initially, for this reason the instructor must first discover new pupils' past riding history, also that of their horses, and their respective problems, as well as their present objectives.

The lesson must always be prepared beforehand. The plan must be simple, logical and flexible. It must have sufficient content for progression and interest, but must not be too complex. The instructor must be content with simple work well done; position and form improvement rather than persevering over too much ground, which inevitably results in confusion and a retrograde performance; there may be a week in which to prepare a lesson; there may be only two minutes – prepared it must be. The stage should always be set in advance and different arrangements of the 'props' required made one step ahead through the course, day or lesson.

Lectures must be prepared and ready, together with any necessary diagrams. Cavalletti and jumps should be set out in advance; consultation and agreement with the other instructors will usually save time and labour and be generally helpful.

The instructor should make frequent spot checks on the tidiness of the vacated stable prior to a lesson and on the manner in which his pupils lead their horses to and from the indoor school; at all times the horses should walk resolutely forward with their shoulders level with their riders' – horses must not be allowed to dawdle idly, hanging back on the reins.

The instructor should also keep a watchful eye on all his pupils whenever they mount and dismount, for slackness here will quickly undo the horses' early lessons; if manners in this respect are not confirmed in the riding school they will soon become bad habits when ridden out of doors, gate opening in a competition, etc. Riders must never allow their horses to move off until they are absolutely ready and give the signal to walk forward in a correct form – on the aids.

Commands – must be clear-cut, unhurried, and audible, they must also be 'human'. A sharp word or two may be necessary occasionally to awaken a dull pupil from a dreamy doze or to avert a disaster, but on the whole severely aggressive shouts should be reserved for the barrack-square, they are not suitable for riders or their horses.

Introductory phrases should be short but complete in their description of the ensuing exercise.

Preliminary commands may be used to forewarn riders of impending action – the longer version being, 'Prepare to—' and the shorter one, 'Ride—'.

Executive commands, the new gait should be commenced on the final word:
'Walk, march' (forward from the halt).
'Ter-rot' (for an upward or downward transition).
'Can-ter'.
The new track should be taken on the final word:
'Now!'

Reward – 'Make much of your horses'. This is a useful cavalry term which conveys more meaning of reward and communication than, 'Pat your horses'. Pupils should be taught how and where to pat their horses together with the reasons for this procedure.

RIDER-CORRECTIONS

All riding faults need thoughtful and skilful analysis by the instructor, he must also be quick and accurate with his assessment of the *root* cause, i.e. one main fault. He must limit his comments to the bare essentials.

Faults may be corrected by two procedures:

i With the pupil halted, at the conclusion of the exercise. The instructor explains and demonstrates, first the fault, exaggerated for emphasis (in a kindly manner), followed by the correct method. After which the pupil will repeat the exercise, trying to carry out the suggested improvements.

ii Instant correction – simple, short commands, given when the rider is in action, to help him to find the timing of his actions in relation to the horse's movement, and thus to improve his *feel*.

The first method is the better one for general use, for it makes the rider think, and it gives him time to understand and to work out how to apply the correction for himself. His brain must be exercised, his intellect stretched, his memory supplied with facts and its retentive strength tested, his confidence and ambition must be fired – that is what teaching is all about.

When correcting riders' faults the Instructor must not beat about the bush, he must be honest and sincere, for in fact, both he and his pupils have the same aim – 'improvement towards perfection':

TAKING OVER THE RIDE

Every new pupil should be welcomed and introduced to the instructor and to the other members of the ride; he should be helped and made to feel 'at home' by all concerned.

All lessons should start with a quick and thorough inspection of tack and turn-out. A ride of experienced riders may be inspected when they are mounted, in the school, or before leaving the stable-yard for outdoor work. Children's rides or those of inexperienced riders should be inspected twice, first dismounted in the stable-yard, and again when mounted, in the school or training area.

Throughout the lesson the horses' tack should remain under careful scrutiny and changes should be made where necessary. The bits must fit and suit the horses and their saddles must fit and retain their position so that the horse's shoulder-blades are free and the riders are placed so that they may easily have a correct influence on their horses. All such inspections should be quick and efficient but never time-consuming.

When the class is mounted the instructor must observe carefully and conscientiously that every pupil's stirrup leathers are of a suitable length, and that their feet are correctly placed in the stirrup irons, i.e. that the stirrups are, 'The right way round'. Correctly adjusted stirrup leathers are of prime importance for correct rider-positions and influences, whether they are riding dressage, cross-country or jumping.

If the whole ride are strangers to the instructor, two possible courses are open to him:

If the ride is of a reasonable size – twelve or less – he should ask the name of each member in turn, noting it down on a postcard, together with some identifying description, e.g.

'John – Police, grey.'

'Betty – Bay, blue bandages.'

'Wayne – Western.'

and so on! It is best not to rely on shirt colours, martingales or gadgets, for the former change frequently, especially in a hot climate, and with a little skill and quite a bit of tact the latter will have been dispensed with by the end of the first lesson!

If the ride is large – over twelve in number – or even 'outsize' – unless the instructor has an outstandingly good memory, he should number the ride off from the front after he has put them into a reasonably suitable order. The first attempt at numbering is likely to be slow, vague and dreary. Repetition will serve the dual purpose of improvement, shaking up the ride and putting them on their mettle, and of emphasising and underlining his number in each individual's mind.

THE LESSON

For the first 5 or even 10 minutes, the ride should work in.

If the indoor-school or training area is near to the stables, the first lesson of the day should start at the walk to warm up the horse's joints, tendons and muscles and to quietly awaken their resilience as well as the riders' and the horses' minds. After one to three minutes they can go forward to trot and canter and work on loosening exercises, e.g. turns on the forehand, transitions and leg-yielding. The riders should push the horses forward at a lively, balanced gait, to accept the rider's aids and a soft contact with the bit. They should not be allowed to run around in a bad form (a 'weak' back) with loose reins and thoughtless riding.

The area used for the first part of the lesson should be reasonably confined, 20×20 metres, or 30×30 metres is suitable for a large ride, out of doors. The reasons for this restriction are: safety, control and better impact of the teaching and concentration and application from the pupils.

Early work in the lesson should include the correction of riders' positions and of their aids, and then at least one of the following:

(a) Balance, suppling and corrective exercises for the riders.

(b) Loosening exercises to improve the horses' form, basic gaits, obedience and control.

(c) Transitions and changes of directions – ridden with very smooth, barely perceptible aids.

(d) School figures.

(e) Early jumping from trot to canter, over low fences. Except in beginners' classes, jumping should not be kept to the end of the lesson by which time pupils, and horses will be feeling a little jaded if not tired. Of course there are times when this reaction can be used to advantage, for instance to make beginners' horses steady and safe and the riders less tense. However more experienced riders and their horses will gain greater benefit from their gymnastic jumping if they have not lost their initial exuberance and enthusiasm by working hard and expending energy on the flat beforehand; in addition, the loosening-effect of the jumping will greatly enhance the impulsion, freedom and ease of the ensuing dressage-work.

All lessons must be specially planned to stimulate interest and to inspire a real, if not burning desire for improvement in each individual member of the ride.

The time allotted to the lesson must be well utilized, without over-taxing horses and riders. Although rest and discussion periods have their obvious value, it is important also to vary the work itself, to use and exert different parts of the body while resting those already tired; thus several of the exercises included in one lesson may all be comparatively taxing as long as they are chosen to employ and develop different sets of muscles and offer a challenge to the riders' minds. Usually the instructor should start with easier work and gradually increase the demand; the time-limit for each exercise, also the degree of its difficulty must of course, be regulated by the conditions and present training standard of the horses and riders.

The early part of each day's work should repeat and confirm a shortened version of the work of the previous day, and then prepare and lead on to new work. The instructor must be very careful not to embark on a new exercise until the previous one has been well understood by his pupils; if there is any sign of doubt, hesitation or confusion he must think quickly of another approach in his explanation or to their carrying out of the exercise, which might provide a quick and easy solution to the problem. On the other hand, he must not wait too long with the teaching of new exercises or the impetus of interest and variety will be lost.

Exercises which have been taught previously must be repeated, revised or tested periodically, with a higher standard of performance expected on each occasion.

VARIETY should be introduced into lessons whenever it is fitting so to do. This may be accomplished by:

(a) A change of activity.

(b) A change of environment or schooling area.

(c) A change of horses.

(d) A change of instructor – in which case there must be a close liaison between the permanent and the temporary instructor.

The instructor should always halt his class in the most advantageous position for all of them to participate; to hear his explanations and answers to their questions and to see his demonstrations, and to be well-placed for the next move or part of the lesson.

He should also take the best advantage of the horses' natural homing or herd instincts, and he should do his best to avoid or at least minimize distractions, e.g. line them up with their backs to any rival activity. When the lesson is out of doors, the ride should be halted with the sun at the side or overhead but never in their eyes; they should be downwind, and as far removed from interruptions and noises as is practically possible.

The instructor must always place *himself* in the most advantageous position for the whole of his class to hear his explanations, to see his demonstration and from which to conduct his instructions or his interrogations. He should time his own positioning carefully; usually taking his place before the ride has finished lining-up, or, alternatively he may give a brief, simple and silent demonstration before coming to a square halt in front of the ride.

Whenever the instructor is taking the lesson in a school he should stand parallel with and near to the centre line, 3–5 metres in from the A or C marker, so that he can see all of his class for nearly all of the time. He should move out to the outer track from time to time to study horses and riders from the front or from the rear as they come or go down the long side. He should make good use of the school-mirrors for they can provide him with 'eyes in the back of his head'.

Alternatively, for work on two circles, or some exercises on the centre line, he should stand with his back to the B or E marker.

Out of doors, the instructor may prefer to stand outside the arena.

The instructor must avoid moving about unnecessarily during the lesson. Movements are often distracting and can cause a wavering in the instructor's own concentration, corrections or commands. If the instructor is mounted and wishes to get his horse on the move, then he may take the ride from the rear, or he may direct one of the students to take the ride for 5 to 10 minutes while the instructor rides, listens and assesses.

Whenever the ride is to be *lined up at the halt* this should be done carefully, the instructor paying particular attention to the manner in which the horses are ridden into their places, that any turning is made smoothly with the weight and leg-aids and not by tugging on the inner rein; that every horse is straight at a right angle with the wall he is facing; that he is at a correct distance from his neighbour, is standing squarely on all four legs in a reasonable form and under the rider's control. Although riders should ease the reins they should never stand in line with completely loose reins due to the obvious risk of an accident from a biting or kicking match – which can easily be sparked off by one unpleasant equine remark or movement by the adjacent horse. Watching a ride which is lined up at the halt can be a very revealing guide to the horses' training and to the riders' education, for much correct work has to have been completed before a rider can stand his horse quite still and straight, in a correct position and form.

Placing the ride is quite an art in itself – student-instructors should frequently be directed to move the ride from one place to another in the most economical way possible. They should preselect the track and the command which is short, simple and most easily executed, especially by the horses, i.e. no short, sharp turns, nor aimless wandering should be allowed. This is a useful task to set while the instructor rearranges a jump or sets out cavalletti – not only does it save time but also it stops any risks of gossiping, and makes the students think, how to organize others as well as themselves.

The ride may be moved off from the halt in a variety of ways, the instructor should choose a method to suit his particular need, always bearing in mind the training standards of the riders and of the horses, and the exercise which is to follow. The simplest methods are either, 'Ride from the right, in close or open order, to the right rein, walk march!' whereupon the rider on the right of the line walks straight forward, followed in turn by the other riders, all riding straight forward before making an easy turn to the right on to the outer track. Or each member of the ride may be called forward by his number or by name – this latter is more informal for children. If he wishes to wake up the riders, to test their control and ability or to rearrange the order of the riders or the horses he may tell the ride to number, 'Ride, from the left, over your right shoulder – number'. He then commands, 'Ride, by numbers, walk or *trot* to take the left rein at distances of five metres – Number *four*!' and so on. Or the ride may be numbered off in twos; after which the 'Ones' are called forward, while the 'Twos' stand still; after a suitable interval the 'Twos' will be called forward. These latter two methods call for careful riding with precise aids from the riders and good manners and obedience from the horses, as the latter must either move forward from the line, leaving their neighbours willingly or stand still and await their turn, all quite independently of each other.

The old practice of turning the ride sharply, on to the outer track from the halt – 'Ride from the right, right turn, walk march!' was a singularly thoughtless practice, it encouraged bad riding and had nothing to commend it.

If some new work is to be taught or a detailed correction is to be described, and made, the ride must first be lined up at the halt so that the instruction may be given to one or two riders while the remainder listen and watch. The instructor must involve the whole ride by asking individuals to explain what they have heard, to comment on the demonstration, on the aims of the exercise or on any faults noted when the first riders tried out the new work. Then it should be ridden by the pupil or class at the walk, before being carried out at faster gaits.

The instructor must remember that every new exercise is more tiring mentally and physically during the initial learning stages than when riders and horses have understood and become thoroughly acquainted with its correct execution.

The instructor must be patient and understanding when introducing new work to his pupils; he must not expect them to carry it out correctly straight away, but must give them time and only gradually raise his standard and increase his demands.

The instructor can again make use of the horses' homing and herd instincts to reduce or increase the demand of an exercise which is carried out individually, e.g. If a rider were instructed to gallop across a field, towards the stableyard and the remainder of the class, he might well lose control and have an accident, if however, he was told to gallop away from home towards and a short distance beyond the remainder of the class, the task would be easier and considerably more safe – and he would have to ride correctly to keep his horse straight.

The lesson should close with easy work to enable horses and riders to 'cool off' mentally and physically.

Before leaving the school or training area, the instructor must ensure that it is left in immaculate order, ready for the next ride's use. If indoors, the fences should all be jumpable, preferably from both directions, and set low. Out of doors, all fences should be restored to a stock-proof state, slip-rails replaced and gates closed, also all divots should be replaced and trodden in. This work should be carried out by the ride dismounted, whilst their horses cool off.

The instructor should encourage thoughtful questions or comments at the end of the lesson and his pupils should acknowledge and thank their instructor for his tuition and help before they break the line and the lesson is terminated.

NOTE   Lessons should always finish on a high note, the last impression is all important.

Regular periods of rest, for reward and assimilation are essential parts of all lessons. These may be provided by:

i   Walking the horses on long reins. This is the best method if the horses have been working at a fast pace and are hot, or if the weather is cold.

ii   Halting the ride, while the pupils sit at ease – but not too easy. Riders must never sit carelessly nor with their reins too loose.

iii   Dismounting and standing by the horses' heads – possibly with slackened girths – not too slack, and they must be tightened if and when the horses are remounted.

These short breaks with the ride lined up at the halt for explanation, discussion, interrogation and confirmation are essential parts of every lesson:

For the riders

(a) Valuable explanations are as dust in the wind if expounded when a class of riders is on the move.

(b) Physical exhaustion eliminates mental assimilation.

(c) With the renewal of energy, pupils can ride their best all the time.

For the horses

These breaks are essential for their physical and mental welfare. Seemingly endless and monotonous work, trotting round and round against the wall of the manège is the surest way to ruin horses' natural gaits and to deaden their minds. By intelligent interrogation and discussion, the instructor should test, confirm or extend his pupils' knowledge while the horses have a respite.

Additional Riding Rules

All trot work is carried out at sitting trot unless the instructor specifies rising trot.

The ride will continue to work at an exercise with an understood discipline of pace and dressing, keeping correct distances for themselves, until the instructor commands a change. This rule enables the instructor to give his undivided attention to the riders' work with their horses.

8 Further notes on the manner and method of instruction

It is up to instructors and student-instructors to inspire their pupils, to help them, and to whet their appetites for improvement in all aspects of horsemanship and horsemastership.

Instructors must remember that they also should never stop learning:
The six most usual methods of teaching riding and stable management are:

  i The lesson

  ii The practical demonstration

  iii The lecture

  iv Discussion, debate, quiz.

  v The book – for reading aloud and study

  vi Visual aids – blackboard, diagrams, films, slides, the epidioscope, videotape, etc; all of these should be employed to complement each other. 'Variety is the spice of life' – there are many different ways of passing on the same message.

All *lesson-plans* should be based on the following pattern:

  i Preparation – homework, organization of facilities and props and placement of class.

  ii Explanation – *what* and *why* introducing the lesson-subject and its aims and objects.

  iii Demonstration – briefly, *what it looks like, how the horse does it.*

  iv Explanation – *How* – the aids, thorough details, stage by stage.

  v Demonstration – of (iv) – and where the exercise will be ridden.

vi Execution – the class carries out the exercise, exactly as described.

vii Explanation and demonstration – faults and their effects; and the correct method again, as the final picture.

viii Re-execution – the class works to improvement.

ix Interrogation and confirmation – *ad infinitum!*

Instruction may be further divided into:

The teaching, and . . . . . practical application.

The oral instruction is always based on the following pattern:

What has to be done, and what it looks like.

Why it has to be done.

How it has to be done.

The teaching must be backed up by practical demonstrations and application.

Instructors' explanations, advice and corrections must be short and to the point – their thinking and speaking must be clear, concise and definite and backed by a sincere belief. Long-windedness on the instructor's part inevitably leads to boredom in his pupils.

The senses of hearing, seeing and feeling should all be involved in proportion to their relative value, e.g. seeing is double the value of hearing, and doing and feeling are the most important of all.

Although pupils' positions in the saddle and their posture must be as near the ideal as possible at all times, this must never be as a result of force, at the cost of natural poise, nor risking any impediment to the rider's feel for the horse's movement.

It is essential that instructors should encourage their riders to develop a trained and critical eye for the correct fitting of their bridles and saddles, that they are suitable, fit well, and are comfortable in all respects. Similarly they should check their horse's backs, girth areas, mouths and teeth daily, making sure there are no sores, wolf teeth, nor sharp edges on the molars, even a deposit of tartar on a tush can cause discomfort and fidgeting.

The bridle – the bit should lie straight in the horse's mouth, with the cheek-pieces buckled on equal holes, or one hole's difference which will enable

FIG.5   TOO LOW   CORRECT - COMFORTABLE

DROP NOSEBAND

a finer adjustment to be made, i.e. half a hole each side with the headpiece pulled through to level the buckles. It is important that the snaffle bit suits the horse and fits snugly, well up in the corners of the mouth. If it is too wide the centre-joint will hang down heavily on the horse's tongue and will slide across the bars as one rein acts. Obviously the snaffle must not be too narrow or it will pinch, but on the whole this latter is a less common fault. The bit must act at the correct angle on the bars of the mouth when the horse is carrying his head correctly. The browband must not be too short or high and all other straps should be fitted correctly, and have their ends secured by the keepers and runners. The drop noseband, if worn, should be fitted a hand's breadth above the top of the nostril and should allow nearly two fingers between the front strap and the nasal bone. If fitted lower it will interfere with the horse's breathing and/or may irritate him. If fitted too tightly, the horse will soon learn to set his mouth against it slightly open, causing an unwanted rigidity in the lower jaw and a dry mouth.

The saddle – should sit well on the horse's back and not be perched above it nor of course, must it press on or even come near to any portion of his spine.

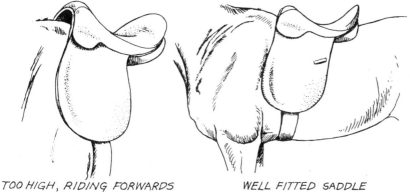

TOO HIGH, RIDING FORWARDS   WELL FITTED SADDLE
FIG.6.

The girth-straps should be fixed far enough forward to keep the saddle back behind the shoulder-blades, this is particularly important on a show or dressage saddle. Whereas a spring tree is excellent for a jumping saddle it is debatable whether it is not overrated when used in a dressage or a hunting saddle. It is an easily proved fact that to carry a rider's weight, a larger, rigid bearing surface is much more comfortable for the horse's back than a small area of constant flexibility. The saddle must have a slight dip in the centre of its top-line, and a narrow waist with only a minimum amount of padding, so that the rider can be as close to his horse as possible and can retain a correct position with ease. It must also fit the rider; a rider with long thighs or a large seat is made too fixed in his position if the saddle is too short, and the flaps must be long enough to reach below the top of the boots when the rider sits without stirrups and with his legs stretched down. A jumping saddle should accommodate the rider comfortably when he rides with shortened leathers, and the girth straps may be farther back, as the saddle is better placed relatively farther

45

FIG.7 SADDLE TOO SHORT

forward. Girths must be clean, supple, safe, attached and adjusted correctly.

Mounting – every horse must remain absolutely still, whether the pupils are mounting from the floor, from a mounting-block, being given a leg-up, or are vaulting into the saddle. The instructors must preserve the horses' training, and teach their pupils the correct principles. Thereafter they must continue to correct any mistakes for even very experienced riders are surprisingly careless in this respect.

Instructors should know and use the recognized school commands in order to place and work the ride and to use the school with maximum safety, ease and efficiency and minimum confusion; but on the other hand, they should also make frequent use of brief exercise-explanations instead of commands as the latter are quickly learnt by the horses so that they anticipate their rider's aids rather than obey them.

The instructor must use his voice to its best and fullest advantage. His words of command must be orthodox and universally recognized for inevitably his pupils will copy his turn of phrase and intonation. Although his sentences should be brief and clear they should always convey a sincerity of meaning to the individual or the whole ride. However mundane and well-worn is the command it should always project interest, enthusiasm and correct application; it should never convey a hint of boredom. When giving a command there should be a sufficient pause between the preparatory explanatory phrase and the executive command in order to give the class time to prepare and ride the movement smoothly. The final, executive word should be clear and just loud enough to be heard by every member of the ride, it should not be shouted too sharply or the riders will overreact and apply their aids too brusquely. The instructor must avoid raising his voice; a moderate, but not too low tone, with variety and emphasis, together with a balanced mixture of humour and authority will sharpen his pupils' attention so that their work is neither dull nor overexcited.

During explanations and interrogations, student-instructors will find it helpful if they are told to imagine that they are standing on the near bank of a fast-flowing river, and their class is on the far bank, thus they must all 'throw their voices over the river' in either direction, so that everyone can hear and be thoroughly involved all the time.

Usually a riding or technical correction is best given individually and yet in such a way that the whole class can learn from it. Occasionally a collective correction will have a better value as a quick aid to general position improvement, e.g. 'Look up and *think*'. 'Relax your hips/thighs/knees', 'Elbows in—'.

When giving lessons in a small indoor school or in a confined space, or for children or beginners, the instructor should be on foot and in the two latter cases he should have at least one assistant. This is another opportunity for student-instructors to start to learn to teach.

If the instructor is dismounted when teaching and wishes to demonstrate some points from his lesson, or faults and how to correct them, he should use one of his pupil's horses, but he should not 'borrow' it for longer than is necessary.

The instructor should avoid keeping pupils or horses in one position for too long, or repeating any exercise too often. On the other hand, there must be sufficient simple repetition to allow assimilation, understanding and feel, and to give confidence.

He should always remember the importance of early lessons, they must be correct in every detail as well as being enjoyable and inspiring. They are the FOUNDATION STONES of the rider's future – only if he takes to the horse willingly and joyously and with interest will he become a good rider.

While the very first riding lessons are best carried out in an enclosed arena, further lessons outside, on a leading-rein are of the greatest importance for the development of ease, feel, confidence and enjoyment, all in the most natural way.

Falls must be avoided. As Mr Jorrocks said. 'A fall is a H'awful thing.'

If a fall does occur it must be reported immediately and recorded in the Accident Book. As long as no harm has been done, the rider should be encouraged to re-mount his horse, he may be led if necessary, to restore his confidence.

For all outdoor lessons, and whenever he may need to demonstrate, the instructor should be mounted on a well-mannered horse. At all times when he is mounted, the instructor must maintain a correct position on his horse, for his pupils will look to him for an example and will imitate his style.

Pupils should carry whips, but should not wear spurs until granted permission to do so by their instructor, i.e. when their seats are independent, correct and established, and they can control their legs.

An instructor must always endeavour to produce a ride of good riders, not a well-drilled ride of a lower standard. He should not keep back the more talented or proficient for the sake of the others.

If the instructor is providing the horses he must select them with care, giving quiet, steady horses to beginners and nervous riders, hot and nervous horses should be ridden by quiet, educated and sensitive riders and he should vary the type of horse for the better riders. The instructor must take into consideration the rider's build and ability and the horse's size, type, temperament and standard of training so that all horses and riders may be suitably paired. When little is known of the individual characteristics of horses and riders at the beginning of a course, the original pairing may have to be amended, however as soon as satisfactory partnerships have been formed these should remain unchanged except for short changeovers within a lesson, unless a particular horse shows definite signs of being unhappy with his rider. Sometimes the instructor may wish to put up a more experienced rider in order to re-school a horse who is not being ridden well enough by his present rider.

If pupils are mounted on their own horse, provided they are sufficiently competent horsemen, it is good to exchange horses for part of the lesson to widen the pupil's riding experience and so that they may watch their own horse working. Obviously, this must be introduced and carried out with tact and discretion.

The instructor should ride the horses himself, from time to time, in order to advance their training, to enable him to know and understand the horses better, to be able to assess any problems and thereafter be better able to help the riders with them, but also to show that what he demands can be done, as well as how it should be done. Only the instructor who can execute himself what he demands of his ride will retain full confidence and respect from them. 'Seeing is believing.'

When a pupil brings his own horse for an individual lesson, the instructor should ride it as soon as he has watched their performance on both reins, in order that he is then able to assess and discuss any difficulties which may not be obvious from the ground.

The instructor must always be aware of his approach to and its effect on horses. The stronger the personality of the instructor the greater will be his effect on the horses with whom he is working. By means of his confidence-giving calm and skilled approach and handling a good instructor will automatically improve the training standard of the horses as well as the riding of his pupils. Although he may well need to stimulate both horses and riders to increased activity and effectiveness, he must never arouse apprehension or fear. The instructor must always be on his guard not to disturb any other horses unwittingly when he is projecting more definite endeavour into one particular horse or the rider.

Properly made movements may be used by the instructor to his advantage, e.g. an instructor may walk between cavalletti, or a grid, or across the back of a low combination in the path of an on-coming horse who has a habit of rushing, in order to make the horse look, and to give the rider a natural situation and objective, to make him want to restrain his horse, and encouraging positive thinking and actions – that is as long as he likes and respects the instructor and does not wish to injure or destroy him! At the other end of the scale, the instructor must be careful not to make thoughtless or abrupt movements, especially if he is carrying a whip and his pupils are riding young or highly strung horses.

Corrections to students or riders may be delivered in many different ways. The instructor should modify his tone to suit the occasion, the extent of the fault and its cause, being most severe if it is an easily corrected fault which

FIG.8   STEADYING A RUSHING HORSE

continues to be uncorrected by the rider's own effort, and being lessened in severity if the fault is small or only recently spotted, or if the pupil or his horse displays anxiety, is nervous, highly strung or over-zealous.

If an individual requires a disciplinary correction, this should be given quietly after he has been called in to the instructor. The next, stronger measure is the giving of a correction within ear-shot of a few fellow riders. Only as a last resort should a reprimand be delivered to an individual in front of the whole ride, at the halt; if the offender has ignored previous warnings or more friendly approaches this last one will usually have a most salutory effect. However, the instructor should always weigh up in his mind whether he could not obtain just as good a result from praising those riders who do good work, thereby encouraging the miscreants to do better.

The instructor should never lose his temper, nor resort to sarcasm especially to force an issue, or he may do lasting, wounding damage. He will invariably win his point sooner and more surely by the employment of tact, intellect, subtlety and reasoning, spiced with at least a speck or two of 'temperament' and humour.

Some instructors have a definite preference either for teaching an individual pupil or a group in a class; it is helpful to remember that both have their advantages.

One pupil taken individually:

(a) Has the instructor's undivided attention.

(b) Riders' problems can be sorted out in private and with minimum time-wastage.

(c) Thus this is the best method for an advanced rider, living a fair distance away from the school.

A class lesson, riders taken as a group:

(a) When covering new ground, lessons or exercises, the instructor only has to give the explanation and demonstration once. Many pupils learn and get the feel of it on the same occasion, and consequently the ensuing question and discussion time is more varied, interesting and instructive.

(b) The learning of a wider aspect of general equitation is helped by riders

49

watching fellow-members of the ride and hearing and seeing their corrections and their discussions.

(c) The horses enjoy company – correctly given class work will encourage horses to think and move forward more freely to the improvement of their gaits.

(d) It accustoms horses to working quietly in company and improves their manners.

(e) A competitive spirit prevails among riders and sometimes between horses as well.

(f) All riders *have* to look up and about them.

(g) An experienced instructor can use the presence of the other riders and horses to his advantage, thus making the chosen exercises more beneficial to all concerned.

(h) It is more relaxing for overanxious pupils.

(i) Commanded riding is very good for all riders, to keep them alert, to make them think and generally to put them on their toes, and it also increases their natural poise, feel and control. Depending on the experience and ability of the instructor it can also be highly beneficial to the horses, improving their impulsion, elasticity and obedience to their rider's aids and their manners and confidence in general.

Instructors must actually *teach* their pupils to watch every horse and rider in the class, and that there is something to be learned from every one of them. Unless this is taught, and pupils' observations and assessments are encouraged and tested, class lessons which provide such excellent opportunities, are partially wasted if the pupils are allowed to free-wheel in their minds and eyes – blankly awaiting their turn.

Finally, a few don'ts and a couple of NEVERS:
Don't bully
Don't have favourites – cliques are destructive to the atmosphere of any school.
Don't be sarcastic – sarcasm is the lowest form of wit.
Don't bore by too much talk, especially in riding lessons.
Don't work horses and/or riders for too long without a break.
Don't distract by moving unnecessarily.
Don't be side-tracked in discussions.
Don't be monotonous, muddled or mumbling in your speaking.
Don't be untidy – in thought, word, deed or turnout.
Never be jealous or disloyal – not in the slightest degree.
NEVER laugh *at* a pupil – laugh with them by all means; the former is despicable, the latter is commendable.
A happy TEAM SPIRIT is a far more precious quality than competition success.

9 Care of the school's pupils and horses

When a new daily or short course pupil enters the school or joins a class for the first time, the instructor must be ready to contact the pupil himself and in a brief, friendly interrogation he must discover:

The pupil's name – how he likes to be called.

His previous riding experience – how long; of what sort; and by whom he has been taught in the past.

The length of the lesson or course.

The aim of the lesson or course.

His main problems – if any.

If he has brought his own horse – as much information about it as possible.

It is imperative that the information is met by an encouraging, warm understanding from the instructor. He should never give the impression of being in the least supercilious or disparaging about the facts presented to him, but should regard this as the first, vital stage of communication and rapport between pupil and teacher. For on the pupil's first impression will the success of the lesson or course depend.

Riding pupils come in a wider variety of age, size and shape than for most sports, and yet all these pupils can be taught to ride. There are several 'Old wives tales' about pupils and why they may or may not have potential as riders; many of the so-called stumbling blocks are completely erroneous.

A widely prevalent notion with regard to the pupil's age is entirely false. Many advisers contend that it is essential to start riding when the child is very young and that if a pupil has not ridden as a child he has missed his chance of ever becoming a good horseman. Sadly the reverse is often more true.

Many children become extremely bad riders and grow up into even worse ones, because their parents have not got their priorities right. Possibly they have tried out their child on a friend's pony, the child has not fallen off (luckily!), in fact he has waxed enthusiastic about the whole idea, and so inevitably the parents buy their child a pony of his own which may be suitable, or it may be young, cheaper and definitely unsuitable. Further monies are laid out for saddlery, transport and other expensive equipment, but very little, if any, is spent on a sound equestrian education. The child will develop a faulty position and concept of riding which will be very difficult to correct at a later date when the instructor is called in to do so. Old riding faults have a nasty habit of reappearing whenever the unexpected occurs, the chips are down and the pressure is increased.

On the other hand, a keen teenager or adult who makes up his mind that he would like to learn to ride is a far better proposition for an instructor to produce as a rider, and often will accomplish this good result in half the time.

The ideal pupil is a child who has been *taught* the ways of horses and how to ride them in a natural, thoughtful and correct manner from the start – then he and his instructor have every possible advantage, and the parents will see that their support is really worthwhile.

The pupil's size is immaterial even if he wishes to compete at a high level, as long as he has a horse to match and suit him. Preferably his knees should come level with the widest part of his horse's rib-cage when the rider sits on his back in an upright position. A very small rider may be very light – this can be a disadvantage in some competitions where a set weight has to be carried and conversely a large rider may be at a disadvantage.

With regard to shape, a study of equestrian photographs will reveal that there is just as much variation in the conformation of the riders as there is in the horses amongst the top flight in all three disciplines in the Olympic Games. In

51

fact some partnerships seem to win their position in the list despite breaking many of the accepted rules of conformation.

A few 'tales' or false theories are listed below – students should be encouraged to think of others for themselves, and to bring them for discussion with their instructor.

'A good leg for a boot' is a phrase used to describe rider's legs which are long and thin, especially below the knee. Maybe this looks elegant and good from the aesthetical and the bootmaker's view, but too thin legs may have insufficient muscle to be effective, and long, thin legs make balance and co-ordination more difficult.

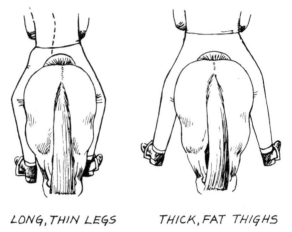

LONG, THIN LEGS   THICK, FAT THIGHS

FIG.9   RIDER CONFORMATION PROBLEMS

'The rider's feet should be parallel with the horse's sides.' A rider who has knock-knees will invariably turn his toes out a little more, whereas bow-legged riders will rarely have this problem. No instructor can turn the former shape into the latter, and if he tries to do so he will create stiffness as the pupil strives against nature for the impossible. Both shapes can make good riders.

'A pupil with flat thighs will make a good horseman, one with round thighs will not.' Rounded thighs can be a disadvantage if their bulk is due to fat, for then they tend to make their owners less stable in the saddle and balance becomes more precarious. If, however, the roundness is due entirely to muscle, those riders can be very stable and secure and can have extremely effective forward-driving aids. These strong-legged riders have much in their favour to make very good cross-country or showjumping riders, but they have more muscles from which to remove constraint for riding a dressage test or for schooling young horses; however, if this problem is understood it can be overcome.

'Riding widens the hips, or broadens the beam.' Many instructors' directives would seem to support this theory, such as 'Get your two seat-bones as wide apart as possible', or 'the broader the base, the better the balance' (Col. Handler). It is true that riding may teach a pupil to spread as he sits, but when he stands the tailor's tape-measure will belie the tale.

'A long back is a disadvantage to a rider.' Logically, a short back should be stronger than a long one. Certainly long-backed pupils do appear to be prone to back troubles. However, people with long backs are also tall, and due to feeling over-conspicuous and shy, they then stoop to seem shorter, rather than holding themselves erect, and thus they are predisposed to having bad backs. However, there are many short-backed riders with troublesome backs, and there are also many good, elegant riders who have long backs. From all of which one may conclude that it is the carriage rather than the length which is of importance.

STUDENT-INSTRUCTORS AND THE HORSES

Every instructor should take the first opportunity to get to know the various qualities, behaviour forms and equestrian background of the students in his ride and those of the horses owned by or allotted to them.

Through a firm but just and benevolent behaviour a good instructor will earn the confidence, attention and respect, which is necessary for the success of his teaching. He must constantly remind himself that most of the faults and shortcomings apparent in his pupils during their lessons are not made because of an unwillingness from horse or rider, but are the result of lack of understanding, or education, or to extra tension due to apprehension or trying too hard, or lack of practical experience or ability. Consequently, the instructor must persevere in his own endeavours, logically and patiently reasoning out the problem and its solution and trying to make himself better understood. By thoughtful use of encouragement and sympathetic correction he will gain his pupils' willingness and interest, attention, obedience and a successful achievement of the desired end result. In ninety-nine cases out of a hundred better results are attained from cheerful encouragement than from reprimands.

From the earliest introductory lessons instructors must teach their students and pupils to THINK, *learn*, *feel* and *enjoy* riding a well-trained horse. If correct basic knowledge is not given to them precisely and clearly in these first lessons, riders will not know from the start how to discern whether the horse has been well brought up, handled and trained.

By following their instructor's good example, pupils will see how the horse regards him as a friend who is respected, as the horse stands squarely, polite and attentive in his loose-box whilst being handled, as well as when being mounted. Thus the seeds of mental and physical control are sown in both horse and rider, and they learn to work in true co-operation with each other from the very beginning of their respective careers as well as during the prelude to every lesson. All horses must be taught to have good manners in the stables and out of them, to pay attention to their riders' demands and to comply to the best of their ability; similarly pupils should respect and pay attention to their instructors. Horses should be taught to walk carefully, not clumsily out of their loose-boxes, to lead well, to stand rock-still while being mounted and many other disciplinary exercises, long before they are asked to carry their riders over big show-jumps, or to gallop, or to execute a series of flying changes, and the

53

same goes for the rider – both species must learn to walk before they can run, and to walk *well* too!

All lessons must be planned and conducted according to every pupils' ability. The riders must not be frightened or disheartened by being overfaced by too severe demands. The pupils' confidence, his belief in his own ability should be awakened, developed and established by a slow but sure development of the demands – only in this way can a bold riding spirit be born. With the fostering of this spirit in his mind, the instructor must be quick to praise improvement and also be ever-ready to notice and recognize warning signs that he has been pushing his pupils too hard by too steep an escalation of his demands, in which case he must immediately revert to easier exercises which are well within the pupils' present capabilities.

While it is an obvious fact that the more senior the instructor, the wider is the range of his responsibilities, junior instructors cannot be expected to appreciate this aspect for themselves, gradually they must be trained to observe and to take an intelligent interest in their horses' and their pupils' welfare, physical fitness, progress and happiness, as well as in the overall running of the school.

Both horses and riders should be fed on a balanced diet which is suitable and adjusted according to the work they are doing and their figures. Neither overweight riders nor horses can carry out their work to their own or their instructor's satisfaction. Alternatively, those who are under nourished, are often 'nervy' and lack inclination as well as mental and physical stamina.

All instructors should supervise and guide their pupils in many spheres which are outside the confines of the actual riding lessons. For example, hard hats must be worn, correctly, and be of a safe pattern, breeches should fit well enough to avoid wrinkling but they must also be of a sufficiently generous cut to allow free play of hip-joints and knees and be thick enough to prevent riding sores and to keep out the cold winter wind. Riding jackets should fit well and be long enough – as a rough length-guide, the lower edge of the jacket should be level with the first joint of the rider's thumb when he is standing with his arms hanging down by his sides. The fingers of riding gloves must be long enough to accommodate the full length of the fingers so that the reins may be held right down at their base. Boots, and spurs if worn, must be suitable and correctly fitted.

Neither an excess of late nights nor of parties will help a rider to assimilate the following day's lesson nor make it easy for him to tune in and ride his horse with sensitivity; this should be pointed out to pupils, particularly if they are attending a concentrated equitation course or are members of a team at a competition. Remember, 'A job worth doing, is worth doing *well.*'

Posture 'He that does not sit genteely upon a horse will never be a good horseman,' and 'No man can be either well or firmly seated on horseback unless he be master of the balance of his body, quite unconstrained, with a full possession of himself, and at his ease on all occasions whatever.' (William Cavendish, Duke of Newcastle, 1557.)

This subject is extremely important and worthy of due consideration.

If a person sets out to do well, or eventually to excel in any sport or in many arts which involve the use of his body, that body must be exceptionally well carried, trained and disciplined in order that any one part of it may be directed to move or to remain still, at will, without this isolated impulse affecting any other part of his body or limbs – only thus can he achieve the maximum effect and result with the minimum effort – and sustain it.

As riders only sit on their horses for a comparatively short period of each day, so it stands to reason that if their posture on a horse is to be good, riders must constantly be aware of striving for and maintaining a good posture for the remainder of their day, whether they are driving a motor car, sitting at an office desk, shopping, or standing up at a cocktail party! ('Everybody talking; nobody listening' – is a foreign judge's definition of an English cocktail party!) They must practice good posture so that it becomes a habit.

In the nineteenth century discipline was superfluously strict, in business, military life and even within the family circle, deportment was aided to exaggeration by tightly laced corsets for persons of both sexes, and young ladies were drilled to walk and turn majestically with piles of books upon their heads.

Nowadays, as we near the end of the twentieth century, 'deportment' and 'posture' are nearly obsolete words; neither parents nor schoolteachers seem to concern themselves with this aspect of education. No wonder that there is such an increase in 'back-troubles' – our chairs and car and 'plane-seats are usually custom-made to slouch in, rather than to support the back when it is upright – so we are encouraged to sit badly, and are rarely taught to stand correctly. Thus modern would-be riders start at a distinct disadvantage. This must be pointed out to them so that they may be encouraged voluntarily to spend more and more of every day practising good deportment, so that less and less time is wasted by allowing their posture to deteriorate. They must be encouraged to develop a modest pride in their carriage and in the way they move. Rounded or unlevel shoulders are obvious disadvantages, and short, stumping walk-steps denote lack of freedom in the hips, and perhaps a deficiency of subtle co-ordination, presence and forward-thinking?

Riders must be mentally alert and as athletically fit as possible – to be fit they must not be fat. Young people doing hard work and taking energetic exercise in the fresh air, out of doors, work up hearty appetites and eat a little more than they need to become good riders. Colonel Podhajsky used to say that a rider should be as fit and have as good muscle-control and grace as a ballet-dancer – and he had not seen Rudolf Nureyev! A weekly application of a weight-chart and a pair of bathroom scales will provide a fair and effective remedy if preliminary cautions pass unheeded.

It is all too easy for instructors to 'nag' at their pupils with regard to their positions when riding; the only alternative seeming to be to continue to nag, to hand over the worst offenders to another instructor for lunge-lessons, or to have a session with the video-tape so that the pupils can see their faults for themselves. The best approach is for the chief instructor personally to give a practical lecture-demonstration to all pupils and instructors on 'POSTURE – How the rider's posture affects both the rider and his horse.'

This also provides a good opportunity to prepare or stimulate the pupils' minds, many of them may have too closed a mental attitude to gain fullest benefit from their lessons unless they receive guidance in this respect, and are helped to feel an urgency to need to learn, to assimilate all the subtle points and finer feelings as well as the obvious directives.

In addition to having a genuine interest in his pupils' deportment and his equitation progress, the instructor must encourage the development of each pupil's individuality, personality, self-confidence and character.

Pupils should be led to realize that just as instructors have to work hard to develop good relations with their pupils, so too must pupils be quick to open their minds and hearts generously.

The instructor must *always* set a good example with his own posture; in this respect, as well as in all other matters; he must realize fully the responsibility of his position.

'Correct upright posture is the consequence of a particular attitude of the mind towards the body; one which promotes both mental and physical poise. Once the principles have been accepted and mastered, the various positions can be held unconsciously with little exertion. There will be no sign of tension and no wasted effort. It is balanced posture, and therefore, is a form of continuous isometric exercise, since the muscles on one side of the body are constantly working against those of the opposite side. Childhood is the best time to learn but it is a simple matter for older people also to master the correct upright posture and derive physical benefit as a result.' (*Home Treatment and Posture*, W. E. Tucker CVO, FRCS.)

'Posture is an active process, and is the result of a great number of reflexes, many of which have a tonic character.' (Rudolph Magnus.)

The chief instructor must train and thereafter remind his team of instructors that the HORSES are of prime importance, for if there is any decline in their standard or performance this will be reflected in the whole of the school's teaching and output. They should look 'fit to go to a show tomorrow'; well-trimmed, in good spirits and condition and going well.

The horses' form and their basic gaits must be preserved if not improved. This is essential both for the horses' welfare and to enable the pupils to learn a correct *feel*; they can so easily be impaired by bad riding and careless supervision by the instructors. The instructors must also safeguard the horses' willing responsiveness to their riders' aids, they will remain obedient without any resistance or thought of evasion if they are worked correctly and thoughtfully at all times.

All horses should be trained and worked in a simple snaffle bridle unless the chief instructor gives other directions concerning a specific lesson for a more advanced horse or rider.

The instructor should examine his horses' legs daily, both before and after work, he should check their appetite and their general appearance and behaviour and immediately cut down the work-programme of any horse who shows signs of overwork and adjust his feed to suit the restoration period.

What might be called the gymnastic modelling, the all-over improvement of the horse's proportionate appearance is effected by the muscular development produced by correct dressage-work.

This work should consist of a gradual and logical build up of demands; it is up to the instructor to keep his eye on exactly how his pupils are working the school's horses as well as their own. All horses should be worked systematically, just enough to tax them a degree or two further each week to produce a continuous improvement and development, as strengthening and suppling gymnastics, but this should NEVER be overdone or abused so that stress is caused from overwork and the horse's mental or physical well-being is jeopardized. That a well-worked and correctly trained and conditioned horse will withstand the exertions of the hunting field or equestrian competitions is true, but there is more to it than that. It is far better as a long-term policy to aim for a fit and healthy horse with clean legs whose spirits and general internal and external systems are not showing signs of wear. A smaller amount of correct work is infinitely preferable to a larger amount of the wrong sort.

Judicious use should be made of rest-for-reward periods at the halt, mounted or dismounted, or at a free walk, especially with inexperienced riders, or young unfit horses, or if the work has been of a strenuous nature. When relaxing at the walk the riders should allow their horses to have free reins but they must also ensure that their horses maintain a good form, particularly that their backs do not drop, weaken or hollow. The walk must remain true, rhythmic with ground-covering strides. A spoilt walk is an extremely difficult gait to recover and a careless or ignorant rider may all too easily and quite unwittingly cause an irregularity in the rhythm, which may quickly develop into a serious fault.

Horses should be worked for at least one to two hours a day, a third of this should be spent walking out of doors, especially if their other work takes place in an indoor school. The working period spent hacking quietly can be extended to three or even four hours during that day. Work and rest should be carefully regulated and distributed according to the horse's age, ability, condition and training standard.

Correct work, fresh air and a certain amount of relaxation are necessary in the horses' daily routine for their proper development and general well-being. By nature, from their ancestors, horses are creatures of the plains; they love freedom and wide open spaces for their minds as well as for their limbs. The horseman can feel and share his horse's contentment as his equine eyes take in far-distant views and activities in the countryside, as he is allowed to pick his own way on a long rein, at a purposeful yet leisurely walk.

The full value of walking exercise is often underestimated; there is no better gait for putting on and establishing a horse's condition, for at the walk the horse moves his head and neck extensively, and all the muscles of his top-line are brought into play and are worked and developed, providing he is ridden correctly, yet at the same time stress and concussion are less than at any other gait.

The instructor must always be on the alert, and be ever-watchful of his horses' basic gaits as well as their form; any work or system of riding which jeopardizes clean and correct rhythmic strides at any gait must cease before it ruins the whole of the horse's training.

Although occasionally the instructor may have to watch and concentrate mainly on one part of a horse he must remember the importance of working the whole horse from his haunches, through his back, neck and poll, to the bit in his mouth. Every part must work together in harmony; conversely, resistance may show in one part of the horse because of tension elsewhere. Excess tension or resistance can only be eradicated from a horse's work when he is on the move; the rider can use the horse's natural need to balance himself to good effect thus eliminating constraint in mind, muscles and joints. Although a mental and physical cooling-off period may be very helpful for a 'hot' horse who is on the point of 'blowing-up' – the rider counting up to twenty while quietly patting – he must not then be misled by the apparent submission, this has yet to be proved by a further, short period of good unconstrained work.

All working periods should finish with an easy exercise, such as serpentine loops on long reins, followed, lastly, by walking on loose reins. Horses should be returned to their stables in a cool, and calm state.

Remember, it is a poor reflection on the chief instructor if his horses look stale, stiff and fed up as they plod round an oval-shaped 'ditch' in a riding school! Horses and pupils should come out of the indoor school looking interested if not animated, and well content.

STABLE MANAGEMENT – HORSE CARE

This is such an important subject that it cannot go without mention. As there are already many excellent textbooks which describe every aspect, it will not be dealt with in any detail in this book.

If the school prepares student instructors for official national instructors' examinations, the chief instructor and his team should use the stable manage-ment headings listed on the syllabii from which to create charts. These should be compiled from the easiest standards upwards to the highest examination. The subjects should remain in the groups as set on each syllabus to guide the students in their own studies and in their teaching later, when they have pupils of their own. All such charts must be up-dated regularly to incorporate new methods, machinery or medicines.

The instructors must encourage their students to keep records of:
> the sections covered by notes taken at lectures or from set textbooks and written up neatly in their loose-leaf files;
> their personal practical experience;
> the lecturing-practices given by the student during his course.

The personal charts and the loose-leaf files should be called-in for checking at regular intervals, and the inter-ride practical tests, mini-lectures, demon-strations, and debates should be organized.

They should also keep their own personal career log-books, listing courses attended, practical experience in the field, e.g. work they have undertaken for the pony club or in showing, horse-trials, jumping, dealing or racing yards, etc.

By setting his own standards high, the chief instructor can expect and obtain a high degree of enthusiastic efficiency from the rest of his team, and their school will soon gain a reputation for producing fit, well cared for and well turned-out horses ridden by educated riders.

10 Rules for the indoor riding school

Indoor schools are springing up (like veritable mushrooms) all over the country; this means that numbers of riders and horses are working together in a much more confined space than many of them are accustomed to. Thus to ensure the maximum safety, enjoyment and employment of a covered riding school with the minimum disturbance, danger or disaster a code of etiquette and procedure is essential.

Quite often riders are labelled 'mannerless ignoramuses' as a result of their behaviour when sharing an indoor school, whereas they cannot truly be at fault for not knowing what is virtually an unwritten code in this country to date.

The following 'rules' have been learned and observed by riders in our hitherto few schools and in the Continental schools for many generations. They are based on the need for safety, courtesy, and a commendable desire to avoid interruption, disturbance, interference and aggravation. 'Equestrian tact demands that every rider should be able to ride or train his horse without disturbing the other riders and thus neither will he be disturbed himself.'

1 All riders, including the chief instructor should always seek permission to enter the school.

2 An instructor already working in the school may not wish to be disturbed; it is his prerogative to refuse permission, especially if he has reserved the indoor school for that period; in practice he is unlikely to refuse.

3 Riders should enter unobtrusively, asking an assistant to open the door quickly and quietly and at just the right moment; make sure the doors are closed. Whoever opens the doors is responsible for seeing that they are fastened securely – this rule applies to leaving as well as entering the school.

4 At the earliest opportunity the senior instructor and the newly admitted rider should exchange acknowledgements or greetings. The instructor should discover the purpose of the newcomer's ride in the school and what help he may need.

5 Peace, quiet and attentive study should prevail in the indoor riding school, therefore shouting, noise or disturbance of any sort should never occur either in the school or its precincts. Conversation should be kept to a minimum and restricted to equine matters of urgency. The school and its galleries should always be tidy, with clothes folded neatly near the door – ready, yet out of the way.

6 If spectators are allowed in any gallery the school may have, they should be requested to sit quietly and still, and never to distract with idle chatter or to make a sudden movement.

7 Riders should select a suitable place from which to mount, e.g. a corner near the door, from a mounting-block of some sort which saves both the horse's back and the saddle tree.

All horses must stand absolutely still while the riders adjust saddlery and dress. No horse should be allowed to move until the rider is ready, has put the horse on the aids and asks him to move forward.

8 The first one to three minutes of ridden work should be spent at the walk on a fairly long rein, yet with the horse fully under control and ridden with a definite purpose in mind. The horse should never be worked at a faster pace immediately after leaving his stable, where he has been virtually motionless for hours on end; his muscles, tendons, ligaments, joints and circulation must be warmed and toned up gradually – alternatively he may be worked quietly in hand. (Major B.'s folk-dance. See Chapter 19).

9 Riders should always look up and stay alert. Keep well clear of any other activity already taking place in the school, and be ready to change the rein, turn or halt as may be necessary for the accommodation of other riders.

10 A group of riders working individually in the indoor school should ensure that there is a distance of at least 1½ metres between each horse.

11 They must keep a watchful eye on all the other riders, to avoid interrupting a faster-moving horse or one which requires plenty of room, e.g. those riding counter-canter, lateral movements, flying changes, piaffe, or on a young horse.

12 Any walking must be executed well inside the outer track to leave it clear for those working at faster gaits.

13 When more than four riders are working together they should all ride on the rein set by the most senior rider present in the school. He is responsible for changing the rein at intervals which are suitable and convenient for the remainder as well as himself. Alternatively they may prefer to work on two large circles. (See No. 20 below.) Every rider should change the rein when led to do so, without waiting for a command.

14 When a small number of horses is working, the riders on the left rein have priority, so that if two riders meet face to face *they pass left hand to left hand.*

FIG.10   PASSING LEFT HAND TO LEFT HAND

NOTE This procedure was laid down in the British Cavalry Manual of 1885 and is still accepted and practised to this day by all the nations who compete in international equestrian competitions.

15 Riders should follow the recognized tracks in the school which are suitable for their horses' present stage of training; i.e. they should be *seen* to plan and ride with thought and reasonable accuracy and should never be caught 'hacking' aimlessly round and round – nor standing 'coffee-housing'!

16 When a rider finds he is getting too close to the horse in front of him, particularly if this is due to that horse playing-up, he should take his horse away from the track in a smooth turn across the school, or in a half-circle or circle, timing his return to the track to fit into a convenient space.

17 Conversely a rider who hears a horse coming up close behind him should quietly turn or circle away if by so doing he will assist the approaching rider, e.g. a young horse learning to carry the rider at canter.

18 Riders should never overtake each other, nor ride two or more abreast.

19 An individual rider may work on a large circle when riding in company, providing the diameter of the circle does not exceed 17 metres thus leaving the outer track clear. Similarly riders working on serpentines should keep inside the outer track.

20 When riders wish to ride on large circles, they should ride on cog-wheels, that is on one 20 metre circle at A and another one on the opposite rein, at C. There should be an evenly balanced number on each circle and they may change the rein out of the circle at X. The senior rider usually commences the changing if no instructor is present.

When working individually on large circles (on opposite reins) or down the centre line, in general riders should circle or turn away on the opposite rein from the horse immediately in front of them – *riders* should not follow each other like sheep, they should school their horses intelligently – thinking riding!

21 The value of halt-periods should be thoroughly appreciated for the horses to rest and the pupils to learn, think and perhaps to watch a demonstration. The class should always be halted in an orderly manner, both for safety, and for ease and efficiency of explanation, demonstration, interrogation and/or discussion.

22 The senior instructor present must choose the most advantageous position for the riders to stand while halted – e.g. on a designated section of the centre line, on the A or C circle diameter line, facing A, C, or X, or wherever may be best suited for them to hear, watch or participate. Riders should halt in line, still and square, at right-angles to the wall they are facing, and leaving the outer track free for other riders or the instructor's demonstration.

23 An alternative method of usefully employing halt-periods is for the instructor to work a portion of the ride while the remainder observes, halted in a strategic position.

FIG. 11   " PARKING"

24 If one rider wishes to halt to rest his horse or himself, or to ask a question, he must choose the moment and place with care. He need not seek the instructor's permission unless he is being worked as a member of a ride. He should halt well inside the outer track leaving the turning-points and the centre line and the diagonal lines free, or he may stand alongside a jump which is not being used.

25 When beginners or young horses are working in the school, all more advanced riders must treat them with caution and consideration.

26 Should a horse or rider fall or should any accident occur all other riders

should halt immediately and dismount if necessary, and any other activities in the vicinity must cease until order is restored.

27 A receptive attitude of mind is an essential quality for any pupil, but particularly so if he is riding in an indoor school; one 'bad mood' amongst the riders can disrupt the atmosphere within the whole school.

28 No rider under instruction should ever argue or comment while his horse is on the move, or the rapport between the horse, the rider and the instructor will be destroyed. All advice offered by an instructor has one common denominator which is to help the rider to improve; in this he should not be impeded by an argumentative pupil. Questions and reasonings must be withheld until the ride or individual is halted.

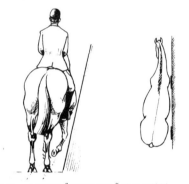

FIG 12   HORSE "HUGGING" THE WALL

29 Every rider is responsible for riding correct tracks and movements when working in the manège. He should never allow his horse to 'free-wheel' along by the wall, for the wall of the indoor riding school has a magnetic effect on the horse. All horses like to 'lean' on the wall with their outer shoulder when being ridden idly, crookedly and without thought, round and round against it, rather than correctly on the outer or other tracks. Therefore this 'system' is to be deprecated as it will quickly have a detrimental effect on the horse's straightness, his gaits and his mental attitude. On the other hand, an intelligent instructor and/or rider can use this wall-magnetism to good effect for the horses and riders in the composition of his exercises, few of which will proceed far along the outer track without a circle, turn, lateral movement or similar variation.

30 The term 'the inner side' always applies to the *horse's* inner side, and does not have any connection whatsoever with the wall of the school or arena. For example, if the horse is moving on the left or the right rein, if he is bent to the right in any part of his body, however slightly, his right side is his inner side.

31 When it is time for rider or riders to exchange, this must be accomplished with a minimum of disturbance. In-coming horses always have priority at the school-doors, to avoid time-wastage or overcrowding and accidents outside the school. The in-coming riders should start to ride-in while the previous riders

are having their final questions answered prior to picking out their horses' feet and departing quickly and quietly from the school.

32 *Lungeing*

(a) Any person lungeing in an area where other riders are working their horses must be very careful and quiet with his whip, voice and tongue-clicking – lack of tact may have dynamic if not disastrous results. The size of the circle must be strictly supervised to avoid accidents. The lunger must keep his horse under control and out of the way.

(b) When young, riderless horses are being lunged they should be worked on the opposite rein to that of the ride – kicks are less likely.

FIG.13   CLASS RIDING IN OPPOSITE DIRECTION

(c) If a rider is having a lunge lesson on a reliable horse they should work on the same rein as the ride – the riders are less likely to knock each other unintentionally.

(d) Initially young horses should only be lunged at a time when they may have the school to themselves, preferably not more than two at a time in a school measuring 20 metres×40 metres or three in a school of 20 metres×60 metres.

The two main reasons for this are:

i Safety; the behaviour of a young horse is unpredictable, as may be his trainer's control.

ii Young horses need plenty of room to be worked on *large* circles or there is a grave danger of straining joints or tendons – or setting-up a chronic lameness.

33 *Basic reminders for junior instructors*

(a) Check the tack at the start of every lesson, particularly with regard to fitting; that the saddle is placed correctly and is securely girthed; that the stirrup leathers are of a correct length – nearly all beginners like to adjust their leathers too short, the firmer feeling of their feet on the stirrups gives them a greater sense of security, that the stirrup irons are of a suitable size for the feet, and are taken up correctly.

(b) An experienced leading file is a great asset.

(c) All work with beginners, or when riders are working on their positions in the saddle or on blankets (without stirrups), should be taken in half the school, on a circle, or on a square where it is easiest to control or to help the riders and their mounts.

(d) Remember that the long side of the school can have an electrifying effect on a horse; hot horses may literally bolt down a long side, alternatively, it may be encouraging to a sluggish horse.

(e) Beginners will often regard cantering and later jumping as a terrifying and dangerous exercise; the pace and or positioning of the remainder of the ride is of the utmost importance. No class should ever be asked to canter together as a ride unless the riders are very experienced.

(f) Quiet, well-thought-out games can be of real instructional value, more so than the usual gymkhana events which can develop into an uncontrollable and frightening gallop. These are designed for capable riders, *not* for beginners.

(g) Cog-wheels and other educational exercises should be used regularly to teach young and novice riders the basics of control, procedure and etiquette, and later to improve the riders and the horses in the most natural way. (These will be described later.)

(h) Thoughtful tidiness is a hall-mark of efficiency.

11 School work

There are a number of tracks, figures and commands, the use and value of which for riding in an enclosed arena are universally recognized in international equestrian circles. They all have a purpose and each has many variations. Because most riders on the Continent have been brought up with and 'educated' to use indoor schools as an equestrian gymnasium or ballet school, thus they ride these school-figures correctly and collectively, as a matter of course. However, in nations which have lovely countryside in which to ride and where the winters are milder, there are comparatively few riders who know how to ride in an indoor school in the purposeful and educating manner which make this work immeasurably beneficial to riders and horses. In these latter countries an indoor school is regarded as an outsize umbrella under which to ride around in safety, and in the dry when it is raining, as well as being a safe and convenient place for an instructor to be seen and heard. This method leads to the mutual boredom of riders and horses as they plod round and round, the former preferring definitely to have the school to themselves – one by one. In fact, as has already been said, both types of riding, the school-work and the cross-country or outdoor riding should complement each other in the education and training of riders and of their horses – neither is complete without the other.

Commanded school-work should never be allowed to deteriorate into a dully plodding, wall-hugging drilled ride of the worst sort, which does nothing for the horses' gaits or the riders' intelligent sensitivity or feel. The true aims of the work must always be foremost in the instructor's mind because he himself fully understands it and believes in its worth.

The instructor must explain and demonstrate painstakingly how to ride the school figures both accurately and smoothly. The ground-plan and the aids for each figure must be taught, confirmed and tested so that correct lines in this work are securely established, and pupils will never more disturb their horses with rough aids due to lack of education.

All beginner-pupils should be taught, and more experienced riders reminded to make their preparations for every change of direction well in advance. Riders must always give their horses fair warning with 'thought, weight and thumb' so that their aids are soft, smooth and easy for the horses to follow, and yet indiscernible to any onlooker.

Correctly applied school-work will benefit:

(a) *The horses:* by intelligent use and interchange of the figures, and of the employment of the correct aids to ride them, exercises may be used to improve all the horses' form and work in the simplest and most natural way, with a marked improvement in their willing obedience, impulsion, suppleness, fitness and manners.

(b) *The riders:* by making them think ahead, with better preparations for the accurate riding of figures and transitions, the riders' influence and co-ordination is improved in a positive yet effortless way. They will learn to ride

FIG.14   TOO CLOSE - THOUGHTLESS RIDING

constructively in the company of other riders, not merely thinking selfishly, for and of themselves alone, e.g. 'Is my horse trotting fast enough?' 'I wish those other riders would not keep getting in the way – I must book this school at a time when I can have it to myself' ... and so on; all of which is narrow, restricted thinking, and will be reflected in their horses' way of going. Whereas, if they are taught to ride as members of a well-instructed ride this encourages forward-thinking; teaches the riders to be alert with their aids; to be aware and open-eyed as well as open-minded; it tests their ability and tact, and quickens and improves the natural harmony of their preparations, actions and reactions, and feel. If there are any more private thoughts they should be critically analytical. 'Is my position as nearly perfect as I can get it?' 'Is my horse going freely forward and on the bit?' 'Are his gaits true and lively?' However, above all else will be the dominating factor of working as a *team*, all riders looking about them as they ride, every member working for a common goal – IMPROVEMENT for PERFECTION.

For the greater part of all lessons, the instructor should work the ride as a whole, in open order, using commands which are easily understood by all riders. For the first 5 minutes of every lesson, providing the pupils are safe and educated enough, the instructor should allow the riders to work their horses individually, without interruption, to give them all time to tune into their horses, and to think and feel and to feel and think. Although at this time the instructor should observe all his pupils' riding-in with acute interest he should keep individual corrections to a minimum concentrating mainly on the ride's dressing, accuracy and forward-riding, and rely on these factors to work their own improvement on riders and horses alike, to the maximum benefit of all concerned in the ride. He must train his pupils to work constructively whilst being aware of and courteous to each other.

(c) *Student-instructors:* By working in a class the student's self-confidence may be sown and cultivated by their instructor, so that they come to find enjoyment, a thrill, and a deep satisfaction from their own teaching, and their pupils, in their turn, will derive richer rewards.

The instructor may lead the students into the instructional side of their work, in a class in the following ways:

i Dismounted practice.

ii The instructor invites students individually to stand with him, either mounted or dismounted, whichever the instructor himself may be, to learn his thoughts, commands, timing and corrections at close quarters, where occasional quiet explanatory asides may further aid his understanding of the teaching.

iii Each student is encouraged to give a few simple commands to the ride, at suitable intervals as directed by the instructor.

An initial period of 10 minutes each is ample time for the students, and for the ride!

In the early stages, if a whole lesson-period is programmed for 'Instructional practice', it is essential that the instructor takes the greater part of the lesson himself to maintain the high standard of its content. The general atmosphere of enthusiasm and interest must be sustained; if it is allowed to wane so will the student-instructor's confidence and control, and this deteriorating will also be harmful to the participating riders and horses.

iv The students help each other in pairs, with simple corrections, from within the ride. Before commencing, the exercise must be explained and the pairs considerately selected, the instructor must explain its objects and likely pitfalls. In this way the students will develop confidence, command, and a discerning eye for, and a pleasant way of correcting faults, as well as a better way of riding – looking ahead and about them, and thinking of others.

v As the students gain in confidence, knowledge and authority, so the instructor may give them various pre-set school figures to teach and command. These must be well-established and students should be given every possible opportunity to assist with beginners' and children's lessons before they are asked to teach even simple riding lessons on their own.

CLASS LESSONS – TAKING THE RIDE

All the following work should first be practised on foot. This gives the students confidence in giving the commands, they learn the tracks and they are not interrupted by their horses nor do they spoil their mouths, form or gaits with clumsy aids while they are learning the figures and the words of command.

When several riders are riding as a group under instruction, in a covered riding school, enclosed manège, or in a field, their lesson may be constructed on any one of the following four basic forms:

i *Riders may form a ride behind a selected leading-file*, as a single ride, as a double-ride, or divided into equal sections.

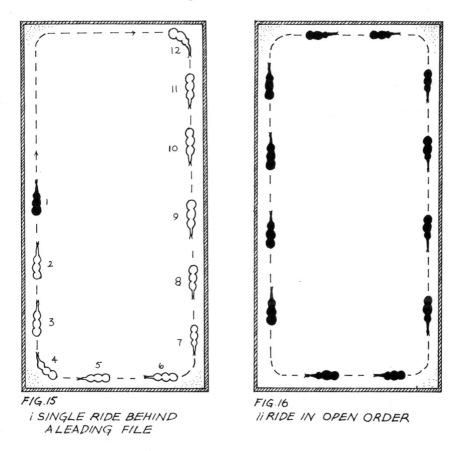

FIG.15
i *SINGLE RIDE BEHIND A LEADING FILE*

FIG.16
ii *RIDE IN OPEN ORDER*

ii *Riders may be in open-order, without a set leading-file*, with equal spacing between horses.

iii *Riders may work independently of each other*, one or more named riders receive instruction in turn, while the remainder carry on with their own work, individually or following a set task.

iv *One-half of the ride works while the other half rests.*

i *In a ride behind a leading-file*

(a) *As a single-ride* – the foremost rider is responsible for the gait, its tempo and speed, and the direction, while the other riders follow him.

To move off a ride which is halted to the left of the leading-file the command is, 'Ride, from the right, forward to the right or left rein, walk march' (or trot), whereupon each member of the ride walks, or trots straight forward at precisely the right time to be in his place in the ride and at the correct distance from the preceding rider as they turn on to the outer track. This method keeps the riders alert and is a good test of their ability. A ride may be formed from any other formation by naming the leading-file and the desired spaces or distances between horses, e.g. 'Form a ride behind Mr Smith, Sarah, or John, on the left rein with two metres between horses.' Each rider chooses a place behind the leading-file and rides there smoothly and without any change of gait or tempo.

Thereafter corners should be well-ridden and the horses kept straight down the long sides, with no shoulders escaping out towards the wall, or hedge. If a rider wishes to make up ground and close up the distance between his horse and that of the rider in front of him he should make a distinct turn across the school before reaching the far end of the long side, thus shortening the school. The riders behind him follow his turning. See Fig. 17.

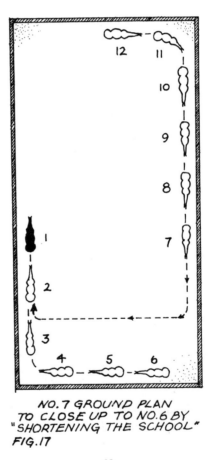

NO. 7 GROUND PLAN
TO CLOSE UP TO NO.6 BY
"SHORTENING THE SCHOOL"
FIG. 17

The ride may be worked as a whole in single-file or one at a time, individually. In the former case the commands may be preceded by the words 'Whole ride'; in the latter case the instructor should specify 'Leading file in succession' or 'Rear-file in succession' when he wishes his pupils to carry out an exercise one by one. In this latter case the instructor must remember to involve the remainder of the ride by inviting comments on each individual round as it is concluded, or giving them a position corrective exercise to work on.

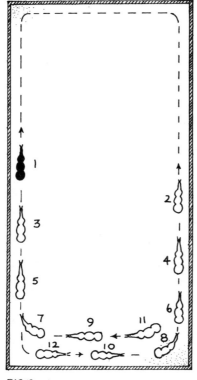

FIG. 18 A DOUBLE RIDE

(b) *As a double ride* – with two leading files, on opposite reins. The leading-file and his ride (odd numbers) are responsible for the pace – speed and tempo. No. 2 and his ride (even numbers) are responsible for the dressing. As a general rule, they will pass left hand to left hand.

To divide the ride, the commands are as follows: with the ride walking on long reins on the outer track, the instructor arranges them into the most suitable order, then, 'From the front, over your inside shoulder, number.' (This may also be done 'in twos'.) 'Ride trot, and take up your reins.' As soon as the ride has settled to a good working trot – not more than once round the school, 'Leading-file down the centre line; divide at A or C (at the opposite end), odd numbers left, and even numbers right,' after which the leading-files

69

should be told to steady the pace if close-order of 1½–2 metres is required, and the instructor should remind both rides of their respective responsibilities with regard to pace and dressing. The rides may be turned down the centre line in pairs, dividing in pairs to the left and the right, and then in fours, etc. If there is no command as they ride down the centre line the riders should automatically divide, and so on, and finally they are told to 'Turn down the centre line in single-file'.

(c) *As a ride which is divided into equal sections* – usually of twos, threes or fours. The instructor commands the ride to number or 'tell-off', as required, from the front, after which he can work them as he wishes. He must remember to return the ride to its original order at the end of each exercise.

ii *In open-order, without a leading-file*

The ride should be evenly distributed around the track, each rider maintaining a good and regular pace and equal distances between the horses. If a rider finds the distance between himself and the rider in front of him varying unduly he must make the necessary correction himself, smoothly and unobtrusively. Occasionally he may ride a half circle across the school to find a more suitable space, and even more rarely should the instructor have to call him out to do so. A ride without a leading file is the most suitable and beneficial form of riding in numbers in a school, especially with experienced riders and young horses, for riders have more freedom of thought and movement and opportunities for individual work and training, under their instructor's guidance. The work may be varied endlessly, all riders working on the same exercises individually as commanded by the instructor, on the outer track for short stretches only, or on other tracks; on large circles, down the centre line across the school, or with one half of the ride usefully halted, while the other half works, and vice versa.

(a) To form a ride in open-order, without a leading-file, from a ride which is halted in close-order, the instructor calls upon each rider by name to, 'Walk march, (or trot), forward to the right rein,' arranging the ride into the most beneficial order for all horses present and distributing his pupils evenly along the rectangular outer track, until they are all out and ready to work.

(b) A ride which is working in close order behind a leading-file may be changed to open-order by one of two methods:

With the ride in walk, the command is given, 'From the front into open-order of . . . metre spaces, ride trot'. The instructor must gauge the number of metres between horses depending on the number of horses in the school. Each leading-file in succession moves forward into trot just as soon as the preceding horse has trotted forward leaving a distance of the required metres behind him.

With the ride in walk or trot, the command is given, 'Form a ride in open-order with . . . metre spaces'. Whereupon the riders disperse along the rectangular outer track in no particular order, making smooth turns or half-circles across the school, remaining on the original rein and forming and maintaining a regular interval behind the preceding horses.

In order to re-form the ride into close order, to change the rein, to turn across the school, or to form or change circles, a leading-file may be nominated, the movement is commanded and executed and then the previous open-order or individual work may be resumed. (It is best to choose a different leading-file on each occasion, to avoid favouritism and to keep all the riders on their toes.)

70

If no leading-file has been nominated, and an exercise is commanded, the rider approaching the specified turning-point or marker commences the exercise and the rest of the ride follow.

iii *When riding individually*, every rider works independently on a task set by their instructor, for a certain period of time. This form can only be used when riders and horses are sufficiently trained, and then it furthers each individual's riding ability to move purposefully yet quietly amongst other horses and riders. Many of the details given in ii also apply to iii.

If the class is being taken in a larger sized school, or in a field, the instructor may divide the ride into two, three or four equal parts and give two-thirds of the ride individual work to do while he gives *special coaching* to two to four riders who will work near to him. All groups will be called in for discussion, rebriefing and exchange at regular intervals – a whistle is a useful, practical means of collecting the ride.

This form of class work is most useful if it is interspersed in the middle portion of a lesson. Its title is self-explanatory and its variations are innumerable.

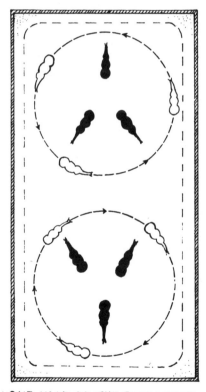

ONE HALF OF THE RIDE WORKS
– THE OTHER HALF RESTS
FIG. 19

iv One half of the ride works while the other half rests.

The resting half of the ride should be positioned thoughtfully by the instructor, they should never be idly scattered nor allowed to feel abandoned. The instructor should tell the resting riders that although their horses are having a period of relaxation the riders are not! If the horses are to remain halted the riders should busy themselves either with some educational practise for themselves, e.g. lengthening and shortening reins or stirrups or for their horses, e.g. dismounting and mounting from both sides, picking up feet, etc. or establishing still halts, all with reward for compliance. Alternatively these riders may be asked to assess the work of the active half of the ride. In the latter case, the instructor must remember to ask for these deliberations before he exchanges the two halves of the ride.

The instructor may use the resting half of the ride to his advantage. Bearing in mind the horse's herd instinct and his gregariousness he can use the presence of the stationary horses to increase the desire of the horses who are working to make smooth transitions from riders' aids which are then virtually invisible.

The resting half of the ride may be told to halt or to walk on long reins on a prescribed circle track or one which is inside the outer track, or they may be halted on the centre line.

This format is particularly useful for novice or unfit riders or horses.

Forming up the ride to the halt

As soon as his pupils can ride easy turns and progressive halts individually, the instructor should teach them to be more thoughtful and to feel *how* their horses come to a halt when they are commanded to 'Form a Ride', on a given line, 'to the halt', e.g. on the centre line, facing B or E; on the A or C circle-diameter line, facing X, C or A; or on the M–H line, facing X or C. The instructor should indicate a line which is well clear of the outer track, is parallel with a long or short side of the school, and is suitably positioned for the ride to see, hear, and then to commence the next part of the lesson. Each rider should predetermine a convenient space into which he may ride his horse in a wide and easy turn round the ride's flank, coming straight into line from the rear of the ride. Pupils should be taught to be smooth with their aids yet precise about their dressing and distances. The horses should come smoothly to a halt with a good and natural balance, straight and still – the riders using minimum rein-aids.

The riders should allow their horses to stand 'at ease' on long reins, whilst they retain awareness, control and responsibility over the behaviour of the horses they are riding; any unsteadiness should be corrected instantaneously, mainly with the leg aids or by a corrective tap with the whip.

Every horse should always be positioned and standing exactly as required, approximately 1 metre apart and at a right angle with the wall or side of the school which the ride is facing.

The instructor should guide his pupils to feel and to get their horses to stand square, on all four legs. The horses' and the riders' feet, hips, shoulders and ears should be level and parallel with the wall in front of them.

If a horse halts crookedly or moves out of alignment, the rider must quietly replace the forehand and should not try to move the hindquarters. If a horse moves forward a step or two out of line then the rider should be told to walk straight forward out of the ride, to turn left or right on to the outer track, to turn across the school beyond the ride, and to time his fourth and last turn so that he is riding on a straight line into his former position in the halted ride. (See horse No. 5 in Fig. 20.)

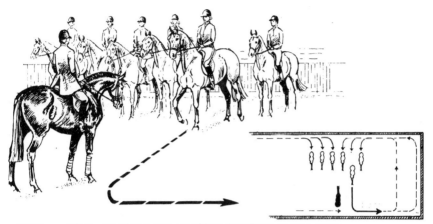

FIG 20   NO. 5   RE-TAKES HIS CORRECT POSITION IN THE RIDE

Leading file take an inner track and halt, or inwards turn and halt. The rest of the ride form a ride to his left (or right) to the halt. In both these procedures the instructor brings his ride to the halt, in their original order and in a neatly closed-up formation. Both these methods provide a quick and efficient means of lining up the ride, which is particularly helpful for beginners and for children on ponies who may or may not be under control, but they do not encourage the independence of thought and movement as well as does the first method, and for this reason they are not so educational to riders nor horses.

'Leading-file halt and inwards turn.' This procedure for halting the ride on the outer track should only be used when it is absolutely necessary. This method is very convenient, for it leaves a maximum area of the school free and available for demonstration purposes or individual performances, and the command and effect are simple. However, this manoeuvre does allow lazy riders to use the impeding presence of the horse in front of them, aided only by an over-strong rein aid to make the short and awkward turn. This, combined with the rider overbalancing to the outside, may well force the horse's hindquarters to swing out, and may even cause damage to his hocks, or to the heels of the horse in front of him, with resultant defensive kicks. Thus it is essential that this useful but more difficult movement is carefully taught, is well supervised, and is only sparingly used thereafter.

Just as an athlete learns the dimensions of a cricket or football pitch, a badminton, tennis or squash court so that he can participate in the sport of his choice, so a rider must learn the dimensions of an arena and also the ground-plans of the various school figures which are ridden inside that arena. In this

73

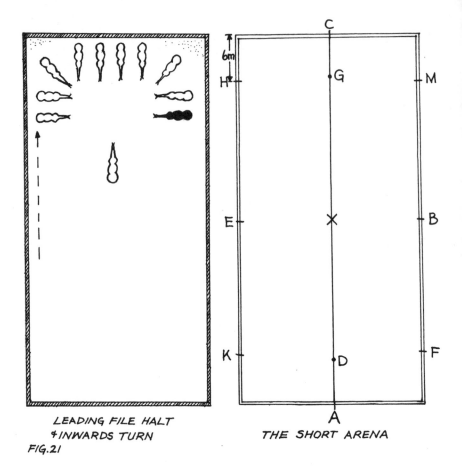

LEADING FILE HALT
 ≠ INWARDS TURN
FIG.21

THE SHORT ARENA

way the arena or its equivalent, teaches him the method of using the school as a gymnasium, it does not restrict his work within its confines.

Universally the following arena-sizes are recognized:

The short arena=20×40 metres. This is often used at national level for novice horses.

The long arena=20×60 metres. This is used for all international events and for most national tests of medium and advanced standard.

The Scandinavian arena=20×40 metres and 20×60 metres, having a common short side at C. This is used at national level for novice to medium horses.

The majority of the test is ridden in the short arena; the long arena being used for medium and extended gaits only, when the greater length encourages the horses to extend forward over the ground. If space is a problem the 60 metre measurement need not be adhered to strictly.

This section contains diagrams, together with brief notes on each figure drawn, to enable student-instructors to learn how to ride them and how to teach them to their pupils. All these figures should be taught to beginners at the walk, in their first lessons.

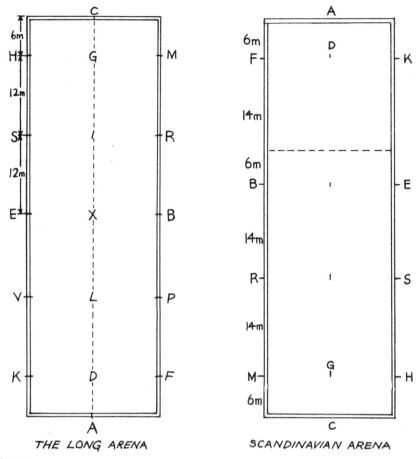

THE LONG ARENA   SCANDINAVIAN ARENA

FIG. 22

If student-instructors are taught that the quality of their teaching will be evaluated by their pupils' riding of the outer track and of the various school figures from, to and within the outer track, it will increase their determination to teach this subject well. The instructor who allows his pupils to trot aimlessly and endlessly round and round the school in an ever-deepening 'track' which becomes an egg-shaped ditch is thoroughly unworthy of his title. He may make a commercial success of his school if he lives in a built-up area or in a rich commuter belt but he will never produce riders and horses of note, nor will his pupils ever learn to appreciate the art of horsemanship.

School figures, terms and commands

1 *The track* is the name given to the path along which the horse moves. Although none of the tracks are actually marked out and are thus invisible, they should be understood and ridden with as high a degree of accuracy as is compatible with the horse's present standard of training.

2 *The outer track* is ridden carefully and distinctly, in a rectangular shape, half to three quarters of a metre inside the wall of the school or manège with

four well-ridden corners. This track is taken on the command, 'Take the outer track, on the right (or left) rein,' or 'Ride, go large on the right rein'.

An inner rectangular track – is ridden on the command, 'Ride take an inner track, two, three or four metres inside the outer track.' This distance must be maintained constantly with four distinct corners until the instructor commands the ride to, 'Go large,' or to take another track.

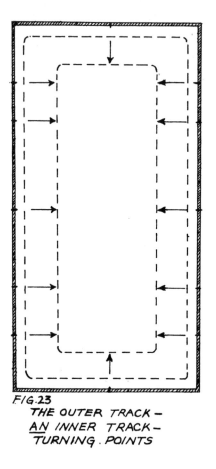

FIG.23
THE OUTER TRACK –
AN INNER TRACK –
TURNING . POINTS

3 *Turning-points* are the places on the track where turns are usually made. The official turning points of the outer track are on the long sides 6 metres from the corner-points, or in the middle of the short or long sides, or midway between the above mentioned points, when riding in a long arena. See Fig. 23. Turns across the school may also be executed from any convenient point on the long sides.

To turn across the school 'Right (or left) turn.' A quarter of a volte or small circle is ridden, and then after riding straight across the school, dressing by the right to keep their line straight, the ride takes the outer track on the right rein

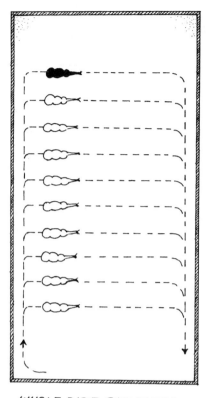

WHOLE RIDE RIGHT TURN
FIG. 24

with the rear file in the lead. This figure should be ridden twice in order to restore the leading-file and the ride to their original order. If the instructor wishes the riders to change the rein, he should give the command, 'and change', before the riders cross the centre line – or better still in a preparatory command, e.g. 'Turning across the school, whole ride ... in sections ... in threes ... or similar – and changing the rein, ride (or first section) right turn.' More advanced classes should liken each turn to a quarter pirouette.

To turn across the school in twos (threes or fours), when the ride is closed-up behind a leading-file, on the command, 'in twos, right turn', the first two riders turn right, ride straight across the school and track right, while the rest of the ride continues until they reach the exact point where the first two riders turned, they then turn without further command, and the next two, and so on.

If there has been no change of rein, the exercise should be repeated once again, in the same numbers, in order to restore the ride to its original order.

Half-circles across the school in twos (threes or fours) may be ridden in a similar way. The instructor must be strict with regard to the correct shape of the half-circle tracks, i.e. that they have three accurately ridden points, correctly spaced out on the circle line. See Fig. 25.

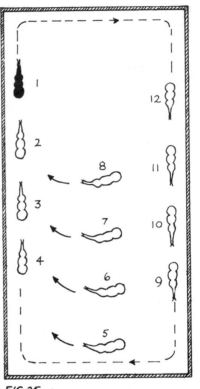

FIG. 25 IN SECTIONS —
HALF CIRCLES ACROSS THE SCHOOL

4 *Corners and/or turns* are ridden as a quarter of a 6 metre circle. The corners should be rounded, or ridden into more accurately, depending on the standard of the riders and of the horse's training and the pace at which the turn is being ridden. The turn should be emphasized least by novice riders, on young green horses, and at extended paces. Every corner or turn is a valuable training exercise; each should be ridden carefully with the thought, 'Straight, half-halt, weight, turn, and push!' The instructor must be quick to reprimand riders who are careless in this respect, for they are then missing so many excellent riding and schooling moments.

5 *The centre line* is the line that runs between the middle points of the two short sides. See Fig. 26. It is taken on the command, 'At A, or C, turn down the centre line.' When the opposite short side is reached, the outer track is followed on the same rein, unless otherwise commanded. If several riders are working on an exercise involving the centre line they should follow it in single file, towards a named end A, or C, – preferably towards a mirror, to check the straightness of their horses, the figure and their dressing. If riders are working up and down the centre line in an exercise which involves passing one another, they will ride on an inner track, $\frac{1}{2}$–$\frac{3}{4}$ metre inside the centre line. Thus, on the right rein they should begin and end with a quarter of a volte or for novices by a

78

suitably sized half-circle from the end of the long side, and the track between the two turns should be absolutely straight and at right-angles to the short side ahead, the horse's and the rider's shoulders and hips axis should be parallel with the same short side.

6 *The quarter and three-quarter lines* are longitudinal lines equidistant to and parallel with the centre line and the long sides of the school. The quarter line is the first one reached on a short side, before the centre line; the three-quarter line is beyond the centre line, half-way between it and the next long side.

7 *The diagonal-line* runs obliquely across the school from a point on one long side 6 metres from the corner (a corner-point) to a corresponding corner-point diagonally opposite, on the other long side. See Fig. 26.

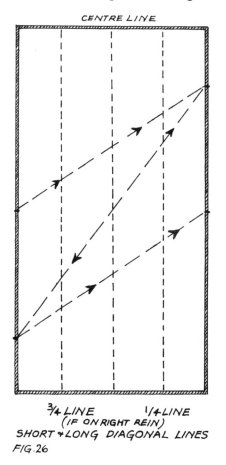

CENTRE LINE

¾ LINE   ¼ LINE
(IF ON RIGHT REIN)
SHORT + LONG DIAGONAL LINES
FIG. 26

In order that they ride this and other diagonal line figures well, the instructor must teach his pupils to ride straight along a diagonal line which finishes 8 metres, rather than 6 metres from the corner, i.e. 2 metres before the actual marker; then their horses' feet will step on to the outer track exactly level with the corner marker. If pupils watch the instructor's demonstration they will soon appreciate the value of this rider directive.

79

8 *Short diagonal-lines* run obliquely across half the school. The diagonal line through the first half of the school runs from the first corner-point on a long side to an obliquely opposite middle-point of the other long side.

The diagonal line through the last (or second) half of the school runs from the middle point of the long side to the obliquely or diagonally opposite second corner point on the other long side. See Fig. 26.

The (long) diagonal-line is followed on the command, 'Through the whole school, right incline.' This command is given when the rider approaches A, or C, on the right rein; if there are two leading files they must pass left hand to left hand, leaving 1 metre between their horses as they pass, and should return to the outer track 8 metres before the corner. If the ride is changing from the left rein they must pass right hand to right hand.

The short diagonal line is ridden following the command, 'Through the first half of the school, right-incline'. The rider, on the right rein, leaves the track at M (or K) and rides straight across to E (or B) where he returns to the outer track on the left rein, *or* 'Through the last or second half of the school, right incline' – in which case the rider continues along the track on the long side until he reaches B (or E), he then leaves the outer track and inclines straight across to K (or H), where he re-takes the outer track on the left rein.

9 *The corner line* is the line that runs from the middle point of the short side and returns obliquely to the middle point of the long side along which the rider has just passed. It is used following the command, 'In the middle of the next short side, turn back to the track.' The riders approaching A, or C make a smooth turn on to the centre line and almost immediately incline back to the outer track at B or E. If there are many riders and there is no room for the leading-files to reach the outer track they will continue on an inner track until the outer one is free. See Fig. 27. This track may also be ridden in reverse order.

10 *Circles or voltes* correctly 'a volte is a circular track', but in most English-speaking countries, a circle is a circle of any size larger than 6 metres, and a 5 or 6 metre circle is called a volte. No circle or volte should be smaller than 5 metres. See Fig. 27. (Volte is pronounced to rhyme with 'colt'.)

The large circle's diameter is usually the length of the outer track along the short side of the school; if a number of horses are being worked in a school which is 20 metres wide, the diameter of the large circle should not exceed 17 metres to avoid interference to riders working on figures which use the outer track.

Every large circle has four circle points, two where the circle crosses the centre line, and two where it touches the outer-track on each side. See Fig. 27. Riders should be taught carefully from the start *how* to ride a circle correctly – their horses 'should breathe on the outer track at each circle-point', they should never be allowed to thump along the outer track with too big a circle – which is flattened out at each circle point by the wall of the arena.

Large, 20 metre circles, are ridden on the command, either 'Ride two large circles at A and C on the left, or right rein,' when both circles are ridden on the same rein, and adjoin at X or they may be commanded on to opposite reins, conjoining at X (cog-wheels). The ride may be told to 'Ride a large circle at B (or E)'.

They will not ride in close-order on the large circles, but will change to and

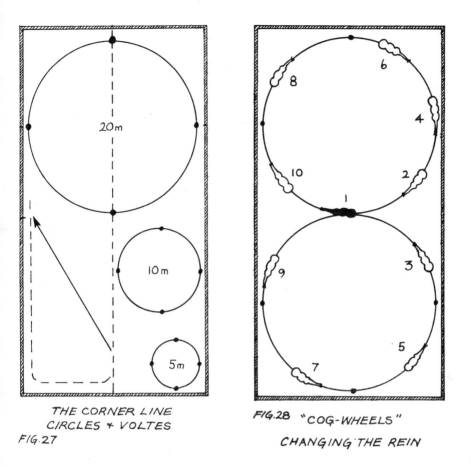

THE CORNER LINE
CIRCLES + VOLTES
FIG.27

FIG.28 "COG-WHEELS"

CHANGING THE REIN

retain equal spacing on each circle and must keep their correct order at X.

To 'change the rein out of the circle' – the circle point where the two large circles conjoin – at X in a small arena – is flattened out to a length of 1–3 metres on the E–B line, where each horse is straightened and repositioned before taking the other circle track.

The instructor should always ensure that every member of his class knows how to ride this movement, i.e. that after passing the outer side-point of the circle, the rider must shorten the outside rein in readiness, he should then shift his weight and adjust his seat early enough to enable the horse to follow this invitation of his rider's aids. At the changing point the rider only has to think of the size of the circle, confirm that his weight is shifted sufficiently to that direction, turn inside forearm and wrist so that the thumb leads the way, while easing the outside rein. The horse will then change direction very smoothly, his hind feet following the forefeet exactly; his ears will be level in height and his central line will align perfectly with the circle line. The rider's forward driving and restraining aids will be carefully measured to retain the horse's interest, form and rhythm. See Fig. 29.

81

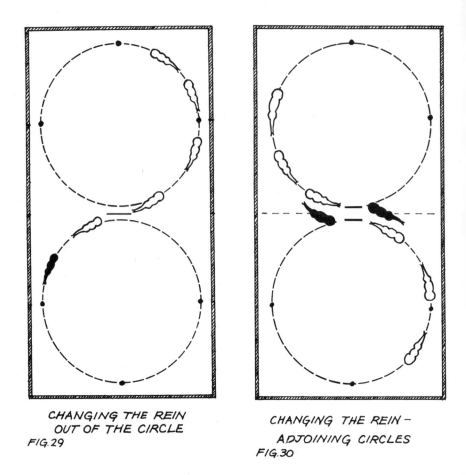

CHANGING THE REIN
OUT OF THE CIRCLE
FIG. 29

CHANGING THE REIN –
ADJOINING CIRCLES
FIG. 30

This figure may be used in a variety of ways – the most usual, with their respective commands are:

(a) In a numbered ride, with a leading-file, the order is given. 'Leading-file change the rein out of the circle.' Whereupon, Number 1 leads the change of rein, straight across X, followed by the rest of the ride in their original numerical order. See Fig. 29.

(b) In open order, on two large circles, two temporary leading-files will be called by name; as they approach C and A respectively, thereafter one rider will pass over X and change the rein from each circle alternately. This is simple if the circles conjoin. If they adjoin then each rider passes and changes the rein behind the approaching rider from the opposite circle. See Fig. 30.

(c) Riding independently, riders should change the rein quite frequently, riding straight on the E–B line for 1–3 metres at X. All riders must keep alert so that the numbers remain balanced in each circle, and that even distances are maintained.

N.B. Strangers working in a ride on circle, will invariably feel hustled; this is usually due to their careless riding of the actual circles. If any rider allows his horse to escape out to the corners, he will constantly have to hurry to make up the lost ground, and will often have the feeling that the horse behind is 'puffing down his neck'. If he rides a true circle it will be easy for him to retain a correct dressing.

A volte is ridden on the command 'Volte, *now*', whereupon each rider makes a small volte, of 5–6 metres, wherever he is at that moment, and then continues in the same direction. Small circles of 7, 8 or 9 metres may be ridden in a similar manner.

To 'Change the rein within the circle' two half-circles are ridden. The first 10 metre half-circle is ridden from the circle-point after the closed side, on to the centre line for 1–2 metres. Here the horse is straightened and repositioned before the second 10 metre half-circle is ridden out to the opposite side circle-point. Thus the horse is facing the short side when he is on the centre line which helps to keep his attention on his rider, far more than would be possible if the figure were ridden the other way round so that he had the greater length of the school ahead of him. This exercise must be ridden smoothly and

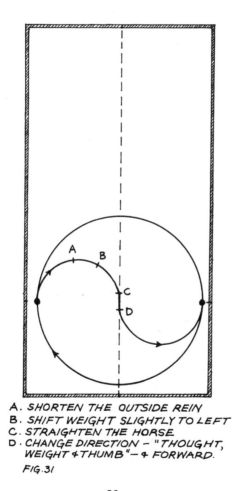

A. SHORTEN THE OUTSIDE REIN
B. SHIFT WEIGHT SLIGHTLY TO LEFT
C. STRAIGHTEN THE HORSE
D. CHANGE DIRECTION — "THOUGHT, WEIGHT & THUMB" — & FORWARD.
FIG.31

thoughtfully – as, in order to have a straight part on the centre line the figure cannot be geometrically perfect. Here common sense and feel must override mathematics. See Fig. 31.

The instructor must warn his pupils to shorten the outside (new inside) rein soon after they start the first half-circle, and to shift his weight subtly, well before reaching the centre line in order that there is no disturbance when changing the direction.

The rein may also be changed by riding a half-circle, or half-volte and return inside the circle. The former, in single-file, behind the named leading-file, i.e. the easier version; half-voltes and return are ridden by all riders simultaneously, on the final word, 'Now.' As half-voltes need a certain amount of collection if ridden at trot, they should not be ridden by novice horses or riders other than at the walk.

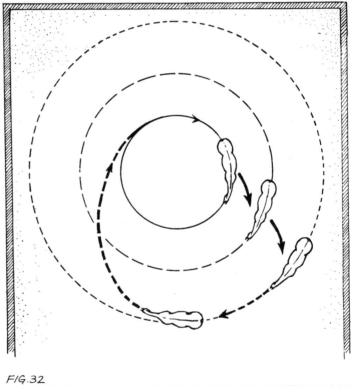

F/G.32

DECREASING & INCREASING THE 20 METRE CIRCLE
(SIMPLEST FORM)

Decreasing and increasing the 20 metre circle – on the command 'Decrease the circle', the horses are ridden individually towards the centre of the circle until 'Enough', or the distance between the horses is only 1 metre, in which case the riders themselves automatically stop reducing the circle, or a 10 metre circle may be specified. On the command, 'Increase the circle', the riders individually move out to the track of the large circle. This exercise should be ridden on a single track to introduce the ground-plan, after which it may be ridden on two tracks, in leg-yielding, with novice horses and later, decreasing and increasing in the more advanced, collected movements of half-pass or travers, and shoulder-in respectively.

11 '*A half-circle on to the centre-line, incline and change the rein.*' The rider follows the outer track to the far end of the long side; he then rides half a 10 metre circle, the centre of which touches the quarter line point on the short side, and returns obliquely to the middle point of the long side along which he has just passed. This is a useful, simple means of changing the rein, in single file, or it may be ridden in sections '8 metre half-circles and return' is a shortened version where each member of the ride rides a half-circle inwards simultaneously on the command, 'Now!' and then inclines back to the outer track.

12 *A reversed half-circle* has an identical pattern to 11 above, but is ridden the other way round, i.e. obliquely away from the middle-point of the long side towards the centre line, before returning to the track with a 10 or 8 metre half-circle. Reversed half-circles, as a ride, ('Norwegian fish hooks') are

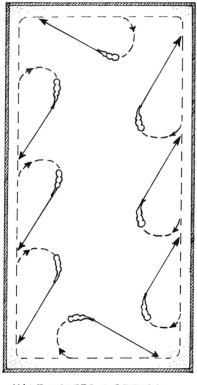

HALF VOLTES & RETURN

FIG. 33

85

'understood' to be of 6–8 metres. This is an excellent exercise for horses and riders alike, especially when ridden on long reins.

13 *A half-volte and return.* A half-volte of 5–6 metres is ridden at a convenient point on the long side, or just before its second corner, after which the rider returns obliquely back to the long side from which he has just come.

14 *A reversed half volte* has an identical ground-plan to 13 above, but is ridden the other way round. (Back to front.)

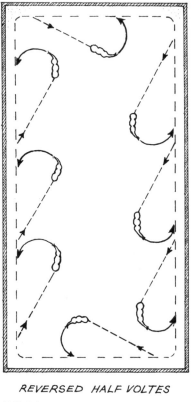

REVERSED HALF VOLTES

FIG 34

Due to the small diameter of the half-circles, the volte figures require a degree of collection and are therefore too demanding for very young horses or novice riders, other than at walk on long reins when they are excellent for confirming the thought and weight aids.

Later, as horses and riders become more advanced, the line returning obliquely back to the track in any of these exercises Nos 10, 11 and 13, may be ridden on two tracks.

15 *A figure of eight* consists of two equal circles touching, and is ridden with continuous changes of rein, out of the circle.

Before they are asked to ride this figure pupils must be reminded of the well prepared and subtle aids for changing the rein out of the circle already described on p. 81. They must be sure to shorten, but not tighten, their outside rein, and to shift their weight to the outside (the new inside) well before the changing point between the two circles, to enable the horses to make very smooth changes of direction and to follow accurate circle lines with ease, maintaining good form and impulsion.

In a large figure of eight the circles are both 20 metres in diameter and are ridden as for changing the rein out of the circle with a 1–3 metre 'flattened' part where the circles join. This is where the horse shows that he has accepted and reacts to the rider's changed aids, particularly those of thought, weight, thumb and an easing of the outer rein.

In a small figure of eight the circles are usually both 10 metres in diameter and are ridden as for changing the rein within the circle, see Fig. 31 with 1–2 metres 'flattened' out on the centre line, facing the short side of the school. Here the horse follows his rider's aids and the rider straightens his horse before repositioning him and changing direction with invisible aids.

16 *A serpentine* is a winding track of regular curves, along one or both long sides, or crossing the centre line. The number and depth of the loops should be specified; they must be perfectly regular and the whole figure fluent and symmetrical.

In a serpentine through the whole school each half-circular-shaped loop touches the long sides of the outer track for approximately one stride before returning across the centre line. The figure should appear artistically curvaceous rather than geometrically angular.

If several riders are working in the same arena, then any rider working on a sepentine through the whole school should only extend the loops to touch an inner track approximately 2 metres in from the wall, thus leaving the outer-track free for the other riders.

A serpentine is ridden on the command, 'Serpentines on the long sides' or 'down the centre line' or 'through the whole school'. In the first two figures the instructor specifies the number and depth of the loops and the ride continues riding the serpentine until the command, 'Take the outer track,' or 'Ride, go large . . .'. In the last figure the instructor enumerates the number of loops – remembering that an odd number of loops returns the ride to the original rein and an even number of loops changes the rein. This figure starts in the middle of one short side and finishes in the middle of the opposite short side – the rider should remember not to ride into the corners of the outer track as part of the first or the last loop of the serpentine.

The instructor much teach his pupils how to ride serpentines with invisible aids, and that, 'Thought, weight, thumb leading the way and ease the outside rein,' should be the unseen theme. Riders of all standards will then find the riding of serpentines miraculously easy, and will thereafter derive increased pleasure, as well as a much greater sense of achievement and togetherness with their horses. The instructor cannot be too painstaking in his attention to detail; he must explain that when riding a serpentine through the whole school, for example from the right rein, as he rides over the widest point of the first loop he should carefully shorten his left rein as this is about to be the new inside rein. Then he thinks very carefully of exactly where he will ride over the ground and how his horse is going, as he slightly shifts his weight to the left (the outside, soon to be the new inside). He may wish to make a suitable half-halt just before reaching the centre line, where he will merely have to turn his left wrist, so that at that point his thought, weight and thumb all combine to lead the way smoothly, as he eases the right (new outside) rein. He asks for a little more bend with his left leg, to soften the new inner side and has both legs in readiness to maintain the impulsion as, when, and where necessary. In no time at all the horse will reach the next serpentine-point and the rider will have to start all over again, shortening the right rein and reversing all the other aids listed above.

When serpentines are ridden in this manner, the horse will remain on the bit particularly well, and will readily display his suppleness because he is completely undisturbed by disruptive rein-aids or unwieldy weight problems, and he can work willingly and happily, in total harmony with his rider. Serpentines are amongst the best exercises to teach riders the real value of invisibly subtle aids, and to feel the improvement in the horses' gaits and form.

Providing that the instructor has been well-trained himself, through correct school-work he can make good use of the influence of the other horses to help the riders and horses to carry out the exercises and manoeuvres in a natural and easy way, which will encourage riders to use only light, smooth and invisible aids, and the horses to comply willingly, all partners enjoying each other's company to the full.

12 Riding out of doors

COURTESY

'Kindness. By favour and not by right.' (Pocket Oxford Dictionary.) This is a motto for all horsemen to remember wherever they are riding, whether indoors or out of doors.

All pupils should be taught to obey the country code and to observe the following rules:

Be courteous to:

Landowners – keep to the offical bridleways. Never ride on anyone else's land without first seeking permission. Take even more care of their crops, livestock, gates and fences than if they were your own.

Drivers of motor vehicles – always thank a driver with an informal 'salute', if he has slowed down his vehicle. Slowing down a big lorry with its trailer can be quite a mammoth operation and if the driver receives no thanks for his endeavours he is unlikely to co-operate again.

Groups of riders should restrict their numbers to not more than three pairs or to overtake them becomes unnecessarily hazardous. Riders should always be alert and helpful to traffic on the roads. They should know the Highway Code.

Hand signals – to traffic must be made in a clear, firm almost military manner. Many good horsemen use a too-soft form of hand signal which is more fitting to a ballet dancer than to a director of traffic.

Instructors should train their assistants and their pupils how to ride cor-

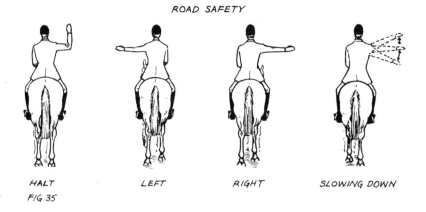

HALT   LEFT   RIGHT   SLOWING DOWN

FIG. 35

rectly on the road before they set out on an instructional hack. Schools should encourage their pupils to take the road safety test, and publicize the test day locally, for the more that other road users understand horses' ways and riders' difficulties the safer will roads become to ride upon.

Pedestrians – remember that many pedestrians are frightened of horses, so never ride too close to them. The same rule applies to cyclists.

Lawns are 'forbidden' territory; this fact must not be overlooked when householders have 'transformed' the road's grass verge, from a jungle of cow-parsley to a neat and tidy extension of their garden.

Greetings and acknowledgements are a warm and friendly country custom.

FIG. 36   NEVER UPSET OTHER RIDERS!

Passing – never pass another rider without asking his permission to do so – he may be on an explosive young horse or an ex-racehorse! If he has an accident it is the overtaker's responsibility.

These are just a few examples of occasions when riders should provide an example of good manners. 'Do unto others as you would be done by.'

Grassland – is an increasingly valuable commodity. Fortunately for horsemen and their horses many landowners and farmers are wonderfully generous in offering their pasture or stubble-fields for riders to ride across or to school on. Sometimes, unfortunately this generosity is abused – their land is poached due to riders using it after recent rain when the going is too soft; gates are not carefully refastened so cattle stray; cows and sheep are harried with a loss of milk and lambs; fences are jumped without permission and broken, yet are neither repaired nor even reported. Crops are ridden across, in careless error, tracks are worn, cutting right through the turf where riders have ridden round and round over the same area, or even lunged 'a perfect circle' for weeds to fill in place of the worn away grass. I have seen parkland desecrated with bald, brown oval shapes cut into the landscape for years to come as a result of a week's Pony Club camp, and seed-fields pocked with giant 'fairy-rings' where horses have been lunged to 'take the tickle out of the horse's feet before the dressage phase'. The real cause of this damage was lack of thought for others and care for their property. A directive from the District Commissioner that all arenas must be moved frequently, and from the owner of the lunged horse to start well away from the horseboxes and gradually to work back over the ground so as not to mark it would have prevented such permanent damage. As a farmer once explained, 'Every footprint is a mouthful of grass for a cow, and every horse has four feet and takes many steps.'

GENERAL RULES FOR RIDING IN THE OPEN

This is the finest form of riding for horses and for riders, it should take place frequently in the farm or moorland belonging to the school or on ground, fields, woods, etc. where permission has first been sought and granted.

All such riding should be conducted in accordance with the rules and code of behaviour as laid down in the British Horse Society's leaflets on Country Lore, Road Safety, etc. Pupils should be taught to think about how to ride outside, with maximum benefit and pleasure for their horses and themselves.

Objects for horses
To improve the scope of their interest in their ridden work.
To improve their ability, balance and surefootedness.
To improve their natural impulsion.
To develop their gaits; undulating ground, stubble or lightly ploughed fields are ideal for this.
To accustom the horses to further strange sights and sounds.
To establish their schooling and their manners in company and alone.
To teach horses to negotiate a variety of terrain and natural obstacles, calmly, freely and with ease.
To further their muscular development – especially on slopes and hills.
To improve their self-carriage and self-confidence.

Objects for riders
To develop their natural, practical ability and feel for their horses' movements, gaits, thoughts and reactions.

To gain a closer acquaintance with and enjoyment of nature and the countryside – at their best when shared with the horse. From his horse's back the rider has a much better view over the surrounding country than the pedestrian ever has, and the natural fear of man is much reduced by the horse's presence which enables the horseman to see wild birds, deer, wild pig and other shy animals at comparatively close quarters.

To practise all the lessons pupils have been taught in the indoor school, without the more concentrated pressures. They have time to think and feel for themselves in closer communion with their horses and with less interruption from the instructor!

To develop their judgment of distance and pace and their control.

Lessons in the open may be conducted in a variety of ways.

As a group

(a) As a ride, using school commands and a rectangular arena.
This is helpful to teach, guide and control children and less experienced riders.

Great care must be taken that a track is not worn in the ground; that horses and riders do not get bored, due to the similarity to their work in the indoor school, that all exercises and work given are safe and well within the capabilities of the horses and ponies and their riders, and yet take full advantage of the open space available.

(b) In smaller groups – working in twos, threes or fours using a much wider area.

(c) Individually, each rider picking his way separately and setting his own pace, keeping sensible distances between horses.

METHODS, EXERCISES AND COMMANDS FOR WORKING A RIDE IN A
COMPARATIVELY LARGE AREA OUT OF DOORS

The instructor must be mounted, and riding a suitable horse.

All the school-movements which have been learnt in an enclosed manège or school may be used out of doors, but both the arena and the spacing must be much larger, in order to:

i Avoid poaching the ground or wearing the grass.

ii To encourage free forward movement in the horses and forward thinking in the riders. This is comparatively easy with experienced riders, but the less experienced may well have to be guided by a few temporary, safe markers. In which case the four corners and the four middle-points should be marked and the ride worked outside them for the majority of their riding time.

iii Working together, in pairs is one of the best forms on which to base work out of doors. The horses and the riders should be thoughtfully matched, e.g. a 'hot' horse with a steady one, a good rider with a novice; and suitable exercises must be selected.

(a) *The whole ride may work together, numbered off in pairs, in open order,* 15–20 metres from the outer edge of the field. After trotting once right round the area, when positions are corrected and horses settled, educational exercises may commence, e.g.

'Leading-files in succession, circling outwards to take the rear of the ride.'

'Leading-files in succession outwards incline, halt, and take the rear of the ride as it passes you.'

'Circling outwards, in rides, 15 metre circles – both rides outwards circle, Now!'

'Odd number ride (or ones), outwards circle, canter at the outer side point and re-take your place in the ride' – and repeat this with the even number ride (or twos).

'Both rides, incline out to give a distance of 10 metres or 15 metres between rides. Rear files in succession outwards circle, 10 metres or 15 metres, canter after the outer side point and canter as a pair up through the centre of the ride, to take the front of the ride.'

(b) *The two rides may work on an outsize circle 30–40 metres diameter*, in opposite directions, in open order, when both rides may work simultaneously, or one ride may rest and observe at walk or halt, while the other ride works using the slow or stationary horses to help them and to test their ability. (Halting by, circling round, bending in and out of, etc.).

(c) *Individual pairs.* The instructor may set the work to be covered – riders' positions; circles; diagonals; canter strike-off; lateral work; etc. and he will then watch each pair in turn as they help each other, *or* he may let them choose their own tasks, for his approval, after which they should come and discuss their progress and problems with him in turn.

Reminders

The posts or markers should be moved frequently; the ride should be worked outside the corner-posts to enlarge the area, to make a change and to help the riders to supple their horses a little more through the corners. They must ride very straight lines between the corners.

Variety and tuition may be combined by the introduction of walking and trotting follow-my-leaders, following a shavings trail, or a scavenger hunt. A willow-leaf, some sheep's wool, a stick of elder – and an extra bonus of ten points for an old tin or jar which must be carried in on foot – the latter is a useful means of ensuring that the field is litter free – but instructors must beware of asking for these items too frequently or some competitive 'bright spark' will not be beyond planting a bottle the night before – in readiness! This is reminiscent of an equitation officer of a famous cavalry regiment stationed in Germany who offered a shilling for every nail found in the shavings in the covered school – one trooper scattered a splendid assortment scrounged earlier from the work-shop, while his mates later picked them up, and collected the reward which was shared out in the evening with much jubilation and a quantity of beer!

Solo riding

Horses and riders should be set off individually, at intervals across a certain piece of country or terrain, to learn to develop an eye for the country, an idea of pace and to learn to ride a horse well on his own.

The riders should be commanded to ride at a slower pace when riding towards the ride or home, than when riding away from them, to avoid the risk of the horses rushing or bolting (herd-instinct, again!).

In all cases of riding in the open, the instructor must have his eye on every member of his ride for as much of the time as possible – *all* the time for novices, and decreasing as the pupils become more experienced. His authority must be such that they can be trusted to ride and conduct themselves as he would wish even when out of sight.

Reminders

Pupils who have achieved a deep seat with longer stirrup leathers in the school may need to shorten their leathers a hole or two when riding in the open to give them a firmer seat, under what may be more exciting conditions!

Riders of all standards must be reminded to improve the use of their weight-aids and to reduce their rein-aids, allowing the horse as much freedom of thought and action as possible; by looking after and balancing themselves both horses' and riders' co-ordination, co-operation and confidence will improve. The riders should school their horses to balance themselves and retain their form on a long rein without hurrying. Instructors must also teach their pupils to alternate a light seat with an upright seat as they ride over varied terrain, so that they are able to maintain their position or change it imperceptibly without any bumping and with a light rein-contact, to keep their horses in good form at a rhythmical, balanced and controlled pace.

The riders must remember that the faster the pace, the rougher the ground and the more hazards and obstacles to be negotiated, the greater will be the need for the horse to have free play and use of his head and neck. The riders should continue to analyse the horses' actions and reactions through a light contact with their seats on the saddle.

When going up steep slopes the horse naturally will want to rush to reach the top as quickly as possible, thus the rider must tactfully restrain the speed to keep a steady pace with less risk of strain, especially to the horse's hocks. He must lean well forward easing the weight off his seat-bones in order to free the horse's back muscles. He should hold the mane half-way up the crest in order to ensure freedom of the horse's head and neck – even a slight backward pull on the reins at the wrong moment could cause the horse to lose his footing and his balance, or even to fall over backwards. A horse can easily bound up a short slope in a few brisk strides, but a long slope or moorland hill should be taken at the walk, zig-zagging to lessen the severity of the climb as long as the hill is not too steep, there is suitable covering and the going is not slippery, e.g. moss or rocks, in this latter case the rider should dismount and lead the horse straight up the slope.

When riding down steep slopes it can be foolishly dangerous to attempt to lessen the severity of the descent by riding it obliquely; if one foot slips, the horse will lose his balance and fall. He must be ridden straight down with his hindquarters aligned behind his fore-hand, allowing him time to look and to have freedom of his head and neck, yet the rider must be ready to guide and control him if necessary. The rider must not over burden the hard-working haunches but neither must he lean forward too far or he will lose the firmness and the influence of his seat.

Young horses sometimes lose their nerve just after they have embarked on a steep slope up or down and they will then try to turn away; riders must be alert, ready to parry any action of this sort, with a light and smooth, open rein aid, or the next step will surely be a fall.

FIG.37   RIDING STRAIGHT DOWNHILL

When negotiating broad ditches with steep sides and muddy or watery bottoms, called rheeins in some hunting countries, the rider must follow the horse's movements instantaneously. He should retain smooth rein-contact until any hesitation is overcome and the horse takes on the obstacle, whereupon the rider must grip the mane so that he is sure not to interfere or get 'left behind'.

If the horse should get stuck in a ditch with a deep, muddy bottom or in a bog, the rider's first reactions must be prompt yet calm. He must size up the situation quickly with particular regard to a possible safe exit for the horse. If this is available the rider should dismount with alacrity, take the reins over the horse's head and with short careful steps get himself on to the firm ground, and immediately and urgently get the horse to make the necessary physical effort to pull himself up and heave himself to safety. If the horse is stuck with no way out then it will be necessary to fetch help and a strong rope. In the meantime the rider must keep the horse as still as possible, as unnecessary struggling will only cause him to sink more deeply. When help arrives it may not be very skilled in which case it is up to the rider to organize the proceedings and to get dirty, which he will. The middle of the rope must be tied securely, using a sheet-bend or non-slip knot, round the horse over the saddle and girth – the rope is pulled round until the knot is under the horse's chest – the two ends are then pulled forwards between his two front legs from whence they can be pulled by men, horses or a tractor very steadily and carefully.

It is amazing what a horse's frame can stand. I remember well as a child out hunting, having ridden for help when a horse had slipped back into a bottomless brook which runs through the middle of the Whaddon Chase country. I returned to the bank near to a particular willow tree which I had noted as a landmark, to see that the horse had moved downstream in his struggles and had also very nearly sunk out of sight – his hapless and bedraggled rider was desperately keeping the double-bridled head just above the water. The carter I had found returning from his ploughing, fastened a thick strap round the horse's neck and fixed his plough-line doubled several times between the strap and the traces of the two work horses. I shall never forget the skill of that carter and the gentleness and strength of their team-work as he and his horses manoeuvred the exhausted horse slowly upstream and out of the mud, back to where the bank was steep and up and out of the river. It seemed quite incredible to me that neither the strap nor the horse's neck was broken and I could hardly believe it could be true when the horse struggled to his feet and stood shaking but unharmed with his shivering owner in the cold darkening winter's evening. Another point to remember from this story – any horse who has been stuck in a bog or a river will be exhausted, shocked and chilled to the marrow; he may also have strained his back-muscles or have displaced at least one vertebra and he must be treated accordingly. Finally, NEVER try to extricate a horse from a ditch by pulling at any part of any of his limbs – by this foolhardy action the horse may be lamed for life.

However, to return to more cheerful scenes.

When riding through a wood, or across rough or stony ground at walk, trot or canter, the horse should be allowed to pick his own way between the trees, bushes or boulders while the rider looks straight ahead at some landmark in the distance. The rider should make frequent use of half-halts to call the horse's attention and to preserve the quality of the gait and to re-balance him, whenever necessary, but should otherwise allow the horse freedom of his thoughts and head and neck to pick his way and to make his own arrangements – remembering three important facts:

1 A horse has four feet to manoeuvre which are a long way from his eyes, therefore the less he is interferred with the safer and happier he will be.

2 It is difficult for a horse to carry an awkward rider burden when the going is undulating, sticky, tricky or treacherous. No horse likes to fall down – a comforting thought surely!

3 This can be further developed into a particularly good educational exercise, by the instructor telling the riders always to pass a tree, bush or rock on the opposite side from the rider in front of him; this teaches the riders to use their thought and weight-aids and their guiding reins correctly and smoothly, and the horses to follow these aids, in as natural a way as possible.

When riding through woods or over heath, moorland or similar common ground, riders must proceed with care, especially where the undergrowth is thick and the going 'blind'; they must keep alert to avoid local hazards which may range from snakes or rabbit-holes to humans sleeping off a picnic lunch.

In boggy, marshy going, the rider should adapt a light seat, holding the mane so as not to tense any unnecessary muscles, he must keep the horse calm and quiet so that he walks forward surely and with confidence. A nervous, unruly horse will often sink down, where a quiet horse can walk across without difficulty. Under very difficult conditions the rider should dismount and allow the horse to follow him on a long rein.

If several riders are riding across marshy ground together they should not follow each other in single file or the path may disappear under the weight. Riders must be warned that bogs may be found in unlikely places, some nasty ones lurk on the top of high, steep hills or on their sloping sides, as well as in the valleys where they might be expected.

If an expanse of water has to be crossed the bottom should first be examined, if possible. If the slope down is very steep the horse should be allowed to pick his way down quietly and confidently because if the bottom is rocky or uneven and he springs out into the water he might easily lose his footing or injure himself.

When riding through water the rider should keep still and calm with a firm seat, being ready to prevent the horse from rushing or from rolling; however he must not impede the movements of the horse's head and neck especially if he stumbles. If the horse should lose his footing and fall the rider should kick his feet out of the stirrups and sit still as the horse picks himself up; if the horse stays down, cast, with his feet higher than his body, winded or injured or just flabbergasted! the rider must grasp the noseband and hold the horse's muzzle up out of the water until he is ready to make an effort to right himself – the rider may have to urge him to do this.

If for any reason a swiftly flowing river has to be crossed, riders should aim for the far bank obliquely against the current.

If the water is so deep that the horse has to swim for a minute or two, the rider should take his feet out of the stirrups, lean forward, hold the mane to ease the horse's back and avoid disturbing him. If the horse begins to swim for any distance the rider should slide off the saddle to the horse's side and hold the mane near to the withers, and if necessary guide the horse sideways with the leading rein held near to the bit.

On a slippery road the horse should be ridden with great care and precision, on the bit, with shortened steps; he will only be entirely safe if he is shod with road-studs. If the horse slips, the rider must sit still, avoid tensing his muscles and allow the horse the necessary rein so that he can regain his balance and his feet.

If the road is exceptionally slippery it may be wiser for the rider to lead the horse on the grit at the edge of the road.

During darkness the horse usually moves more alertly than he does in daylight, and his night vision is far superior to that of a human being. Thus the horse is able to move about surefootedly even over rough going, provided he has sufficient freedom of his head and neck to look out for himself. When riding on small roads or lanes it is wise to keep to the middle in order to avoid loose stones, gutters and overhanging branches. On major roads, the rider should keep well in to the near side and he must carry a strong torch or wear reflectors on his stirrups and/or reflector bandages on his horse's legs; a reflector jerkin, a white jacket or mackintosh is also useful to show up in motorists' headlights – many of these lights are not at all sufficient when dipped.

Chief instructors should make a rule that every rider for whom they are responsible informs some person in authority where he is going and for how long before he goes out unaccompanied. In general it is best if riders go out hacking or schooling in pairs or in small groups so that someone is at hand should a rider encounter difficulties or have an accident.

The object of this section is not to make potential riders and instructors change their careers midstream for a sport or art which is less hazardous, injurious or dangerous such as croquet or bowls or painting – it is solely to warn riders of horses' ways, their instinctive reactions and possible evasions so that, should the need arise, they can be successfully parried with minimum effort and maximum effect.

Success in any of these possible 'adventures' leads to a deeper involvement with Nature and the countryside, a sense of achievement and a better understanding and respect within the horse and rider partnership; the thrill, pleasure and contentment of riding a good horse over a lovely piece of country is surely one of life's best experiences which has to be felt to be believed. Jumps of any kind, even over very small fences, add variety, 'the spice of life', and give extra bonuses in the form of a freshening up of enthusiasm, the blowing away of all mental cobwebs, and of improving the horse's gaits. Frequently we are asked the question 'Do you jump dressage horses?' 'Yes, of course we do!' – but keep it SAFE!

Doctrine

13 The rider's seat – his position

INTRODUCTION

The phrase 'the application of the aids' has been written in too many English books on equitation to enumerate, and all the descriptions therein are very similar. They are for the most part simplifications of classical methods used through the centuries in the training of horses, but here is the problem, this very simplification has cut out several subtle and important facts, changed the emphasis and thus the meaning and the method. As a result of these omissions and inadvertent alterations much of the early teaching given to our young riders has been insufficient or even incorrect. Lessons learnt when young quickly become subconscious habits and as such are extremely difficult to change, or to re-school. If we wish to produce classically *educated* yet natural horsemen, who get the best out of every horse they ride and are capable of improving all manner of horses, the foundations must be correctly taught from the first lesson.

To give a few examples of some bad directions, complications or mistranslations which have led to wrong thinking, teaching and application:

1 '*Grip* with your knees.' I can remember the disgrace, as a child, of returning at the end of riding an exercise, having lost the flat green leaves put under each knee to see if my grip was good enough to keep them there! We now know that the rider's hips should be supple, that the thighs should be flat but not tight, and that the knees should lie softly against the saddle, gripping only in an emergency, riding fast across country, or jumping.

2 Pupils were taught to 'Sit up *straight*' which they did, perched on top of their saddles like ramrods, with a stiff if not hollow back, tight hips, tight thighs, tight knees – excess tension everywhere! We now know that the rider's back should be straight over supple hips, and that the *shoulders* should be straight and level with the head erect above them, all without any constraint.

3 There has often been incorrect, complicated teaching of the aids themselves – and even a change of meaning due to a change of order or emphasis. For example, to circle to the right – the aids are given as follows:

'the right rein bends and directs,

'the left rein controls the pace and supports the action of the right rein,

'the right leg, on the girth, creates impulsion,

98

'the left leg, behind the girth controls the hindquarters, the weight stays central.'

How simple the above instruction sounds, but is it not insufficient as well as being incorrect? For there the rider is told to guide and influence the horse mainly with his hands, with the result that they both move or even pull backwards. If we wish to abide by the classical and accepted principle of influencing our horses mainly with our thought, weight- and leg-aids, and as little as possible with our hands, then it is more helpful to the riders and their horses and thus more correct if they are taught:

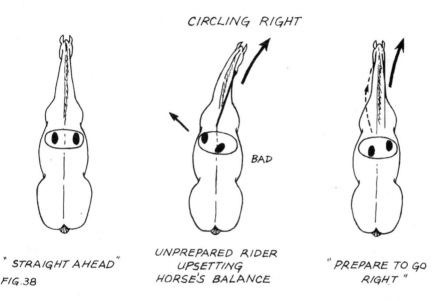

CIRCLING RIGHT

BAD

" STRAIGHT AHEAD "

UNPREPARED RIDER
UPSETTING
HORSE'S BALANCE

" PREPARE TO GO
RIGHT "

FIG.38

To circle to the right – first the rider thinks – he plans the circle's ground-plan and transmits his thoughts to his horse. The rider then shifts his weight slightly to the right moving his right seat-bone forward, and lightly pressing his right knee and heel down. Both legs are in contact with his horse's sides near to the girth. The right leg will usually be needed on the girth, and the left leg may be required a little farther back to prevent the hindquarters from swinging out, or forward on the girth to prevent the outer shoulder from falling out and to improve the quality of the strides of the gait. The left rein must give just enough to allow the horse to stretch his left side and his central line to follow exactly the curvature of the circle, without losing the contact, while the rider keeps a similar, smooth, light contact with the horse's mouth through the right rein.

4 Another misguiding statement is: 'The hands control the forehand; the legs control the hindquarters.'

Once more this directive over-emphasizes the influence of the rider's hands and also it divides the horse into two separate parts, the front and the rear. If he has to be divided it would be far better to halve him down his central line. The same applies to the rider, for his weight influences either side, depending to which side it is shifted, his right leg supported smoothly by the right hand and his left leg supported smoothly by his left hand. Even this though, would only be a part of the truth, for the horse is a whole, living creature and must be influenced as such by the rider. All the movements of a well-trained riding horse must come truly, easily and fluently from his hindquarters, through his back and neck to the bit, and thence to the reins and the rider's hands, back and seat. To this end *all* the rider's aids must co-ordinate and work in unison at all times – with his horse – both living beings in harmony together.

5 One more example, where simplicity is this time replaced by illogical confusion: To walk or trot forward, the rider is told to 'ask for impulsion with his inner leg, to follow the movement of the horse's head and neck with his hands and to control the pace with his outside hand.'

This prompts the question, 'If the rider wishes to ride straight forward, out of the stable-yard which is the inner leg and which the outer hand?' No! this cannot be correct; all horsemen will agree with the age-old saying that:

'The most difficult task in equitation is to make the horse go *straight*.'

Thus the horse must accept and respond to all the rider's aids which must themselves be simple, finely balanced and constant in their conversation and direction – from the mind and 'feel', to the seat and legs and thence to the hands.

As Colonel Händler, the late Director of the Spanish Riding School of Vienna told us, 'The rider's aids and influences are many and should be used with infinite variety – they may be compared with the keys of a piano, there are many possible chords or combinations.'

6 Examples of mis-translation to be found by the dozen in our much revered textbooks:

Starting with the ordinary trot (see p. 145); to referring to 'passaging' when riding a half-pass; to 'shoulder-out' for travers, and to 'shoulder-in' for renvers, while shoulder-in in its correct form did not exist!

Thirty years ago the only uses for a snaffle were as 'the first bit for a very young horse, and, to raise the horse's head'.

Until quite recently the turns on the forehand and on the haunches were both thought to have a stationary inside pivoting leg, which was actually supposed to swivel or screw round on the ground! This was a view I had been taught and so shared until Dr Rau explained to me 25 years ago that at both the 'turns on the spot' as he called them, it is essential that all four of the horse's feet maintain the rhythm and sequence of the walk, with either the fore or the hind feet describing a very small half- or full circle, or marking time on the spot, while the other pair of feet move in a symmetrical arc or circle around them. To turn in any other way would be of no value to the training of horse or rider, in fact it could be detrimental, whereas both turns carried out correctly are excellent exercises for horses and riders – as will be further explained later in this book. No wonder our horses were confused, for they were reprimanded at the walk for moving the pivot-leg, and at the canter received the same treatment for *not* moving it!

These examples of mistaken directives, variations of them, or other mis-translations have been taught in this country for nearly a hundred years, and I believe they are responsible for much of the confusion and even narrow-

100

mindedness which exists in our system of training young horses today. Too many riders have thought (and worked) too little – now is the time to mend our ways.

The horse is a living creature with highly sensitive mental and physical feelings; he is not mechanical with an engine, gears and levers. Both rider and horse must learn a common, systematic build-up of education, so that their grammar and vocabulary are logically and progressively developed over a reasonable length of time. This schooling-period should be short enough to stimulate interest and mental assimilation, and to foster a sense of achievement, and long enough to understand the new work, to establish confidence, and to avoid confusion and discomfort from mental muddles or muscles over-taxed and aching from over-exertion before they are sufficiently strong to withstand the demand.

Horsemanship of a higher order cannot be 'instant' as with coffee, sugar or tea! Seemingly small details of the various aids must not be sacrificed but must be thoroughly read, studied and digested, and taken as a sincere endeavour to make riding and being ridden, in even the more advanced or difficult movements, a comfortable and enjoyable experience for both the partners involved – the rider and the horse. Only by consistently correct work will our horses' gaits, form and performances be improved.

THE RIDER'S POSITION OR SEAT ON A HORSE

This is one subject, above all others, that the chief instructor himself must teach. So much of the instructors' and the pupils' time, thought and mental and physical effort will be saved if every detail of the rider's correct position, his aids and influences are explained with maximum expertise, sincerity and inspiration in the very first lecture.

Yes, I use the word 'lecture' here, on purpose, for the more instructing I do the more convinced I am that the chief instructor must give at least one initial talk to the class when they are dismounted, in the peace and quiet of the lecture-room. However experienced and successful a newly joined pupil may be, he will find it far easier to assimilate new ideas, to sift and sort his present riding position and to feel how to make certain movements if he is seated on a static chair, rather than on a horse whose very action of breathing causes a slight diminishing of the rider's own personal awareness and concentration; if that same horse gives a sneeze or cough, rubs his nose on his knee, or makes a rude remark or gesture to the next horse, this movement can tear apart all the rider's threads of thought and feelings for position or poise.

The lecture should be programmed to take place when as many of the school's instructors as possible can attend it – they cannot hear it too often, and if the chief instructor is worthy of his title he will have found several new nuggets of gold from horses, pupils, conferences or books so that the work improves in value and interest with every telling.

I never cease to be astonished in my travels round the world, to discover how little thought and discipline is given to the rider's position in the saddle – either by the riders themselves or by their instructors. The disturbance, disruption and disorder which even experienced riders cause to their unfortunate mounts due to misalignment or even gross carelessness with regard to the placement or

101

misplacement of their weight on the horse's back seems to be a universal fault, the magnitude of which is rarely appreciated.

All trainers and medical experts of the human species agree, whether their pupils or patients are athletes, gymnasts, footballers or ballet dancers, that concentration, muscle-control and balance are essential to the co-ordination, employment of energy, and equilibrium necessary for maximum output and performance. These experts also agree that the positioning or movement of a human being's head and neck has a real effect on every other part of his body. There can be no denying this fact, nor that, if we go a stage further and talk about humans and horses:

the human must move in equilibrium,

the horse must move in equilibrium – and does so in his natural, unburdened state,

the human head is comparatively small yet heavy, its position affects man's balance, structural stress and his movement,

the rider is not small when compared with the horse he rides; therefore any alteration in his weight must have a substantial effect on the horse's balance, structural stress and his movement.

the horse's head and neck together form his balancing-pole; if he is to use them to maintain his equilibrium their movement must not be restricted or disrupted by the rider's rough or unsympathetic hands.

If at this point the lecturer encourages his class to remember that the horse's problem is far the greater, for at least a man's head is a part of himself, whereas the rider is an entirely separate entity from the horse, the pupils will be convinced that they should try to emulate centaurs, rather than monkeys on bicycles; if they ride God's creatures they should do so to the best of their ability.

This complaint is not a new one. In 1733, François Robichon de la Guerinière, often called the Master of Modern Dressage, made a plea that horsemen should be more graceful when riding their horses. He explained, 'By gracefulness I mean an air of relaxed and easy competency that a rider must be able to maintain with correct posture and an independent seat in all of the movements a horse is able to make.

'This exacting balance depends on the rider's strict attention to the use of his body as a counterweight, yet while doing so, his movements should be so subtle that they serve more to improve the appearance of his seat than to look like too obvious aids to the horse.

'This fine point of the art (of riding) has been neglected. Because of this, it is scarcely any wonder that horsemanship has lost some of its former lustre' – how applicable this is nearly 250 years later!

The Seat

The rider's position or seat on the horse should ensure security in the saddle, coupled with the ability to accompany closely all the horse's movements and to apply the correct influences, with maximum ease and effect from minimum effort. The rider's seat must be adjusted to suit the purpose of the work he is proposing to do, and his posture must be adapted according to the circumstances. Due to the variations in human conformation, it is not possible for all riders to achieve a classically elegant position; they should strive to do so but never at the cost of losing their natural fluency. For this reason instructors must guard against over-insistence on the correct positioning of every part of every rider, as this will only cause unwanted excess tension.

There are two main variations of the basic balanced seat
   i The straight (upright) seat – when the upper part of the body is vertical.
   ii The light (forward) seat – when the upper body is inclined forward to remain in harmony with the horse's centre of gravity when he is galloping or jumping. The rider should be able to change swiftly and smoothly from one variation of the balanced seat to another at will; abrupt changes and exaggerations with regard to the movement of the upper body must be avoided at all costs – as always, the rider's movements must partner those of his horse in fluent harmony.

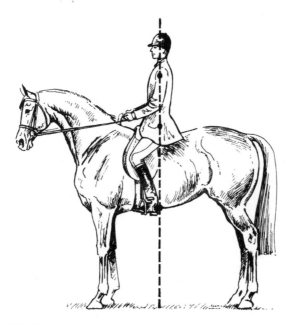

FIG.39   *CORRECT BALANCE*

The straight, or upright seat, or what is often referred to as 'the Classical Dressage Seat', is based on or guided by a vertical-line, i.e., the rider's ear, shoulder, hip joint and the back of his heel should be as nearly as possible on the same vertical line; this seat should be used for all dressage work.
   The rider should sit well down in the centre of the saddle on both his seat-bones and on the surrounding muscles, without excess tension, the whole width of his seat resting on the saddle, straight over the horse's central-lines (longitudinal). Present day, tight breeches often detract from this basic requirement of a good seat as they do not allow the desired spread of the muscles and tissue surrounding the seat-bones. The hip-joints and seat bones

103

at the base of the pelvis should be well forward and the points of the hips vertical over the seat-bones – as a rough guide the upper end of the breeches' side seam or zip should never be in front of the vertical. The horizontal line of rider's hips should always be parallel with his horse's hips. The seat-bones should never press back and down, into the horse's back, instead they must always be positioned and ready to ease forward, to allow the horse's back-muscles to work freely under them.

To guide his student-instructor's eye and his pupils' understanding, the instructor can ask them to compare the under-surface of the rider's seat-bones with the rockers of a rocking-chair. If the pelvis is exactly upright the rider's weight is neutral, allowing the horse to feel the influence of the leg-aids without interruption. If the top of the pelvis is tipped very slightly back by an elastic bracing of the rider's back muscles, a feeling of 'over-drive' is transmitted to the horse. If the top of the pelvis is tipped slightly forward, fixed, stiff and hollow backed, with the front of the seat bones down in the saddle, a virtual 'hand-brake' is automatically applied to the forward impulsion, or this sensation may cause an oversensitive horse to panic and bolt. In this position it is physically impossible for the rider to retain the necessary elasticity in the small of his back. Even a slight hardening of the rider's seat inevitably results in a reflected stiffness in the horse's back and a deterioration of his natural gaits.

Sometimes experienced riders imagine that they are always sitting in harmony with their horses' movements and they will register disbelief, if not indignation, when the instructor tells them that they must improve their positions, so that their seats and their weight aids may be correct, assisting their horses rather than impeding them.

The rider's spine should be vertically above his horse's spine, when riding on a straight line, and when checked from the rear. When riding on a curved line the rider must not allow his seat to slide to the outside, but rather he should be sure to be in balance in the direction of the movement; in other words he should think of sitting a little to the inside, the amount being dependent on the pace and the degree of the curve or circle; remembering that the smaller the circle and the faster the pace the stronger is the pull of centrifugal force, pushing the rider's seat outwards, and this he must guard against with the utmost care using forethought and feel.

From their first lessons, riders must be taught the importance of good posture and fitness with controlled relaxation, of putting and keeping themselves in balance with their horses, and of the use and value of their weight as an aid. The rider's hips must invite and allow the horse's back muscles to move freely underneath them. The rider must be able to move each hip forward and to shift his weight to one side or the other, easily and precisely, at will, so that the horse can carry him with maximum ease and efficiency.

It is essential that the instructor is patient, persevering and utterly persistent in his teaching of this invitation of the rider's hips, for balance, harmony and invisible aids are utterly dependent on it. He must explain exactly which part of the hips he is talking about – i.e. that he is referring to the hip joint and seat-bone area, where hip-measurements are taken by the tailor, and not the top of the hips where the hands may be rested for a knees bend exercise. The instructor should also explain the similarity of leading with the hips when riding a motor-bicycle across country, when ski-ing in a slalom race and he will be able to find many photographs to illustrate this positioning in any western-riding magazine. See Fig. 40.

When instructing in Jamaica I was fascinated by the size of the burdens carried on the heads of the coloured Jamaicans. Pots and suitcases of alarming dimensions, and packages and bundles of infinite variety – 'chicken-in-the-basket,' out there was a very different dish – six at a time, alive and clucking and all carried on one person's head along the dusty track from the corrugated iron

FIG.40   WESTERN RIDING

hut which was 'home' to the market town several miles away. Balance – how easy it is for our horses to carry us if we keep in balance – but how often riders slide out of balance because they have not been well taught initially, or because they ride without sufficient forethought.

Finally, no description of the rider's position or seat on a horse, can be complete without a mention of the rider's chest, for if this is not well-carried, proudly as if arrayed with several medals, the lower edges of his rib-cage will depress the front of the rider's middle-part, and his spine, his pelvis and hips will not be free to move as required. This cramping will also affect the rider's lower-back muscles and the play of his seat-bones. That these are no new thoughts on the seat, may be seen from the following quotation, written over three centuries ago by our famous and great equestrian master, the Duke of Newcastle, 'The rider's breast ought to be in some measure advanced, his countenance pleasant and gay, but without a laugh, pointing directly between the horse's ears as he moves forward. I don't mean that he should fix himself stiff like a post, or that he should sit upon his horse like a statue; but, on the contrary, that he should be in a free and easy position, as it is expressed in dancing with a free air,' and 'A good seat is of such importance, that the regular

105

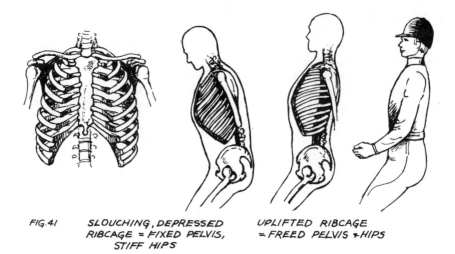

FIG.41   SLOUCHING, DEPRESSED   UPLIFTED RIBCAGE
             RIBCAGE = FIXED PELVIS,   = FREED PELVIS +HIPS
             STIFF HIPS

movement of a horse entirely depends upon it, which is preferable to any other assistance; therefore let it not be despised.'

The thighs

The top of the thigh-bone (femur) should be well turned on the hip joint so that the flat inner sides of the thighs rest steadily on the saddle with the fleshy muscle behind the thigh itself, enabling the rider to sit close to the horse to feel his back and to work in harmony with him. The knee-caps should face as straight forward as nature will allow. This positioning of the flat of the thigh also enables the rider to grip against the saddle-flap should the need arise, e.g. horse bucking, or 'playing-up'.

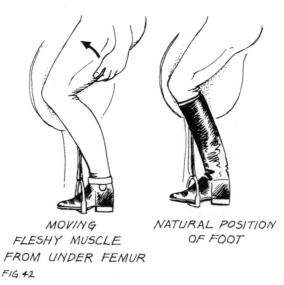

MOVING   NATURAL POSITION
FLESHY MUSCLE   OF FOOT
FROM UNDER FEMUR
FIG.42

The knees should be slightly bent, forming supple hinges without any excess tension (loose, rather than gripping), so that the rider can keep his lower legs in light contact with his horse's sides, in an effortless way 'thinking of wrapping his lower legs around his horse like a wet cloth' to quote Colonel Händler. If the fleshy part at the back of the thigh is turned in against the saddle the knees automatically come out and there can be no gripping-power should it be required; nor is it possible for the lower legs to retain a close yet easy contact. The rider's toes inevitably stick out also which is the most obvious indication of the fault to the instructor; any excess tension or false-gripping with the knees will cause a similar unwanted tension in the seat.

If the knees are pulled up too high, the thighs will push the seat to the back of the saddle and the result is a 'chair-seat', if they are too low and too far back a 'hanging-seat' on the fork and off the seat-bones results; both these deviations from the correct position diminish the rider's security and his influence on his horse. Under normal conditions his hip, thigh, knee and ankle muscles and joints must be without constraint so that they do not restrict or upset the suppleness and controlled relaxation of the horse's back muscles. Any excess tension in these areas will have an adverse, stiffening effect on the horse's form and gaits. The correct positioning of the middle part of the rider is the key to the whole of the rider's position or seat on a horse.

The lower legs should hang relaxed yet controlled, free yet still, and close to the horse with the feet in a natural position, pointing mostly forward, not turned in unnaturally, nor should they be allowed to turn out too much. Both faults cause an awkwardness which restricts the influence of the rider's legs.

When riding without stirrups the sole of the boots should be approximately horizontal, if the toes are forcedly pulled up or down this will cause tension in the ankles, affecting the legs and hips above. Riding with stirrups, the heels should be kept slightly lower than the toes, this also lowers the knees and the rider will find it easy to keep his lower legs in close yet supple contact with his horse. The feet should be positioned so that the toes are in a vertical line with the knee-cap. One third of the foot is placed in the stirrup and the whole width of the sole at the ball of the foot rests on the stirrup bar. The feet must be flexible at the ankle-joints and tread smoothly, lightly and springily in the stirrups which should serve only as supports for the soles of the feet and the balance, but should not carry the rider's weight. The rider can check that the length of his stirrup leathers is correct by two methods, firstly before putting his feet in his stirrups he should note that when his legs are hanging down naturally the stirrup bars should be just below the ankle bones. When the rider stands up in his stirrups with straightened legs the fork should be four fingers width from the centre of the saddle. When checking the adjustment of the stirrup leathers, the rider's experience, his build, his horse's action must all be taken into consideration. The leathers should not be longer than the above description or the rider will be striving continually to 'keep' them, he will tip forward on to his fork and lose the effectiveness of his lower legs. The rider's lower legs should be close to his horse's sides at all times so that his leg-aids may be as fine, discreet and instantaneous as possible. Gueriniere's teaching in this respect is worth remembering, 'the heel should be turned a little more in than out to guide the spurs easily and without constraint to that portion of the horse's belly which is just four fingers behind the girth.' As the spurs in those

107

times were longer than are many modern spurs, the riders legs must have been very close to the girth rather than far behind it as many modern instructors recommend.

The back and loins should be straight without excess tension; a hollow (sway) back or a rounded (humped) back are very serious faults and must be corrected. There should be a controlled suppleness in the back which absorbs and follows the movement of the horse's back without lessening the rider's influences which can easily 'escape' through a direct or a lateral 'wobble'. A nodding head may be a sign of a stiff back, rigid hips, a depressed diaphragm or of shallow, tense breathing. A rider should sit easily *in* the saddle and not be perched on top of it, as even the slightest bumping or lack of harmony can cause deterioration of the horse's gaits. If bumping pupils are told to 'stick to the saddle and try to push it forwards with a straight but elastic back, in rhythm with each stride', it may help them to release some of the pelvic tension, which will enable them to feel and accompany the horse's movement and stride, so well, with supple hips, that no outward effort or disorder shows.

At a later stage, when a pupil has acquired a correct posture on a horse, and has gained in experience, riding many different horses, developing feel, and an appreciation of correct form, his instructor may explain how to brace his back. To improve the quality of a horse's gait, the rider may fractionally increase the tension of the flexor muscles of the shoulder girdle and the deep muscles of his back – nothing should be visible, but the horse will feel it – and hey presto! the rider will feel the effect. 'Brace the back!' 'Straighten the spine!' Yes, that is all there is to it – both phrases are applicable and are true descriptions, provided that they are explained correctly and the pupil's position and experience is good enough for him to be able to understand and to apply this invaluable aid.

The shoulders and chest. The shoulder girdle should be definitely yet elastically braced by its flexor muscles. The shoulders themselves should be lowered to an equal level and slightly pulled back, straight and squared, without excess tension. The shoulders should never be raised and rounded as if hunched against a chilly wind, for this inevitably leads to a stiff, unstable seat with hands to match. The diaphragm should be lifted, (as in a singing or elocution lesson), so that the chest, without being noticeably forced forward, has a natural poise. If this 'uplift' is forced, overdone or tense it is apt to cause a hollowed back and stiffness in many joints. The instructor must remind his pupils to breathe naturally, and deeply, especially when riding a new exercise, or in a dressage test when he is apt to try too hard.

If the rider's rib-cage is not kept straight or if one side is pulled in, it gives the hip below it a 'collapsed' appearance and the seat becomes crooked. In fact, this cause and effect is usually reversed; the seat being displaced to the outside is most commonly the root-cause of a collapsed inner hip and dropped inner shoulder. To correct this fault the instructor should tell the pupil to sit to the inside and imagine he is breathing only with the lung on that side. If the crookedness is very marked, the pupil may be told to 'sit to the inside and lean to the outside' – this exaggeration will make him straight as well as balanced and safe, but as with all corrective exaggerations it must not be overdone.

The rider's shoulders should always be level and parallel with his horse's shoulders. When riding turns or circles, the instructor must watch that his pupils' outer shoulders are brought forward. As a useful guide riders should be taught to invite the directing of the horse's forehand by a subtle turn of their own shoulders so that they are at right angles to the intended track.

The instructor must make a habit of checking the rider's position from behind to see that the following are level – ears (neither human nor equine heads must tilt!) shoulders, elbows, hips, knees, ankles and feet.

The head and neck should be carried naturally by and out of the shoulder-girdle, with a feeling of growing tall up the back of the neck, combined with an ease of posture. There should be no stiffness in the rider's neck, or forward push of the chin. This latter, rather common fault may be due to the rider's strong, subconscious desire to urge his horse into a faster pace than he can achieve with his as yet ineffective forward driving aids. The pupil should be mounted on a free-moving horse and be told to pull his chin in slightly, feeling the back of his collar with the nape of his neck, while he makes one or two double chins without a vestige of force . . . 'as if the top of your head were linked to a star' (W. E. Tucker).

A correct head-carriage is most important because of the effect it has on all the rider's influences on his horse. The rider should look freely about him, well ahead, and at his horse's poll but *never* aimlessly downwards at the ground; he should constantly pay attention to his environment as well as to his horse. He must be acutely and sensitively aware – concentrating, observing, reacting and listening, while thinking, looking and riding forward!

The upper arms should hang down freely as if with weighted elbows; they should be kept steadily close to the body without 'squeezing' or having any excess tension in the shoulder-joints – 'the upper arms belong to the body'.

The elbows should lightly brush the rider's waist or his hips, depending on the length of the arms and the depth of the rider's seat. They should always have an elastic 'hinge' when viewed from the side, and should *never* be pulled back so that the upper arms are behind the vertical, this is a sure indication that the reins are too long – 'the elbows belong to the hips'. They should be level and supple when viewed from the rear.

The forearms – should as a general rule, form a nearly straight line with the reins to the horse's mouth, both when viewed from above and from the side. See Fig. 43.

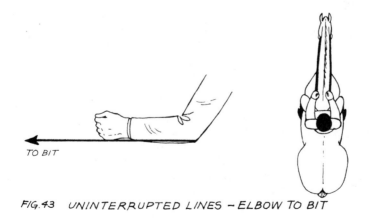

TO BIT

FIG. 43   UNINTERRUPTED LINES – ELBOW TO BIT

The correct position, carriage and movement of the rider's forearms are important factors which should be taught carefully in early lessons. The pupils should be shown diagrams illustrating the two bones which comprise this part of the riders' arms also one of the muscles. See Fig. 44 and they will then understand why they must never turn their hand, wrist and forearm into what Müseler damningly calls 'the English position', for by so doing they cramp the

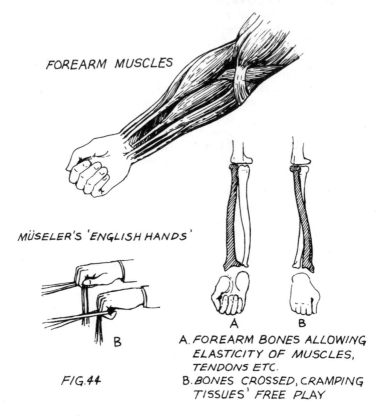

FOREARM MUSCLES

MÜSELER'S 'ENGLISH HANDS'

B

FIG.44

A

B

A. FOREARM BONES ALLOWING
   ELASTICITY OF MUSCLES,
   TENDONS ETC.
B. BONES CROSSED, CRAMPING
   TISSUES' FREE PLAY

free-play of the forearms' tissues and they will have heavy hands. Instead they should keep de la Gueriniere's illustrations of the rider's hands clearly in their minds. See Fig. 45. The latter are carried with poise and grace, from the back of the shoulders, and are thus superbly light yet finely controlled, to give correct, soft, smooth and elastic influences.

The hands. The backs of the hands should form a continuation of the line of the forearm. When viewed from above, the forearm itself is slightly curved as are most of nature's best works, and this curve should be continued through the wrist and balled hand to the base-knuckles of the fingers. The fingers should lie flat, across the cushion below the thumb and should not be curled up within the hand; the tip of the thumb should rest on top of the rein as it lies over the first joint of the index finger – stiff, straightened thumbs reflect stiff wrists. The hands themselves should be held straight up and down with the thumbs

M de la Guérinière's pupil demonstrating
correctly carried hands as he rides shoulder-in.

Fig. 45.

P.M.S.

uppermost, the middle knuckles of both hands turned towards each other, fairly close together but not touching, approximately the width of a bit apart, so as not to interrupt the flow between the rider's seat, the reins and the whole horse.

The reins are held right down at the base of fingers which are then free to move, with very clear, direct, yet sympathetic movements within still hands. Usually the hands should be level and held fairly low and steady without resting on the horse, i.e. 'carried' hands, one on each side of the neck; they must never jostle up and down, cross over the neck, nor be pulled backwards. The hands may be turned smoothly so that the fingernails are uppermost when they are acting, or with the base-bone of the little fingers turned towards the horse's mouth when they are giving or yielding, but riders' hands should *never* be allowed to hang on the reins in a solid, passive pull with the backs of the hands uppermost – the heavy or ham-handed position. See Fig. 44 B.

111

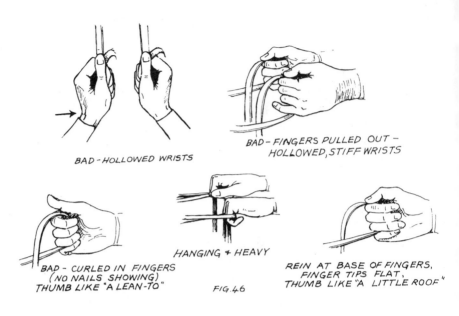

BAD - HOLLOWED WRISTS

BAD - FINGERS PULLED OUT -
HOLLOWED, STIFF WRISTS

HANGING + HEAVY

BAD - CURLED IN FINGERS
(NO NAILS SHOWING)
THUMB LIKE "A LEAN-TO"

FIG. 46

REIN AT BASE OF FINGERS,
FINGER TIPS FLAT,
THUMB LIKE "A LITTLE ROOF"

The rider must be made aware from the first, and reminded frequently, that there is a horse's mouth at the other end of the reins; he must always be very smooth, sensitive and careful with his rein-aids on the living mouth in front of him; all rough or stiff hand actions will be reflected right through the whole horse, thus instructors must be particularly vigilant that all rein-adjustments as well as rein-aids are made very smoothly.

All parts of the rider's body, from the top of his head to his toes should combine harmoniously, so that horse and rider are 'as one' – with an easy poise, and thus may enjoy each other's company to the full. Instructors should teach that excess tension and stiffness are the worst enemies of fluency in the horse's gaits and in his performance, and for this reason a word of explanation and encouragement will be far more beneficial to a genuinely diligent rider than a sharply spoken correction. Instructors should train and encourage their pupils to think for themselves very carefully about the placing and control of all parts of their bodies, just as top-class athletes, gymnasts and ballet-dancers are trained – particularly that they are only using the muscles they need and mean to use, and that they purposely relax the others so that the muscles do not oppose each other, thus causing unwanted tension; this is particularly important in the middle part of the rider – the seat area, from the bottom of the rib-cage to the knees.

Pupils may be told to imagine that every horse they ride has two big elastic bands, one on each side, which runs from the heel of the horse's hind foot, up over his sesamoid-bones, the back of his hock, the outline of the hindquarters, and loins, along his back, under the saddle, over the withers, along the top of the neck to the poll and thence to the mouth. (See Fig. 47.) These 'bands' work separately yet in co-operation and harmony together, and their elasticity and fluency must never be impeded by a static blocking from the rider's pelvis, hip-joints or seat-bones, or from his hands. The sooner pupils are taught to

112

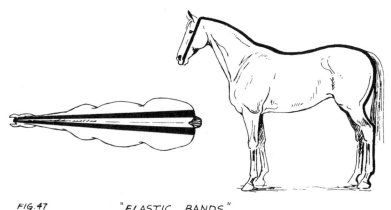

FIG. 47   "ELASTIC BANDS"

appreciate this all important movement, the quicker will be their progress as riders, and in later lessons they will comprehend more easily what is meant by a horse being on the bit and the different effects of the rider's seat – that it may allow, follow or develop the horse's movement. Their weight-aids will then be all the more effective and co-ordinated yet invisible, and they will be able to improve the gaits of any horses they may be privileged to school.

Increased firmness of the seat and strengthening of the aids.

Sometimes the rider has to ride unwilling horses which refuse to go forward and on these occasions the rider has to assert his will, aids and intentions, or the experienced rider may reach stages in his horse's training when he wishes to exert extra influence on the haunches to obtain increased bending of the joints of the hindquarters and to give extra freedom to the forehand.

On all these occasions the rider must increase the firmness and the power of the forward-driving aids of his thought, his seat and lower legs. He achieves this by bracing the muscles of his shoulder-girdle and the deep back muscles which in turn will influence the muscles of the lower back and pelvis, on one or both sides, so that the seat-bones are pressed more forward on the saddle, while moving well with the horse's movement. The rider must be particularly careful to preserve the uplift of his chest and the poise of the upper part of the body which should remain practically vertical. It is equally wrong to crouch, or to lean back, because by this exaggeration the rider will put an increased load on to the hindquarters, and he will hamper the freedom of movement of the horse's hindlegs, rather than increasing their activity. If the rider mistakenly stiffens and hardens his back so that he bumps on the saddle it will have a very adverse effect on his horse whose back he will render just as hard and stiff as his own, to the detriment of the horse's true natural gaits.

The light (forward) seat

For normal riding across undulating country, at slow paces, in good going the upright seat should be used, but for riding over marshy ground at walk or trot, or across country at a faster speed, for instance out hunting when hounds

FIG 48 LIGHT OR FORWARD SEAT—
EXPERIENCED RIDER

are running, in hunter trials or during the cross-country phase of a horse trial, the rider will adopt a more forward position as follows:

The stirrup leathers should be shortened by two to four holes, in order that the rider may be perfectly balanced when his upper body is inclined forward with the shoulders and knees more or less in the same vertical plane.

The angles of the hip, knee- and ankle-joints being more closed, due to the shorter stirrup leathers, give greater elasticity and range of movement to the rider's seat so that he may follow the horse's athletic movements with fluency and ease. The seat should remain lightly on the saddle to ease the horse's back. In this way, the rider's centre of gravity is brought forward to match the horse's when he is moving at a faster pace. There should be a more definite grip with the knees, and the calves should stay in steady contact with the horse's sides; to do this the pressure on the stirrups should be slightly more on the inner than the outer half of the tread. The rider may slip his feet 'home' in the stirrups to minimize the risk of them slipping out when riding a fresh or fractious horse, over rough going, between trees and bushes, or over drop fences. As stated earlier, the rider must make any seat adjustments unobtrusively to remain in as complete harmony with his horse as is possible. At no time should the rider's seat bump on the horse's back as he rides fast across country, for this reason cross-country riders must be very fit.

The balanced seat may be modified farther forward by experienced riders, if required, e.g. the steeplechase phase of a horse trial or show jumping against the clock. While riding at a faster gallop, on good going, over higher jumps on an onward bound horse, the rider must shorten his stirrup leathers a further hole or two, or even more if racing, in order that he may maintain an even further forward position, to match the horse's centre of gravity and to give his back absolute freedom. Within reason, the shorter the stirrup leathers, the freer the horse's back. A word of warning must be added here; the shorter the stirrup leather the less the rider's seat and leg aids can be used to direct and control his horse and the less secure he is in the saddle. This must be borne in mind when show-jumping over big fences in a comparatively small arena, for here the rider must adjust his stirrup leathers so that they are long enough to allow him to use his seat and legs for accurate regulation and placement of his horse's stride and take-off.

The light or forward seat will be explained in further detail in Chapter 16, which is devoted to riding over fences.

(a) The snaffle reins should be held one in each hand, between the fourth, the ring finger, and the fifth or little fingers, and as far down at their base as possible, with the flesh ('wrong') side of the reins towards the ring fingers. There should be no twists in the reins and the ends should hang over the first

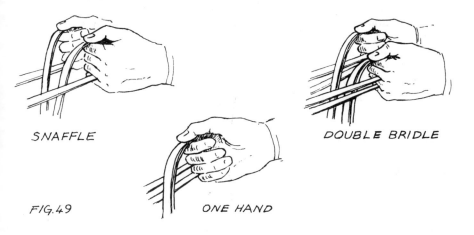

SNAFFLE

DOUBLE BRIDLE

FIG. 49

ONE HAND

joint of the index finger and thence down between the rein and the horse's neck. The hands should be kept softly balled with the end finger joints (nearest the fingernails) nearly straight and the finger tips resting on the fleshy part of the hand below the thumb; the tips of the thumbs rest on the flat of the rein, and hold it securely without gripping unnecessarily. The rider's thumbs should 'make a little roof' – of a house, not of a lean-to (see Fig. 46). If the tips of the thumbs are raised it is a sure indication of excess tension in the elbow, forearm and wrist. No joint or sinew in or connected with the rider's shoulders, arms or hands should be stiff or tense, or this will be reflected in the form of the horse he rides.

NOTES: i The base-bone of the little finger is too short to encompass a broad snaffle rein, thus if the little finger is tucked inside the rein, it will be straightened out by the width of the rein, and this in turn will nullify the elasticity of the hand itself and may even stiffen the wrist and arm as well. Instructors should be careful to explain this to their pupils when they first teach them to hold the snaffle rein between the ring finger and the little finger, and even more so when they correct a pupil who had previously ridden with all the fingers inside the rein.

ii Instructors should advise their pupils to wear gloves which are supple, thick enough to be comfortable but not cumbersome, and which possess long fingers. The fingers of many ladies' gloves are far too short to enable the wearer to hold the reins correctly, down at the base of the fingers.

(b) To ride with both snaffle reins in one hand, one of two methods may be adopted. Usually the left hand is the bridle hand, but both snaffle reins may equally correctly be carried in either hand. In the first method the little finger and the ring finger separate the two reins and the ends of both reins hang over the middle joint of the index finger, as with a single rein, the hand being held in the correct up and down position and centrally in front of the rider. In the second method, the whole breadth of the hand is between the two reins, with the left rein coming up the palm of the hand from below the little finger to hang over the index finger, or it may be brought out between the index and middle fingers. The right rein enters the hand over the index finger, passes down the palm, over the left rein and lies in the opposite direction. The ends of both reins hang down the horse's near shoulder, and the rider's hand is held with the back uppermost. This second method gives the rider more differentiation between the rein on each side of the horse and therefore he has easier control of a fresh or half-trained horse, although he will forfeit much of the elasticity, lightness and sensitivity due to the heavier positioning of his hand.

(c) When riding with a double-bridle, each hand holds a bridoon (snaffle) and curb (curb bit) rein separated by the rider's little finger, the bridoon rein the lower of the two and the curb-rein slightly looser to avoid moving the curb-bit unintentionally.

For riders with small hands and fingers, or riders who persist in overtightening the curb-rein, it may be easier and less confusing for them to separate the bridoon and curb-rein with the fourth or ring fingers instead of the fifth or little fingers, as this places the broader rein round a longer, more accommodating finger base-bone, as well as putting the bridoon-rein in the usual snaffle-rein position in the hand, thus they will use the bridoon-rein instinctively.

It is important that the rider keeps his thumb quite firmly on the bridoon-rein where it passes over the middle joint of the index finger. The curb-rein should lie over the centre of the index finger's base bone. The rider must be very aware of each rein's feel and action at all times and he must be quick and smooth in making all necessary adjustments.

(d) The reins of a double-bridle may be carried in one hand in either of the two methods described in paragraph (b). In both methods the reins will remain in their usual order. In the first method the reins are divided by the lowest three fingers with the ends hanging over the first joint of the index finger, and in the second method the reins cross over in the palm of the left hand with the little finger separating the left reins and the index finger separating the right reins.

(e) *To shorten the reins*
  i To take up relinquished reins or to shorten loose reins: The rider takes the whip and the centre of the slack of the rein in his left hand. He picks up the buckle at the end of the reins with his right hand and places the left hand on top of the reins just in front of the withers, sliding the ring finger between the reins to divide them. With his right hand he then pulls the reins, through the left hand to the required and level length. Finally he lets go of the buckle and takes

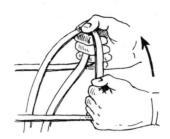

TAKING UP THE REINS

FIG. 50

up the right rein with his right hand and carries both hands correctly in front of him, maintaining smooth contact through the reins with the horse's mouth.

ii To shorten the reins after they have been taken up, before preparing for a transition, movement, or change of direction:

If the rein or reins are to be shortened they must be gripped by the thumb and index finger of one hand immediately behind and inside the other hand, which is then pushed forward to take a new grip. If, when riding with a double-bridle, only one rein needs to be shortened, it is taken as above, and is pulled through to the required length. Pupils must never be allowed to creep or scrabble up their reins, making a series of jerks, or dropping the contact as they go; one hand must always help the other hand, and the light contact must not be disrupted in the slightest degree. The correct smoothness of this action is rarely taught, checked or corrected with the care and consideration it is due. The same principles apply when the rider wishes to reward his horse for work well done by patting him spontaneously on his neck, he must take both reins in his outer hand and quickly and smoothly obtain an equal contact before he pats the horse with his freed hand.

(f) *To lengthen the reins*

If the rider wishes to lengthen his reins, he allows them to slide out between his fingers to the required length. When riding with a double-bridle, and when only one rein needs to be lengthened the rider may use the opposite hand to pull the rein through from the front of his hand.

(g) Instructors should always insist that the ends of the reins hang down under the rein, i.e. between the rein and the horse's neck. If this is not corrected, even in the earliest lessons a bad habit will be formed, as the ends of the reins make an interrupting disturbance on any reins over which they hang.

When riding in a show-ring the ends of the reins should always hang down on the horse's shoulder which is farthest from the judge, so that his view of the horse's forehand is not obstructed.

(h) A whip may be held in either hand with a snaffle or a double-bridle. It should be carried lightly between the thumb and the first joint of the index finger, about 10 cms from the butt end. When the reins are held in one hand, the whip is usually held in the same hand, while the other hand hangs down outside the thigh.

(i) Pupils should be taught how to hold and manipulate the reins, together with the actions and their respective effects *at the halt*, with many repetitions, in order that good habits may be formed from the start. The hands must be carried correctly and rein-adjustments made smoothly and competently at the halt before the pupil should be asked, expected or allowed to do any riding on the move with rein-contact. The instructor must check frequently that pupils of all standards carry their hands and use their rein-aids correctly. It is very important that the rider keeps his fingers 'through the reins', and places his thumbs on them as described.

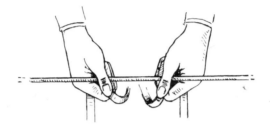

FIG. 51   WHIP— TESTING THE HANDS

A simple test, at the halt initially, may be provided by placing a thin whip or stick under the rider's two thumbs where the joints form the 'roofs' so that it lies across, parallel with the ground. The thumb nails may nearly touch each other or they may be up to 10 cms apart. The whip should remain quite still when the rider quietly and smoothly asks for a slight positioning of the horse's head to the left and straight; to the right and straight, and so on. The whip will prove to be a distinct 'give away' if the rider's rein-aids are marred by stiffness, or awkward or abrupt movements. He must turn his wrists smoothly, to bring the little fingers towards his body, to *act*, or forwards, towards the horse's mouth, to *give*.

(j) Instructors should teach their pupils to ride with their reins in one hand quite frequently in order to develop and emphasize their thought, weight (seat) and leg-aids and thus improve the independence and lightness of their hands. Instructors must be watchful that the straight and level position of the seat and shoulders is not disturbed and that the rider's bridle hand remains in quiet, smooth and equal contact with his horse's mouth.

N.B. A correct *seat* is the only foundation from which good hands can be developed. A good motto to give pupils to memorize is: 'Above the hips grow tall; below the hips stretch down.'

The reins should not be too thin or narrow or the contact between the rider's hands and the horse's mouth will be indefinite, or even sharp and erratic; slightly thicker reins give a more consistent feeling enabling the rider's rein-aids to be as smooth and soft as possible. As a guide, the reins of a snaffle-bridle should not be less than 2 cms in width for adult riders, though children may need slightly narrower reins. Although rubber covered reins are excellent in wet conditions across country or show-jumping, they are too stiff and cumbersome for dressage-work; plaited reins do not have a smooth enough surface. For wet weather, reins may have a fine and supple lace down either side, but under normal conditions plain, well-kept, leather reins are by far the best type.

14 The rider's influences on the horse

The aids – the language shared by horsemen and horses as they live and work together.

'The aids' is the term generally used for the set of signals by means of which the rider conveys his wishes and intentions to the horse; and which the horse in turn is taught to understand and obey. By means of correct training combined with diligent application and correction for perfection, the basic language of the aids becomes a more subtle, unobtrusive 'influence'. There is a motto from the French School, 'a seen aid is an exaggerated aid'. This is a good ideal to have, although there may be times when it is difficult to live up to it! The school's motto should be, 'Keep it simple, and keep it natural'.

The foundation stone for accurate aids and smooth influences is a correctly positioned, yet supple seat which enables the rider not only to be with the horse's every thought and movement, but also to indicate clearly the next move ahead without disturbing the horse mentally or physically.

The aids may be best summarized as follows:

1 The rider's will – disciplined, trained thought, concentration, communication, determination, and the many other facets of the mind.

2 The weight – the placing and subtle shifting of the rider's weight; his seat on the horse's back, leading, aiding and providing support for the legs and hands.

3 The legs, comprising the upper legs (thighs and knees) and lower legs (calves and heels – the latter may be refined or reinforced by spurs). When applied on the horse's sides, the leg aids have a mainly forward-driving influence; they may also move the horse sideways.

The whip – used to increase the effect of the rider's legs, as a correction, and also occasionally as a punishment, e.g. if the horse kicks out at another horse.

4 The hands – provide the human link in the rein aids which act from the rider's shoulders and through his arms not only on the horse's mouth, but also on the whole horse, mainly yielding, guiding, restraining or regulating, supporting the weight and leg aids.

5 The voice – is used to translate, to quieten or sooth, to warn, to encourage, to urge forward or to reprimand – depending on a variation of the intonation rather than the actual words used.

Tongue-clicking has a very effective forward-driving effect, and must be used with discretion.

6 FEEL – the tactful co-ordinator, combined with the senses of balance, timing and rhythm.

The aids co-ordinate to have three main effects, i.e. forward-driving; sideways-moving; or restraining.

Some further points to remember:

(a) The forward-driving aids are usually of greater importance than the restraining ones.

119

(b) To have his horse properly between leg and hand, the rider must have his horse going forward with good impulsion, gradually coming from the hindquarters, through the back and neck to the reins, thereby giving the rider the feeling that the horse is 'in front of his legs', and truly *on the bit.*

(c) The strength and firmness with which the aids are applied depends on each individual horse's sensitivity, willingness and stage of training. An aid that a sluggish horse hardly notices may be felt as a punishment by a sensitive horse. The aids given to a young or unschooled horse have to be clear and definite, even to the point of exaggeration; however, as his training advances the aids should become finer and less noticeable until the horse eventually obeys the rider's wishes from 'invisible influences'.

(d) Planning, preparation and positioning are all essential factors in the effective and economic application of the aids to indicate to the horse what he should do. If tasks are well presented, the horse will accept them with a natural willingness.

(e) One aid should never be applied on its own but should be combined with and be supported by the other aids. Only by close co-operation between thought, weight, leg and rein aids can a horse be brought to the willing obedience and the form* which correct training, or dressage requires. The desired result is achieved by judicious use of the various aids, and not through thoughtless expenditure of energy or force.

(f) Harmony and fluency – are both important factors.

(g) Accuracy – but never at the expense of any of the above mentioned qualities.

1 THE THOUGHT AID – THE INFLUENCE OF THE RIDER'S MIND

The rider's will, his mental and psychological forces comprise the first group of aids.

The rider plans his work-schedule to foster his own improvement as well as that of his horse. He signals his wishes to his horse; he analyses the effects of the work, and he employs his mental resources to the full, e.g. his brain, his will, his memory, his sympathy, his concentration, and even perhaps his telepathy, for horses do become extremely sensitive to their rider's thoughts.

Before giving any aid or signal to his horse, the rider must think what he is going to do, and how and where he is going to do it. He must make intelligent preparation in order that all his influences may be used precisely, distinctly and in harmony, so that he asks for a reaction in the way and at the moment at which it is easiest for the horse to comply smoothly and fluently with his rider's wishes.

The thought aid can be applied in many, subtly different ways, all at practically the same time, but pupils should not be confused with too complicated a barrage of ideas on this subject, at first, for all thoughts must be simple, sympathetic and straightforward.

Riders of all ages must be taught to THINK. This would seem to be an obvious

* The word 'form' is translated from the Swedish, where it means not only the horse's outline and his being correctly on the bit, but also the way in which the horse goes as a whole, mentally and physically; how he moves, and what he feels like to sit on, as a ride, in all his gaits. It is a small, simple word with a large and complex meaning.

principle but in fact, it is often omitted altogether from the teaching programme.

A simple formula to give to pupils at the start of their career, is that whenever they are riding they should think and look in three main directions:

FIG. 52

(a) In the direction in which the horse is travelling, with positive thoughts, giving confidence to both horse and rider with regard to the next move – and the one after that.

(b) At and near their horse's ears and poll, for this is the vulnerable and vital transmitting area; from here the rider can receive and read the horse's thoughts (if the rider is receptive), and, for his part, the horse has an acutely sensitive receiving corridor immediately behind his poll, through to his brain. The rider should concentrate and maintain a consistent and assured line of communication open between himself and his horse.

(c) Awareness of the environment – of the terrain, of the proximity and activity of other riders, and so on.

The second direction, by the horse's poll, is most important but this must not be confused with the common fault of looking down at the ground in a purposeless, negative way, nor must it be overshadowed by direction-finding which can be falsely developed into a stiffening stare, nor must awareness be used as an excuse for lack of concentration.

The rider must constantly think and feel and feel and think what is happening under him; he must allow sufficient time and space for the horse to interpret the aids, warning him with an imperceptible movement of a muscle – only the muscle which is needed – so that the horse can prepare his body to respond to the rider's next request. This sequence of thoughtful signals is of vital importance to the horse's improvement and to his enjoyment of his work.

In order that a rider may become educated he must train his mind to assimilate knowledge. Initially he must study all aspects of equitation with an enquiring mind, taking every opportunity to watch, listen, read, imitate and feel for himself until his horsemanship advances and he can become more discerning and can 'sift the corn from the chaff'.

Controlled relaxation is just as important for the rider's mental state, as it is for his physical system. Excess tension in the rider's mind, from nervousness, over anxiety or from trying too hard, will cause a similar excess of tension in his body, and this in turn is bound to be reflected in the mind and movement of his sensitive partner – his horse.

Self-control and discipline may be unfashionable or even distasteful words in this day and age, but without them no rider can hope to be successful, nor can an instructor be a first-class trainer of riders and horses.

General L'Hotte's famous motto – 'Calm, forward, straight,' is excellent as a maxim for the training and discipline of the rider's mind as it is for his riding and the training of his horses.

Calm – the great confidence-giver, keeping a cool head even when under duress; but never degenerating into dullness, thanks to an underlying spark of courage and inspiration – think calm.

Forward – thinking ahead, positively, with a measured degree of determination, consistently and smoothly with unwavering optimistic concentration. This forward thinking should be applied to the broad spectrum of planning and preparation, as well as to the lightning rapidity of split-second reactions – think forward.

Straight – a clear and true understanding of the aim and the means to attain it; steadfast but not detrimentally dogmatic nor complicated; a certain integrity – think straight. '*Believe* it – and you will *do* it!'

Finally, a word of warning:

The more experienced the instructor or the rider is, the stronger will be the influence of his mind and will on the horses with whom he works. He must be aware of this and use it kindly to his advantage and never allow its effect to be to his disadvantage. For example, if the instructor walks away on the landing side of a fence the horse will probably jump it as if following him; if the instructor stands on the landing side, facing the jump, watching the horse and wondering if he will jump it, in all probability the horse will refuse. Horses are ultra-

FIG. 53A

FIG.53B

sensitive creatures and telepathy is a strong force which should never be underestimated.

2 THE RIDER'S INFLUENCE WITH WEIGHT-AIDS (SEAT)

The weight (seat) is listed as the first of the rider's physical aids, not because I believe that it should be used and seen to be used as the strongest aid, but because without any doubt it is the most important aid to think about and to get right – first and foremost.

If the brain is the instigator or the commander-in-chief, the rider's seat is the foundation or the executive headquarters of all his communications with his horse when he is riding. Any instructor who teaches a system of riding which fails to recognize the importance of the correct use of the rider's seat renders a grave disservice to the riding of the country in which he practices. In fact, it is equally dangerous to teach too little about the seat and its weight-aids as it is to tell pupils to over emphasize their weight aids or the use of their backs. If any of these influences become distorted, mistimed or rough, they can cause chronic damage to the horse's back.

If the instructor omits or postpones careful teaching on the correct position and use of the weight as an aid, from the start of their pupils' riding career, then due to lack of thought and discipline, the seat's position and influence become incorrect and cause confusion and counter-action to the rider's leg and rein aids which then will have to be used in an exaggerated manner in order to override the faulty weight-aids. Instructors and riders must remember, invisible aids should be the aim of every true horseman. If the rider is not taught about the weight-aids until later on in the programme of his riding lessons, not only will he have a gap in the foundations of his training, but also, at a later date it will be much more difficult for him to assimilate and use these aids in the most correct way. A good position, weight aids and balance must be established as a natural habit from the very first lesson.

A young horse may be directed and assisted to carry his rider most easily by a

123

correct placing of the rider's weight – the novice rider will be inspired by the magic of his horse's response to simple weight aids – and eventually there will be many advanced movements which an experienced rider may execute in the best, most refined may on a well-trained horse by using imperceptible weight-aids alone. All the top trainers, riders, instructors and judges at international level agree on this, so let us commence by giving the seat the consideration, thought and training which it deserves and so badly needs.

The term 'the seat', or 'weight-aid' has a far wider meaning than is generally understood, for the following are all incorporated:

    i The rider's head.

    ii The rider's weight – including his whole stance as he sits on his horse, from the top of his head to his feet, but particularly the middle part of his body, from his waist to his thighs.

    iii The seat:

    (a) The area of the small of the back, the loins.

    (b) The pelvis, with the point of the hip as its uppermost edge.

    (c) The hip-joint, at the top of the thigh-bone (femur).

    (d) The seat-bones.

    iv The muscles – all of them thoughtfully employed, the chief 'operators' being those:

    (a) Of the shoulder girdle.

    (b) Running down each side of the spinal-column, especially at the loins.

    (c) Of the abdomen.

    (d) Of the pelvis.

    (e) Of the buttocks, or 'hams' as referred to by the Duke of Newcastle!

    All of these play their part individually or together in the giving of a seat-aid.

For instance, the importance of the rider's head is often neglected by riders and instructors alike. In fact it has three essential roles to play. Firstly, it must be employed to the full, thinking, learning, planning, trying, analysing, believing and willing. Secondly, the rider's mind is also capable of setting-up a strong telepathic ray with his horses. Thirdly, it has a distinct effect on the rider's weight-aids. Physically the rider's head is a comparatively heavy part of his body – if he had the misfortune to fall from the fourteenth floor of a multi-storey building he would land head first, because of the weight of his head. This fact is the reason why a correct head-carriage is so important for the rider – a small inclination of his head can go down through the rider to his seat on one side or the other. This may be felt by riders when they are lined up at the halt. They should be told to look first at a spot one or 2 metres to the left of their horse's forefeet, and then to look up, straight ahead, and notice the change on their seat-bones. They may then try the exercise to the right side and repeat the whole procedure. Soon they will be confirmed in their belief of their instructor's insistence on a good, straight head-carriage above straight yet supple shoulders and a tall neck, and will fully appreciate that it is essential for riders to look up in order to prepare, to feel and to use their aids in harmony, correctly and with maximum ease and efficiency.

Although looking down at the ground is a grave rider-fault which is relatively common, especially with rather shy, diffident riders, instructors must mete out their corrections in this respect in careful measure. Over-sharp or too frequent admonitions of, 'Look up!' may well be exaggerated by an over-zealous pupil until the rider's head-carriage, his eyes, and the mind behind them deteriorate into a stiff-necked and meaningless gaze, which disallows freedom and positive mental communication between the rider and his horse. The pupil must be encouraged both to be aware of his environment and to look at and think through the horse's poll; the mental bond must be forged and fostered; it should never be broken by over-forceful instruction.

Often the weight-aids are used only to support the leg and rein-aids if they are used at all, whereas they should be regarded as the most essential and effective of all the physical aids. For instance with a very green young horse or with a well trained horse, the rider may make larger or smaller turns solely by the employment of the weight-aids, and in many show classes in this country horses go forward with remarkably good impulsion and form for riders with long reins and lower legs stuck too far forward to apply leg-aids. In these latter cases the riders' seats supply the only forward-driving aids and very effective they are.

A moving horse's centre of gravity is constantly changing and a rider should be able to follow every movement smoothly and in such a way that his own and his horse's centres of gravity remain as close together as possible, in perfect harmony. This is something which with correct initial training, should come quite naturally, requiring no effort; so that through his trained, natural ability the rider subconsciously remains with his horse's changing centre of gravity.

However, if the rider purposely places his weight in a certain way in order to change his horse's equilibrium then he is using his weight-aids.

To give a simple example, imagine a rider sitting upright, placing his weight straight over the middle of a horse who is moving straight forwards; the rider may be trying either to retain his horse in equilibrium or to bring him into it.

If the rider shifts his weight to one side or the other he indicates a turn towards that side, because in order to balance himself and his rider, the horse likes to move himself towards the rider's changed centre of gravity. When the rider is using this sideways-leading weight-aid to circle or turn his horse, he must check that he is sitting slightly to the inside, and not at all to the outside. He should move his inner hip forwards and lower the inner heel, and he must sit more firmly on his inner seat-bone while thinking of lifting a little weight off his outside one.

Major Boltenstern explains the similarity of the rider with a conductor, as follows:

'A rider who sits centrally on the saddle at all times, his weight merely *following* his horse whenever he changes direction is like a novice (or bad) conductor standing on the rostrum in front of an orchestra, his baton merely following their music; he gives no leadership, there can be no thrill, and the orchestra's performance will never be more than mediocre. On the other hand, a rider who uses his weight-aids by making an imperceptible but positive shift of his weight in to the direction he wishes his horse to take *before* he asks for the actual change of direction, and who moves his inner seat-bone forward fractionally in advance, thereby invites and leads his horse, and thus his riding resembles the work of a trained conductor who is always a fraction of a second *ahead* of the orchestra. In the latter case, the musicians follow the conductor, and in this way he can improve their performance – if he is talented and dedicated as well as being trained he may even inspire them up to world-concert pitch.'

The rider must never exaggerate the shifting of his weight or make a rough alteration, for example when correcting an outwards-sliding seat, or he will upset his own equilibrium as well as that of his horse, instead of leading him in the easiest and smoothest way.

The instructor must frequently check that his pupils' lateral weight-aids are correct. Even experienced riders can be surprisingly forgetful or negligent in this respect. The rider's inner side must never be 'bent', leaning inwards with a collapsed inner hip and a lower inner shoulder, these are sure signs that his seat is displaced to the outside and this major fault entirely disrupts both the positioning of the rider's hips and his weight-aids. It is usually particularly well demonstrated when a rider looks down to the inside as the horse canters off on the wrong leg.

Leading international instructors, and judges are all agreed that there are two major faults which they *never* wish to see:

1 The hollow-backed, fork-seat – the most serious rider-position fault, where the top of the pelvis is tipped forward and the rider's influences are directed backwards instead of forwards.

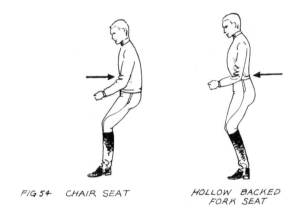

FIG 54   CHAIR SEAT   HOLLOW BACKED
                                        FORK SEAT

2 The chair-seat – due to too short stirrups, and the rider's lack of posture, the back is rounded and the rider's 'tail' and buttocks are tucked underneath him.

Both of these faulty positions cause the rider to be stiff and to have hard and ill-timed influences with consequently disastrous effects on the forms and the gaits of the horses they ride.

A smooth, thoughtfully controlled suppleness in the rider's back, loins and seat is an essential quality for every rider who wishes to acquire the natural ability to follow his horse's every move fluently, and to apply all his aids with tact, minimum effort and maximum result.

The importance of the influence of the rider's seat (weight and back) is sometimes ignored or even rejected, due to misinterpretation or misunderstanding. The two best known attempts to translate the widely used continental term 'anziehen des kreuzes' into English are 'bracing the back' or 'straightening the spine'. The first translation fell into disrepute due to incorrect explanations and demonstrations showing a hard, forceful, even leaning-backwards posture resembling a tin-soldier, and the second was often depicted as a sway or hollow back, as may be seen in a naughty child who is suddenly told to, '*sit up straight!*' The result of these misinterpretations, both of which caused riders to bump hard against their horses' backs, was that the horses thus abused hollowed their backs in an endeavour to escape the discomfort or even pain from the harsh bangings, and thus the riders and some of their instructors become frightened of that which they had misinterpreted.

In fact, the second phrase, 'straightening the spine' was thought out by the late Mrs V. D. S. Williams, one of our top Olympic dressage riders, together with the late Colonel Podhajsky, the Director of the Spanish Riding School of Vienna for a quarter of a century, both of whom knew rather more than most people about good riding!

Both the phrases, 'bracing the back' and 'straightening the spine' were carefully chosen and employed to describe a very small but also very important and even powerful action of the rider's back whereby the rider elastically contracts the muscles of his shoulder girdle and those on either side of his spine, down to the small of the back, to increase the firmness and strengthen the forward-driving influences of his seat. This tightening of the muscles slightly straightens out the natural hollow in the rider's back and is combined with a thoughtful preservation of the correct, upright poise of the upper body, especially the shoulders, and with a feeling of pushing the hip-joints forwards, so that the rider's weight is slightly further back on the 'rockers' (seat-bones) at the base of the pelvis.

From their first lessons on this complex subject the pupils must be taught that these movements should be felt and not seen, they must be applied with tact, delicacy and great feel, and never with force, or even a vestige of stiffness or constraint.

Müseler has provided the basis for two excellent dismounted exercises which will give pupils the feel for using their backs. In the first exercise the rider lies on his back on the floor with his knees slightly raised and bent. After tightening the muscles across the back of his shoulder blades, he lifts his hips forward off the floor, one at a time and then both together, while he carefully analyses the

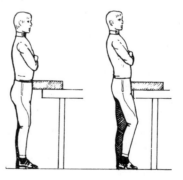

FIG. 55   MOVING THE HIPS FORWARD

use of his muscles. The movement need only be slight; it is the thought and feel that counts, for when a pupil applies this action to his riding it should be a secret message to his horse with no action visible.

In the second exercise the dismounted rider stands facing a table on which there is a small pile of books. The topmost book needs to be slightly larger so that it juts out a little and it should be exactly level with the rider's hip-joint. If, while keeping a good posture, the rider edges the book forward 1–3 cms with his hip-joints, one at a time and then both together he can feel for himself the subtlety and fine control required. Once more the hip movement should be co-related with a tautening of the back of the shoulder girdle.

Müseler's idea of tipping forward a light stool is also helpful, but I do not advocate the use of a garden swing, for although the following action of the back is a good simile, most people tense the buttocks under their seat-bones in order to push the swing forward, and this can be mistranslated into a chair seat.

The forward-driving influence of the seat which is provided by the rider's back above the middle of the seat area may be felt to a lesser degree when the rider walks his horse straight forward from the halt. By the very fact that he corrects his own position, (and posture) and pays attention, before using the forward-driving leg-aids of both legs by the girth, he will have used his back in a natural and correct way and quite sufficiently for the purpose. Gradually, as their education is developed, more experienced riders may be given the feel for a stronger forward-driving back and seat by using transitions to and from the medium trot, preferably on the open side of a 20 metre circle where the riders' aids and feel will be naturally softer than they will be on a straight line. There should be no apparent or forceful change in the rider's aids, often a quiet reminder from the instructor to, 'straighten your shoulders', will suffice. The look of amazed joy which comes on to his pupils' faces as, each in turn, feels his horse move into 'over-drive' at the first side circle-point, will always provide highlights for the instructor's day.

This increased firmness in the seat must only be used when it is needed, with carefully measured strength and great sensitivity and tact. The rider's seat must remain softly 'stuck' to the saddle throughout, staying in absolute harmony with the oscillations of the horse's back and all larger, stronger movements, under the saddle. A correct forward-driving influence of the rider's seat can only be achieved if the rider is able to maintain a correct yet easy carriage of his upper body above a seat which is settled deep yet softly into the centre of the saddle, and if he has the ability to activate his back and loin muscles exactly as and when necessary. The rider must have absolute control of each and every part of his body, as a ballet-dancer or gymnast is trained to do, in order that he can prevent any part of it from making an involuntary or unwanted movement, as well as being able to place and use his body exactly where he wishes; this latter, even despite the horse's contrary actions and movements, e.g. when he is playing up.

The desired quality of 'sitting softly on the horse's back' is another requirement which must not be misconstrued, so that the rider's back loses its poise and degenerates into a wobble, the looseness of which negates the rider's control, both of himself and of his horse.

Another fault which is slightly similar is that of a falsely following back, when the softness is cancelled out by a too firm, driving seat. This fault is sometimes seen in the show-ring when a show rider tries to impress the judges with his horse's spectacular movement. Owing to a tightening in his seat, there is too much muscle-tissue tucked under his seat-bones and his pelvis is 'locked'; he drives his horse up to over-restraining rein-aids and the nett result of all this is that the horse moves spectacularly with his forelegs but hardly at all with his hindlegs as the movement cannot pass in a genuine way through the horse's back. This is a particularly sad state of affairs as due to faulty riding some really lovely horses with marvellous conformation quickly lose their good, natural action, become hollow-backed, and thereafter can never realize their true potential.

For whichever purpose the rider is using his weight-aids, be it forward-driving, sideways-moving, leading, allowing or following, his seat must always be supple in order to accept and encourage the arching and swinging of the horse's back, as he works forward, on the bit, from the heels of both hind legs equally and powerfully.

Thus to sum up, a rider with a classically good seat, who sits straight over the middle of his horse, with supple ease, and correct timing and use of the muscles of his back and loins, has achieved the essential basis for correct influences with his weight-aids which in turn are of paramount importance in the language of communication between the rider and his horse. Nevertheless, it is essential that all instructors should continue constantly to remind their pupils to walk, stand and sit *well* at all times; good posture will not arrive as a result of a few good lunge-lessons, it can only be acquired through constant practice on the horse and off it – all day and every day!

NOTE Quote from FEI Rule Book; 'Only the rider who understands how to contract and relax his loin muscles at the right moment is able to influence his horse correctly.'

3 THE RIDER'S INFLUENCE WITH LEGS, SPURS AND WHIP

Due to the historical and technical differences mentioned earlier many English riders became confused with regard to the use of their legs on their horses. For many decades a firm grip of the thighs and knees was considered to be of paramount importance and extra polish was added to the picture by the instruction to put more weight on to the inside of the stirrup, so that the instructor could see the sole of the boots as his pupils rode by; the lower legs were used as an obvious signal when necessary, but most of the movements required demanded little finesse. Thus many riders rode, and a few still ride, with tightly gripping knees and with their lower legs sprung away from their horse's sides, which in turn become unaccustomed to any contact from them – thus all riding signals are given with the hands, and occasionally banging legs. How often is heard the defence, 'Oh, but my horse goes mad if I use my legs on him!' It is hardly to be wondered at – he suffers such a surprise when they thump his sides out of the blue, as if to say, 'Go faster – *hurry*!'

When General Viebig came over from Germany in 1971 to judge the dressage at the Badminton three day event he remarked on the extraordinary lack of leg-influence between riders and horses. As yet another horse retreated across the arena jogging and wavering instead of showing an extended walk, with the rider's legs sticking out, well away from the horse's sides, not daring to touch them, he said, 'If only these riders realized that their legs must be *close* to their horses' sides, keeping the horses on the aids,' and later he added a little picture which explains the feeling so well – 'the rider's leg-influence to his horse is like a mother's hand, holding her child's hand as they cross a busy street – so few of these riders "held their horses' hands" and gave them confidence through communication with their legs.' Since those days there has been a marked improvement, but even so it seems to be fair comment that in many English-speaking countries hand-aids are far too obvious and strong, while weight and leg aids are singularly lacking.

The pressure of the rider's lower legs starts from the seat, and works through the thighs, knees and inside of the calves, and thence, if necessary, to the heel and spur. If the rider's leg-aids are to be of maximum benefit they must be used in the right place, with an appropriate measure of pressure and at exactly the best moment. This precision and tact can only be achieved if the rider's lower legs are kept close to the horse, yet not clamped in any part. The second factor to emphasize to pupils is that although they must realize and remember that strong leg-aids can only be given by a rider with a firm, balanced and independent seat, the rider must guard against tightening his hips, thighs or knees, as any tension in these areas would automatically 'freeze' or nullify the influence of his lower legs, which will then probably flap or bounce in a meaningless and deadening manner. A flapping lower leg often indicates tight hips and knees, in which case the instructor must immediately tell his pupil to *ease* his thighs and knees.

To apply a leg-aid the rider eases his knees while closing his lower legs supplely and distinctly around the horse in the girth area near the intercostal nerve – where the abdominal muscles have their source. The rider should have a feeling of enclosing the horse's middle with his legs, and even of 'lifting it up', in the case of a weak or hollow-backed horse.

The actual manner of applying the leg-influences has many variations; the pressure may be from alternate legs as in the walk; it may be prolonged and distinct with both legs, or short and lightly squeezing either in rhythm or syncopated. Different horses, in differing circumstances, at different paces and moments in time will call for these fine variations. The horses themselves are the best tutors, combined with guidance from a perceptive and experienced instructor.

A well-trained horse will only need a light touch from his rider's legs. If the horse does not respond to such a delicate aid, the rider must use more pronounced aids, by pressing his legs (and spurs if necessary) against the horse's sides once or repeatedly. If the horse is sluggish and still unwilling, the rider must free his legs in order to bang them quite forcibly against the horse's sides, backed up by a sharp tap with the whip, applied behind the rider's legs. In this 'last resort' the knees should not be lifted away, but they and the leg above them should remain in the correct position. If the spur is to be used to emphasize and strengthen the leg-aid, the toes may be turned out a little. However, it must be remembered that ultimately all activity of the rider's legs should be as invisible as possible.

The rider must not clamp his legs, nor flap or bang ceaselessly with his legs, nor press continuously with his spurs, as the horse will then become insensitive or even resistant to the leg-aids, and the rider will become unduly tired, if not exhausted! As soon as the rider feels that the horse is going to obey his request the influence of the leg must be reduced and that of the spur removed.

The rider's upper legs from the hip-joints to the knees should remain quiet yet supple and still on the saddle; this part of the leg should not be tense but occasionally it can be used, with a downwards and backwards stretch, to control the horse's hindquarters. The lower legs from the knees down provide the main influence; they must be movable and under easy yet complete control so that their positioning and activity can be used exactly when, where and how the rider wishes, without disturbing any other part of his body, i.e.

behind the girth – not too far back, between one and two hands' breadths are quite sufficient,
by the girth,
immediately in front of the girth – a very effective forward-driving area due to the proximity of the intercostal nerve.

All these positions are fractionally variable, depending on where the influence is needed at the time.

Whenever an instructor gives a lesson, lecture or correction which involves the leg-aids he must ensure that his pupils know of the existence and invaluable effects of the horse's intercostal nerve. He must explain, preferably dismounted with a saddle horse, that the intercostal nerve is nearest to the surface just in front of the girth, half-way between the lower edge of the saddle-flap and the horse's elbow. This nerve instigates an arching reaction in the horse's lumbar vertebrae, as well as a strong forward reach of the hindleg on that side. The instructor should invite his pupils to feel this reaction for themselves, placing their hand lightly on the horse's back immediately behind the saddle while he gives two or three well-spaced, definite presses (nearly 'pokes') with his thumb or the butt-end of his whip in front of the girth, just above the horse's elbow. The intercostal nerve is most unprotected and therefore sensitive in this spot, whereas farther back, in the horse's rib-cage, it is obscured by a covering of muscles and flesh. All of which confirms the reason for the effectiveness of leg-aids given by the girth, or even in front of it, and why the rider should avoid using his legs too far back where they will tend to irritate the horse rather than to stimulate him.

According to the placing of the rider's leg-aids, and the simultaneous or various pressures thereof, together with the co-operation of the other aids, the rider obtains:

a forward-driving influence,
a sideways-moving influence,
a regulating influence,
a bending influence.

Equal pressure of both legs by the girth is forward-driving; if at the same time the reins restrain, the rider will obtain a degree of collection.

By differing the pressure of the legs the rider can obtain a sideways movement from his horse whereby the horse yields, and moves away from the leg making the stronger pressure. To stop or regulate this sideways movement the other leg must meet it with contra-pressure, and thus a regulating leg-aid is produced. The sideways-moving leg and the regulating leg are usually applied just behind the girth, but they can be used slightly forward if the rider wishes to influence the horse's shoulders. When the rider increases the pressure of one leg the other leg must not be loosened away from the horse's body.

The bending leg-effect is used when the rider wishes to bend the horse's body, it can only create this effect with the close co-operation of the other leg, used a little farther back to control the horse's hindquarters, and with all the aids smoothly blended together.

The horse is most sensitive to his rider's leg-aid at the moment when the hindleg on the same side is lifted off the ground; a sensitive rider instinctively uses this moment to influence his horse. This rhythmic leg-activity cannot be taught until a rider is reasonably experienced; it will happen naturally, encouraged by discussion with his instructor, when the rider's feeling for balance and rhythm in the horse's movement is sufficiently developed.

The spurs are used to emphasize or intensify the leg-aid and can also, on rare occasions be used as a punishment. Spurs should be used with delicacy and discretion. They should only be worn by riders who have achieved a correct and independent seat, have complete control of their legs and who have sufficient knowledge, practical experience and ability. The spur is one of the most effective aids in obtaining immediate response to the rider's legs and for advancing the horse's training; however, if misused, they can ruin everything.

Spurs should be strapped so that they lie along the top seam of the heel of the boot, pointing straight back. The ends should never be pointed, and if rowelled these should never be sharp or fixed.

Normally the spur should be applied discreetly with the inner branch touching the horse's side. If there is an occasion when the spur is used as a punishment, then it must be used with quick but cool determination, with the toe very slightly turned out. As with a whip, the spur must NEVER be used when the rider has lost control of his temper.

'Spurs and whips should only be worn and carried when walking on foot, to and from the riding lesson, until such time as riders are pronounced by their instructor to be proficient enough to wear and use them when riding their horses.' (Swedish Cavalry School directive.)

The whip There are several varieties of whip, all specially designed to suit different purposes. The two most generally used in the riding and training of horses are a long schooling whip and a thicker, shorter jumping whip. There are also hunting whips, showing canes, racing whips and many others beside, each with their own uses and methods.

There are three main uses for a whip: it may be used to reinforce the influences of the rider's legs and spurs, to help to explain the aids to a young, green horse, or very occasionally, as a punishment.

A schooling whip should be a little more than 1 metre in length so that it can be used behind the rider's leg without noticeably altering the rider's hand position or feel on the reins. It must not be too thick or heavy or it will interfere with the manipulation of the reins and upset the balance of the hand, whip and reins. Alternatively if the whip is too thin and 'whippy' the rider has no control over where and when it will touch his horse. These whips can be quite an expensive item; however, most birch or hazel hedges grow excellent schooling whips which can be 'had for the asking' at hedge-cutting time.

When riding, the whip is carried with the thicker end uppermost and pointing up and partly forwards, held between thumb and forefinger with the end of the thumb on the reins not on the whip. The thinner end of the whip should point down and backwards, lying across the middle of the thigh. The whip should balance well, with only approximately 10 cms projecting above the rider's thumb. A longer projecting portion can be dangerous for the rider's eyes, front-teeth, or chest, should the horse jump or play-up.

As a general rule the whip is carried in the inner hand, if riding in an indoor or outdoor school, so that the rider can use it to reinforce his inside leg-aid. However, this is by no means a hard and fast rule; for example when riding a young horse on a large circle out of doors, the rider may require his whip in his outside hand to prevent the horse from having any nappy inclinations towards other horses or the stables, and, as will be shown later, there are several occasions when it will help the pupil and the horse if the whip is carried and used in the outside hand during various school movements.

Whenever the whip is moved, or changed from one hand to the other this must be carefully turned and done as smoothly as possible so as not to disturb or frighten the horse. All riders should practise changing schooling whips and jumping whips, first when dismounted, and later when mounted, at the halt, until they are adept at it. The schooling whip is changed by turning the wrist, bringing the thin end up to move in an arc straight over the horse's withers and down to the opposite side. The jumping whip is pulled quickly through the hand from one side to the other. See Fig. 56.

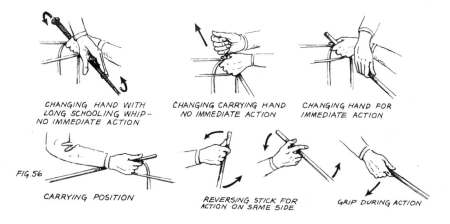

CHANGING HAND WITH LONG SCHOOLING WHIP – NO IMMEDIATE ACTION

CHANGING CARRYING HAND NO IMMEDIATE ACTION

CHANGING HAND FOR IMMEDIATE ACTION

FIG. 56

CARRYING POSITION

REVERSING STICK FOR ACTION ON SAME SIDE

GRIP DURING ACTION

If the whip is to be used to reinforce the aids, the rider gives the horse precisely the right sort of tap exactly to suit the circumstances, either on his side just behind the leg, or occasionally on the shoulder. The action is executed by a quick turn of the hand akin to a flick of the wrist; the rider must be very careful not to move his hand backwards or outwards, either of which would disturb the rein and the bit in the horse's mouth.

If the whip is going to be used as a powerful aid or as a punishment, the rider

133

must first adopt a firmer seat, being ready to hold up the horse's head to prevent him from bucking or playing up, and think in which hand the whip will be used to best advantage – all this is completed in a split second. He then puts the reins in one hand, takes the whip reversed with the thinner part uppermost, in a firm grip and gives the horse one or two whacks on his side immediately behind the rider's leg, or occasionally farther behind, on the thigh. The rider should never hit his horse under the belly or in the groin, and of course *never* on the head.

While the horse is being reprimanded thus, the rider must use his outer aids strongly to prevent the horse from avoiding the whip. It is imperative that the rider remains cool and calm yet deliberate throughout; not only must he never hit a horse in temper, but also he must recognize submission and stop instantly, being ready to give as soon as the horse is willing and eager to obey, and then he should reward him for doing so.

The rider should be adept at using the whip equally with either hand, exactly as required, in the right place and at the right moment to have the maximum beneficial effect. He must always be just, and quick to forgive after the battle is won.

4 THE RIDER'S REIN-AIDS

'The rider's legs and seat create impulsion, the hands prescribe the manner in which it shall be directed.'

'Think of the weight and leg-aids holding the horse on the required track – the hands only indicate.'

'Think weight and leg *before* hand.'

Much has been written about the riders' hands, perhaps too much, and possibly this is contributory to so many riders guiding and governing their horses by means of their hands, to the detriment of the horses' mouths, backs, action and movements. A second yet greater reason for the predominance of the rider's hands when influencing his horse is that the human race has been ordained by Nature to DO most things with its hands. If aspiring horsemen were to take up writing, painting and basket-weaving with their toes perhaps they would then ride far better, with only minimum hand influence. This latter, very basic fact should be considered and deliberated upon by all riders in order that they keep the influence of their hands in correct proportion and perspective, i.e. they use them as little as possible. From their first lessons riders must be taught to make all rein adjustments and rearrangements with utmost care and smoothness; they must never cause a disturbance to the bit in the horse's mouth, nor a purposeless or abrupt change in the contact. All necessary manipulations should be taught in detail at the halt and thereafter instructors must check frequently that their pupils' rein adjustments are made thoughtfully and smoothly, and that they themselves set a good example in this respect. As a general rule riders should try to preserve two unbroken (nearly straight) lines from their elbows to the bit; the first line viewed from the side, and the second line viewed from above. See Fig. 43.

The instructor must teach, and remind his pupils frequently, that the rein-aids are supplementary and complementary to the weight and leg-aids and that the control of the rein-aids originates from the back of the rider's head, neck and shoulders; the muscles at the top and the back of the shoulder-blades are of particular importance and must be stable, pliant and precisely controlled.

If the rider is to have correct, sensitive rein-aids he must have flat and level shoulders with his head and neck carried straight above them, and his upper arms close to his sides; the whole body stabilized, dependant on the rider's seat and having a correct, yet easy and elegant posture which is in complete harmony with his horse.

If pupils have a problem and are 'ham-handed' or lack co-ordination with their rein-aids, the instructor may find that it helps their understanding and feeling if he suggests they hang an imaginary coat-hanger across the back of their shoulders. He must tell them to imagine that this coat-hanger has a long hook and hangs from the back of the base of the skull, and that the hanger itself lies approximately 15 cms below the top line of the shoulders. They can then think of their rein-aids working from this 'coat-hanger', with weighted elbows lying close to the hips, and with very smooth, well-greased pulleys within the elastic joints of the shoulders, the elbows and the wrists – this will invariably help them to obtain a correct feel for soft and ultra-smooth rein-aids which co-operate fluently with the weight and leg-aids. He must also explain that the rider's seat is the secure foundation of the rider's back, the 'wall' from which the 'coat-hanger' hangs.

The rider's correctly carried hands influence the horse through the reins to the bit, which acts mainly on the horse's lips, his tongue and/or the bars of his mouth. However, the influence of the reins is not restricted to the forehand as many riders imagine; the influence of the rider's rein-aids must be felt through the whole horse, without any interruption at the withers. See Fig. 57.

FIG 57   STIFF ARMS, HARD HANDS

As the feeling on the reins, or pressure, is smoothly increased so there is a restraining effect; and if it is decreased there is a giving or yielding action.

Once more Gueriniere gives excellent definitions and descriptions with regard to the rider's hands.

135

The light hand is that which does not feel any contact at all of the bit on the bars of the horse's mouth.

The gentle hand is that which feels a little of the effect of the bit without giving too much contact.

The firm hand is that which holds the horse in full contact with the bit.

'It is a great art to know how and when to use these three different effects of the hand. Their use depends on the nature of the mouth of each particular horse. The effects must be applied without constraining the animal and without suddenly abandoning contact with his mouth. Stated another way, after yielding, which is the action of a light hand, the rider must gently take in the reins looking for the feeling little by little, until he has a soft contact with the bit in his hand. This is followed by the firm hand which restrains more and more and keeps the horse in stronger contact.'

After this to reverse the procedure from the firm hand, the contact is gradually and smoothly diminished through the gentle hand before passing back to the light hand. The gentle hand must always precede and follow the firm hand.

NOTE In modern parlance the meaning of a 'light hand' has become superimposed on that of a 'gentle hand' which tends to diminish the degrees of refinement – and of true lightness.

De la Gueriniere concludes 'The rider's hand should never resist or yield abruptly; to do so will ruin the horse's mouth or cause head-tossing,' or other resistances, or faulty gaits.

Whenever the horse is working, the rider should concentrate on his horse maintaining a steady, lightly held head-carriage, submissive yet proud, quietly accepting a nice contact with the bit. The rider's hands should never hang, passive and heavy, on the reins. The ring-finger of one or other hand should keep up a softly murmuring vibration with one side of the horse's mouth or the other whilst the horse remains straight or when positioned, turning, flexing or bending to the left or to the right. By 'asking' in this way, the rider tactfully invites the horse to submit and to chew softly on the bit. This is a measure of the whole of the rider's influences on the whole of his horse.

Reminder – The rider must always think, 'Weight and legs *before* hands.'

Occasionally, by a tactful and temporary alteration in the height of his hands the experienced rider can suggest a better head-carriage to a badly trained or upset horse. By raising his hands the rider can have an elevating effect on a too-low head-carriage, and by lowering them he can encourage a star-gazer to lower his head into a position where it is then easy and comfortable for him to accept the bit and the rider's rein-aids. These suggestions must always wait upon a willing response to the rider's forward driving aids.

Partly through the alternate actions of the reins and very occasionally due to the reins touching the neck, a rein-action is achieved which is either guiding, restraining, regulating or supporting.

Both hands must co-operate with each other; when one hand acts by guiding or leading, restraining or supporting, the other hand regulates; both retain a smooth contact with the horse's mouth and are co-ordinated with the weight (seat), and leg-aids, these being the primary aids – primary both in timing and in importance.

Generally speaking a rein is termed a supporting rein if it supports or helps the rider's leg which is on the same side of the horse, i.e. the rider's left rein supports the action of his left leg in its sideways-pushing, regulating or restraining effect. Too often pupils are taught that a supporting rein only supports the action of the other rein; 'left rein, supported by right rein' appears over and over again in our English textbooks and this causes an over-emphasis on the importance and strength of the rider's hand aids, as opposed to those of his weight (seat), and legs, and implies that they are used separately from them rather than in close co-operation with and of secondary importance to them.

All influences with the reins should be made with smoothly supple yet softly elastic wrist, hand and finger-joints, combined with an easy poise and suppleness in the rider's shoulders and elbows. The reins should not be allowed to slide out through the fingers incessantly, nor on the other hand should the rider constantly retain a hard or over-firm grip, with rolled-in fingers. The reins must be lengthened or shortened as is required, frequently if necessary.

To obtain a desired result without causing any resistance or worry to his horse, the rider should apply a smoothly gripped pressure which must be prepared and made with tact and thought, sufficiently early so that the rein-aids are based on and subsidiary to the weight- and leg-aids. The rider receives the forward impulsion and the horse's suppleness into his hands which then cherish them – both these qualities and the gaits themselves can be destroyed all too easily by the rider's hands if they are stiff or over-assertive.

If the horse fails to obey the pressure on the rein immediately, the rider must not resort to forceful pulls to impose his will. Through alternate restraining and giving and with co-operation from the other aids, combined with a judicious use of helpful exercises, resistance will eventually be overcome. However, there may be moments when the horse resists forcefully himself, in which case he must be brought up against a matching strength in the rider's restraining aids. As the horse leans, resists, jerks or pulls, the rider must restrain, keeping his hands absolutely still, as if they were tie-rings in a wall, set in concrete, his elbows close to his hips and his seat forming a sure base for the restraints, and he must always be ready to give instantly in the exact second that the horse gives – thus the horse will soon learn what is required and he will submit and work forward on to the bit in a correct and happy way. On these occasions of bad, rough, behaviour on the horse's part, the rider must be firm to be fair and to teach the horse. It would be entirely incorrect for the rider to give and allow and to follow the horse's head, or he will quickly learn to treat his rider's hands as if they were a yo-yo or similar toy, for his amusement, and a bad habit could quickly develop into an uncontrollable vice. To give when the horse jerks or sticks his nose out against the bit would teach him the wrong thing, whereas a still hand will teach him the right thing, for in the latter case the horse will soon realize that he is making the discomfort for himself and will discard the bad habit. This method, combined with loosening exercises, such as turns on the forehand and leg-yielding will soon reform a spoiled horse.

As soon as a horse gives a sign that he is going to follow a rein-aid he must be rewarded immediately with a subtle give from the rider's hand, and thus he will quickly learn what his rider wishes him to do. With a well trained horse this restraining and giving is quite invisible, as it becomes a tiny communication between horse and rider within the rider's apparently quite still hand. James

Fillis was a famous international instructor and horseman of the last century. He was a true cockney by birth, he lived and learned in France, and trained the Russian Cavalry. As well as schooling sixteen horses a day and training some to canter backwards on three legs, he left us with a very useful thought or two. His saying on hands is one that particularly springs to mind at this juncture, 'Good hands give when the horse takes and take when he gives; educated hands take when he takes and give when he gives.' This explains rather well that hands should be still yet lively within themselves and that they should never be dead, lazy and hanging-on or heavy. That it is far better to give than to take, we are told in the Bible, so that is no new thought.

For a rider to be told that he has 'good hands' is perhaps one of the greatest compliments he can be paid. The term itself incorporates a mixture of several essential factors:

(a) A balanced seat – the rider being entirely steady and easy for the horse to carry. Good hands can only come from a steady seat which does not disturb the horse.

(b) Feel – that intangible 'something' which stems from a natural talent and enables the rider's hand influences to be instantaneous in the timing of their actions, reactions and responses.

(c) Education – even the best natural riders must have a fund of correct knowledge to call upon – 'to know the reason why', to know the correct feel, and to appreciate thoroughly the dangers of misuse, especially of heavy, unsteady, overactive, stiff or restrictive hands.

(d) The reins must be adjusted correctly – if too long, the rein-aids will be clumsy and inaccurate.

(e) The hands should be carried and used in a correct, up and down position with the thumbs uppermost and the wrists slightly rounded. To act, the wrists are turned very smoothly, bringing the fingernails upwards. To give, the little finger knuckle turns towards the horse's mouth. If the hands are held with the backs uppermost and flat wrists, with the thumb instead of the little finger turning and moving towards the rider's body, the finger, hand and wrist-action is made stiff and insensitive (heavy hands).

(f) The rider's hands must be steady and completely independent of the seat, so that if necessary they can be kept quite still (never jostling up and down), or they may be moved very smoothly at will.

(g) They, together with the joints and muscles of the shoulders and arms must be controlled yet very supple, so that they can increase or decrease the effect of the bit smoothly and softly.

(h) The wrists should be capable of turning as if they contained well-oiled ball-bearings, enabling hands to be light and acutely sensitive, in order to feel and retain the lightest contact with the bit.

(i) The hands must be allowing so that while retaining a soft contact on the reins to the bit, they do not restrict the natural movements of the horse's head, but rather they should invite him to give and to stretch; this is especially obvious and important at the walk, when riding a curved line, and when jumping.

(j) The rider's hands must be quite independent and controlled yet free in order to be able to change their position or influence immediately, as the circumstances require.

If, especially when riding young horses, the rider's hand movements have to be apparent rather than invisible, he should still abide by the important rules that he was taught in early lessons, i.e. each hand must remain on its own side of the horse's central line, with approximately the width of a bit between them. Hands should not pull backwards and should never be used across the withers towards the rider's opposite hip. The rider's guiding and supporting rein-aids will be most effective when the wrist is moved away from the withers and is turned so that the thumb faces outwards and the little finger is brought under and up towards the rider's body and hip on the same side. The rider's upper arm must be kept close to his body. That this is a light hand action should be explained by the instructor to his ride when they are halted; he should ask them to put their reins in their left hands and to move their right hands as if giving a sideways guiding aid firstly by lifting their right hands out, backs uppermost,

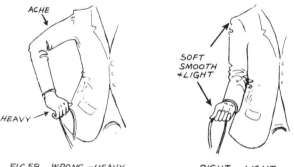

FIG.58   WRONG –HEAVY   RIGHT – LIGHT

with the little finger part of the hand leading and elbow out, when the arm and hand will soon prove to feel weighted and heavy. Then they should feel the comparative lightness of the softly turned forearm and wrist with the thumb leading the way and the elbow close to the hip. This simple exercise will quickly prove the point and convince the pupils of the right way to give a guiding rein aid. Thereafter the word, 'thumbs' will suffice to remind them, during turns, circles and serpentines to move the guiding hand softly outwards, the thumb leading the way and the fingernails uppermost. (Almost as if 'thumbing a lift'.)

The instructor must introduce the theory and practice of the horse being on the bit as soon as the pupil is ready and able to receive and understand it. If this lesson is postponed, the most fundamental principle in equitation will have been evaded; without it the pupil's riding cannot progress and the horse's training, form and paces will deteriorate rapidly, and thus a vicious circle is set up, for although pupils can learn to sit on a horse's saddle, they cannot learn how to *ride* unless their equine schoolmasters give them a correct feel.

On the bit

The term 'on the bit' is described in this section as its quality is evaluated by the rider's hands through the feel on the reins; the rider however, must be taught to understand that his hands merely test the end product, and that

139

without the correct use of the thought, weight and seat and leg-aids the rider will never receive the correct feel into his hands. He must have the horse on the bit in the true sense, which involves the whole of the horse, his form, his mental attitude and his movement.

The horse is said to be 'on the bit' when the hocks are correctly placed or engaged, the neck is straight at the withers and is more or less raised and arched according to the stage of training and the extension or collection of the gait, and he accepts the influence of the rider's hand with a light soft contact and overall submissiveness so that the action of the reins passes smoothly and fluently through the horse's whole body. The horse's head should be carried in a steady position with the nose slightly in front of a vertical line by his eye, with a supple poll which is at the same time the highest part of the neck. The horse should always be willing and eager to do as his rider wishes and should offer no resistance to his influences. His lower jaw should be relaxed, there being no sign of constraint, evasion or resistance; he may quietly champ the bit or his mouth may be still, but never set; the mouth should be moist, showing a little salivary cream in the bit-area. Generally, he should have a calm yet willing interest, and a happy expression. The horse should be on the bit at the halt, and in all his work, except when resting, on loose reins.

It is most important that instructors understand the full meaning of the FEI's definition and the requirements thereof. 'Accepting the hand' should not be used as a substitute phrase for it only refers to a part of the full meaning. When a horse is on the bit his whole being is affected from the heels of his hind feet up to the two elastic bands mentioned on p. 112, along his top-line, through a supple poll and lower jaw to his mouth, and thence returning along the same route to the hindfeet.

A horse is brought on to the bit by all the rider's influences co-ordinating tactfully together; he is then ready, attentively listening to the slightest indication from his rider, and is willing to respond instantly yet confidently to his wishes so that the horse and rider can work together in complete harmony.

Instructors must be on their guard constantly that no pupil has misinterpreted the term 'on the bit' to mean a forced, false positioning of the horse's head and neck only, which the rider obtains by pulling on the reins, and even fixing his hands somewhere below the horse's withers, with the backs of the hands uppermost, tense wrists, elbows and shoulders, and stiffly straightened arms.

When circling or turning the rider must never move his inside hand inwards towards or across the horse's withers for by so doing he would 'short-circuit' the elasticity, the impulsion, and the whole flow of the horse's movement. Instead, he must shorten the inner rein well beforehand, and must 'lead the way with his thumb' turning his fingernails uppermost in order to retain the soft elasticity of the sinues of the forearm and the consequent smooth lightness of the rein-aid.

Pupils must be taught to put their horses on the bit by using their forward-driving aids, i.e. both legs and an elastically braced back pushing the horse forward on to softly restraining hands, so that the horse brings his hindlegs forward underneath his body, enabling all four legs to provide a well-balanced support through a strong but resilient back. The rider should sit softly as the horse thinks and moves forward, being influenced from behind to the front, and gives a sure, steady yet light contact on the bit, as he quietly champs or 'chews' the bit. If the horse's forward urge and resolution diminish, or his mouth goes dull or dead, or he evades contact with the bit, the rider must strengthen his aids until the horse is on the bit satisfactorily.

The instructor must watch that his pupils move their hips and seat-bones well forward with their horses' movement, that there is no stiffness in their backs and that they do not sit heavily, especially if a horse has a weak back or hindlegs, and that their lower legs are en garde, close to their horse's sides, to be applied instantly as required yet with minimum effort and movement, and that their hands give correct and smooth rein-aids.

As his pupils progress, the instructor should teach them the meaning of flexion – 'The willing give in the horse's lower jaw, poll and neck'; bending and straightness should also be given careful consideration. On the latter subject, instructors should impress that top priority must always be given to the following qualities:

Mentally, the horse must be straight and forward-thinking, happy in his work, willing and eager to please, calm, confident and attentive.

Physically the horse must be straight, forward-going and in suitably good condition; he must be on the bit, balanced and supple, working with a good rhythm, loose shoulders and bold, free yet co-ordinated movement.

Pupils should be warned that an over-emphasis on bending often causes a major fault whereby the horse bends too much to one side and not enough to the other, whereas if the horse is straight with freedom in his shoulders, it is quite easy to bend him equally both ways. Activity behind, or engagement of the haunches cannot be obtained unless the horse has been loosened in his shoulders and is straight, so that the movement can go truly through the whole horse. The haunches cannot be engaged properly or fully nor can the movement go through to the bit if the horse is tense or crooked.

The influence of the reins, when the horse is ridden in a snaffle bridle

As already stated, hands and the rein-aids must be smooth and soft at all times and the rider should always carry his hands correctly, with his shoulder and arm joints and muscles supple and unconstrained, and his reins carefully adjusted to a suitable length.

The horse recognizes a restraining influence through an increased feel from the reins to the bit on his mouth.

Usually a well-trained horse does not need any excessive or even noticeable restraint. His rider just closes his fingers a little more firmly on the reins to establish a light contact with the bit. If the horse does not respond to this action the restraint should be increased by a barely perceptible and ultra-smooth turn of the forearm, wrist and hand, bringing the fingernails uppermost, the little finger slightly closer to and the thumb away from the rider's body, thus increasing the ring-finger's pressure on the rein. If this is still not enough, the rider must first ensure that the reins are short enough and tighten the muscles at the back of his shoulder, move his hands softly and smoothly straight backwards without bending the wrist joint. The whole arm should be brought into play, without any tension in the shoulder joint.

The rider may occasionally need to carry his hands a little higher when riding a horse with too low a head-carriage, and conversely he should sometimes lower them slightly below the normal height if the horse goes with his poll too high. However, at no time should the rider try to correct a faulty head-carriage by force from his rein-aids or by setting his hands. Instead he should employ a quietly gripping pull with moving fingers, the tips directed straight towards his body, or, if he is using a rein-aid to support a sideways-pushing leg-aid then he directs his hand towards his hip on the same side. In both cases he turns the wrist, turning the thumb part of the hand slightly away from the horse, the fingernails uppermost, and the elbow staying close to the hip.

Restraining influences should never be made solely by the reins, they should always be aided by tactful forward-driving leg-aids and a firmer seat. A fairly extreme example of this can be illustrated simply by imagining a pupil riding a horse who is leaning heavily on the hands and pulling, whilst increasing his pace; in this case it is imperative that the instructor tells his pupil to 'sit down' in order to strengthen his seat and leg-aids and enable his restraining rein-aids to be effective. If he is allowed to be pulled forward so that he loses his seat, he will in all probability lose control as well.

When downward transitions and halts are correctly ridden, the rider's rein-aids should be almost, if not quite invisible, and so instead of having to strengthen his seat he should think of lightening it by pressing down his heels and by imagining he is stretching the top of his ears straight upwards. Thus he transfers a little of his weight on to his stirrups and thereby allows his horse to have more free play of his back muscles, to engage his haunches fully and to round rather than to hollow his back as he comes softly, smoothly and squarely to a halt, without any apparent signal from his rider.

The rider recognizes a giving influence from a diminished (but not departed!) feel of the bit. This giving is achieved firstly by a lighter grip on the reins, secondly through turning the hand so that the little fingers are eased away from the body, and lastly by the rider moving his hands and arms forward. In other words, give means that the muscle-work of the hands and arms is more or less decreased, but it must be remembered that every give of the rider's hands must always be followed by consistent forward-driving aids, tactfully measured to suit the circumstances and the horse.

As a general rule, a give in the reins should not be made so that the delicate contact with the horse's mouth is lost. However, when riding young horses, or when re-schooling horses who have been spoilt by faulty training, an exaggerated give with the marked loop in one rein only may prove to be very beneficial. It is of course imperative that young horses should also be ridden across undulating country, in the woods or over the moors, with loose reins so that they may develop their balance, their stride and acquire self-carriage and confidence under the rider.

A raising rein-action

By raising his hands momentarily, the rider can encourage his horse to adopt a higher carriage of his neck and head. This particular rein-aid should be executed by a smooth raising of the hands, and a liveliness of the fingers within these hands and this action must always be supported by active forward-driving aids in order to engage the haunches. The rider should think of raising the horse's withers, then the top of his neck and lastly his head. If, while he does this, the forward-driving aids are neglected the rider will make his horse raise his head with a false bend in the neck, against which the horse will hollow his back and trail his hindlegs inactively behind him, or he may plunge his head down with his nose tucked in, becoming beyond, as well as behind the bit. The rider must drive the horse forward so that he is 'in front of the rider's legs'.

The influence of the reins when a trained horse is ridden in a double bridle

The principles of bitting when a horse wears a double bridle may be summarized briefly as follows: The bridoon acts in the horse's mouth in the same way as a snaffle bit. The action of the curb-rein is transmitted in lever-form through the shanks of the curb bit and thereby increases its power. The curb bit consists of a lever whereby the power A is supplied by the rein to the ring at the bottom of the shank, the resting-place of the mouthpiece in the horse's mouth on the bars, B and the support is given by the curb-chain C which must be flat and exactly in the chin-groove, and attached to the eye at the top of the shank. See Fig. 59.

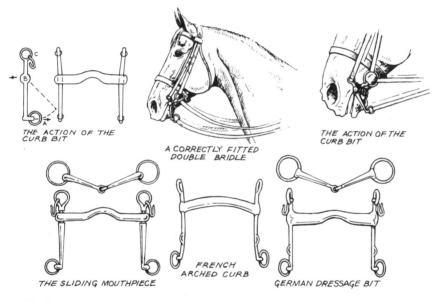

THE ACTION OF THE CURB BIT

A CORRECTLY FITTED DOUBLE BRIDLE

THE ACTION OF THE CURB BIT

THE SLIDING MOUTHPIECE

FRENCH ARCHED CURB

GERMAN DRESSAGE BIT

FIG 59

A long lower shank thus increases the severity of the curb bit, and this is intensified if the mouthpiece is thin and the upper shanks are long too, the pressure points then being sharper on the bars of the mouth. Finally the severity of the curb bit is increased if the space for the tongue is enlarged, because the tongue is relieved from pressure of the mouthpiece which is then transferred solely on to the bars. To conclude, the mildest form of curb bit has short shanks, a relatively thick mouthpiece and slight accommodation rather than complete freedom for the tongue. Generally, the lower shanks should not be more than twice the length of the upper shanks. Horses have a variety of shapes and sizes of mouth, jaw-space and tongue, and these too must be taken into careful consideration when selecting the right bits for a particular horse. A

143

sliding curb mouthpiece tends to make some horses fussy with their tongues and mouths. My personal preferences are for, either the German dressage double bridle or, for horses who find these thicker mouthpieces too much of a mouthful, a French arched curb bit which suits most horses with narrow lower jaws.

When riding with a double-bridle, restraining and giving rein-aids are applied according to the general principles already described when riding with a snaffle-bridle, but if anything, the rider must be even more careful of the movements and actions of his hands. He should give all rein-aids with the bridoon-rein, the pressure on the curb-rein being only very slightly in evidence. The more experienced rider must be well taught, corrected, and given plenty of supervised practice in the skill of riding a horse in a double bridle. He must be conscientious and careful that the curb-reins are not shortened inadvertently, neither should he allow them to slide out through his fingers so that the looping reins cause the curb bit to jangle in the horse's mouth with resultant, obvious disturbance to it.

> 'Be gentle, my children, in using your hands,
> Touch lightly, and let the chief effort be mental;
> The will is the power that guides and commands.'
>
> *Philpotts Williams*

5 THE VOICE AID

The rider's influence with his voice, and tongue-clicking

The rider's voice is a natural aid by means of which he conveys many messages to his horse, particularly in the early stages of training and when working him in hand. Chiefly by variations of its tone rather than by the actual words used, the trainer's voice may be soothing, encouraging, praising, forward-driving, steadying, warning or admonishing, as well as educational, e.g. words of communication and of command in the stable, on the lunge, and as a translator of the rider's aids when the young horse is first backed.

Tongue clicking is a subsidiary to the voice aid. Its forward-driving effect is quite remarkable, and it is particularly useful when working a horse without a rider. The strength of the clicking sound should be modified to suit the requirement and as it tends to have a fairly galvanizing effect on some sensitive horses, great care must be taken when working in company with other horses and riders.

The voice-aids should be quiet, short yet meaningful. A spate of words, mumbled phrases or obtrusive shouts are all valueless, for they merely arouse confusion or fright in the horse's mind.

As the horse's training progresses so should the use of the voice decrease. The rider will lose marks or may even be disqualified for using his voice when competing in a dressage test.

Instructors will find that there is another very important use for the voice which is not always recognized to the full. Any pupil who is too tense will be helped to relax, and to feel his influences and his horse's reactions and movement if he is encouraged to use his voice in some suitable way, e.g. beginners counting the rhythm of the gaits; children singing as they go down a grid; or even an advanced rider having a problem maintaining extended trot, passage, etc. The reason for the resultant relaxation is logical rather than magical! If the muscles of the lower jaw are moved they are no longer tense, and this relaxation passes to the muscles at the back of the rider's neck and thence down each side of his spine to his seat; also of course, having to say something relieves much of the pupil's mental or nervous tension, and with a careful choice of word or phrase the rider's feel for rhythm and co-ordination in general will be improved.

6 FEEL

The rider's ability to feel, in every moment of every stride exactly how the horse is moving, to discern which aids are required within that moment, coupled with the ability to co-ordinate them to the right degree to improve the rhythm and the quality of the gaits, and to judge what the horse is thinking – all this is called the rider's FEEL. The natural talent in this respect varies tremendously between different riders, but well-developed and refined sensitivity is an essential quality for success in the riding and training of horses. A lack of feel can be overcome with patient guidance and correct training as long as the rider has a natural sympathy and compassion; a mental, emotional and physical sensitivity; a generous heart and an intuitive belief – all of these are vital components of FEEL.

15 The horse's gaits and the rider's influence
– how he applies the aids

The beginning of this section is perhaps the best place to explain the recent changes in the modern terminology used to define the horse's paces or gaits. To simplify the picture as much as possible, the trot will be taken as an example and the types of pace within the trot will be listed according to their length, from the shortest to the longest.

Prior to 1971, here in England we had three different sorts of trot: collected, ordinary (everyday, basic trot) and extended, and on these three our training programmes and national dressage tests were based. On a personal note, in the 1950s during our years in Germany when my husband's Regiment was stationed in a particularly 'horsey' area near Celle, in the North Hannover district, the German national dressage tests enumerated five types of trots: collected, short working, working, middle and extended.

The two working trots were used in tests up to Elementary level, and collected, middle and extended trots for tests above that standard. It was not until I was lucky enough to be given the opportunity to compete internationally in Rotterdam in 1970 that I realized that there was a vast difference between the English and the Continental interpretation of the word 'ordinary'.

On the first day, when the Prix St Georges Test was being ridden, I went up to the arena on foot to watch the earlier competitors, to get my eye in. I was astonished at the energetic, rounded, near-extension the horses were showing between the markers where ordinary trot was asked for in the test. 'Right, if that is how they do it, we had better try to do the same,' I thought, but I was

145

puzzled. The last day's Grand Prix test-sheets solved the problem, for one of my own particular sheets was printed in German and where the English versions demanded, 'Ordinary trot' the German equivalent was 'Mittle trab' (Middle trot) – so there were two entirely different meanings for the same word. I believe there must have been a misunderstanding when the tests were translated in Brussels due to our only having three varieties of trot. When I first queried this point, I suggested perhaps we might have four trots which would be collected, ordinary, medium and extended for economic as well as traditional reasons, but Colonel Gustaf Nyblaeus, the Chairman of the FEI Dressage Bureau, decided in his great wisdom, that as the ordinary trot had two meanings and was '*too* ordinary anyway' that word should die and be buried and erased from the equestrian language. So now, officially, nationally and internationally there are four trots; listed according to their respective lengths of stride, from the shortest to the longest, they are: collected, working (replacing our old national ordinary), medium and extended.

The descriptions of the gaits in the following paragraphs are adapted from the FEI Dressage Rule Book (1975). The phraseology has been modified to suit instructors and their pupils, rather than the expert international dressage judges for whom the rules were primarily written.

The halt
At the halt the horse should stand absolutely still, that is the foremost

FIG.60   THE HALT

requirement of all – the immobility. He should stand straight, and square with his weight evenly distributed over all four feet. The forelegs should be vertical and abreast as a pair, the hindfeet should also be abreast and stand directly under the horse's hip-joints. The horse should be willingly attentive to his rider's wishes, rather than sleepy or nervously alert and inattentive. He should be on the bit, accepting a light contact with the rider's hand and should be ready and willing to move off at the slightest indication from his rider. The neck should be carried freely with a natural elevation from the withers to a supple poll, with the fore part of the muzzle slightly in front of the vertical. The elevation of the forehand will be dependant on the engagement of the

146

haunches; whereas an advanced horse will show this additional graceful quality, a novice horse must show a form relative to his standard of training.

The instructor must be careful that by teaching the requirements of a correct halt, he does not lead his pupils into disturbing their horses' immobility by trying to make them 'square-up' their feet; he must insist that they stand absolutely still, or ride forward again in order to make a new and better halt.

The halt is one of the most useful and important exercises in the training programme of any riding horse and as such it should be practiced frequently. A perfect halt is the result of correct, careful and systematic training, combined with educated riding.

To bring a moving horse to a halt. The halt may be progressive, e.g. canter, trot, walk, halt; or direct, e.g. canter, halt, depending on the horse's and rider's ability. The rider's forward-driving aids must be tactfully active while the thought, weight and rein-aids carefully restrain. From the first lessons, the instructor must sow 'the three pea-seeds' which must be cultivated in all subsequent lessons which include halting, so that the rules become part of the rider's subconscious reactions:

i *Predetermine* – plan well ahead *where* the halt will be made.

ii *Prepare* – in plenty of time, the horse and rider must be balanced and co-operating well together. The gait must be active, rhythmical and suitable. Half-halts to improve the horse's balance, contain his impulsion and maintain his form are indispensible when preparing to make a halt.

iii *Posture* – even as he approaches the pre-determined spot, the rider should retain a good posture, thinking of growing tall ears and pressing slightly more on his stirrups as he rides smoothly into a good, square halt, rather than making a last-minute stop as if at a suddenly-red traffic light!

When the hindlegs are brought under the horse he should give at the poll and quietly champ the bit with a closed, or nearly closed, mouth. The rider should give sufficiently without losing the contact with his legs or reins, to allow the horse to 'alight' to the halt softly and easily. The horse should place his legs vertically and maintain a good form or natural bearing throughout. Occasionally minor adjustments may be made forwards – they should *never* be made backwards. The rider's legs should remain close to the horse, lifting up his middle, to retain his form and prevent him from stepping backwards or to one side. If a slight give of the rider's hand is neglected the horse will probably stand with his fore or hindfeet under him too much, like an elephant standing on a tub in the circus, he then loses his natural bearing and cannot stand with the required ease, and elevation of his head and neck.

If the rider's forward-driving aids have been insufficient or incorrect the horse will leave his hindlegs out behind him as he comes into the halt, he will lower or hollow his back and will lean heavily on the rider's hands which will then resort to a dull (or despairing), heavy pull on the unfortunate horse's mouth.

Pupils should be taught to ride boldly yet softly into the halt; to maintain their horses' form and their attention during the halt; and to move forward well, 'on the aids', from the halt. These three phases are important and should be carefully taught initially and insisted on at all times by the instructor. 'Why not?' as General Viebig would say – one of his favourite questions which was at once excellent, thought-provoking, or maddening, and entirely unanswerable!

To be able to ride correct halts is a very important exercise for all riders, as it tests their knowledge, tact and feel. Pupils should be taught to feel the more obvious faults for themselves, and can test each others' assessments, but the more subtle faults must be corrected by the watchful instructor. The pupils must not look down to check that their horses are standing absolutely square, nor should the instructor be over-particular about this, for pupils must learn the importance of an attentive immobility whenever they bring their horses to a halt.

Unless pupils are taught that halts are important movements, they tend to disregard them altogether, almost as though to stand still is a waste of time as they have suddenly thought of something *far* more interesting or 'advanced' to do. Their thinking – or non-thinking, can be transformed if the instructor recommends the adoption of a general rule, 'Whenever you ride your horse to a halt, count twenty before you ride forward into the selected gait . . .?

The instructor should keep an eye on every rider and horse in his class, even when they are halted as a ride, in front of him for questions, discussions or explanations. The horses should not be kept at attention throughout a more lengthy halt, but should be allowed to stand 'at ease', on long reins. The riders should sit straight with an easy poise, they should never lounge or move about thoughtlessly on their horse's backs, nor should the horses be allowed to move out of alignment, or to rub their noses on their knees, eat grass or bite or kick their next-door neighbour. Pupils should prevent these lapses by quicker anticipation, and by leg aids, *not* by using their hands – other than to give a quick tap with a whip to call the horse to order.

To move forward from the halt the rider must first determine the gait at which he will proceed, and he must be sure that the horse's form is good, that he is on the bit and attentive before he asks him to move straight forward. The rider then applies carefully measured forward-driving aids particularly with both legs on the girth, to achieve a clear, active and calm transition, whilst simultaneously his hands allow the forward movement without losing the soft, smooth contact with the horse's mouth. The rider must prescribe and maintain the correct rhythm and amount of impulsion from the first forward step, he should then adjust his aids to maintain the horse's form at the desired gait. The horse should remain on the bit, but this factor should never be allowed to jeopardize the freedom and fluency of the horse's movement and steps.

If the horse is sticky and does not answer the rider's aids willingly and instantly, the rider should strengthen his seat and his forward-driving aids, using both his lower legs farther forward, nearer the magic spot, (the sensitive intercostal* area) just in front of the girth. He should also ride the horse forward with his hands, even if doing so does cause a momentary loss of contact.

The half-halt

This is the name given to one of the most valuable and delicate 'keys' to the partnership of a rider and his horse, whereby the attentiveness and balance of both partners is improved within the briefest possible moment.

There are many degrees of half-halt, from the obvious ones which live up to

---

* See Chapter 19.

the description of 'a halt within the gait', as may be seen given by dominant riders on heavily built horses, to the finest half-halts which are invisible to the observer's eye, yet are understood perfectly by the horse.

The educated rider indicates his leadership to his partner by means of half-halts on many, many occasions whenever he rides, whether he is hacking in the countryside, out hunting, riding a cross-country course, or even when show-jumping 'against the clock'. All riders should be taught how, why, and exactly when, to use a half-halt, relatively early in their equestrian education, for without a thorough grounding in this work it is difficult, or even imposs-ible, for them to develop a correct feel of the co-ordinating influences of their aids, nor of the horse's movement; instead they will learn to hang on the reins while the horse runs along on his forehand. This soon causes the horse to lose the balance, rhythm and freedom of his natural gaits, and the sensitivity of his mouth as well.

The FEI explains the half-halt as 'a hardly visible, almost simultaneous co-ordinated action of the rider's seat, legs and hands with the object of increasing the horse's attention and balance before the execution of movements or transitions to lesser and higher paces'.

By momentarily shifting slightly more of the horse's weight on to his hindquarters, the hindlegs are engaged with a consequent lightening of the horse's forehand and his whole balance is improved. The rider must not lean the upper body back or he will overload the haunches and may easily disturb the rhythm of the gait. The rider must not tip forwards or stiffen, particularly in his back or hips, or he will overload the forehand and cramp the horse's back so that he will not be able to bring his hindlegs actively forward under him.

There are two equally important components in the riding of a half-halt,

i The rider makes an especially careful check that his own position is correct, and applies his weight, legs and rein aids, clearly and sensitively, whilst lengthening the distance between his heels and the top of his ears, in order to allow the rounding of the horse's back.

ii He asks the horse to improve his balance and form.

Both these adjustments are made simultaneously, during a fraction of a second; a half-halt must be quick, light and tactful, it should never be a forced, heavy-handed, nor a prolonged affair.

Thus, to sum up, the half-halt may be used at all stages of a horse's training to restore his equilibrium whenever it is lost, to increase the horse's alert attentiveness, to improve the quality of the gait in which he is working, to prepare him for certain movements and to balance him if necessary, within them, e.g. turning, slowing down, halting, upward or downward transitions, lateral movements, etc.

FIG. 61   THE WALK

The walk

The walk is a four time gait. (Four hoof-beats.) There are four steps to a stride, the sequence of footfalls being:

1 Right fore.
2 Left hind.
3 Left fore.
4 Right hind – or the sequence may commence with a hind leg.

At the walk the horse should march deliberately and regularly in a well-marked and even four-time beat which is maintained consistently throughout all his work at the walk. The horse should retain a good form, carrying himself and his rider with ease and a natural balance.

When the four beats cease to be distinct, even and regular, the walk is faulty, being hurried, awkward, disunited or broken. The walk is the most fragile of all the horse's gaits, it can easily be spoiled by incorrect training or riding. Asking the horse to walk on the bit too early in his training, or worse, collecting the walk before he is ready, can quickly destroy a horse's natural walk. If a young horse is constantly ridden by a rider whose hands and seat do not follow his horse's movement this will soon impede the natural fluency of the gait. The whole of the rider's middle-part must be supple, particularly his hips and lower back, and his hands and his lower legs should ride the horse forward, asking each hindleg to step farther forward alternately, left and right, rhythmically and not urgently or stiffly.

The following walks are recognized: collected, medium, extended and free.

(a) The collected walk is a comparatively advanced movement. From the first, instructors should emphasize the dangers of asking for any collection in the walk before horse and rider have achieved collection at trot and canter, and even then it must only be sought 'little by little'. The hindlegs are engaged with good hock action by the rider's forward-driving aids used in conjunction and careful co-ordination with restraining rein-aids. Each step is higher and covers less ground than at the medium walk, due to the increased activity. The horse moves resolutely forward, on the bit, and with his neck raised and arched firmly from the withers. Due to a supple yet high poll, the front line of the horse's head is nearly vertical. The horse's head remains steady, his mouth maintaining a light contact with the rider's hands as he quietly champs or chews the bit. His bearing is confident and proud, he shows no resistance or irregularity in the rhythm or sequence of the gait. The hindfeet touch the ground either in or just behind the footprints of the forefeet. The more collected the walk, the less obvious is the movement of the horse's head or of the rider's hands, seat and legs.

(b) The medium walk, the every day walk is called 'medium' rather than 'working', to emphasize the desired ground-covering quality. It should be a free, regular and unconstrained walk of moderate extension. The horse remains on the bit while he walks energetically yet calmly with even and determined marching steps, the hindfeet touching the ground in front of the footprints of the forefeet. The rider's forward-driving aids enable him to maintain a light, constant but allowing contact with the horse's mouth.

(c) The extended walk. Here the horse lengthens his stride so that each step is of maximum length. The walk should be purposeful, covering as much ground as possible, without haste, without losing his balance in the slightest degree, and without disrupting the rhythm or regularity of the gait, the hindfeet touching the ground well in front of the footprints of the forefeet (over-tracking). The rider's hands allow the horse to stretch his head and neck out, and to move them freely without however, losing contact with the horse's mouth, and his forward-driving aids ask for bold ground-covering strides, particularly from the hindlegs, without causing constraint or bustle or any loss of equilibrium or rhythm.

(d) The free walk. The free walk is used for relaxation and reward, and the horse is given complete freedom to lower and stretch out his head and neck. The rider has no contact with the horse's mouth and there is an obvious slackness in the reins. Here again, every part of the rider should be seen to follow well the movement of the horse; any vestige of stiffness in the rider will automatically impede the freedom of the horse's walk. The horse is guided and controlled by the rider's thought, weight and leg-aids alone. The instructor must be careful that his pupils understand that they must lengthen the reins by allowing them to slide out through their fingers freely, and must then carry and move their hands forward well with the oscillations of the horse's head and neck, rather than sliding their hands backwards to the buckle-ends of the reins, and then leaving the hands stationary behind the front arch of the saddle and behind the horse's movement, which they will then hamper rather than encourage. The instructor must also watch that his pupils re-take the contact with their reins with well-prepared and smooth adjustments. He should warn his pupils not to make an immediate transition to a faster gait, but to ride several steps of medium walk first, or to trot while on long reins and then to take up the reins. In this way the instructor will preserve his school-horses' training; they will not learn to anticipate an upward transition whenever the rider takes up his reins, but will await the rider's decision.

FIG. 62.   THE TROT

To walk forward from the halt

The rider corrects his position and ensures that the horse is on the bit and attentive before he applies forward-driving aids and allows the horse to move straight forward with a give of his hands, he then adjusts his aids to maintain the horse's form at the desired gait.

Should the horse not respond willingly to the rider's forward-driving aids, if the pupil is inexperienced the instructor should help tactfully, while an experienced pupil should strengthen his aids, and if necessary use his whip with a quick hit just behind his leg. In this latter case he should repeat the halt and move-off, without the whip, and be equally quick to reward the horse for obeying.

A good ground-covering walk is essential for a riding horse of any type. The horse should carry his tail reasonably high and it should swing to the tip like a pendulum, in rhythm with the horse's stride. The walk should be easy yet purposeful and in no way be disturbed by the rider, who must have a correct and following seat, forward-driving legs, and sensitive smooth hands which invite the free movements of the horse's head to enhance the rhythmical flow of the whole gait. If the rider's hands do not give each time the horse's head is lowered, the stride will be shortened and the pace become restricted, if not irregular. Although a well-trained horse can walk while the rider's hand is fairly immobile without losing the rhythm of his walk, a good ground-covering walk cannot exist without a full give of the rider's hand, a movement which should start from his shoulders. (Thinking of the coat-hanger, see p. 135.)

To trot forward from the halt

The rider prepares as above but thinks, 'trot' instead of 'walk'. He then applies his aids nicely adjusted to ask the horse to lift up his middle part and then to trot forward with a bold two-time trot rhythm from the first step forward.

To canter forward from the halt

First the rider must be proficient at moving off at the trot and at obtaining good canter-departs from trot and from walk. After making correct preparations at the halt, the rider should think, 'Canter, right' and apply the correct aids while looking up and ahead. The first stride must be a true canter stride, with the required leg leading.

152

All transitions from the halt must be smooth, balanced and *straight* as the horse moves foward willingly, confidently and on the bit.

The trot

The trot is a two-time gait. (Two hoof-beats.)

There are two steps to a stride, the sequence of footfalls being:

1 Left-fore and right-hind together (left diagonal).

2 Right-fore and left-hind together (right diagonal).

There is a brief moment of suspension between each step.

The trot should be free, active and regular and should be moved into smoothly, clearly and without hesitation and be concluded in a similar manner.

The quality of the trot is judged by the general impression, or form; the horse's acceptance of the bit, the easy activity and the regularity and elasticity of the steps, all originating from well-engaged hindquarters and a supple back, poll and jaw. The rhythm must remain constant and well-defined as if a metronome from the top of a piano were carried on the horse's poll, and he should maintain a natural balance and carriage throughout all his trot-work. Riders must be taught as soon as possible how to supervise and sustain the horse's form when he works at trot, so that the rider's feel and the aids maintain a good rhythm and impulsion, and the horse chews quietly as he remains on the bit.

When riding in the school or in a dressage test the rider should ride at sitting trot, remaining quietly in the saddle, following the horse's movement well and allowing the horse's back to swing freely, unless rising trot is demanded.

Beginner pupils should always be taught the sitting trot first, and this should be well established before rising trot is introduced. To teach the rising trot prematurely invites an unstable rising seat rather than one which sits naturally, well down in the saddle – one might say here that deeper thoughts lead to deeper seats!

Rising trot

When the trot is ridden rising, the rider follows the horse's movement and softly rises and sits on alternate diagonals, to ease his horse's back and himself. If he sits as the left diagonal pair of feet come to the ground he is said to be riding on the left diagonal. To change the diagonal the rider sits for one extra beat. It is most usual for riders to ride on the left diagonal when riding on the right rein and vice versa, as this helps the rider to balance himself and his horse better on the inside hindleg and to activate this leg on large circles and wide turns. Occasionally experienced riders may find a change to the inside diagonal will help, e.g. when retraining a horse with a hollowed back – but this is the exception rather than the rule.

Instructors should teach their pupils to be supple rather than gymnastic in their riding of a rising trot and they should encourage their pupils to think and be accurate about commencing on the required diagonal, and to change diagonals quite frequently when riding out of doors, as well as whenever they change the rein in a manège. In the latter case pupils should be taught to change the trot diagonal in the stride that crosses the centre line when riding across it at an angle of 70°–90°, and in the stride which actually changes the rein when riding down the centre line or along a diagonal line. They should not change diagonals at X in the latter cases or they risk upsetting the regularity of the rhythm at that point, and will teach their horses a bad habit which will be even more apparent at medium or extended trot.

The following trots are recognized: collected, working, medium and extended.

The collected trot is a comparatively advanced movement. A short working trot is a useful step towards it but is by no means the real thing. A good collected trot has qualities which are a joy to feel and to behold. The horse's hindquarters are well engaged, the swing of his back is unimpeded and his head and neck are raised in a smooth curve, rising from the withers to the poll; these three factors enable his shoulders to move with greater ease in any direction. The horse remains willingly and steadily on the bit which he quietly champs, or chews, with a relaxed lower jaw. His steps are shorter and higher than in the other trots, and he is more light, active and mobile. The rider achieves the required spring and elevation of the steps of the collected trot by a careful balance and co-ordination of his forward-driving and his restraining aids. It is very important that he maintains a correct position himself, with a pliant back and supple hips, that his lower legs are effective in their demand for engagement of the horse's hindquarters, and an elevation of the horse's middle part, forehand and steps, and that the rein-aids are smooth, soft and light and yet consistent.

The working trot is the basic, everyday trot, the steps of which are longer than those of the collected trot yet not so long as those of the medium trot. It is the trot used most in the schooling of both young and trained horses. The range of variety of working trot is greater than that of any other gait. Working trots vary according to the horse's natural balance and movement which are dependent on several factors but mostly on his individual characteristics of conformation and temperament, his present standard of training and on how he is ridden. The instructor must guide his pupils to discover the best working trot tempo for each individual horse. Free forward movement, rhythm, balance, suppleness and impulsion are all important qualities, and the horse must accept the bit and the rider's influences willingly, without resistance.

It is here that riders most frequently confuse speed with impulsion. I recall our eldest daughter's amazement when I was judging the dressage phase of a Three Day Event, when she was asked by a harassed competitor, 'Does your mother like a fast test or a slow one?' Obviously, the competitor had had

'Insufficient impulsion.' written on one test sheet; had gone faster in the next test only to be criticized for 'Hurrying – too fast'! Instructors must remind their pupils frequently that impulsion is the energy created in the horse by the rider's forward-driving aids and restrained and regulated as required; this store of impulsion within the horse facilitates the easy activity so vitally necessary in all his work.

'The horse should go forward in working trot with even, elastic steps and good hock-action' – this last requirement has been added by the FEI to their definition in order to emphasize the importance of impulsion originating from the activity of the hindquarters rather than the flat, inactive, almost dreary 'ordinary trots' of which were so dreadfully 'ordinary' in all too many instances in former times. Collection is not required. Movements in working trot are not included in advanced dressage tests; it is ridden in the earlier, easier tests which are for horses who are not yet trained sufficiently to produce collection. In many countries a short working trot is used as an intermediate step towards the advanced collected trot, this is a helpful addition for horse and rider.

The medium trot comes between the working and the extended trots, but it is more 'round' and is not so extended as the latter. The horse goes forward in good self carriage with free and moderately extended steps and an obvious impulsion from the hindquarters. The horse must remain on the bit as the rider allows him to carry his head a little more in front of the vertical than at the collected or well-balanced working trot, and allows him also to lower his head and neck slightly without losing his balance on to his forehand, in order that he may lengthen his strides. The steps should be even and maintain a constant rhythm, the whole movement should be balanced and unconstrained. The rider must move well with the horse in all respects, his upper body should not be left behind the perpendicular, nor should he lean forward with a rounded back, a collapsed diaphragm and stiff hips. The instructor must guard equally against the passive pupil who does not ask enough, and the over-zealous ambitious rider who over-drives his horse with an element of force and tension, in which case the latter will pass through the rider's back to the horse's back and will show clearly in his steps – these same principles apply to riding the extended trot.

The extended trot is the trot with the longest strides; with each step the horse covers as much ground as possible. Maintaining a constant two-time rhythm, he lengthens his steps evenly and to the utmost as a result of great impulsion from the hindquarters. The horse remains on the bit as the rider allows him to lower and extend his head and neck, just sufficiently to enable him to stretch in a good, though longer, form throughout his whole body. The instructor must teach his pupils to guard against any tendency for the horse's action to become high or false, the hind legs to straddle, moving 'wide behind', or any irregularity in the rhythm or length of the steps.

Contact with the rider's rein-aids should be consistent; the horse should not lean on the rider's hands – he should carry himself with ease. The horse's forefeet should touch the ground on the spot towards which they are pointing, they should not be flipped out beyond it first. Exaggerated movement of the forelegs which is not matched by the angle of the cannon-bones of the hindlegs is an artificial product of forced training and as such has nothing to do with true

155

dressage. It is usually indicative of excess tension and a poor form with a hollow back.

All transitions from longer to shorter strides must be smooth and fluent and never abrupt and the aids should be soft and unobtrusive. Transitions play an integral part in the training of riders and of horses, and in the development of an extended trot.

If, when a more experienced pupil is schooling a horse towards extended trot, he breaks into a canter, the rider must not check him immediately, or the horse will quickly learn to evade the exercise by breaking into a canter instead of exerting himself as required for the extended trot. Instead the pupil must be taught immediately to apply his forward-driving aids to push the horse on to the bit at the canter, establishing a good canter before bringing him back to the trot and trying again for a lengthening of the strides.

Further points on the rider's position and influence at the trot

When pupils are riding at sitting trot the instructor must insist that they think and feel the horse's movement and that they keep a good posture. They must keep their shoulders straight and level, their hip joints and seat-bones well forward, retain a smooth suppleness in their spines, especially in the lower part of their backs, and a well adapted contact of thighs, knees and calves, not gripping but remaining with the horses' movements, thus they will be able to 'stick to the saddle' rather than being lifted and bumped – which is bad for both horse and rider.

Pupils must be watched constantly that they do not tip the upper body forward and displace the seat towards the rear of the saddle, with deflated diaphragms, and shallow breathing, in a false endeavour to minimize their weight and movement in the saddle. This attitude will in fact have the opposite effect as the hips, pelvis and spine will be cramped if not locked, which will cause disastrous bumping on the saddle and the horse's back.

Whereas in sitting trot the rider sinks into the saddle with every step, in rising trot this only happens on every alternate step. Mainly due to the horse's movement, and also to a slightly increased support from knees and stirrups, the rider is lifted up by one of the diagonal pairs of legs; he remains over the saddle during the next step with supple knees and ankles and then sinks down again softly as the original diagonal pair of legs comes to the ground, and he is ready to receive the upward impetus once more and the cycle is repeated. The horse should move the rider, the rider's weight should not thrust off the saddle and return with a resounding bump – a horrifying thought, and yet is a 'happening' which occurs frequently in most fields of equestrianism. The gravity of this fault is borne out by the following true story. When Colonel Paul Rodzianko, the famous Russian instructor, was taking a course for young British officers in Germany, just after the Second World War, he became quietly very angry. He halted the ride, told an offending pupil to dismount, lie face down in the manège, then in his riding boots he jumped up and down on the pupil's back – and he was not a little man! Colonel Rodzianko said, 'You did not like that, did you?' A muffled 'No' came up from the tan floor, 'Well neither does your horse – remount and do not bump down in the saddle ever again.' Certainly he proved his point!

During the rising trot the horse's balance and carriage must not be impeded

156

or lost. Through a correct seat and influence of the rider's aids the horse should be kept active, balanced and on the bit. Thus the rider must be careful to retain a correct firmness and carriage, his upper body moving smoothly up and down. The rider's movements should be fluent and harmonize perfectly with those of his horse, they should never be abrupt nor off-balance. As the rider is lifted he should keep his pelvis well forward without any obvious movement and when sitting down again his seat must return precisely to the same correct place in the centre of the saddle; this return to the saddle must be made softly without a vestige of bump or bang. In the school, the rider uses an upright seat at rising trot, while out hacking he may adopt a slightly more forward posture.

The rider's knees and lower legs must be kept still; the light tread on the stirrups must be directed vertically downward, not forwards nor outwards – both of these faults result from carelessness or excess tension and stiffness in the hips; and cause the rider's lower legs to become unsteady and to lose their contact with the horse's sides.

The rider's hands must not follow the movements of the upper body blindly, with stiff arms which will badly affect the horse's mouth and his action. Instead the smooth contact with the reins must be retained by correctly carried hands with a soft suppleness in the rider's shoulder and elbow joints, which will be further reflected in his wrists and fingers.

In rising trot some riders pull up their shoulders and elbows, and thus lose carriage, balance and 'follow'. This is a result of a mistaken endeavour to lift themselves out of the saddle instead of letting the horses' movements do it for them, and is commonly caused by being taught rising trot too soon.

The purpose of the rising trot is to make trot-work easier for the horse and his rider, not only by halving the number of sitting-beats but also by moving the rider's weight a little more on to his stirrups on the alternate steps. When a rider rises at trot his weight changes during every stride which has an influence on the gait itself. When the rider is lifted with the knees as a steady anchor, and the thigh as a lever, the point of gravity is moved very slightly forward, and during the next step when the rider sits, it will be moved back again. In the first step the horse goes forward while the rider is above the saddle, in the second step the horse carries the rider forward with him as he sits in the saddle. Thus at the rising trot it is quite easy for the rider to put the right rhythm into the horse.

Most of a young horse's trot work is ridden in rising trot unless the young horse has a particularly strong back. As the muscles of his top-line develop, so the rider may increase the amount of work in sitting trot. More experienced pupils who are schooling young horses at sitting trot must be reminded to follow the horse's movements softly, with their seats at each rise and fall of the gait. When riding out of doors, the rider may incline his upper body a little farther forward, with a moderately light seat, as the horse will have more natural impulsion and will require less urging with the forward-driving aids. It is very important that the rider remains exactly 'with the horse' whichever form of rising trot he adopts and that his movement is as soft and unobtrusive as possible.

NOTE In dressage tests *all* trot work is executed sitting unless otherwise specified.

FIG. 63   THE CANTER

The canter

The canter is a three-time gait (three hoof-beats). There are three steps to a stride, the sequence of footfalls in *the right canter* for instance is:

1. Left hind.
2. Right hind and left fore together.
3. Right fore (the leg after which the canter is called).

There is a brief moment of suspension between each stride, where all four legs are in the air.

When riding on a curved line, in an enclosed arena or school, the canter is called true and united when the inside legs are leading, and counter-canter when the rider asks the horse purposely to canter with the outside legs leading. The canter is incorrect when the horse misunderstands, or goes against the rider's wishes, and canters false, on the wrong leg. There is a rather pointed definition of the difference between counter-canter and cantering on the wrong leg – 'The first is done by the instructor; the second is done by the pupil'. After quoting that the instructor must never make a mistake in his own canter aids! The disunited canter is a faulty pace when the horse changes the canter with either the fore or the hindlegs, for example he canters with the left foreleg and the right hindleg leading at the same time.

When he changes to a disunited canter the horse guides the instructor – the horse will change in front if the rider's rein-aids are abrupt, too strong or incorrect, and he will change behind if the rider's seat becomes displaced so that his weight and leg-aids are incorrect, or if the rider hangs on the inside rein.

A well-trained horse should move forward into the canter from any gait or position smoothly and without hesitation; the canter itself should be free, active and regular.

The quality of the horse's canter is judged by the general impression and form, the regularity, fluency, spring, and lightness of the three-time gait, originating from the engagement of the hindquarters, and the willing acceptance of the bit (without any tension or resistance), combined with a constant rhythm and a natural balance.

The horse must always be straight when he carries his rider in canter work, his shoulders must be exactly in front of his hindquarters, on straight lines, and relatively so on circle lines; there may be a very slight bend at the poll in the direction of the leading-leg. However, occasionally, for training purposes, the

instructor may tell his more experienced pupils to ask for this bend to be away from the leading-leg in order to give them a feel for the desired straightness, and for the best way to correct any horse who may be inclined to canter crookedly, with his hindquarters to the inside. If the pupils ride counter-canter with the 'wrong' bend down the long side, they will then learn how to use the wall in the right way – to keep the horse's haunches in line under him.

The following canters are recognized: collected, working, medium and extended. As was the case with the trots, the canters are listed according to their relative lengths of strides, i.e. from shortest to longest. The order bears no relation to the order in which they are introduced into the training programmes of riders or horses.

(a) The collected canter is a comparatively advanced movement and as such is only used in the later stages of the training of riders and horses. The horse strides forward, on the bit, with his head and neck raised and arched, from the withers to the poll, and the nose steady, just in front of the vertical. The strides are shorter than at any of the other canters but the impulsion is greater, thus making it possible for the horse to maintain regular and lively foot movements in an even three-time rhythm. The collected canter should show a noticeable engagement of the hindquarters and lightening of the forehand. The shoulders should be free and mobile, and the haunches must be very active, and the whole horse should be supple, showing no resistance to his rider's influences.

The collected canter should only be ridden by experienced riders on horses who have been sufficiently prepared for this demanding work. The rider shortens the canter strides by increasing the activity of the horse's hindquarters with his forward-driving aids while at the same time he catches the forward movement of the steps with quick light half-halts which are given mainly with the outside rein. These half-halts and their accompanying gives must be made in rhythm with the canter strides and should be used sparingly, so that they encourage rather than diminish the added animation and activity and consequent lowering of the haunches. The rider will soon learn to feel and appreciate the required, powerful springing of the horse's hindlegs, and he must be very careful to keep his own hips well forward and his pelvis and back supple and pliant to absorb the movement, and to facilitate this action of the horse's hindquarters; any stiffness in his seat will eliminate it.

(b) The working canter is the basic everyday canter, the strides of which are

159

longer than those of the collected canter, but are not so long as those of the medium canter. It is the canter most used in the schooling of young and more trained horses. Many of the remarks made earlier concerning the working trot also apply to the working canter. The individual variations and their causes, the required qualities of free forward movement, balance, ease and impulsion, acceptance of the bit and of the rider's influences are all identical, added to which the horse 'should go forward with even, light and cadenced strides and good hock action'. It is simplest to quote the FEI's explanatory note here: '"good hock action" does not mean that collection is a required quality of working canter; it only underlines the importance of an impulsion originating from the activity of the hindquarters.' Instructors must watch that their pupils do not mistake inactivity for smoothness. Movements at working canter are only asked for in dressage tests of medium standard or below.

(c) The medium canter. The strides of the medium canter are longer than those of the working canter but shorter than those of the extended canter. The horse goes forward when requested to do so by the rider's soft and fluent forward-driving aids. He should cover the ground well, with free, balanced, regular and moderately extended strides, and good impulsion from the hindquarters. The more the strides lengthen the more the rider must allow his seat to go with the movement, for only by so doing will he be able to preserve the horse's form, the roundness, and the resilience of the horse's back muscles. The horse should remain on the bit while the rider allows him to carry his head with his nose a little farther forward in front of the vertical, than he does at the collected or working canters. The rider also invites the horse to lower his head and neck slightly as his strides lengthen evenly; he must not lose the contact or allow the horse to become unbalanced on to his forehand. He should make judicious use of half-halts to ensure that the horse is balanced and straight and that the action of the reins still goes through the horse's body from his hind-heels to the bit.

(d) The extended canter. As a result of great impulsion from the hindquarters, activated by the rider's forward-driving aids, the horse lengthens his strides to the utmost, covering as much ground as possible. He remains on the bit while the rider allows him to lower and extend his head and neck, and his nose stretches a little farther forward than in medium canter. The horse should maintain the same rhythm and remain light, calm and balanced during the extended canter and its transitions.

Transitions within the canter should always be soft, fluent and accurate and not in the least harsh or abrupt. Instructors must impress upon their pupils the importance of transitions both within the canter and to and from it, for well-ridden transitions are an invaluable exercise for improving the quality of the canter strides.

Before starting canter work, especially if there is any problem or imperfection in the pace, it is always beneficial to ease and calm the horse with helpful loosening exercises such as leg-yielding through increased pressure of the inner leg, whereby the horse goes forward and is prevented from bringing his hindquarters inwards and the rider will gain much pleasure from the smoothness of the transition – the horse will feel happy too! The exercise of decreasing and increasing the circle on one and two tracks respectively can also be used to help the transition to canter, the rider asks for the strike-off in the moment

160

when the horse regains the track of the big circle. Many horses find the transitions from walk to canter and canter to walk much easier than those from and to trot. The instructor must train his pupils, little by little, to be diligent and practise all transitions.

The aids to canter on a named leg – the canter strike-off, or canter-depart

Introduction. There are probably more varieties of 'correct aids for the canter-depart or strike-off into canter' in this country than anywhere else in the world, and in consequence the proportion of smooth transitions to canter seen in our schooling-grounds, show-rings or dressage arenas is disappointingly small. It is extraordinarily difficult for aspiring horsemen if instructors and the various available textbooks all teach different methods. Even a brief research will reveal that at the beginning of this century, whereas we had a smattering of knowledge of the ground-plan of the movements which might be ridden, we had no traditional foundation of classical training giving directives of *how* to ride them or how the horse should move when carrying out these movements and transitions. Thus many teachers and authors had 'pot-shots' at issuing instructions; riders were told to 'move their weight back and to the outside', to 'weigh down the outside hind leg and lighten the leading foreleg,' they were told to 'lean the weight of the body forward over the horse's inside shoulder,' to 'bend the horse's head away from the leading leg', or to 'move the inner hand over the withers to turn the horse's head towards the leading leg.' They were told to 'start the canter from a rising trot on the opposite diagonal from the desired canter-lead' or, on the other hand, some instructors were adamant that a horse should only ever be asked to canter from a collected (sitting) trot – and so on. One's heart bleeds for riders and horses alike – no wonder riders were confused and horses became 'over-nagged' and soured by over-ambitious, unmethodical training methods, and dressage itself gained a bad reputation.

It is in a sincere endeavour to blow away the mists and cobwebs that this particular movement is described in minutest detail so that no misunderstandings will impede the rider's actions or the horse's reactions, and so that clarity, ease and smoothness will prevail.

Some of the aids described hereafter differ slightly from or even directly oppose some aids which have been taught in English-speaking countries for a long time. However they do follow principles which have been officially recommended and recognized internationally for literally hundreds of years. I well remember a special meeting being held after Captain Edy Goldman, when commanding a most polished demonstration at the National Equestrian Centre, was noticed to instruct his riders to 'ask for the canter with the inside leg'. Although in practice the results of this apparently revolutionary idea were excellent, the theory was rejected loudly and immediately because it conflicted with our traditional doctrine of 'outer leg back to ask for the canter and to prevent the hindquarters from swinging out'. Personally, I can well understand this attitude, for in the 1950s I was typically British and dogmatic (obstinate?) on this very subject when told in Germany to use my inside leg predominantly for a canter-depart – until I was offered a very good horse to ride in British and German competitions and he would only strike off into the required canter if I used my inside leg distinctly and strongly on the girth!

161

Thus my conversion began, and in more recent years Colonel Podhajsky and Major Boltenstern have warned us not to demand the canter strike-off solely with the outside leg as this provokes a crooked strike-off and canter. Other instructors from the Spanish Riding School and those recommended to us by the FEI have taught us the finer details of their methods which again were identical to the first-mentioned great international instructors and these are the aids which are outlined in the following paragraphs.

Before and during the strike-off into canter the rider must keep the horse full of impulsion and going forward well on the bit. If the strike-off is asked for from a walk or a trot the rider must call the horse to attention with a half-halt, the reins acting very slightly towards the outside hindleg which makes the first beat of the canter, and thereby causing no obstruction to the forward movement of the inner fore or hindlegs. The rider moves his weight slightly inwards by lowering his inner knee and heel and putting a little more weight into that stirrup, and moves his inside hip-joint and seat bone slightly forwards, while keeping his upper body straight and the shoulders level. The inner hip should be kept well forward and the outer shoulder must not fall back. The rider's inner lower leg should be by the girth and the outer leg ready immediately behind the girth, with the knee kept back and down, not rising. Both legs are used tactfully, indicating the strike off into canter with the horse's inside legs leading. The rider's inside leg is used to free and lighten the horses shoulders, to lift up his middle-part, and to animate his inside hindleg, causing it to step farther forward to take the horse's weight securely, to enable him to start the canter with the outside hindleg. By this action the sequence of the present gait is changed and the horse is asked to start into canter, the rider's outside leg supports on the horse's body and keeps him straight.

The rider should think 'canter' as he eases the weight off his outside seat-bone and he should look up very slightly to the outside, to help to make his position exactly right – he should never look down to the inside or his seat and all his aids will be disrupted and unintentionally he will give wrong signals to his horse. The rein-aids must remain smoothly consistent. Just before the canter-depart the inner rein may ask for a slight positioning at the poll towards the leading leg to ensure that the horse is soft on his inner side, and the outer rein may limit the forward reach of the outer hindleg with small finger movements when necessary.

It is of the utmost importance that the horse is kept absolutely *straight*, before, during and after the strike-off into canter; he must never start on two tracks, nor be allowed to canter at any time with his hindquarters to the inside.

Whenever the horse strikes off into canter willingly, eagerly yet calmly, the rider must immediately give sufficiently to allow the horse not only to start but also to move well in the new gait. The rider's upper body must remain vertical yet pliant so that he follows the horse's movement fluently, while both lower legs maintain the impulsion with alert control. He should keep his inside hip and his outside shoulder well forward and use his forward-driving aids to develop and maintain the bounding quality of the canter strides.

Eventually, as he becomes more advanced in his education and responsiveness, the rider must refine his aids, so that the horse understands influences which are well-nigh invisible to the observer's eye. In most cases the quieter and smoother the strike-off, the smoother and more unconstrained, and rhythmic the horse will be during the canter itself.

A good rider, sitting correctly on a well-trained horse will merely have to think 'canter', lift his outer seat-bone imperceptibly, and it will happen – with no visible aids.

The easiest place for a pupil to ask a horse to canter on a named leg is when he is riding on a 20 metre circle at A or C in an enclosed arena. If the rider asks for the canter strike-off as soon as the horse has passed over the centre line and is on the last part of the open-side of the circle, approaching the long side of the

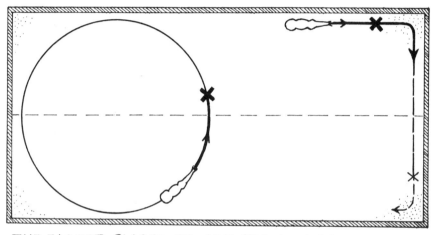

THE EASIEST PLACES TO ASK FOR A CANTER DEPART
FIG. 64

school and the closed side of the circle, the horse will wish to comply with his rider's request, as the enclosing walls of the school 'point the way' for him to canter on with the inside legs leading (see Fig. 64). If the horse canters on the wrong leg the instructor should tell the pupil it is wrong and direct him to trot and try again. He should not expect a novice pupil to know whether or not his horse is cantering on the wrong leg, it is up to the instructor to guide him to feel the sequence of the horse's legs under his seat; pupils must never be allowed to look down for the leading foreleg.

If a rider or a class is riding on the outer track of the school, another easy place for horse and rider to be asked for a canter-strike off is just before the first corner of the short side. Here the horse sees the short side ahead of him guiding him round, and what is more, he can see that in a comparatively short space of time he has another corner to negotiate in the same direction, thus both corners invite him to strike off with the inside leg leading. Horses are not fools when it comes to balancing themselves; it is invariably the rider who makes the mistake in a 'wrong canter strike-off'.

The most difficult place to ask for a canter depart is at the beginning of a long side of an enclosed school. After completing the constricting turns of the short side the horse is invited to change his equilibrium towards the outside in order to straighten out down the long side, and thus he is encouraged to strike-off into the canter with the outside legs leading. This fact will be proved time and time again when working horses loose in the school and may be used to advantage in later lessons when riders and horses are learning counter-canter.

Rider faults at the canter-depart

The fault most seen during the strike-off into canter is that of looking down. Prevention being better than cure, it is essential that instructors are meticulously careful to teach this transition correctly from the first beginner's canter lesson. Pupils must be taught to think, and helped to feel through their seats, the movement of each hindleg and which of the horse's shoulders and forelegs is reaching slightly farther forward.

The most common rider-faults at the canter-depart are as follows:

(a) The rider looks down, along the horse's inner shoulder, as if hoping to will the foreleg on that side to appear as the leading leg, or to see whether his efforts have been successful. Unfortunately, this leaning forwards and inwards will not produce the desired results for the rider's seat is displaced to the outside with the inner hip back; the weight-aid becomes entirely incorrect and the rider's legs lose contact with the horse's side or the inner leg is displaced backwards. All this usually results in the horse striking off on the wrong leg, and probably in his being reprimanded for doing so.

If a pupil has a real problem, a mental block over discerning with which leg the horse is leading at canter, he should be taken quietly aside and be given individual coaching. The instructor should encourage him to retain a good posture, to keep breathing naturally and to close his eyes for a few steps before he asks for the canter, this may help him to feel, and to think of the feeling more easily. He should open his eyes as soon as the horse is moving at canter. Obviously, the instructor will let the pupil try the blindfold effect at the slower transitions first, e.g. from walk to trot to get accustomed to the new sensation and to gain confidence. The instructor must exercise discretion and not overlook any possible dangers – the lesson must be safe.

(b) The rider's inner leg is not applied at the girth to ask the horse to strike-off into canter, instead the inner leg is stretched forward with a stiff knee, so that it will be applied too far forward – if it is applied at all!

(c) The canter-depart is asked for by the rider's outer leg alone which is also pulled backwards, this may well cause the horse to kick out against so rough an aid. Inevitably this faulty aid results in the horse being made crooked, with hind-quarters in, and his fore and hind feet on two separate tracks, the first strides at least will lack impulsion and the horse is unlikely to retain his form.

(d) Too strong rein-aids, the rider 'hanging' on the inner rein which bends the horse too much in his neck and prevents the forward reach of the inner shoulder and hindleg – this will often cause the horse to lose his balance or change legs behind.

(e) The rider fails to *think*. He selects a bad place, such as the beginning of the long side of the arena, or when circling away from other horses or from the direction of their stables.

(f) The rider does not *feel* and therefore does not balance and position the horse sufficiently before asking for the canter, or misses the exact moment.

If the horse starts the canter with the wrong leg leading he must be brought smoothly back to trot or walk at once, using mainly the outside rein and leg; the horse must be straightened then positioned correctly while being pushed forward on to the bit and into the canter, again with both legs, the inside leg on the girth clearly asked for the preparatory step for the correct canter-depart. This correction must be ridden forward – inside the outer track to avoid the risk of the magnetism of the wall making the horse crooked, and of disturbing other riders.

A sensitive and experienced rider will usually feel and thus anticipate a correct or an incorrect strike-off to canter, so that in the latter case he can rebalance and correct his horse before he actually commences the wrong canter.

The rider must constantly check that the posture of his upper body is good and that his seat is correctly positioned with the hip-joints pushed well forward and a lowered inner knee, and while the horse is cantering he must follow the horse's movements in perfect harmony. In his endeavours to keep his balance when turning at canter the rider must avoid bending or collapsing his inner side, because his seat will then be pushed outwards. Instead he must sit slightly to the inside before the turn, in order to invite the change of direction; he must keep his inner seat-bone and outer shoulder forward. The knee and ankle-joints must be softly flexible. The rider's upper body must be kept steady, vertical and with a smooth following throughout the spine, the hips and the lower back in order to absorb the movement. The upper arms must be kept close to the body, which retains a good posture with straight, level and supple shoulders and an erect neck and head. The outer shoulder must never be allowed to fall back.

The most common rider-faults at canter are as follows

(a) An unsteady seat, with flapping, unsteady legs and jostling hands, causing disruption and discord to all the rider's aids and to the horse. This is usually due to incorrect or lack of early teaching; the rider having been allowed or even encouraged to canter before his seat is established and steady at the walk and trot. If a pupil is taught the rising trot too soon this can also be a contributory factor to faulty riding at canter. These pupils must not be asked to canter until they are competent and confident when riding transitions and school figures at sitting trot.

(b) The rider's upper body is held behind the vertical; this generally results in non-following hands which hang on to the reins, and the horse's mouth.

(c) Stiff knee and ankle-joints, and/or a stiff back so that the rider is ejected out of the saddle with every stride, falling back into it with a bump just in time to be pushed up again by the next stride, to the detriment of the horse's and the rider's backs. At the same time, the effect is transmitted to the arms and hands which become stiff and unsteady. An unhappy situation which must be carefully coached through getting a correct position and feel for very short periods (a few strides only of sitting trot and of canter). Stiffness may well be the result of nervousness.

(d) The rider's upper body is tipped forward, usually with a hollowed back so that he is in front of the horse's movement; whereupon the rider's aids become confused and he may well lose control of his horse.

(e) Insufficient forward-driving aids, particularly the rider's inside leg failing to demand engagement of the hocks and impulsion, or pupils mistaking inactivity for smoothness.

(f) Tension or speed spoiling the canter – either being mistaken for impulsion.

(g) Sitting crooked, or to the outside.

When the horse moves in a smooth yet active canter, yielding to the rider's hands, the reins become practically passive, retaining a light yet steady feel with the horse's mouth.

During all canter work on straight lines the rider must keep his horse straight, and on the bit, in order to develop the best possible gait for each individual horse, so that it is regular, with easy, long, ground-covering strides, yet is perfectly balanced over all kinds of ground, whether it be the smooth turf of a dressage arena, a show-ground or a polo-field, along a woodland path or over a light, ploughed field. From this active yet easy canter a powerful gallop or a good collected canter can later be developed.

Circling or turning at canter. The rider must be taught first to prepare both himself and his horse, and he should map out the ground-plan well ahead. His own preparation consists of *thinking*; of correcting his position and adjusting his seat an appropriate degree to the inside, with the inner hip and outer shoulder well forward, straightened shoulders, and elbows, particularly the outer one, close to the body. To prepare the horse the rider should think and feel, checking that the gait is sufficiently active, balanced, and – if the diameter or angle of the circle or turn requires it – collected. If necessary the horse should be rebalanced with a half-halt or series of half-halts, before the circle or turn is commenced. For many lessons, if not years, instructors must patiently persist until these preparations are made as a habit and quite subconsciously, by their pupils.

The most common faults made by riders when circling or turning at canter are:

i The rider's seat slides out, and his inner hip goes back due to a weak position or to a lack of preparation – this fault may also cause the horse to change legs behind and become disunited in his canter.

ii A heavy, insensitive pull on the inner rein which invariably causes the horse's outer shoulder to be pushed out, and the horse to swerve out of the true line of the movement, to lose his balance and to change legs behind.

iii Over-strong rein aids will restrict the forward movement of the horse's inside hind leg and block the co-ordination and elasticity of the canter strides.

To make a downward transition from canter to trot, walk or halt, the rider prepares as if for a circle or turn with the horse well on the bit. He uses one or several half-halts, and when the horse's canter, form and balance are good he then uses restraining rein-aids, starting from the back of his shoulders. He moves the fingers within his inner hand with a little more pressure in order to impede the forward reach of the inner (leading) foreleg, thinking of shoulder-in, to soften the horse's inner side, the outside rein then indicates the transition down. He moves his inner leg back very slightly, and down, to keep the horse straight, preventing the hindquarters from swinging inwards. The rider should press slightly on his stirrups while 'growing tall', with an inflated diaphragm, his hips well forward, and an elastically following back and hips allowing the horse's back muscles to move powerfully and freely, bringing his hindquarters well under him.

If pupils are told to 'sit down', or to 'push to a halt', there is a grave risk that they will round and stiffen or harden their backs, causing their horses to hollow their backs away from the discomfort, and to leave their hind legs out behind them, all of which are bad faults and detrimental to the horse's training.

If when making a downward transition, the horse *leans on the hands*, the instructor must first check that the rider is not using tactless, heavy rein-aids with his elbows sticking out, and that he is not stiffening his back or hips against the horse's movement. The instructor should tell the pupil to plan to ride an 8–10 metre circle in from the outer track, and to ask for the downward transition as the horse is finishing the circle, just before he returns to the outer track. This will make the horse wish to make a downward transition for himself, because the small circle is arduous work, and he will also feel happy to slow down as he comes back to the wall with its magnetic, speed-reducing effect. Later the rider may use frequent and well defined half-halts or a loosening exercise (such as leg yielding), decreasing and increasing the circle immediately prior to the downward transition, and by these means together with spontaneous reward, the rider will soon effect a cure and the horse will become calm, obedient and light.

When his pupils seem reasonably competent at cantering on a named leg, the instructor can give them the following exercise to test their ability and to develop their feel and understanding.

The instructor tells his class to take the right canter, then when the horses have settled, the riders change their own positions, moving their right legs slightly back and their left legs a little forward. They will immediately feel out of tune, with the result that when they replace their legs in the correct positions they will really appreciate how good it feels.

By this simple exercise, the instructor will achieve two objectives, firstly the pupils will realize how necessary it is for the riders to sit so that it is easy for them to feel comfortable and to be as one with their horses. Secondly, the pupils will learn to feel and to know on which leg their horses are cantering, and, even more to the point, to feel on which leg their horses are about to canter – before they strike-off into the gait.

Rider faults to be corrected when making a downward transition are:

i Forgetting to plan ahead, to prepare for the transition with half-halts so that the horse may be ready, in good form and in the best possible balance. The rider's aids are abrupt and rough.

ii Excess tension caused by lack of confidence, certainty or by trying too hard, e.g. for accuracy, in a dressage test.

iii Hard, backwards pulling hands, instead of soft and smooth rein aids coming from the shoulders, back and seat.

iv Not maintaining the canter rhythm through his co-operating aids. The rider must continue to *think*, to *breathe* and to *feel*, 'canter, canter, canter,' right through his transitional aids, until the horse makes the first step in the new gait.

To improve the balance and the quality of the horse's canter pupils should be taught how the school wall may be used to help the rider. If the rider uses the centre line, riding a 10 metre half-circle on to it and a half-circle away at the far end, during the second half-circle, towards the wall, the horse will naturally develop balance, suppleness and further engagement of his haunches for himself, in order to re-take the outer track easily and safely. In this way the horse will start to collect himself, the rider will merely have to sit correctly in balance, keep his horse well on the bit and enjoy feeling his horse's canter improve.

When pupils are first taught to change from one canter lead to the other, the instructor should explain, demonstrate and teach them to trot and walk for a few strides before restarting the canter on the other lead. Although it might seem simpler for both horses and riders if the instructor were to direct the change of lead to be made through trot only, in practice the riders will invariably forget the half-halt and push their horses into the new canter without balance. If the downward transition is progressive to walk, the half-halt is given free, and is rewarded by a much more supple transition to the new canter.

In a true *simple change of leg* the horse makes two direct transitions, from canter to walk for one to three steps, followed by a direct transition to canter with the other leg leading.

As the horse's training and the rider's experience progress the number of intervening strides may gradually be reduced until the new canter can be restarted after only one walk step. The rider must be quick yet supple and readjust his aids, moving his new inner seat bone forwards and exchanging the position of his lower legs so that the new inner leg is on the girth and the new outer leg is eased back just behind the girth. If the change is asked for on a curved track, between circles or serpentine loops, the horse must be thoughtfully re-balanced and repositioned. Eventually the change may be made within the period of suspension between two canter strides, in which case it is then a flying change of leg or change of leg in the air.

The counter-canter – is an excellent suppling and straightening exercise which also improves the horse's balance and willing obedience to his rider's aids, during which the horse canters on the right rein with the left (near) legs leading and vice versa, this being purposely demanded by the rider. On the other hand, although the leading legs are also towards the outside of the arena when the horse is 'cantering on the wrong leg', this is due to a mistake on the rider's part.

In counter-canter the horse remains slightly bent or positioned, at the poll only, to the side of the leading leg, although the line he is following curves in the opposite direction. His hindfeet should follow in the track of his forefeet and must not swing out. The horse's conformation makes it impossible for his spine to be bent to correspond with the circle line when he is cantering with the outside legs leading. It is these facts that develop and test the horse's straightness, suppleness, balance and obedience, and the rider's feel, his ability to follow his horse's movement, and the correct use and co-ordination of his aids. Thus the counter-canter is an excellent training exercise for both the rider and his horse.

NOTE It is very important that from the beginning of their lessons in counter-canter the instructor emphasizes that the pupils must never punish any horse for changing his legs in any way, for 99 per cent of the time the rider is at fault. If a horse is unfairly reprimanded he will remember this, and will be afraid to give a flying change when he is asked for one in later lessons, for fear of being punished again.

Progressive exercises for counter-canter

i Inexperienced riders will get the feel of counter-canter in the simplest way by means of riding one shallow loop of serpentine 3–5 metre deep, down the long side of the school.

The ground-plan should be ridden at the walk first and then at the trot, the instructor being particular that the pupils leave the outer track immediately after the first corner of the long side; that they are already starting to return to the outer track as they cross the E–B line, and that they have completed the return one horse's length before the corner marker at the far end of the same long side.

The instructor must explain that the rider must keep his position, still yet pliant, and retain his aids for the original canter lead. He must not get worried or lose his nerve in the least, for any tension will affect his seat and will be felt by the horse; although he may look to the outside, and it may well help him to do so, he must never look down to the inside, or he will disrupt his seat and aids, and cause the horse to change his legs.

To the inevitable question. 'How do you make your horse go back to the outer track without changing your aids or his legs?', the instructor must remind the pupils that the thought aid must be most dominant and will usually suffice; any change in the physical aids must be tactful, subtle and absolutely invisible.

'*Think* exactly where you wish to go,
believe it, and
you will go there!'

The ride may then be commanded to execute an exercise consisting of continuous serpentine loops of 3–5 metres one down each long side, in open order, until the instructor commands, 'Ride go large', and walks them on long reins with intervening circles and transitions as he sees fit.

The instructor must watch closely for any sign of excess tension or over-ambition; the pupil asking for too deep a loop too soon, before his horse's suppleness or his own ability are capable of achieving such a demand. He must also be ready to warn any rider who is failing to control his horse's hindquarters.

ii Experienced riders on young horses, and pupils who have successfully established the counter-canter exercise (i) should ride counter-canter down the long side, in the following manner.

If the rider knows that his horse canters most easily with the right legs leading, he should proceed in an active working trot on the left rein, on the outer track, riding well forward on to the bit. As he passes the middle of the short side, the rider shortens the trot, makes a half-halt and rides well out into the corner. As he completes the corner he makes the first of two smooth changes of direction, turning in slightly to a distance of approximately 2 metres from the track. Then he points the horse smoothly out again towards the outer track, and it is at this precise moment, just before making this second change of direction, that he asks the horse to canter right with the usual aids for doing so. This is the ideal place for the horse as he will feel quite content, having the whole of the long side ahead of him along which to canter easily with the outside leg leading. Before he reaches the far end of the long side, the horse should be brought smoothly to a trot and be rewarded before being restarted into a canter with the left leg leading (true canter). If the horse does not

169

understand, often because the rider has been too late or unbelieving in his request for the counter-canter strike-off, and they have not achieved it by the middle of the long side, the rider should remain in trot and start again from the beginning at the middle of the next short side. Gradually the bend in the line can be diminished, until the strike-off can be made immediately after the corner and when the horse is positioned very slightly towards the outside of the arena, on a straight line.

When this first stage has been established on both reins, the counter-canter should be continued round the short side, ridden as half a 20 metres circle, to the end of the next long side. The rider must be very careful to maintain a correct position with constant yet quiet aids, and to follow his horse's movement well, particularly with his seat, keeping his horse well forward on the bit, so that the movement does not deteriorate, especially on the short side of the school. Later the pupils will be able to ride once or twice right round the outer track.

iii The instructor can then vary the work by exercising the pupils and the horses in counter-canter and true canter on the large figure of eight, in which case he should ask for the downward transition to trot or walk on the true canter circle, i.e. the right circle when the right foreleg is leading or vice versa, as this is naturally easiest for the horse, added to which he should not be taught to make a downward transition in the middle at a counter-canter exercise.

iv The counter-canter may be entered by a preceding half-circle or half-diagonal; in either case the horses should be returned to true canter before they are asked to make a downward transition.

Instructing tips – 'keep him on the outside rein'. 'Don't get worried – it's easy!' The instructor should reassure an over-anxious pupil by reminding him how often and how easily a beginner rider or a young horse canters false, often on a small circle, quite happily, blissfully unaware that he is cantering on the wrong leg! It may ease the problem if the pupil is told to put the rein and whip in the hand which is on the same side as the leading leg and to pat the horse just behind the saddle-flap with the free hand. This ensures that the rider does not tense up and change the positioning of his hips – a fault which even experienced riders may make, without realizing that they are doing so. The pupil should then be told to ride the canter with the reins in his outside hand, to hold the whip in his inside hand, hanging down just behind his hip-joint, and to think of pushing his inner hip and seat bone forward with each canter stride. Alternatively the outer hand should hold the whip and the reins while the inner hand is balled into a fist, the knuckles of which are pushed lightly against the back of the rider's seat, just behind the inner hip-joint, from whence it can give a rhythmical reminder to that hip and seat bone to keep moving forward in time with the movement of the horse's back muscles and haunches.

Lengthening and shortening the canter strides

This exercise is practised in the riding school to develop the rider's ability and his feel for impulsion, rhythm, tempo and speed, and to confirm and test the poise and effect of his positions and influences. It will also improve the horse's impulsion, his willingness to go forward and will develop his balance, his gaits and his general athletic ability, physique and condition. The distance and the extent of the lengthening of the strides should be chosen to suit the standards of both the rider and the horse. The transitions must be soft and fluent; the horse must be kept well forward on the bit and in good form throughout the exercise. The rider must never be at all brusque with his aids in an endeavour to show off distinct transitions, for by these means he will create tension and resistant habits in his horse.

This exercise should be practised out of doors on all types of good going – including up and down hill. The instructor must ensure that calmness prevails or exuberance and excitement will cause tension and an upset to the horses' temperament and to their training.

The instructor must watch the riding of the *transitions* with especial care. If the rider tenses, or forgets to keep his diaphragm and rib-cage well raised, and his elbows close to his sides, his hips and back will stiffen, their movement will be blocked and so will that of his horse's back, to the detriment of seat, aids and of the horse's canter. Pupils should not be expected to ride extended canter in a school which is less than 60 metres in length.

To lengthen the canter strides the forward-driving aids are increased and the hands give just enough to allow the horse sufficient freedom for his head and neck, and to round and lengthen his strides. The rider follows the movement well, adjusting the position of his upper body to suit the standard of the horse's training, the speed and the terrain.

He maintains the desired impulsion, form and an even tempo by making and retaining a nice balance between his forward-driving and restraining aids.

To shorten the strides or decrease the speed: the rider must *think* 'how and where'; he should adopt a slightly firmer yet supple seat, while tactfully and smoothly increasing both his forward-driving aids and his restraining aids to maintain the horse's form, and by means of repeated half-halts to lower and engage the horse's hindquarters and to ensure that the action of the reins goes through the horse's body. He may use a circle to help the horse to want to slow down. As soon as the horse obeys he must be rewarded by an imperceptible give from the rider's hands and legs, which must not, however, be so much that the horse's form is even partially lost. If the horse resists by holding the bit, setting his jaw, rolling up his tongue, or if he goes against the bit, the rider must obtain a give to his hand from the horse by using a firmer seat. He must use his forward-driving aids whilst making repeated restraints and gives with the reins, moving his fingers within his hands, and then be ready to cease these demands at the exact instant that the horse complies.

In every change of gait or pace, the forward-driving and the restraining aids should be adjusted and balanced with thought and feel so that clearly visible transitions will be executed softly and smoothly with invisible aids.

The instructor should watch his pupils' riding of the transitions from a position which is in front or behind, as well as from the side – both rider and horse must be *straight*. If the lengthened strides are being ridden down the long sides of the arena, with a decrease at the end and shortened strides through the short side; the danger-spots are at the beginning and during the latter portion of the long side. It is here that the riders must be particularly careful that they do not lose the posture of their upper body. They must be reminded to keep their elbows down by their hips, their shoulders low and straight, and chests raised, their inner hips and outer shoulders forward and their hands correctly carried. Their horses must not be allowed to try to evade the work by coming

171

FIG. 65   THE GALLOP

off the bit, flattening their backs and losing their form on the upward transition. If the riders are encouraged to think of keeping their horses' shoulders in front of the inside hind leg it will help them to preserve the straightness with vigilant outside aids.

Rider faults to be corrected when lengthening and shortening the canter strides

i 'No difference shown!' is a comment often written on a competitors' dressage sheets.

ii Insufficient preparation – especially pre-planning and half-halts.

iii Trying too hard, tensing and using too visible aids, any small degree of stiffness will prevent the movement from coming through the whole horse.

iv Forgetting to maintain the horse's form throughout.

v Crookedness – the rider not adjusting his weight-aids sufficiently before a coming corner or change of direction.

The gallop is a four-time gait. (Four hoof-beats.) It is an extension of the canter; as the horse stretches forward and lengthens his stride over the ground, the pace becomes four-time, the sequence of foot-fall in the right gallop being:

    1 near hind,
    2 off hind,
    3 near fore,
    4 off fore,
      followed by a period of suspension.

The two main categories of gallop referred to and used in the training of riders and horses are the half-speed gallop and the fast gallop – both titles are self-explanatory. In the latter the horse moves at the fastest possible speed at which he can maintain a good rhythm and tempo. This is very taxing for him and therefore he should never be asked to gallop faster or farther than his present standard of training and of fitness will allow.

All lessons on the gallop should be given in as unrestricted a space as possible, out of doors where the going is level and reasonably resilient. The good old turf of a permanent pasture is ideal; some sandy beaches are inviting, but sand is hard and not always consistent; it can provide treacherous going, and of course holidaymakers must be avoided! A big field is good, providing the riders are taught to round out the corners smoothly, and a preliminary inspection for ruts, holes, poached ground or other hazards is carried out by the whole ride before any fast work is commenced. A large field has an advantage over the wide open spaces of the downs, in that its confining boundaries facilitate the recapturing of loose horses, and the controlling of any

172

whose 'brakes' are questionable. Before riders are allowed to gallop they must be taught to circle in the middle of the field if, at any time, they feel the horse getting too strong for them to control. Instructors must remember that to be bolted with is a very frightening experience, and that 'to be forewarned is to be forearmed'! Horses should never be taken into a field and galloped straight away; they and their riders must prepare with some quiet loosening up and mannering work first.

The aids to gallop – The rider develops the gallop from a canter with the required leg leading, by urging the horse forward with his forward-driving aids until he is moving at the desired speed. The rider's hands give fractionally to allow the horse to lengthen his stride and outline, he retains a light contact to maintain and regulate the horse's balance, rhythm, impulsion and endeavours, with tactful use of his co-ordinating aids.

Even at the gallop the horse must be on the bit. All details laid out in the section on lengthening and shortening the canter strides apply to the riding of the gallop.

The rider must be physically fit himself in order to be stable, light and strong, to steady, support or to urge the horse forward. The rider may adopt either an upright seat, a moderately light seat, or a light seat; the instructor should teach his pupils all these variations of the balanced position.

The upright or vertical seat – is taught first, it is the best position whereby the rider can use his influences on his horse, particularly the forward-driving aids. For this reason it is the seat most usually adopted when riding young, green, sticky or nappy horses, horses who buck, or when showing a horse off, with nonchalance in a showring. The rider's position and influences remain identical to those for the canter.

The moderately light seat – refers to the rider's position when it is in between the upright and the forward seat and when the rider does not wish to be fully committed to either. It may be adapted to either of the more extreme versions instantly, fluently, and effortlessly, as required.

The light, or forward seat – may be used by more experienced riders on free-going horses when galloping farther than a comparatively short distance.

Before he may ride with a light or forward seat, the rider must shorten his stirrup leathers as many holes as may be necessary for him to adopt a forward position with his upper body and to move his centre of gravity forward to match that of the horse. The rider closes the angles of his hips, knees and ankles and puts more weight on to his knees and stirrups. He keeps his seat just above

173

FIG. 66   THE JUMP

the saddle, his back and shoulders remain firm and flat and he looks ahead between his horse's ears. He must adjust his reins so that they are short enough for him to remain in perfect balance whilst retaining a light contact with the horse's mouth. He must not use his reins as a support nor must he ever bump down in the saddle. The rider must be well aware of easing his weight forward off the horse's back, and of helping him to maintain his balance and rhythm and to use himself to the utmost. The rider must also be ready to use his judgement and restrain the horse if conditions require this, e.g. fatigue, or false footing.

Instructors must be sure to warn all pupils of the dire results of dropping the contact while allowing the gallop to peter out like an unwound toy; this foolhardy practice is almost guaranteed to end in injury of some sort to the horse, and he risks straining a tendon or joint, if he does not break down completely. This applies particularly when finishing a cross-country course or a race, with a tired horse. Riders must be taught how to reduce speed smoothly, maintaining his form, retaining a contact and supporting the horse when he most needs it. Riders must keep their horses on the bit until they have reduced the pace to a walk – then they should walk on loose reins to allow the horse quietly to regain his breath and his mental and physical equilibrium.

16 Jumping – or riding over fences

The subject of jumping, or 'riding over fences' is a wide one, ranging as it does from the first jumping lessons for children or beginner riders, to riding to hounds or to the specialist forms of jumping such as steeplechasing, show-jumping or riding in the cross-country phase of a one or three day event. All have the same foundations and principles from which any more specialized advancement may be made.

Basic general purpose jumping of small fences is an essential ingredient in every aspiring horseman's training programme; there is no finer exercise to teach and practise the rider's feel, and to develop, test and perfect the co-ordination of his aids, his natural horsemanship and his control.

Instructors should include jumping regularly in their pupils' lesson pro-grammes. They should be diligent and imaginative in the composition of

174

courses. Although fences should always be comparatively easy and inviting for the horses, they should stretch the riders' mental and physical capabilities in accordance with their experience. A good instructor will rarely need to build really big fences which may risk damaging the horse by injury or strain, or by sickening him of the sport. Whereas the less talented instructor will have to rely on high or spectacular fences to impress his pupils and hold their respect and attention, an experienced instructor will rely on a variety of approaches, obstacles and distances to provide the necessary challenge and thus his riders will make correct and constructive progress while the horses remain sound, fresh and enthusiastic – and both will jump with improving confidence, style, fitness and effectiveness.

If a pupil wishes to specialize in jumping, his riding and work on the flat must be correct and confirmed both in theory and in practice so that he follows the principles of good horsemanship even under difficult circumstances – they must become as second nature to him so that they remain steadfast even if an unexpected upset or a major problem arises. That a rider must have a well-established independent seat with quiet but effective influences, particularly those of his weight and legs, holds good whether he is riding a dressage test or a show-jumping round; in both cases the rider must know what he wants from his horse and have the knowledge and skill to maintain it. Within his horse he must have:

Impulsion – good willing activity coming from a forward thinking mind and well-engaged haunches.

Balance – at all times – fluent and easily adjustable.

Communication and control – the horse must be co-operating willingly, being on the bit and obedient to the rider's aids.

Gait – this must be of good quality, and quickly adaptable in the lengthening and shortening of the strides and outline to develop his scope. Whereas the quality of the gaits is very important in the early stages of jumping – a deficiency often denotes stiffness for some reason – this purity of the gaits may have to be sacrificed occasionally in the tension of a competition, especially in a jump-off, but must be re-established first and foremost, when schooling at home.

Rhythm – as consistent as is relatively possible.

175

Straightness – between the rider's forward-driving, regulating and restraining aids and straight on the line of the track, whether this is straight or curved. The horse's hips and hind feet must always be aligned behind his shoulders and forefeet in order to have the maximum, most effective, propulsive power from the hindquarters.

Smoothness, confidence, calmness, awareness and concentration, co-ordination, harmony. (All these are also essential qualities for the horse and the rider, individually, and between both members of the partnership – mental and physical working *together*.)

Physical fitness and athletic ability – resulting from correct work and gymnastic exercises on the flat and over cavalletti and fences.

Suitability of the fences, and of the work – for both horses and riders.

Knowledge and skill – acquired through correct training originally, sage observation and thoughtful, supervised practical application.

Feel – the most important key to success in horsemanship and in instructing – the rider must feel the horse's thoughts and movements and be quick to adapt his style to suit each horse he rides. Similarly, the instructor must feel for each and every one of his pupils and their horses; he has to have maximum perception in maximum direction!

The worst crime an instructor can make in a jumping lesson is to overface any horse or rider so that they lose their nerve, even in the slightest degree. A good instructor will inspire by building-up confidence, he will foster the horses' natural desire to please and the riders' ambition, dedication and determination to improve their technique and thus their performance.

More experienced pupils who wish to specialize in dressage should never spurn the chance to participate in a jumping lesson. Providing it is being given by a good instructor their horses will enjoy the fun of this gymnastic work and will be loosened mentally and physically by it as well as receiving a recharging of their 'impulsive-batteries', and many rider-faults which remain hidden during work on the flat are magnified, obvious and easy to correct when small fences are introduced into the work.

Sometimes the chief instructor may tell the riders to work together in twos, helping and correcting each other. Obviously this must be done discreetly, for the indoor school or outside schooling areas should never sound like the shallow-end of the public swimming pool on a bank holiday! It is interesting to note how much better riders ride and their horses perform if 50 per cent of their concentration has been diverted towards helping another rider!

Instructors must never forget that many riders of all standards may be frightened of riding over fences. There is no disgrace in this, as Mr Jorrocks said, 'A fall is a h'awful thing', and many more spectacular falls are seen over fences than are ever experienced riding on the flat. A good instructor will always ensure that his pupils enjoy their lessons, and this they will surely do if understanding and confidence prevail when lessons include jumping. Novice pupils should be given opportunities to observe more experienced riders riding over fences before they embark on this themselves, and again later, at regular intervals during their subsequent training. The instructors' ride, loosening up their young horses over low fences in the indoor school, will provide ideal demonstrations, as here the pace will be slow and jumping should appear easy, interesting and problem-free.

176

The lectures

Although riding over fences is essentially a practical subject, there are many aspects which must be introduced and further covered by teaching the theory of the rules and techniques, in the lecture room. The content of each lecture must be carefully pre-planned and delivered with sincere belief and enthusiasm in order that all the facts are remembered when students or pupils watch demonstrations and may be readily applied in the practical jumping lessons.

As well as ensuring that his lecture is well put-over and thus equally well assimilated, by using a variety of visual aids to add to the impact of his words, the instructor must keep his explanations as simple as possible. It is very important that he makes the subject of riding over fences sound easy, safe and enjoyable, and not at all complicated or hazardous, as first impressions are always retained.

For the content of his lectures the instructor should work methodically through the following pages. He should also keep his mind, ears and eyes open for opportunities to back up his lectures by asking permission to take his class to watch another class receiving jumping instruction, or to other suitable local activities.

List of Subjects to be covered in the lectures:
(a) Descriptive jumping terms.
(b) The nine phases of the jump.
(c) Equipment, and some safety rules.
(d) Fence construction – brief notes.
(e) How the horse jumps the fence.
(f) The rider, over the fence – a brief outline of basic facts and then, in detail.

(A) TERMS

The various descriptive terms – pupils should be taught these terms in an early lecture, to increase their vocabulary, their education and their understanding.

The track – the track is the line the rider selects for the horse to follow whenever he is ridden over one or more fences. For show-jumping competitions this track is measured carefully to and from the centre of the fences, with well-rounded corners and the times are then calculated and set accordingly. The track of a cross-country course is a far more complex affair for the track chosen will be determined by the respective advantages of footing, gradients, approach, take-off and landing levels, the fence itself and the get-away after the fence, all balanced against the shortest possible track.

The Fences – The dimensions of a fence are:
The height – measured on a vertical line from the highest edge to the ground.
The spread – measured from the front to the back of the fence, from the nearest and farthest outside edges of the top poles or jump elements.
The width – measured across the face of the fence.
Fixed fences – are those which are solidly built and remain in position even when hit by the horse as he negotiates them.
Show jumps, or knock-down fences – self-explanatory! There are many official statistics for the former, which are carefully laid out in several BSJA

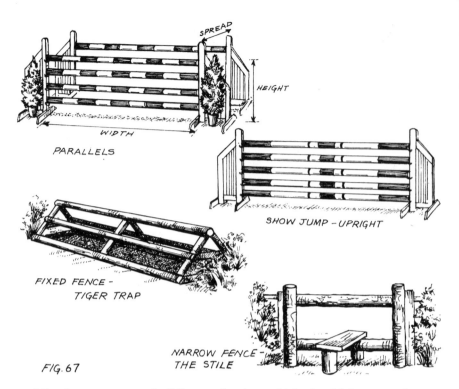

PARALLELS

SPREAD

HEIGHT

WIDTH

SHOW JUMP – UPRIGHT

FIXED FENCE –
TIGER TRAP

NARROW FENCE –
THE STILE

FIG. 67

publications on course building and rules, which should be part of every instructor's personal library.

Even the most simple fences should be varied as much as possible; variations may be provided by alternating or mixing the following three basic forms:

Upright – vertical fences – built for height.

Spread – e.g. parallel bars, oxers, hogs-backs, tiger-traps, ditches and water.

Narrow – a reduced width tends to increase suspicion especially in young horses; the confidence gained in quietly overcoming this improves their boldness. A stile is a comparatively easy example; a narrow place into a dark wood is a really tough demand.

Ground line – the lowest discernible line on the take-off side of the fence. A good helpful groundline is one which is in advance of the height of the fence. A false groundline is one that is behind the height of the fence; this is misleading and unfair fence building. Very occasionally the false groundline principle may be used to advantage when schooling a careless 'old hand', or a hunter – for few farmers are concerned about groundlines when they are building fences to keep in their stock. For training purposes this is a specialist schooling aid and should only be used by an exceptionally skilled and experienced trainer.

Schooling fence – an inviting and easier version of the type of fence the horse will be asked to jump when he is fully trained.

Practice fence – at every competition the organizers will set up at least two practice fences for competitors, over which they may warm up and supple their horses, and perhaps even school them over before they ride in the event. Usually one is an upright and the other a spread fence.

Flags – all competition fences are flagged with a red and a white flag respectively on the right and the left of the fence. The rider may only jump that fence from the one direction, i.e. so that the red flag is on his right – if he jumps it in the wrong direction he will be eliminated. This rule also applies to the practice fences.

The take-off zone, or platform – the area of ground in front of a fence, from which the horse can take-off to clear the obstacle with maximum ease and efficiency. The lower the fence the larger the take-off zone or area; the higher the fence the smaller the area. See Fig. 68.

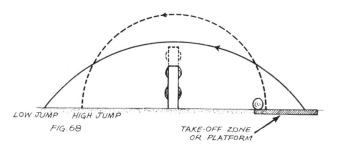

LOW JUMP   HIGH JUMP

FIG. 68

TAKE-OFF ZONE
OR PLATFORM

Coming right at a fence means that the horse and rider have arrived at the fence with perfect balance, impulsion, and rhythm and they take-off within the zone.

Coming wrong at a fence, describes the opposite effect, a 'happening', which if acute can cause many faults of style as well as an anxious moment (or heart acrobatics).

An eye for a stride – a rider and/or horse who sees a good stride is one who can appreciate the situation from a fair distance in front of the fence. Miss Pat Smythe was remarkable even among top international show jumpers for being able to see a good stride from an incredible distance before arriving at the take-off zone. Some riders have an exceptional talent for this, but a seeming weakness in this respect can be brought up to a good standard by careful training, confidence and endless practice. The rider must NEVER be allowed to fiddle his way into fences as this will only distract the horse. The more the pupil worries about seeing a stride the longer it will take him to develop 'a good eye'.

Rider left behind – a fault whereby the rider fails to move or remain forward, in balance with his horse as he takes off and jumps the fence. See Fig. 77.

Rider getting in front of the movement – if the rider adopts an exaggeratedly forward position at any time he will automatically weaken his influence, especially the forward-driving aids and will upset the horse's equilibrium, his rhythm and his confidence. This fault is often caused by unnecessarily short stirrup leathers, and is most usually shown during the approach, as the horse takes off, and as he lands, as well as being most disrupting on turns.

Bascule – the rounding of the horse's top-line as he jumps a fence. If a horse jumps with a good bascule, he jumps in good style with plenty of scope, springing well off his haunches and making fullest possible use of his back as well as his neck and head.

To stand-off – a style of jumping whereby the horse takes off early before the

179

take-off zone. This can provide an exhilarating sensation for the rider, and an experienced horse may 'get away with it', but it should not be encouraged in show-jumpers nor in hunters as accuracy is diminished as is the ability to spread farther to clear the fence, or any unexpected hazard which may lurk on the far side of the fence. Horses who stand off must be given exercises with poles, cavalletti or related fences to teach them to come in closer to their fences, on to the platform, and eventually to back off in order to gain extra height.

Backing off – a style of jumping when the horse has developed his athletic ability sufficiently to be able to take off close to the fence, thereby making maximum use of the thrust from his powerful hindquarters to propel and project his body upwards and over the fence.

Putting in a short one, getting too close, or getting under the fence – are all terms used to describe a faulty jumping style when the horse takes off too close to the fence for his present standard of training and ability. This fault can be eradicated by an experienced rider giving the horse corrective gymnastic work over cavalletti and grids and by the use of placing fences. If allowed to develop, the horse will inevitably 'take a fence by the roots' and give his rider a bad fall.

A refusal – the horse refuses to negotiate the fence – usually due to fear or pain, to seeing other horses refuse, or to bad schooling on the flat or over fences.

A run out – the horse disobeys his rider by leaving the intended track leading over the fence; instead he veers off to one side or the other, thus by-passing the fence.

A peck – when landing over a fence the horse makes a mistake and momentarily loses his footing or stumbles.

A fall – when one of the horse's shoulders and hip on the same side touches the ground simultaneously. When this occurs the rider must roll up into a ball – an extended limb is easily broken. He should roll clear of the horse, if possible, regain his feet and then get hold of the reins. Bad accidents can occur if the rider hangs on to the reins while he is still lying on the ground.

(B) THE NINE PHASES OF THE JUMP

Pupils should also be taught the nine phases of the jump, to start them *thinking* in the right way, and to provide a concrete list for future reference, thought and discussion.

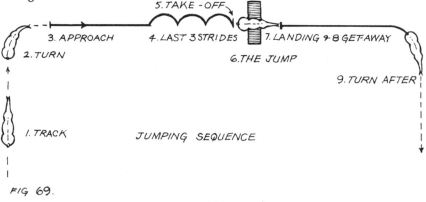

FIG 69.

180

The nine phases are:

1 The track towards the fence, through a course of fences, and when going away from them – including before the start and after the finish, in a competition.

2 The turn towards the fence – carefully gauged to meet the jump's central line at the most advantageous spot.

3 The approach.

4 The last three strides.

5 The take-off zone and the platform.

6 The jump – the period of suspension – the airborne leap.

7 The landing.

8 The riding away after the landing – the get-away.

9 The turn after the fence.

The details of the horse's and the rider's actions during each phase are described later in this chapter.

All jumping lessons must include progressive instruction in the correct riding of the nine phases of the jump; these should be taught constantly and then be confirmed, tested and improved, with continuing emphasis on the riding of the track between the fences, particularly turns, changes of direction, riding forward off corners, and making the best use of the arena or terrain, before the start and after the finish.

(C) EQUIPMENT

The instructor must teach his pupils to be very particular with regard to the equipment they use – it must be: SAFE, COMFORTABLE, SUITABLE.

Pupils should be taught the danger points to watch, e.g. stitching, webbing, rolled or covered leather, etc. Once taught they must be checked periodically to keep them up to the mark, for pupils remain the instructor's responsibility.

Equipment for the horse

Bridle – preferably a snaffle. (Children mounted on keen ponies may be better with a double-bridle, to preserve their feel for light rein-aids as well as their confidence.)

The reins are generally best if they are of medium width with either a pliant rubber covering or a supple leather lace woven down each side. Plain leather reins are excellent for normal schooling when neither the horse nor the weather are wet.

For cross-country competitions, or when hunting, it is advisable to have two reins on the snaffle-bridle, especially if a running-martingale is used. It is unwise to rely on one rein which might break, thus terminating the round!

The reins should have a knot in the end, for security (never trust a mere buckle) to prevent the ends of the reins from slipping under the front edges of the saddle, and to shorten them and thus eliminate any danger from the rider's toe being caught in the loop of the end of the reins.

The headpiece of the bridle should always be securely fastened to a plait at the top of the horse's neck in a cross-country competition; a brown shoe lace makes a neat 'fastener'.

Saddle – a general purpose or jumping saddle is best. It should fit both the horse and the rider. It should not have too high an arch at the back or it can be dangerous to the rider's back if the horse falls; it can restrict the rider's movement; and if the rider should be badly left behind over a fence he will have great difficulty in regaining his seat in the saddle. The girth straps and webbing must be sound.

The ends of the stirrup safety-bars should NEVER be turned up.

The stirrup leathers – must be sound, and have sufficient holes, but should never have extra, intermediary holes punched in them for these weaken the leather. They should be correctly 'set' before the rider takes the stirrups.

The stirrups – should be made of good quality stainless steel and must be of the correct size.

A surcingle – should always be worn for jumping. A horse can make an unexpectedly stupendous effort over an innocently small fence and burst his girths or straps or webbing, in which case the surcingle will save the day. The surcingle should be fitted snugly on the front of the saddle's waist and over the girths. It should never be put through the stirrup leather keepers – even though some saddlers may recommend this; nor must it pass over or ensnare the stirrup leather ends. Surcingles may be made of webbing or leather; the latter are the more reliable but not so comfortable to sit on.

A breastplate – should always be worn for jumping over a cross-country course where the horse may run up a bit light by the end of it, also for all jumping if the horse is herring-gutted or does not have a well-defined girth place, and in hilly country.

FIG. 70   BREASTPLATE

I have seen too many unpleasant accidents due to saddles slipping back ever to allow a pupil to ride without a breastplate if it was needed.

There are two varieties; the better version is the everyday hunting pattern which gives added stability at three points, i.e. on each side of the front of the saddle and to the girths. Breastplates should not be fitted too tight; they must allow free-play to the horse's shoulders when he is galloping and jumping.

Protective boots – Overreach boots (bell boots) are a good safeguard for most horses but they are essential for loose or free movers, most long-striding thoroughbred horses need them, ponies seldom do.

182

Whether to use tendon, brushing or overreach boots is a more debatable point, particularly for cross-country events if horses are jumping into water, as a few grains of sand or a piece of grit from a churned-up river bed caught inside a boot can do terrible damage to the horse's tendons by the end of the round. An ordinary crepe-bandage over thin gamgee probably takes a lot of beating but in this case the bandages *must* be put on by an expert and the ends of the flattened tapes securely tied and sewn.

Shoes – must be carefully checked for security and that there are no sharp edges, particularly inside the toe, nor risen clenches. Studs should not be necessary for schooling, but are often used in competitions. Usually smaller, spiked studs are best for hard going and larger studs give a better grip on soft ground.

A neckstrap – a broad, short stirrup leather makes a good neckstrap for novice riders on horses with hogged manes. It should be fastened so that it stays half-way up the horse's neck – if fitted as for a martingale it is too loose and therefore lies too far back to be of use to a nervous, novice rider when he is jumping a fence.

A crash hat, which is safe and stays on when the rider falls off is a vital necessity. All the rest of the rider's clothing must be suitable and safe.

A back protector – may be worn under the jersey or colours when riding at speed over fences.

A jumping whip – should never be fastened to the rider's wrist or person in any way, it could easily be trapped to the saddle if he falls.

NOTE From the above list, it would seem as if I favour far more protection for the horse than for the rider!

N.B. Few young instructors will have seen a rider being dragged. It can be a most sickening sight – prevention is better than cure. If a rider falls he will probably be dragged if:

i The stirrup iron is too narrow for his foot to escape from it, or too wide so that his foot slides right through and is trapped.

ii The safety-bar ends are not down to enable the stirrup leather to be pulled off.

iii The stirrup leather is incorrectly twisted due to the rider's foot being wrongly placed in the stirrup iron.

iv The surcingle is fastened over any part of the stirrup leather.

v The rider is wearing shoes or boots with cleated (ridged) soles or which have no heels.

vi The stirrup iron is caught on the spur strap buckle which was on top of the boot's instep instead of down the side of the foot. See Fig. 71.

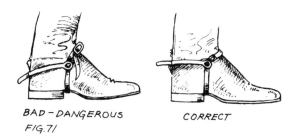

BAD – DANGEROUS
FIG. 71

CORRECT

Some basic safety rules:

i Secure, and well-fitting hard hats must always be worn.

ii All equipment used must be safe, e.g. saddlery, fences, etc.

iii The jumping area must be of a suitable size, with sound perimeter fences and good going underfoot. All entrance-gates must be securely closed.

iv The horses must suit the riders – in size, shape and temperament, and the riders must be able to control them.

v The instructor must have every pupil under his eye and discipline at all times – safety is of maximum importance. Pupils and students should *never* be allowed to jump without permission, *nor on their own*, in case they have an accident.

vi All jumping lessons should be based on the lesson plans and principles described earlier. See p. 43.

vii Fences should be well-built, low and varied.

viii No rider or horse should ever be over-faced.

ix The instructor should always dictate the pace to suit the training standard, the present exercise, the fences and the going.

x In the majority of lessons it is better to increase the spread of the fence rather than its height – the former improves style, the latter increases the strain. At a more advanced standard an upright fence will improve the horse's bascule and the techniques of both horse and rider.

xi Horses should never be sickened by too much jumping. Jumping lessons should consist of a large proportion of work on the flat and over ground poles and cavalletti.

(D) THE CONSTRUCTING AND SETTING OUT OF FENCES

This must be carefully taught to student-instructors, and the chief instructor should supervise and check both the theory and the practical lessons regularly.

The following basic rules must be listed and explained:

1 Fences must be built to improve the confidence and the style of riders and horses.

2 Fences should be set low at the beginning of every jumping lesson, or competition practice.

3 All fences must be well built, they must be:

(a) SAFE – all the materials used must be reasonably solid and in good repair, no projecting nails, no worn or rusty metal parts which might become jagged if hit.

Rail cups – should have shortened, rounded-off pins so that there are no sharp spikes sticking out.

Rail cups should contain a rail or be affixed to the upright underneath cups which are holding rails. Alternatively they should be removed and stored outside the jumping paddock or arena.

All instructors and riders should be warned of the dangers of either leaving rail-cups empty, fastened on to the jump upright above the top element of the fence, or if they are dropped on the floor. In the first instance, the horse may catch his leg on it; in the second he may tread on it, if it is overlooked when the fence is moved, or if the rider falls off he may land on it and suffer severe injury.

184

(b) INVITING – this means that the fence builder must imagine that he is a horse, with a horse's limited eye-sight, with a large, long and cumbersome body, with a suspicion towards the unexpected, the unusual or the unknown, with trot steps approximately 1.25 metres in length and canter strides which average 3.25 metres if he is moving in a good form at an average pace!

So, fences must look possible for a horse to negotiate; they must appear to be *solid* so that they are easily seen by the horses and do not give the impression that they could easily be knocked down. This last point will make the horse *want* to clear the fence, as his natural instinct of self preservation will tell him that if he does not jump well he might hurt himself.

The siting of each fence must allow the horse plenty of time to view the fence, to size it up, and to organize himself to negotiate it safely, and so that the rider can see and ride a smooth track which will teach them a feel for fluency.

The actual shape of the fence should invite the horse to jump well. It should have a ground-line which is slightly in front of a perpendicular line at the front of the fence, especially for inexperienced riders and novice horses. The fence can also have guiding lines, consisting of crossed or sloping rails to encourage riders and horses to take the fence at a central point. See Fig. 72.

FIG.72   LEADING · IN RAILS

(c) ECONOMICAL – in that maximum care is taken,

Of the horses – that they are not asked questions which might cause injury to them or to their training. The fences should work and test the *riders* more than the horses; they should make the riders think, feel and practise, rather than tiring out the horses.

Of the fences – the solid or frame elements of walls or hedge-boxes should be protected by a sloping rail, as they are expensive to repair or replace.

Of the land – riding land is a rare and valuable commodity, especially if it is grazing or borrowed land, therefore fences should be constructed so that they are easy to move and they are sited with forethought for convenient removals before the turf is worn and the grass roots are killed.

(d) EDUCATIONAL – their thoughtful construction improving the education of riders and horses alike.

185

(e) IMAGINATIVE – yet reasonable. Initiative and variety tempered with caution and common sense.

4 The fence builder must always give due consideration to the nine phases of the jump.

5 The track must have a good, free line both before and after the fence and between all related fences or those which may later be related.

6 The distances between related fences, cavalletti and ground-poles must be suitable, although they need not be identical.

7 During lessons the demand should be increased only when the pupils and the horses are confident and ready. Any increase must be gradual and well-judged to improve the riders' ability and the style rather than increasing strain, wear and tear on the horses.

8 The siting of temporary fences of a show-jumping type, in an enclosed manège should be planned to leave at least the outer track and the centre line free from obstruction. Fences built near the outer track should be set up at least 3 metres clear from the wall, so that two horses and riders may pass each other in opposite directions, and so that the fences never squeeze the horses out towards the wall.

The siting of cross-country fences should always be fair, and all fences built on an incline should be comparatively low. Horses receive too many shocks and strains in competitions; at home their confidence must be strengthened and ambition fired by many pleasant experiences.

9 At the end of every lesson the instructor must see that all the fences are reset at low heights and that their footing is levelled so that they are ready for the next lesson.

(E) HOW THE HORSE JUMPS THE FENCE

During the approach – the horse sees, accepts and sizes up the fence to be negotiated.

During the last three strides – he lowers and stretches out his neck and head, in order to utilize the muscle-power of his forehand to lift and round his back and to bring his hindlegs well in under the bulk of body-weight, to lift it up over the jump.

For the take-off – the horse shortens his neck, and raises his head to lift his forehand from the ground, with folded up forelegs. He then stretches his neck and head in order to spring upwards and forwards off his powerfully pushing hindquarters.

The leap – in order to make a suitable flight and landing, the horse stretches his neck and head to their fullest extent. He should jump with a good bascule with his head lowered, his back rounded, and his hindlegs well folded up under him. His forelegs unfold after he has cleared the topmost elements of the fence.

Landing over the fence – as he lands, the horse raises his head and shortens his neck in order that his forelegs may be stretched forward to enable him to make a soft landing with the minimum of shock and concussion and to swing his hindlegs clear of the fence and forward under his body weight. He usually lands on the non-leading foreleg, followed closely by the leading foreleg, and then the two hindlegs.

The stride after the landing – the 'get away' – during this stride, the horse has to make a major readjustment, to re-establish his balance as he takes to the flat; to feel and adapt to the quality of the going underfoot; to use the change of momentum and pull of gravity to develop a powerful ground-covering gait, or to prepare for a further spring, as may be necessary. Most of these are spontaneous reactions, sparked off by his propreoceptive sense, and need untrammelled, split-second judgment and action. The horse can brook no interference from his rider, although he may well benefit from his close leadership, co-operation and support. Above all, the horse must have freedom to stretch his neck and head forward, and be encouraged to round his back, in order to engage his haunches to establish himself in the new gait. The skilled rider will prescribe the canter lead, merely by thought and indiscernible weight-aids.

(F) THE RIDER

A brief outline – A detailed description follows:

During the nine phases of the jump the rider will adapt the balanced seat to suit the requirements of the demands.

Having been taught the balanced seat myself by British instructors two of whom had attended officers' courses at the Italian cavalry schools; having discussed jumping seats and methods with successful trainers and competitors from other nations, principally Germany, Russia, Sweden and the USA.; and having taught it to innumerable successful pupils in this country and abroad, I have not found any system to better it.

The basic variations of the balanced seat are three-fold:

1 *The upright position or seat*

(a) The stirrup leathers may be reasonably long.

(b) The rider's upper body is vertical.

This position of the body enables the rider to use all his influences with maximum effect. It may be used when riding on the flat between fences to re-establish the horse's mental and physical equilibrium.

2 *The moderately light seat*

(a) The stirrup leathers are one to four holes shorter, depending on the legs and the stirrup leathers.

(b) The rider's upper body is inclined slightly forward from the hip-joints, with a flat back, ready to swing upright or farther forward as required. The slight shortening of the stirrup leathers increases the angle and spring of the hip, knee or ankle joints and adds to the rider's stability and security and to the ease of mobility of the rider's upper body.

This is the best position for all general purposes.

3 *The Light or forward seat*

(a) The stirrup leathers are two to six holes shorter than for the moderately light seat.

(b) The rider's upper body is inclined farther forward; his seat is just above but very close to the saddle.

This position should be reserved for good riders riding at faster paces on experienced, free-going horses. Due to the shortened stirrup leathers the rider's seat is moved farther back on the saddle, on to the structurally weak part of the horse's back; therefore the rider must be extra-careful about what he does with his seat. It must be exactly poised, centrally, just above and very close to the saddle. His weight-burden must be very thoughtfully controlled so that it is as easy as possible for the horse to carry, it leads the direction (weight-aid), its return to the saddle is soft and smooth, and it NEVER bumps down on the horse's back, or disturbs his rhythm, efforts or equilibrium.

This position should only be taught to student-instructors or pupils when they are sufficiently experienced and fit, showing competence and harmony when riding with a moderately light and balanced seat over courses of small fences, taken from walk, trot and canter, over varied terrain – it is not for novice riders.

Details of the rider's position when he adapts the balanced seat to a more forward position, i.e. to the moderately light seat, or the light or forward seat.

The rider's legs remain firm and steady, the lower legs being by the girth. They should not impede the horse's movement by applying a vice-like grip which would also exhaust the rider. The lower legs should carry on a normal forward-driving conversation (influence), soft or strong, depending on the need. The legs should be strong, ready and able to grip in emergencies.

The rider's hip-joints must be flexible, 'well oiled' yet well controlled. The efficiency of the balanced seat depends on the rider's ability to close and open the angle at this joint exactly how and when these variations are needed, with a natural precision.

The rider's upper body should swing forward supply from the hips exactly as required, fluently going with the horse's movements as he follows the track of the rider's choice, striding over the ground and jumping the fences.

The back – ideally it should be straight, or slightly hollowed, rather than rounded.

THE BALANCED SEAT OVER FENCES

FIG. 73

The shoulders must be straight and level. If pupils have been taught to retain a good posture when riding on the flat, and when walking and sitting in yard work and lectures, the muscles of their shoulder girdles will be well disciplined. Rounded shoulders signify weakness and/or stiffness in that area and are a very bad riding fault.

The arms from the shoulders to the hands should keep a light elastic contact with the horse's mouth, with shortened reins enabling the whole arm to be balanced and to move freely forward to invite the horse to stretch or to match his requirements exactly.

The neck should be straight, rising freely from the shoulders.

The head should be well carried, the eyes looking ahead for the track and considering, and leading the horse's thoughts, feelings and reactions. The rider's thoughts should reinforce his horse's courage and resolution or calm him if he is worried. They should make cool calculations well in advance, while constantly referring to a natural *feel* – for the horse, and his form, the footing, the pace and the track over the fences.

The overall picture should be one of an outstanding *partnership* perfectly balanced at all times and full of controlled zest.

If novice riders are taught to ride with slightly shorter stirrup leathers, so that they can adopt a moderately light seat, and can follow their horse's movements naturally, as they have started to do over cavalletti, then they will come on to riding over small fences in a very natural way, without any marked changes in their riding, feeling or thinking. They will learn the basic principles of rhythm, feel, balance, movement, timing and control with growing confidence, and then, as the demands are increased, they may shorten their leathers a little more, or considerably if they are galloping fast over fences with a light or forward seat.

The rider's aids when riding over fences

These should be kept simple throughout all jumping lessons. The rider's forward-driving aids should be effective but tactful, whilst his restraining aids must be well judged and never restrictively interfering or ill-timed. Pupils should be made aware of how to lead their horses in the desired direction with their thought and weight aids so that they ride their horses in a very smooth way always to land on the required lead at canter, and through accurate changes of direction, and eventually, short turns at speed. Riders must strive to combine their forward-driving and restraining aids with instinctive judgment and tact to ensure that their horse's form and his gaits are of good quality so that he can use himself with maximum agility both between and over the fences.

The instructor should remind his pupils to seek in their horses:

Impulsion – good, willing activity coming from a forward urge – of mind, and hocks.

Rhythm – each horse has his own 'best rhythm'.

Straightness – on straight or curved tracks.

Balance – half-halts must be used, not forgotten, even when the pace is faster.

Confidence – based on a trust in his partner's judgment and his riding.

Fluency.

Calm-willingness.

Co-ordination and harmony – the rider's mental and physical; the horse's – and both together.

189

FIG. 74

The riders remembering within and to themselves – *think and feel – feel and think*.

NOTE The use of the whip. This should never be used in temper – as it often is when the rider feels his pride has been damaged. The whip may be used, if necessary, to strengthen the rider's forward-driving-aids of thought, seat and legs. If the whip is needed it should be used to create more impulsion going *towards* the fence; it should not be used to punish the horse when he is moving away from the fence, after a refusal. The horse does not reason as a dog would, this foolish rider-reaction only seems to make the jump even more 'nasty' to the horse.

A brief outline of the rider's behaviour over the fence

During the approach – the rider sizes up the fence, traces his track exactly to the spot selected for the take-off, and with a tactful combination of his forward-driving and restraining aids, he ensures that the horse's gait is of good quality. His mind and heart must be full of conviction, sympathy and courage. He sits in a natural, balanced position, either upright or with a moderately light seat unless he is travelling at a fast pace. His hips should be supple, his shoulders level and flat, arms elastically bent, the hands fairly close together,

low and near to the horse's crest, but not leaning against it. The rider's head should be kept erect and he must think and look ahead, either over the top of the fence or following the track on the far side of it, whilst retaining a close communication with his horse's mind. Looking down during the approach is the best known method of inviting a horse to refuse to jump the fence.

If the rider is likely to be galloping a great deal, he will ride with shorter stirrup leathers in order to close the angles of his hip-, knee- and ankle-joints further, to enable him to retain a light seat, easing his weight forward to match the horse's centre of gravity. He will incline his upper body further forward from the hip joints, while keeping his seat bones close to the saddle in order to feel and to be able to influence his horse, without a vestige of a bump or other disturbance to the horse's back or mouth.

During the last three strides – he must sit quietly and softly, his rhythm and resolve being switched calmly 'forward', and strengthening those of his partner, the horse. He should incline his upper body forward.

For the take-off – the rider must synchronize his movements precisely and fluently to be exactly with his horse. He should keep a steady contact with his legs and the reins, while the latter must allow the horse to use the balancing pole of his neck and head as he wishes. The rider keeps his shoulders flat as he

191

swings his upper body fluently forward, closing the angles of the hips, knees and ankles, and keeping down, close to his horse. His main thought-theme must be to, 'stay with him, and allow him freedom of his neck and head and of his back.' This theme continues during the leap – the rider stays quietly forward – with and allowing – and keeping in fluent yet alert control of his own body and limbs, and thinking and looking ahead, preparing for the landing and rejoining the track.

Landing over the fence – the rider must remain exactly with his horse. His contact and influences should stay constant and with reserves 'at the ready'. His upper body should remain forward with the seat-bones returning to the saddle extremely softly and smoothly as the grounding is completed.

The stride after the landing – the novice and even the more experienced rider should concentrate on remaining in balance while preparing for the next move. Carefully he should adopt a more upright position, ready to steady the pace, improve the impulsion, re-establish the balance, or to ride a smooth turn or downward transition.

An experienced rider travelling at a fast pace must co-ordinate his forward-driving and restraining aids with careful balance and split-second timing in order to assist the horse to rebalance himself and to re-establish his best rhythm within this stride – so that seconds are gained, not lost. They will need to apply their tact, training and talent to use this stride to their best advantage; it will provide a test of their horsemanship – from it their horses must go FORWARD, CALM and STRAIGHT to meet the next challenge.

THE NINE PHASES OF THE JUMP – IN DETAIL

Much of the following text is for more experienced pupils. However, if these important facts are taught to student-instructors and introduced into the earlier lessons, they can be recognized and confirmed whenever the opportunity arises in practical sessions.

1 *The track – before, between and after the fences*
The instructor must make his pupils aware of this very important but often forgotten phase of jumping. Many refusals and even accidents are caused from inexperienced riders' ignorance in this respect. Quite simply they have never been taught about it, but inevitably it is the poor horse who suffers the blame and often the punishment too.

If the instructor reminds his pupils of two indisputable facts they will realize for themselves the importance of working out the best track before, between and after fences, and this will become a natural habit. He must remind them that:

i Horses are not jumpers by nature.

ii Horses are physically incapable of seeing a fence clearly when they are really close up to it, thus it is unfair to expect them to negotiate a fence if they have not had a chance to size it up first from a reasonable distance.

The planning of the track requires intelligence, knowledge and feel, and is an integral factor to the success of the day whether the rider is out hacking, using logs and ditches to enliven the ride, is out hunting, is schooling over fences round the farm, or is jumping in a show-jumping or cross-country competition.

By teaching his pupils to realize that there *is* a track, and to think about it, to plan and to use it, the instructor instigates an educated format and style into his pupils' manner of riding over fences. Harmony and fluency will develop naturally from the start.

When riding the track, all the usual disciplines and principles of riding on the flat apply; the rider must be smooth and correct in all his aids and influences as has been fully described earlier. His awareness of the track gives him an added incentive and challenge, that of pitting his brains and his skill against the problems put in his path by Nature or by the course builder. He must plan, to use the paths and turns to the best advantage to improve his horse's schooling, to add to his experience, or to test the training to date as well as to enable the horse to negotiate the fences cleanly and well.

The horse should maintain a correct form and gait, as well as balance, impulsion and a calm yet eager willingness. He should follow the track and negotiate the fences smoothly and accurately, guided by imperceptible aids from his rider, so that together they form a picture of effortless ease.

Just as a good horseman will always plan and ride the best track, so will a good instructor develop his pupils' skill in this phase, and a really first-class course builder will set at least as much of his test in the riding of the track as in the demand provided by spectacular fences – i.e. he will tax the riders rather than over-taxing the horses.

As his pupils progress the instructor must teach them that when riding a course of show-jumps or a cross-country course, *the start* and *the finish* should both be given and ridden with the respect and care due to any fence on the course. Lack of tidy consideration of either of these 'ends' can cause a competitor to lose the whole competition. At the end of a course of fences, the rider should *never* 'ride a finish' on a loose rein – this is one of the easiest ways to break down a tired horse; instead he should complete the job properly, keeping the horse on the bit and between the aids, through the finish and then allowing him to slow down and 'unwind' appropriately – both mentally and physically, before either horse or rider may safely relax.

2 *The turn towards the fence*

This is perhaps the most important area for riders to contemplate, weigh-up, and to arrive at with their horses going exactly as they wish, and then to use to their advantage – and yet it is another area which is often neglected.

The instructor must remind his pupils of the directive he has given them during their work on the flat, 'Collect, weight, turn and *push*!' This should be applied for riding the turn before the fence. Whether the turn is rounded or accentuated it is always important, and especially so when a competition causes an increase in the demand in a small arena. Careful plotting of the track and skilful riding of turns can make all the difference between winning or losing a competition.

The turn itself can be used to improve the horse's balance, engaging his hocks and bringing him off his forehand. The rider compresses the spring (the horse) to increase the power within the horse, he 'rides off the turn', directing this power towards the fence. By enabling the rider to gain an extra metre or two of ground a well ridden turn can be the deciding factor between 'arriving right' or 'arriving wrong' at the fence, particularly in a small arena.

Fluency, harmony and co-ordination should be combined in the horse and rider partnership. As they make the turn towards the fence *all* the desired qualities should be evident, in readiness, in exactly the right proportions. Naturally this is the ideal – the eventual goal towards which the lessons must aim. 'Practice makes perfect', but practice is only possible after full realization and appreciation of the project.

3 *The approach*

The rider should approach the fence with calm determination, he must be reminded of the importance of the rider's will and the telepathic transfer of his thoughts. The instructor should point out that anxiety and hesitation are immediately transmitted to the horse and may make him run out, refuse or make a bad jump.

The rider must look for and size up the fence, trace his track exactly to the spot selected for the take-off, and point the horse straight forward to come in at right angles to the fence. During the approach the rider must assess the pace and the length of the horse's strides. If they are not suitable he must adjust them as required, well before he reaches the last three strides before the fence. The horse should be kept in balance and well on the bit by the rider's thought, seat, leg and rein aids. When the horse moves towards the fence with willing eagerness to jump it, and he has accepted it, so to speak, the rider should feel pleased and remain quietly with the horse offering no interruption, but keeping him well on the bit (and up to the mark).

An inexperienced rider often loses confidence when his horse seems over-willing or keen to jump and approaches the fence at a disconcertingly fast pace. In an endeavour to slow down, the rider will pull back with his hands with increasing force. When the horse is thus prevented from lowering his head and stretching his neck to judge his stride and take off he becomes fractious, 'hot', or even unwilling to jump at all. Here the best cure is for the instructor to effect a change of horses, putting the novice rider on a quiet, steady horse, and an experienced rider on to the upset horse, in order to restore both confidences.

The novice rider can also learn a very useful lesson in equestrian tact by watching the result of patience and good riding in the re-schooling of his horse, he should be allowed to appreciate this quietly of his own accord, over-emphasis of it could damage his pride and dissolve his self-confidence.

The rider can approach the fence either at the walk, trot or canter – depending on the training standard and the eventual aim, the position and size of the fence, and the going. The speed must also be adjusted to suit various other conditions; high upright fences without a ground-line must not be approached too fast. When approaching big spread fences, usually the rider should ride forward in a strong onward-bound rhythmical canter. It is however wrong in this latter case to increase the speed too early as it will then be more difficult for the horse to calculate the take-off and the power needed for the spring of the jump will be reduced, he must keep some 'in hand' or in reserve. When approaching a high spread fence the rider must not make the approach too slowly, as the horse, in order to negotiate such a fence, needs a certain energy and power for the last strides before the fence. When the horse is nearing the fence he should as a rule, be allowed to regulate his stride, choose the take-off point and make his own arrangements for himself without being disturbed by the rider.

Normally the horse should be allowed to keep as even and smooth a tempo, speed, rhythm and stride as possible. If the horse hesitates at all or seems sluggish or unwilling, he should be urged forward immediately and energetically, with seat, knees and legs, and if necessary with spurs and whip, as educated aid reinforcements, never as rough bullying means. If the whip has to be used to build up sufficient impulsion on the track between the fences it should be reversed and used meaningfully immediately behind the rider's leg – quickly, coolly and efficiently, so that impulsion, balance, pace and rhythm, and the rider's position are restored before entering the approach-zone of the next fence to be jumped.

Occasionally if an experienced rider has to use his whip at the last moment it may be applied with a quick turn of the wrist, smartly on the shoulder. Experience, timing and tact are required to enable the rider to use the whip just before the jump without disturbing him and doing more harm than good.

The disadvantages of taking the reins in one hand in order to apply the whip behind the leg increases the closer the rider gets to the fence, for often the horse will run out, away from the whip. The whip should not be used during the moment the horse takes off – or after he has already left the ground, both timings are too late, and may cause the horse to flatten, and drop his legs on to the fence, thereby knocking it down or injuring himself.

If the horse wants to rush towards the fence, the rider must not disturb him by raising his hands or hanging on the reins. If he is unsuccessful in slowing down the horse early enough by repeated half-halts, before entering the approach-zone, he must give with his hands and allow the horse freedom to make his own assessment and arrangements to negotiate the fence. The rider will do better to pray than to pull, for if the horse is resisting strongly against the rider's influences his attention is diverted from a safely judged negotiation of the fence and thus the rider prevents him from adjusting his take-off in time, which could have very unpleasant results.

4 *The last three strides before the fence – 'belong to the horse'*
The horse must be allowed to concentrate on negotiating the fence. This rule should be observed by all riders. Only really experienced riders have a right to vary it. The rider should give his horse the slight freedom of rein which he wants, while his forward-driving aids maintain the impulsion. The rider's hands should always offer the horse an invitation to stretch forward; if they follow they are a fraction too late. They should be kept low, moving towards and maintaining a smooth contact with the horse's mouth.

The instructor must correct any sign of excess tension in this phase, for this will stifle confidence, rhythm and the consistent urging of the riders' forward-driving aids – in fact, the lower legs may even spring away from the horse's sides. Many pupils will hold their breath and should be encouraged to speak out aloud during the lesson, but not at a competition.

From their earliest jumping lessons pupils should be taught to be aware of their weight-aids; how to invite the canter lead required on landing, by keeping their inner hips well forward and looking up and slightly to the outside rather

195

than down and to the inside. They should also learn how to guide their horses on a curved line by slightly shifting their weight to the inside and keeping it there, neatly poised, with the inner hip and leg fractionally farther forward, throughout the jump.

Well-chosen gymnastic exercises using cavalletti, a placing fence or combinations of fences with nicely related distances, provide excellent means for developing pupils' feel for rhythm, co-ordination, and an eye for a stride during the approach and with an increase in confidence they will overcome the temptation to interfere with their horses' prejudged arrangements during the last three strides.

5 *The take-off*

When the horse comes up to the fence and wishes to lower his head and stretch his neck in order to make an accurate take-off, the rider must ease his hands forward giving the horse the necessary invitation and freedom of rein. During this moment the rider's upper body must be moved forward fluently by a supple closing of the angles of the hips, when the horse takes off, to enable the rider to adjust to the horse's changing centre of gravity and to remain with him as he thrusts upwards and forwards. This forward swing of the rider's upper body will enable him to stay exactly in balance with his horse and at the same time, will relieve the horse's back from any actual pressure from the rider's seat-bones. The weight of the body remains central and is partially transferred to the rider's thighs and knees, and his lower legs remain steadily in position by or just behind the girth.

The soft contact with the horse's mouth must never be lost for the horse must be kept well on the bit and between the aids, throughout the whole performance. The rider should keep his eyes on the other side of the fence, so that already he is selecting the track he wants to follow after the fence has been jumped – or, if jumping-off against the clock, he may well be sizing up the next fence.

If, just before the horse takes off, the rider leans or falls forward abruptly, thus reducing or even losing all contact with the bit, his influence is lost and the horse is disturbed at the very moment that he most needs confidence in his rider's weight distribution, and their united balance and co-ordination, i.e. during his calculated take-off. Owing to the disruption he will be forced either to jump badly, to run out, or he may lose his nerve and stop. On the other hand, the rider must not try to 'help' the horse to take off by lifting with his hands, digging with his heels, or interfering in any way, instead he must allow the horse to select the correct moment and make the required effort by himself.

When, at the take-off the horse leaves the ground with the forelegs (see Fig. 74) the forward tilt of the rider's body will ease the seat-bones slightly from the saddle; however, the seat must not be elevated exaggeratedly, only enough to enable the rider to follow the horse's movement smoothly. The rider's back should be kept strong and flat yet pliant. The lower legs must be kept still, close to the horse's sides, asking the horse to retain his form and to jump with a good bascule. The heels should stay down, allowing the knees to retain stability on the saddle, and the rider to stay in perfect unison with his horse.

196

6 The jump – the air-borne leap

As the horse soars over the fence, the rider must follow the whole movement fluently.

The rider should look ahead with an erect yet easy head-carriage and quick yet cool thoughts.

The invitation to stretch, with a good bascule, must be offered during all phases of the jump by moving the slightly opening hand forward towards the horse's mouth and easing the fingers as much as is required, yet retaining the contact and the communication of the rein-aids. The exact degree to which the upper part of the rider's body should be inclined forward, to obtain the necessary 'follow through' cannot be laid down as it must depend on and be relative to the dimensions of the fence in question, the speed at which it is being taken and the jumping style of each individual horse. When riding over low fences the rider should lean slightly forward; when the fence dimensions are greater and the speed is faster, the forward inclination of the rider's body must be increased.

7 The landing

The force with which the horse's fore feet hit the ground as he lands over the fence will depend on the dimensions of the fence, the speed at which it has been jumped, the horse's style of jumping and to these factors will be added the relative level and slope of the ground on the landing-side of the fence. Ideally the rider should stay in close co-ordination with his horse, allowing him to make his own adjustments without interference or disturbance from his rider. However, it will greatly assist the rider to achieve this aim if he is reminded of the following points:

He must again ride into his knees – they should absorb most of the shock of landing.

He must retain the secure and steady position and contact of his lower legs.

His seat should return smoothly and pliantly to the saddle as the upper body becomes more upright, the rider's centre of gravity coming back in time with that of the horse.

The smooth contact of the rein aids should be carefully preserved.

He must guard against making any rough movement, or stiffening in any part of himself.

He must not upset the horse's mental or physical balance nor impede the fluency of the stretch forward and the re-establishment of the gait on the track.

8 Riding away after the fence – the get-away

As soon as the horse has landed over the fence he should be ridden straight forward at the required gait, rhythm and speed, contained well between the aids, the rider being ready to urge the horse forward with his seat and legs, to engage the haunches and lighten the forehand, to decrease or to increase the speed as may be necessary. Both during the landing and immediately afterwards, the rider must avoid resorting to any form of roughness, particularly with his hands, he must not drop the contact nor must he forget his poise.

Whenever he is riding young or nervous horses the rider must be quick to reward with a word or a pat on the neck; this must be an immediate reaction, completed within the first few strides after he has landed, or the horse will not realize and understand that it is the jump that is being praised.

9 The turn – after leaving the fence

Any turn which is made after the horse has been ridden forward and away from the fence should be ridden according to the principles for riding turns, i.e. 'Collect, weight, turn and *push*!' This is particularly necessary if there is a marker-flag, gateway, tree or some similar object requiring a close and accurate, time-saving turn.

When young horses are being schooled in company, over single fences, each horse should be ridden away and turned in the opposite direction from that taken by the horse in front of him in order to improve his co-operation and obedience.

The same procedure is excellent for riders to make them *think*, and to ride with clear yet smooth aids.

In conclusion –

At the risk of boring with repetition – remembering that to many pupils repetition leads to absorption of facts (in a sort of self-defence), I will start as I mean to finish. The qualities which the instructors should foster and that the rider should seek throughout the nine phases of the jump are:

In the rider – a flair consisting of courage, confidence, cool judgment and a vital dash of enthusiastic enjoyment. A position in the saddle as correct, supple and steady as his standard and conformation will allow, being in balance with his horse, and directing and controlling him with correct, smooth and effective aids.... Thought, weight, leg and rein aids.

In the horse – a matching boldness, suitable impulsion, balance and surefootedness, rhythm, and calmness. He should accept the rider's aids willingly, be on the bit, move forward freely and be in a good 'form'.

Riders' faults when jumping – and their corrections

Faults must be corrected as they occur, but as with all corrections, they must be made with care and tact so as not to create tension or stiffness, nor to impair any individual's natural talent, flair nor fluency. The most common faults to be observed and corrected are:

i Riding with the stirrup leathers too long or too short

If the stirrup leathers are too long the rider's position will be weak and his aids will be inaccurate and ineffective. He will probably bump about in a most unhelpful manner on his horse's back. If the fault is really bad it can injure the horse's back.

If the instructor tells the pupil to shorten his stirrup leathers a hole or a few holes, as he thinks fit, the pupil will then have his thighs and his knees further in front of him which gives him greater security and control of his position and of his horse – a vital factor if the latter is an onward-bound bold type.

Too short stirrup leathers must be avoided because the more the rider's knees are raised above the middle bulge of the horse's rib-cage, the less he is

198

COMMON RIDING FAULTS
OVER FENCES

LOOKING BACK

STIRRUP LEATHERS TOO LONG
HOLLOW BACK
TOO UPRIGHT-STIFF

FIG.75.

STIRRUPS TOO SHORT
SEAT TOO HIGH –LOOKING DOWN

able to wrap his legs round his horse, and consequently his security in the saddle and his influence on his horse are weakened, if not jeopardized altogether.

If these pupils ride and jump low fences without stirrups they will come naturally to a more suitable length for their stirrup leathers.

ii *Riding with the reins too long or too short*

The majority of riders make the mistake of jumping with too long reins from a subconscious desire to give their horse a free head; instead they risk upsetting their own balance and being behind the horse's movement throughout the jump and thus being disruptive with all their influences – if not, in bad cases, destructive to their horse's back teeth as well as to his back.

If pupils are told to ride over low fences with their hands reversed along the reins, this will usually cure these problems and encourage soft, smoother rein-aids.

REINS REVERSED FOR SOFT REIN AIDS
FIG.76

iii Rounding the back and looking down

This is a common fault of less experienced riders and is usually due to being left behind, which may be the result of a lack of enthusiasm on the part of either partner. The rider's seat and his influences are considerably weakened, and he loses all fluency over the fence and/or course of fences.

The instructor should advise, 'More impulsion, find a good rhythm and keep it; get forward and hollow your back' – this last exaggeration is necessary temporarily to eliminate the fault.

iv Exaggerated or clumsy movements during any phase of the jump

These are not only pointless, they are also disturbing to the horse.

The rider may lift his seat too high up out of the saddle with straightened legs as he leans right forward up the horse's neck. This exaggerated form of 'give' serves no purpose, it may even disturb the horse, and if the rider returns to the saddle with a bump he may injure his horse's back, or put him off the sport altogether. If the horse twists over the fence or makes a mistake as he lands, the rider may part company from his horse!

The rider may move his hands either too high, towards the horse's ears which may prevent the horse from lowering his neck, or too low, down the horse's shoulders which may prevent him from stretching his nose forwards, or, worse, he may try to hoist him up with his hands at the moment of take-off. These faulty hand-actions interfere with the horse's natural movement.

If the rider pushes his feet forwards this will automatically displace his seat to the back of the saddle, and in all probability he will be left behind, hanging on by the reins.

If the rider's lower legs are drawn too far back during the jump, this is an equally bad habit for not only are the legs put out of action when they are needed to urge the horse forward on landing, but also if the horse makes a mistake the rider will invariably be catapulted 'out of the front door'!

Notes:

When jumping down a drop or into water the rider's legs should be moved a little farther forward, to the front edge of the girth, to counteract the extra shock of the more acute landing.

The racing seat used when riding in point-to-points or steeplechasing is a specialized seat with much shorter stirrup leathers.

Looking back to see if they have negotiated the fence correctly, or to assess the damage done is a very bad habit, for in turning the head the forward thinking is switched off, the rider's shoulders and hips often turn too, then the rein, seat and leg influences are disrupted, the weight is displaced and the horse's balance is upset, just when the horse should be concentrating on the next fence.

Stiffness, hesitancy and lack of impulsion and rhythm are often caused by the rider inadvertently holding his breath, due to over-concentration or exertion; to apprehension, or to his trying too hard. This is always alleviated if not overcome if the instructor tells all the pupils to say some word or phrase in rhythm with the horse's stride as they negotiate the jump, grid or course. The instructor should listen with careful perception, as often, changes in the voice's pitch, or its total disappearance will tell him exactly when the tension is worst!

Whatever the cause, if pupils are intent on going hunting or competing before these faults have been eradicated, they must be told to hold the mane half-way up their horses' necks. This will add to their confidence, enable them to concentrate more on improving and strengthening their own positions and to appreciate and follow the horse's movement – and above all, they cannot then catch or hurt their horses' mouths.

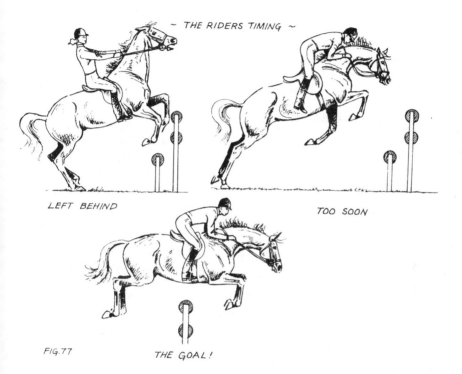

~ THE RIDERS TIMING ~

LEFT BEHIND

TOO SOON

FIG.77

THE GOAL!

v *The rider's timing is at fault* so that he is not absolutely 'with' his horse at the moment of take-off.

If the rider is left behind the horse's movement, he may cause him to hit the fence with his hindlegs, upset his landing and generally provide him with an unpleasant experience.

If the rider throws himself forward too much or too soon he will upset the horse's balance by putting too much weight, suddenly, on his forehand; this may spoil the horse's performance during the take-off, over the fence and as he lands.

It is imperative that a pupil with a timing problem realizes that the horse must have freedom – of his head and neck, for they are his balancing pole. He must be reminded of the responsibility of his weight burden. His whole position must be kept completely under control to allow the horse to utilize his muscle-power to the best of his ability. The pupil should be reminded that his seat should remain central on a straight track or leading the way before and during a curved line. He should keep his seat as close to the saddle as possible as

201

he swings his body forward and his legs should remain in close and steady contact with the horse's sides, by the girth.

Most of all, the pupil with a timing problem must be encouraged to speak out aloud from the start to the finish of his round, so that he cannot hold his breath and he makes himself concentrate on his horse's rhythm and movement in a natural way. To avoid his feeling conspicuous and tense the whole class should be told to carry out the exercise in turn.

vi *The rider exaggerates the 'give'*, he drops the contact and the horse – into the bottom of the fence. Although it is certainly better to give too much than to restrict the horse by not giving enough over the fence, it can be dangerous if the reins are dropped suddenly, abandoning contact at the very last moment, as the horse will invariably be thrown off balance.

vii *A bold keen competitive pupil may 'hurl' his horse at the fence*, in an endeavour to override the horse's hesitancy, unwillingness or lack of obedience to the aids, thus making the common mistake of confusing speed for impulsion. Here confidence and rhythm must be regained tactfully, over lowered, straight forward fences, and with instantaneous reward for good work.

viii *Crookedness* – this is a bad fault which may be due to lack of correct tuition, to stiffening against the take-off, nervousness, holding the breath, or pain from an injury. This is a major fault because it makes the rider-burden an extremely awkward one for the horse to carry.

As with all rider-faults, the instructor must return to early demands in order to improve the rider's straightness and technique before he is asked to jump even a course of low fences again. A straight grid ridden without reins and stirrups on a steady horse will prove invaluable for these cases.

ix *Lack of intelligent thought* – of any of the nine phases of the jump or of his horse, his thoughts and actions.

All these faults need thoughtful and skilful analysis by the instructor; he must be quick and accurate in his assessment of the *root* cause.

Faults due to a lack of thought or technique (position and aids) are best corrected when the pupil or class are halted. The instructor explains and demonstrates – while the class cogitates.

Faults which are the result of inexperience or weakness of co-ordination or timing may be overcome more readily by spontaneous coaching given when the pupil is in action – the instructor virtually 'riding the horse' verbally. This method must be used sparingly.

The instructor must use his discretion in each case; usually the first method is the better of the two, being clear, more effective and therefore long-lasting, and a number of pupils can learn from the instruction at the same time – they all have to THINK.

The worst crime an instructor can commit in a jumping lesson is to overface any horse or rider so that they lose their nerve, even in the slightest degree. A good instructor will inspire by building up confidence, he will foster the horses' natural desire to please and the riders' ambition, dedication and determination to improve their technique and thus their performance.

Refusals should not occur; if they do the instructor should ask himself at once, 'What was my error of judgement or directive?' The most common causes of school horses refusing are:

i Bad instruction – lack of feel, over facing riders and horses.

ii An uneducated pupil who has never been taught the basic principles, e.g. the nine phases; the rider's correct behaviour over a fence; how the horse sees, sizes up, reacts and jumps the fence.

iii A nervous rider who has little heart for riding over fences.

iv A badly-ridden approach – crooked; too short; over-ridden, un-balanced; or over-shortening, right up to the take-off zone.

v Insufficient impulsion, weak or purposeless riding. Novice riders and/ or horses should not be expected to jump fences when going away from all their comrades; there should always be at least one horse being ridden in sight, on the landing-side and well beyond the fence to be jumped.

vi The horse's training over fences may have been inadequate.

vii The horse may have been sickened by too much jumping, especially if this has been on either hard or slippery ground. He may have too many memories of pain caused by bad riding, particularly from being caught in the mouth or banged on his back, or from hitting his legs due to a rider's mis-direction or interference. He may have been hurt by badly-fitting saddlery, or he may have been expected to carry riders who were too large, heavy and cumbersome, over fences.

viii Some horses are naturally 'chicken', lacking courage, and react immedi-ately to a rider who is too passive, weak or nervous, or when they see another horse refuse a fence in front of them.

Refusals must be dealt with calmly, firmly and immediately. The instructor should teach all his pupils the basic techniques to be followed whenever a horse has refused a fence.

(a) Determine the cause and use this discovery to aid the cure.

(b) If the horse runs out, to the left for instance, he should be halted immediately and turned back on his track to the right; a turn on the forehand will help to remove constraint. He may be shown the fence and reassured of its simplicity, before he is taken away, re-presented to and ridden determinedly over the fence. (The instructor must warn his pupils that they must never turn their horse to look at the fence in a show-jumping competition, or they will be eliminated, nor must they dilly-dally for by so doing they will accumulate even more penalties – for exceeding the course's time-limit.)

(c) Should a second refusal occur, or should the instructor have the slightest doubt about the rider's ability or the horse's willingness, he should lower the fence and direct a rider on a free-going horse to give a lead.

(d) If the horse persists in running out to the same side, i.e. to the left, and the rider is bold and reasonably experienced, then he should angle his approach to come in from the left, thus making a left-handed run-out almost impossible. See Fig. 78. The instructor must warn his pupils never to over-do this angling of the approach or they may upset the horse and teach him to run out to the right.

Novice riders are nearly always over-ready to blame their horses for making jumping faults whereas almost invariably it is he, the rider, who has not give his horse a chance to make a good, clear jump over the fence. The reader has only to stand near a hunt jump, or at the ringside of a restricted show-jumping event

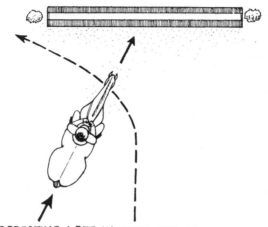

FIG. 78 CORRECTING LEFT-HANDED RUN-OUT

to see countless examples of bad riding and brave, generous horses – 'Why do they go on jumping when they are made to suffer so much?' one is led to ask.

Jumping can evolve into a great sport, which in many ways has a parallel in skiing. Balance, use of the weight, elasticity of the hip-, knee- and ankle-joints, and thrills and spills as you wish or dare! Riding over fences has several advantages, the greatest of which is that the enjoyment is doubled by having a living partner, which can also double the skill-requirement and the challenge.

Man's moral responsibility to the horse with whom he works should never be superseded by overambition or greed for competition success of financial gain. Out in the country beyond Los Angeles there is a statue of a lone horseman. It is of one of the members of the Japanese three-day event team, and was sculpted and erected in recognition of his humanity and horsemanship, when, despite the overwhelming pressures of his team-membership, he retired his horse in the middle of the cross-country phase as he felt it was unfair to ask his nearly exhausted equine partner to finish the course. The Japanese are very proud of that statue – and rightly so.

Lesson reminders – for the three basic class standards

All lessons must be SAFE, foster love and understanding for the horse, instil correct techniques, practise and progress, and be stimulatingly enjoyable – FUN!

In lessons for novice riders when the class is lined up facing the low jump, it is imperative that a horse and rider be posted 15 metres to 25 metres beyond and in line with the landing-side of the fence, to ensure that from their very first lesson, riders ride straight forward after the fence, and the horses remain well-schooled in this respect.

A horse who rushes back to the ride as soon as he lands really is a disgrace to the rider and to the school who owns him.

The importance of patting the horse, singing a song or saying a phrase must be remembered, in order to dispel nerves, to ensure that pupils keep breathing normally, to develop their rhythm, confidence and feel in as natural a way as possible. The pupil's voice also acts as a 'nerve-barometer' which is very easy for the instructor to read.

The correct riding of easy turns after, before and between fences should be taught at this stage because if a rider is allowed to develop the bad habit of sliding his seat to the outside it is so much more difficult to correct his position, balance and consequent fluency later; in fact a really bad riding fault is often impossible to eradicate once it has become established. Thus a correct weight placement to the inside, to guide and balance the horse must be taught from the very beginning so that it is established as a natural subconscious reaction when riding the track between fences. This is an all-important foundation-stone but it is one that is too often overlooked.

A novice rider should never be pushed or over-faced, his progress will be much more sure if the instructor has the patience to wait for the pupil to request an increase in the demands. Fences should never exceed 80 cms in height for this standard.

First jumping lessons are of great importance and should never be taught casually, although the manner in which they are conducted must never be too formal or tense.

The instructor must have a limitless supply of course or work-out plans and keep adding to it. The common aim of all these courses is to develop the pupils' general horsemanship over low fences, combined with school figures and transitions, using barrels or similar markers to help them to find and ride a good track. Fluency, harmony, invisible aids – well-ridden turns – half-halts; keeping the horse moving forward in a good form – all these must be praised, not merely their riding over the fences.

In the middle stage of their training, the pupils' ability, suppleness and control are developed by jumping in open order, from a trot; the use of combinations, grids, spreads; jumping from an angle and unusual fences such as corners and stars, small drops, banks, ditches, water jumps and so on. The fences at this stage should average 1 metre in height; higher fences serve no purpose, on the contrary, they may cause a serious set back.

The middle stage is the most important one in every jumper's career. Plans, programmes, courses and problems should be purposefully varied. Riders should ride and jump in groups in open order, each taking their own line, so that they look up and about them naturally and of necessity to avoid collisions. The instructor must watch that his pupils guide their horses smoothly and thoughtfully, mainly with their thought, weight and leg aids, and lead them to appreciate and feel for rhythm, balance and tactful control as confidence and ability improve. Poles on the ground and low cavalletti strategically placed across the outer track or in the centre of the school and ridden over at walk, trot and canter, are invaluable aids to correct riding for pupils of all standards – if there is a weakness in their positions, weight placement, rhythm or co-ordination this exercise will show it up and present a fair challenge.

More advanced jumping

Only when confidence, experience and ability have been built up and established, should pupils and horses be asked to shorten their stirrup leathers further, to negotiate larger obstacles, and fixed fences at speed, and even then they should only do or for short periods once or twice a week, to develop their scope, eye, experience and confidence. They should return to the middle stage frequently and regularly, to ensure that they are never sickened by being overtaxed.

N.B. The value of reward for the horses should be taught and re-emphasized frequently at all standards. A reward bag should be kept at hand, and although a student who is acting as a jump steward may lift the bag the rider should always give the tit-bit from his own hand – a reward is a very personal matter!

PART C

Early Riding Lessons

17 General principles

Teaching beginners can be excitingly rewarding work for any grade of instructor; unfortunately it is often regarded as a boringly tedious chore which may be palmed off to any novice student-instructor. This must be a false, shortsighted policy, for good instruction has the triple-edged advantage that the pupil learns to sit on a horse and to ride him correctly, the training standard of the school horses is not lowered, and the school soon earns a good reputation.

It is extremely important that the chief instructor teaches this phase carefully and thoroughly to all the instructors. He should prepare and give a series of lecture-demonstrations himself, and he should keep a constant eye open to see that his instruction has been understood and is being implemented.

If the quality of instruction is really good there will be several very important and long-lasting results:

i The foundation of the pupils' equestrian way of life or career will be correct and sound, and will stand him in good stead for as long and as far as he may wish to ride.

ii He will learn, from the first, how a horse 'ticks'; he will be made aware of the horse's mental and physical sensitivity.

iii He will learn to observe and to assess the horse's form and movement.

iv He will be stimulated by small successes, and his ambition will be fired.

v He will not form incorrect attitudes of mind nor of position which are so much more difficult to correct once they have become firmly rooted, faulty habits.

vi His nerve will remain staunch, for his well-trained instructor will never have overtaxed it.

The four-fold aim of SAFETY, CONFIDENCE, FUN and IMPROVEMENT must always be prominent in the instructor's mind, together with SIMPLICITY in the format of the lesson.

Unless the instructor possesses the qualities already enumerated in Chapter 5 in full measure he will not be able or fit to teach beginner-riders adequately!

The instructor must always bear in mind how he felt when he first learned to ride:

(a) A horse is a large animal, and by his very size and seeming unwieldiness he can arouse feelings of alarm or even of extreme fear in children or adults who have had no previous experience with horses.

(b) Very few beginner-riders are able, naturally, to manage or cope with a horse, unless they have been born, bred and brought up to a country life with an equestrian background. As this ideal horseman's upbringing becomes more and more rare so does the riding instructor's responsibility increase; from him his pupils must learn the correct methods from the start. They must be taught all the most rudimentary facts about horses and their general behaviour; how to handle horses quietly, fairly, yet firmly, and that they must never make sharp or sudden movements, or be rough, loud or unjust.

The instructor should never assume knowledge; ignorance can easily be the cause of an accident. 'Prevention is better than cure'. Pupils must be fore-warned of the hazards, e.g. a horse's shod hoof treading on a human foot can be excruciatingly painful, as can a bite or a kick from a horse.

At least 50 per cent of every early lesson should be spent dismounted, while the pupil learns how to handle, to lead, and to look after the horse or pony. He should be taught how to make friends with the horse while he is in the stable, or is being grazed on a head-rope; to observe how he expresses his feelings; how he breathes, eats, drinks; and what he eats. The pupil should be encouraged to help to look after the horse, picking out his feet, brushing, saddling, unsaddl-ing and leading him about, always under supervision. He must be taught how to move horses about and how to move about them in a way which horses understand, expect and respect.

Time spent in carrying out simple tasks with the horse is always well spent – it is never a waste of time – e.g. beginners love to be allowed to help to catch up the horse or pony from the field and to lead him back to the stable-yard.

Attention to detail should be carefully applied so that it inspires rather than interrupts. When pupils are beginning to learn to ride they are most receptive and learn quickly and well. It is up to the instructor to teach them all the small details as well as the more obvious, major tasks, in order to foster their interest and perception as much as their practical ability.

Pupils should be encouraged to *think* from the start and instructors should encourage their pupils to read, to draw or to trace diagrams of the points of the horse, of the saddle and bridle, of the arena and its figures, etc. remembering that the knowledge and not the artistry is being tested. Whereas some aspiring horseman may be fortunate enough to have an artistic flair, others not so endowed may be embarrassed by their inability to draw; they should be encouraged to trace or to be diagrammatic.

As often as possible the early lessons should be taught by the same teachers, human and equine, in order to establish maximum rapport, confidence, enjoyment and progress with the pupil.

Beginners' *horses* should be carefully selected to suit individual require-ments:

(a) They should be kind and quiet yet willing and obedient, and be reason-ably well trained.

(b) They should move forward freely, but not too freely, and only when asked to do so.

(c) They should lead well, both from the ground and from another horse to either hand.

(d) They should get on well with other horses.

(e) They should be comfortable to sit on.

(f) They should be the right size for the rider. Generally a horse which is too small is preferable to one who is too big, the former's back is not so far up from the ground! A wide horse will stretch a novice rider uncomfortably; a narrow one gives a less stable feeling, lessening security and testing balance.

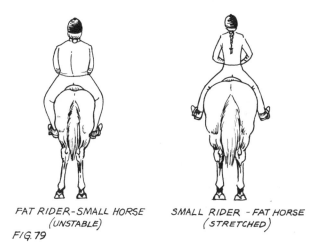

FAT RIDER-SMALL HORSE (UNSTABLE)   SMALL RIDER - FAT HORSE (STRETCHED)

FIG. 79

(g) They should have comfortable gaits, the strides being neither too long (throwing), nor too short (stumpy). Both for the teaching of feel and for ease of understanding, slightly longer strides are preferable.

(h) The horses' schooling should not be allowed to deteriorate; they should be ridden, preferably out of doors, by experienced riders at regular intervals to preserve their enthusiasm, generosity, sensitivity and the standard as well as the quality of their gaits.

(i) Beginners' horses should never be young and partly broken, unduly quick or sharp, nervous, stubborn or bad-tempered.

The preparations must be thoughtful and efficient. e.g. The stirrups and stirrup leathers should be gauged for size before the horse is saddled. The assistants should be forewarned and ready, and their horses tacked up, if needed, i.e. the stage must be set well before the lesson is due to start, so that the pupils may be welcomed on arrival and the tempo of the lesson itself is maintained at an inspiring level, and is not lowered by unnecessary interruptions.

The whole atmosphere and tempo of the lessons must be confidence-giving.

The environment must be both safe and peaceful.

All lessons should be based on the format of:

Explanation

Demonstration

Execution

Interrogation

Repetition

Confirmation

(All six of these items must be incorporated into every lesson.)

The instructor should use either this simple form or the more detailed version described earlier, in Chapter 8.

The horse must be correctly saddled and bridled. A neckstrap should be fitted if required, and the leading-rein attached as required. All of this should be taught to and carried out by the pupil before the final adjustments are made by the instructor, after which he teaches and helps the pupil to mount.

From the first time the pupil sits in the saddle, the instructor must be doubly aware of his pupil's reactions – he must feel with great sensitivity both for and with his pupil.

The early lessons should never be hurried or over-demanding, the pupil's nerve must be preserved. If a pupil is in the least apprehensive the instructor should be prepared to spend the whole of the mounted period at the halt. Even if a horse or pony shakes his head to remove a fly, the sensation can be quite disconcerting for a new rider, and much can be taught at the halt, e.g. adjusting stirrup leathers, girths and reins, and a few easy exercises.

It is a wise and a good instructor who waits for the demand for new work to come from his pupil:

'May I see what it feels like to walk?'

'May I learn to trot, please?'

'Do you think I could come off the leading-rein?'

'Are we jumping today?'

These are typical guiding requests for which the instructor should wait.

The instructor must exert tactful restraint on the overambitious pupil who tends to think his ability and expertise are greater than they are. 'Pride comes before a fall,' and the latter is good for neither the rider nor the horse. Overconfident riders will usually comply willingly to a limiting of their activities if the instructor explains that the requested exercise would not in fact be good or comfortable for their newly found friend – the horse.

If an instructor is teaching a class of beginners he must have reliable assistants preferably one leading each pupil's horse. These assistants need not be qualified, but they must be keen to learn, and be quickly receptive in order that they may act exactly as the instructor wishes; they must be competent and effective in their handling of horses, and diligent in their quiet help to the pupils.

The instructor must always aim at producing good natural riders, and he must remember that this can only happen if his pupils genuinely enjoy their lessons. They must have FUN – but that fun must be educational and SAFE. A touch of humour always enlivens the scene and is a sure way of removing any excess tension and of improving the pupils' confidence.

The reasons, and advantages should always be taught whenever a new method is introduced, this increases its acceptability. In later lessons, common faults and any disadvantages may be pointed out to invoke a greater depth of thought.

The early lesson-subjects should be listed for the instructors, together with details of the most important points to be taught and faults to be avoided. The subjects should be set out in a logical sequence and each one should be taught and confirmed before new work is introduced.

Junior instructors must be warned against over-persuasive, bombastic parents whose false pride and personal ego makes them force the pace, often against the true wishes of the child or his instructor. These parents must be persuaded to support their children with patient interest; overambitious parents who are constantly pressing for competitive performances must be persuaded to regard riding as a craft which has to be learnt thoroughly as is the craft of a carpenter, surgeon or chef. Hopefully they will wish their children to become good riders.

The work must be regulated with the utmost care so that it enables the rider to feel SAFE, well-balanced, secure and at ease. Lessons must be stimulating and enjoyable; they should not be:

boring,

over-demanding,

intimidating – in any way.

It is essential that beginners 'make haste slowly'.

All assistants must be well briefed about the forthcoming lesson so that they may back up the teaching by repeating the explanation if necessary.

The instructor should make imaginative use of props such as strategically placed barrels or by incorporating conveniently growing trees, bushes or plants, and of short tests on school figures ridden at the walk, to give purpose and variety as well as practise of his teaching, to all his lessons.

Clothing must be suitable – it must be protective, safe, hard-wearing, neat and tidy. Children grow quickly and specially tailored riding clothes are expensive; thus a hard riding hat is an essential item but long leather riding boots are not. Although a jacket is necessary for formal occasions, a jersey is better for lessons as a jacket can conceal a multitude of position faults or can be slighly restrictive, especially when nearly outgrown. A shirt or jersey reveals the rider's outline and movement and any faults which may exist. For riders of the female sex a supporting, stabilizing bra is a *must*.

Riding 'bareback', the saddle replaced by a small folded blanket and a web surcingle, is excellent for all riders, providing that the horses are reliable, they have comfortable backs and gaits, and the lesson is conducted with great care. The riders must never be over-taxed.

Correctly fitted side-reins, as loose as possible, may be worn by beginners' school horses for trot and canter work, so that they may be ridden with minimum rein-aids in the early lessons. When the pupils' balance, position and confidence are sufficiently established, to enable them to carry their hands steadily enough, they may be permitted to take up a light contact with their reins, and the side-reins are then removed.

There is a well-known school on the continent which has a particularly clever, psychological approach to unsteady hands. To the visiting rider's question, 'Why does my horse wear side-reins?' the reply is given, 'Because we have not yet seen whether your hands are good enough to ride with a rein-contact.' This gives an immediate challenge to the visitor to prove his good hands, and have the stigma of the side-reins removed as soon as possible! The threat remains, ensuring correct hand positions, carriage and influence with no careless jostling or ill-effects, and the instructor is spared the chore of having to give repetitive, time-wasting corrections or reminders.

The chief instructor should involve all his student-instructors in these early riding lessons, for they themselves cannot be reminded of the correct basic work too often. Even if they are presently working on more advanced equitation in their own riding lessons, a frequent return to 'the basics' will not only be very good for them as a matter of principle, it may also sort out some little puzzle or mystery as yet unsolved in their more advanced work – all this, providing that the calibre of the teaching is good enough!

The chief instructor should exchange the students' responsibilities in these lessons from time to time, but he must not change them over for change's sake. The beginner-rider will make quicker progress if he is allowed to get to know the student who helps him, his confidence and prowess will advance much more readily if he can rely on the same friendly person to help him at every lesson. Occasionally, in the testing or teaching of stable management for instance, the 'conveyor-belt system' is the most efficient and it is here, particularly, that the duties must be exchanged. For example, because Mary is an ace at plaiting up a tail – and enjoys revealing and teaching her craft, she must teach the other students to be equally good and then she herself must be moved on to another task such as, 'fitting saddlery' or a quiz-session 'find and list the faults in the stable, horse and tack-room'. All the students should be thoroughly conversant with the school's methods and have a staunch conviction in their rightful success which is well supported by sound reasoning. If they know how and why to teach all the early lessons it will establish their own understanding and belief even more securely and they can then be relied on to teach in exactly the same manner themselves when their turn comes.

The chief instructor should test the beginner riders himself periodically; both in their theory and in their practical work; this puts his instructing team on their mettle. The knowledge that their teaching is being put to the test ensures that they will do their best to prove that they have been teaching the correct methods, aids and ideas *well*. The chief instructor must never take this for granted or one day he could be gravely disappointed – he must keep all his instructors, horses and pupils, physically in a good form, and mentally – on the bit.

Handling horses

Practical lectures and instruction on handling horses which are kept out at grass should not be skimped, for these early lessons contain much important matter.

Students should be taught: How to encourage horses to come to them when they call. Not that the countryside should be disturbed by riotous groups carolling and whistling early in the morning, for that would not be the best way of remaining friends with one's neighbours. They should be shown how to train their charges to come to the gate at a specially welcoming call, and the promise should be fulfilled by a reward of a slice of bread, apple or carrot. A catcher is guilty of cheating if he does not offer the willing horse a small token of appreciation.

How to put on the headcollar or bridle; how to wait for or help other catchers; how to manoeuvre the horse through the gate; to CLOSE the gate, so that it is not open all day – inviting two or four legged trespassers, and being warped out of shape as its considerable weight is supported only by two comparatively small hinges at one end.

How to lead the horse in hand with a bridle or a sound headcollar and secure head rope. All students should be warned against ever leading a horse without a lead rope, for if the horse were to jerk up his head in alarm at some real or imaginary object or noise, the leader will lose his grasp on the headcollar, and the horse – with modern traffic, that could result in a serious accident – and a dead horse. It has happened, too often – the risk should *never* be taken. Stout gloves should be worn, to protect the hands from the rope and during fencing repairs or other field tasks.

Road and traffic procedure must be taught; emergency first aid procedures for horses and riders; how to inspect the horse and his shoes, how to clean and generally care for him.

FIG. 80   BAD TURNING OUT

Students should be taught how to turn horses out in the field at the end of the day, after every vestige of saddle and girth marks have been sponged or brushed off. How to inspect fences for gaps, slack wire, and to check the field for dangerous tins, bottles or plastic bags and poisonous plants. How to release the horses one by one, turning their heads towards the closed gate and making sure that they are standing still and calm before sliding the bridles over their heads very carefully. Any pupil who is seen to be careless when unbridling should be asked to feel the narrow, unprotected bars of a horse's mouth and he should be told how easily they may be bruised, chipped or splintered; it is then unlikely that he will ever repeat his thoughtless roughness. Finally they should be encouraged to gain more satisfaction from seeing a horse walk away from the gate quietly and contentedly, rather than departing in a flurry of heels, at a mad gallop instigated by a flourishing headcollar or bridle and seeming to signify, 'Thank God, we are free from those humans for a few hours at last.' This latter mode of ending the day is neither very satisfying for the humans concerned, nor is it very complimentary!

The catching up and turning out of horses is an excellent exercise to teach student instructors to think and organize themselves. Besides learning never to leave or turn out one horse by himself, and never to forget or lose the key to the padlock, students can learn to help each other, e.g. 'We'll catch all the horses this morning while you people get on with the yard duties, and then we will reverse proceedings in the evening.' It is interesting to note that this simple

213

solution usually has to be worked out by the instructor at the beginning of every course – students rarely naturally think for themselves.

Handling the horse. There are many suitable and simple lessons on this subject for junior or assistant instructors to teach. They themselves must realize the full importance of the subject-matter, and must be diligent in the passing on of their knowledge.

From the moment the pupil enters the school's stable-yard and is welcomed and taken charge of by a designated member of the teaching staff he should be encouraged to learn, even though it is not yet the official start time for the lesson. Opportunities for observing horses' behaviour and for supervised work amongst them should never be wasted.

Pupils must be taught how a horse moves about and reacts both in the stables and out of doors, they must be encouraged to spend as much time with them as possible.

Horses are remarkably receptive to thoughts and moods, which is why a horseman should have a happy and optimistically confident disposition, should be sympathetic (with extra sensitivity) and possess a quietly enquiring and perceptive mind with a gift for remaining calm and installing that quality into others in times of stress. Much of this attitude of mind and mood will be copied by the pupil as he works with his instructor.

The instructor must explain that the horse is essentially a very kind animal who is usually very anxious to please his human partner but that he is also highly sensitive and is easily upset by sudden movements, quick approaches and loud noises. If the horse is upset or frightened, his instinctive inherited defence system of flight, kick or bite will immediately rise to the fore despite many generations of domesticity.

Using only quiet and trustworthy horses or ponies, pupils should be taught how to carry out the following simple tasks:

(a) How to approach and touch the horse, in the correct, acceptable way, as well as a demonstration of how not to do it together with the probable, invited dangers. He should learn the points of the horse – and little by little, salient facts about conformation.

(b) How to put on a headcollar.

(c) How to untie and tie up a horse, using a quick release knot; the correct length of rope and why. Selecting suitable objects to tie a horse to out of doors. (Using a short length of strong but ultimately breakable string, tied round a stout branch of a tree for a fixing for the head-rope rather than a projection on a light portable hen-house!)

(d) How to lead the horse in hand, taking a pride in how well he can encourage the horse to walk with him, shoulder to shoulder, from both sides, with the instructor helping as he may be needed. This is one of the best opportunities to sow the seeds of communication between the rider and his horse, and it is an opportunity which is often omitted, because its possibilities are not realized. Later the pupil should be taught how to trot the horse out in hand and to stand him up for inspection; when he can observe and feel how the horse moves.

(e) How to pick out the horse's feet.

(f) How to groom him – basic grooming tools and their uses.

(g) How to saddle up, being careful of the horse's spine. How to fit the saddle

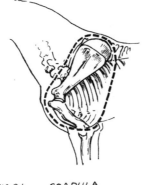

FIG 81　SCAPULA
(SHOULDER BLADE)

well behind the horse's shoulder-blade, and how to pull each fore leg forward to stretch out any wrinkles in the skin under the girth, behind the elbows, which if left could cause girth-galls. How to remove the saddle and how to sponge off, rub dry or slap up the horse's back.

(h) The basic rules of feeding, and how to give food to horses, when stabled and when at grass. How to sort, shake out and fill nets or sacks with hay. Discerning good quality fodder.

~ BRIDLING ~

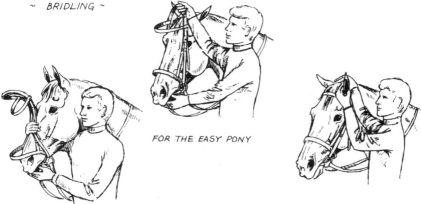

FOR THE EASY PONY

FOR THE MORE DIFFICULT PONY

FIG. 82

CAREFUL!

(i) Bridling, fitting and taking off a bridle – being particularly careful of the horse's mouth, eyes and ears. The pupils should be shown both methods of bridling and be warned never to make a horse 'head-shy'.

(j) Care of tack (i) immediately after use – bit washed and dried; sweat and grease removed from leather-work with a damp cloth before hanging up. (ii) a thorough clean – at the end of the day.

(k) Mucking out and setting fair – with variations of materials and methods.

STABLE
BANDAGE

EXERCISE
BANDAGE

BANDAGING

FIG. 83

(1) Rugging up, bandaging, setting fair and all yard duties should be introduced and taught, in fact everything to do with horse care.

There are innumerable early lessons on handling horses which should be taught for horse care is a specialist craft. Instructors must remember that they too had to learn once upon a time, that any and every lesson can be interesting providing that the instructor is good enough – and that they must NEVER ASSUME KNOWLEDGE.

Homework should be set, e.g. drawings, tracings and diagrams of points of the horse, of the saddle and bridle, and of the under surface of the foot, of the grooming tools. Junior instructors can think out and run mini-tests to suit the lesson covered.

18 Understanding horses – how the horse 'ticks'

'A horse is not human and the greatest barrier to the understanding of any animal is anthropomorphism, that is to say, attributing human personality and behaviour to animals.' (*N. H. Blake*)

The sooner pupils are taught to observe and learn about the ways of horses the sooner will they be able to develop a sympathetic understanding without which they will never become horsemen. Unfortunately there are many people riding today who would be better riding a bicycle than a horse, and certainly their horses would be far happier if they did so! The fault does not always lie with the modern 'horseback riders', more often it lies with the teachers of those riders, their parents, a hiring-stable or even books which they have read.

Although we are known as a 'nation of animal-lovers', spending more money on saving animals from being badly treated than we do on protecting battered babies, sometimes the true image is of an over-large elderly person feeding an outsize old cat – which might cause us to wonder who is the most over-indulged. Seeming-kindness and ignorance often go hand in hand, and sometimes there is a happy outcome, but when the kindness is replaced by competitive ambitions or other egoistical elements then the realms of cruelty are

216

entered. As in the human world, mental cruelty is often worse than physical cruelty, but when the two are combined they make a most pernicious evil.

Pupils of all ages should be taught the basic facts of the background history to the modern life-style and psychology of horses, in the simplest terms possible, from their earliest lessons.

To support this teaching the instructor should recommend suitable books for his pupils to read. Beside the textbooks of the BHS and the Pony Club, there are many excellent children's books. *Black Beauty*, *Moorland Mousie*, *Older Mousie*, *Flicka*, *Smokey*, and those written by Pat Smythe, Moyra Charlton and Josephine Pullein-Thompson are amongst our family favourites. Adult pupils have a wide selection from which to choose – from the horse-psychologists of ancient China, to Xenophon (so 'modern' and sympathetic in his approach), to the many present-day writers who have touched on this subject, and maybe there are equine psychic lands as yet undiscovered – who knows?

'Life from the horse's point of view' is a subject which should be referred to often during equitation and stable management lessons, for if pupils are to become successful riders or horse-masters they must understand as much as possible about the horse's natural instincts, his nervous system, his mind and the signals by means of which he reveals his thoughts and feelings.

Native ponies, or larger ponies who are nearly descended from native stock, have a definite advantage as 'school-masters' for beginners because their natural primitive instincts are well-preserved and are more easily observed and read than are the reactions of the larger, more domesticated horse. Some pupils' parents can be quite offended if their child is mounted on a pony rather than on a horse, especially if they come from a country which does not have any native pony breeds. For them a small pony seems inferior to a tall, prestige-giving horse. However, children and well-trained ponies usually build a strong rapport which will surprise and delight the parents, providing that they are patient for a week or two; their patience will be given additional incentive if the instructor also explains the practical logic of 'The bigger the horse the further and harder the fall'.

Lecture-demonstrations on 'How the Horse ticks' should be included regularly in the school's programme, as well as in every demonstration to which a more general audience is invited. The more civilized we become the less country customs, manners and laws are passed on from parent to child and in schools. Many spectators at these demonstrations know very little about horses other than that 'they are dangerous at both ends and uncomfortable in the middle', or they might know how to 'start, steer and stop' – but usually they find simple facts about the psychology of the horse an absorbingly interesting subject.

As repetition can be boring, care must be taken to vary the introduction and the approach or the slant of the lecture. There are many ways of opening proceedings, e.g. a mare with her foal at foot; a yearling or a 2 year old being handled; a young horse being trained on the lunge or under a rider ('breaking', 'broken', or 'breaking-in' are obsolete terms which are not applicable to modern horsemanship) or a group of young ponies being worked through some obedience tests can provide variety.

Any of these, or similar scenes will stimulate audience-interest and sympathy due to their own special appeal – to the spectator's eye, mind and heart.

First the instructor must remind the audience of a few of the known facts of the horse's ancestors' way of life, when they were wild creatures of the plains. In those far off times the instincts of the equine species were fundamentally so strong that most of them survive to this day although the dire need for them no longer exists. These instincts and the tools whereby they could be implemented were:

1 *Survival*
(a) Warning system:
Sense of smell – acute, through flaring nostrils.
Sense of hearing – acute, good mobility of ears, pricking to catch sounds and vibrations.
Sense of touch – a 'foreign body' sparks off two main instant reactions, 'Buck it off!' or 'Squash it off against some solid object!'
Sight – a wide visual range even when grazing, for distant, moving objects.
Warnings of a trap ... of being confined in a place from which there is no escape (a natural cause of a horse refusing to load into a trailer or to jump a ditch or coffin type of fence).
Wariness of snakes ... distrusting ropes and poles on the ground.
Wariness of sudden movements, especially if they are too close for the cause to be seen clearly and identified.
(b) Defence system – against wolves and other predators, and early man.
Flight – galloping and dodging at speed, preferably back to the herd.
Bucking off.
Squashing.
Striking or kicking with fore or hind feet.
Biting.

2 *Sustenance – Food and Water*
Roaming – in search of nutritious grass or plants and a fresh water supply.
Sense of smell – enabling them to discover new, young green grass and good water.
Hunger, combined with a sense of taste – differentiating between good and harmful fodder and water – as a rule. Surprisingly, domesticated horses are often careless in this respect and will readily prune a yew tree or hoover up sand from a shallow stream – both with fatal results.
Because of his need to roam to find further food supplies, the horse has a relatively small stomach which is a very important factor for horse-owners to know in order that they may feed and work him in the best way for his welfare. In the First World War army horses achieved incredible marches and manoeuvres of amazing length and speed without food and water for as long as 37 hours in desert heat and warfare. In fact they even outstripped the indigenous camels – 'the ships of the desert', with their specially built-in 'reservoirs'. Those horses' success must have been due to their *courage* as much as their hardiness; it is to be hoped that whereas their achievements will never be forgotten, that sort of trial will never again be required of horses by man.

To suit his special digestive system we must feed little and often; water before feeding (if a horse is not eating his hay this is often because he is thirsty), we should never work the horse immediately after a full feed: we must give plenty of bulk, feed good quality fodder, give variety, adhere to regular times of feeding and routine; give some succulent fodder every day and a minimum of one hour a day running free in a field; all these well-known feeding-rules are based on the horse's natural, primitive needs. The actual actions of grazing and roaming are strongly embedded necessities of a horse's life style. All stabled horses should be hand-grazed if it is impractical to turn them loose into a field every day.

3 *Herd membership* – supplying the horse's need for congenial company. Horses are very gregarious creatures and will not thrive happily if kept shut up alone. This herd instinct is a strong influence; it must be appreciated and it may be used in the horse's training.

Safety in numbers is the other herd-factor. The communal defence procedure of a herd of wild horses was copied by the early settlers. The horses used to form a ring with their heads (and vulnerable jugular veins) in the centre and their heels on the outside ready to deliver rapid and powerful life-saving kicks. Similarly the settlers used to drive their covered wagons to form a circular barricade from the cover of which they could fire at the marauders.

These are two aspects on which the instructor should elaborate:

(a) It is unfair to keep a pony in solitary confinement in a small paddock or a stable. Although horses are the ideal company, cattle, sheep, a goat or frequent visits from his child-owner will serve to fill the void, but if the befriending child goes away to boarding-school or on holiday, the pony should be given some substitute company; cattle in an adjoining field will suffice. A pair of ponies turned out or stabled together can prove to be a mixed blessing, especially if they are of different sexes, for they can become very devoted and present a problem of raucous whinnying, total lack of attentiveness to their riders and possibly of nappiness when the ponies are parted at a later date.

(b) Nappiness is a direct result of the horse's natural urge to stay with the herd, and should be understood as such. If a young horse exhibits signs of being nappy it must be dealt with fairly and firmly with immediate and generous reward for compliance. With confidence will come obedience and then nappiness will disappear, unless it was caused by bad training originally and then the cure will require expert handling and much more time.

4 *Courage*

Although a trained horse is a remarkably courageous creature, by nature he is timorous, suspicious and afraid of the unknown, of sharp or sudden movements or noises, or that which he does not understand. This wariness stems from the primitive need for self-protection or the survival of the species. So the basic natural instinct is not courage, it is FEAR. If a horse is frightened his natural reactions are to run for protection amongst the herd, to gallop away, to kick out with a hindfoot, to rear up and strike with a front foot, or to bite.

In the domesticated horse, the stable becomes the substitute for the herd, and the majority of horses are more free-going when returning to their stable-yard than when going away from it even though they are more tired on the return journey. However, the two strong instincts of herd-membership and fear can combine disastrously if there is a stable-fire, when horses will resolutely refuse to leave the burning building, in fact, they will dash back into it. Pupils should be warned of this and told that a damp sack or jacket, thrown over the horse's head may be the only way to rescue horses from their burning stable. The damped cloth will effectively block the horse's senses of hearing, sight and orientation so that instead he will focus his attention on to his human friend and allow him to lead him to safety.

In a horse, there is only a very short space of time and of occurrence between fear and panic. If a frightened horse is not reassured and calmed he will quickly enter a state of panic wherein he becomes insensitive to feeling, sight and sound. Genuine fear can be conquered by disciplinary measures; the frightened horse must be comforted, soothed and calmed, and then he must be given confidence. Bad or vicious horses are never born that way; if they become so it is always due to a lack of understanding or tact, or to some form of human mismanagement. A horse who trusts his rider is bold, reliable and happy – a wonderful companion.

5 *The Homing instinct*

Horses have a strong homing instinct which probably descends directly from ancient native rules of herd-territories and grazing-rights. The modern, domesticated horse can find his way home even across unfamiliar country. There are many stories of ridden horses who, when left to their own devices, have carried their riders home, through dense fog, swirling mists or even an alcoholic haze! The horse's homing instinct is far stronger than that of Man, who has to rely on landmarks in order to find his way. Man's sense of orientation is far better developed than is his bump of locality.

6 *Pleasure in pleasing*

Although this is not a natural quality for a wild, native pony, horses have been captured, used and worked by man since 2,000 BC so 'an earnest desire to please', may justifiably be called a primitive domesticated instinct, and very important it is too in the training of the horse and to his life in general. Prompt reward for work well done is the surest way of preserving the horse's willingness.

Reward – an impromptu quiz, 'How do you reward your horse or pony?' will wake up and involve the audience, and promote a stirring of thoughts.

The best reward of all for a horse who has done well in his ridden work is for the rider to dismount and give him a tit-bit, whilst 'making much', patting him on his neck and speaking to him with obvious pleasure at his effort. However, such a major demonstration is not always possible, in which case more subtle means are preferable, e.g.
the thought 'well done',
the word, 'Good',
a pat on the neck,
a halt – sustained, 'at ease' for a few minutes,
a halt and a long slice of carrot, a lump of sugar or similar tit-bit, proffered equally from either hand.
The horse should be trained and ridden according to the principle of 'reward

and correction' – a horse should very rarely be punished, for the mistakes he makes are usually due to an error on the human's part. If he does deserve punishment it must be instantaneous.

Footnote It is advisable to explain and demonstrate how to give a horse a pat on the neck and how not to do so, together with the whys and wherefores. The rider should free the patting hand by placing those reins in the other hand, quickly yet smoothly, making no disturbance to the horse's mouth and retaining a light, level contact with it. If the rider is riding with a light seat at the time, or if he wishes to give his horse an added reward of easing his back, he should bend forward slightly in order to pat his horse in the centre of his neck. This is the best spot because the contact of the rider's hand is felt spontaneously by the whole horse, from his brain to his hind-heels, for under the centre of the neck are the cervical vertebrae, the spinal cord which widens at that point, and the central nervous system. Also located there are the initial or subsidiary attachments of the main ligaments and muscles of the horse's forehand, his middle-part, and his hindquarters. Thus a pat will convey congratulations and also will provide a mini-massage, relaxing any excess mental or physical tension.

There is a second good spot for a rider's rewarding pat, this is just in front of the withers. The better the horse's training the more sensitive will he become and the more complex may his work programme be – in which case, the second pat-style will be preferable. In this case the rider pats his horse with his freed hand under the reins, immediately in front of his withers, at the top of the base of his neck on the side opposite to the patting hand. This is an easy place for a rider to reach quickly without disturbing his seat or posture in the least; it is a natural, horse-to-horse caressing place for mare and foal or grown horses nuzzling each other, and the well-developed trapezium muscles of a fit horse whose neck is well set-on will receive and help to transmit the kindly message spontaneously all over the horse's body.

The quality and strength of the pat is important too for it must be 'just right'. If the pat is too soft, superficial and 'tickley' its message is equally superficial – like a limp hand-shake. Alternatively a hearty, hay-wisping thump is too heavy, sharp and alarming to convey a genuine message of, 'Thank you, well done'. A happy medium is the answer. Under no circumstances should the rider cause disturbance to the horse's mind, mouth or back by thoughtlessly rough movements or pats.

Timing is extremely important. Patting should be done whilst the horse is actually performing the work correctly or immediately afterwards – later is too late.

Thus a pat must be thoughtfully given if it is to be of full value, communicating the rider's pleasure directly and meaningfully to the horse's mind and body.

The horse's brain – this is not the small, insignificant, inferior part which it is often said to be before the speaker then dismisses the horse as a creature of little or no intelligence.

The horse's brain weighs about 650 grams (nearly 2 lb), it is approximately 17 cm in length and is made up of a veritable labyrinth of highly complex nerves – literally hundreds of them, the conformation and construction of which take nearly one hundred textbook pages to describe.

To keep the lecture as simple as possible the instructor should explain that

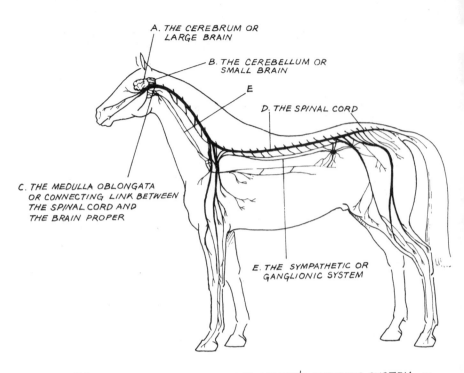

A. THE CEREBRUM OR LARGE BRAIN

B. THE CEREBELLUM OR SMALL BRAIN

E

D. THE SPINAL CORD

C. THE MEDULLA OBLONGATA OR CONNECTING LINK BETWEEN THE SPINAL CORD AND THE BRAIN PROPER

E. THE SYMPATHETIC OR GANGLIONIC SYSTEM

FIG. 84   ~ THE HORSE'S NERVOUS SYSTEM ~

the horse's brain is the horse's communications headquarters from which the whole of his nervous and muscular systems are organized and on which his very life depends.

There are two main physical parts to the nervous system:

The voluntary system – which is dependent on messages to and from the horse's brain, and which is subdivided further:

(a) The sensitive nerves ... receive messages from the body's surface and send them in to the brain.

(b) The motor nerves ... on receipt of a signal from the brain, the motor nerves activate the muscles as directed.

The involuntary system – which consists of sympathetic or para-sympathetic nerves which arouse or diminish excitement respectively.

There are several parts to the psychological aspect of the horse's brain, much of which is due to his built-in receivers.

A horse cannot reason with human logic but he has an astonishingly good and long lasting memory. Riders must realize that bad, awkward or inconsistent riding will teach the horse bad habits in his way of going – for the horse will remember the wrong methods just as well as he will learn the correct ones – he cannot differentiate between the two! He is also amazingly receptive to the mood and the deeper feelings and emotions of the human being attending to or riding him. It is much more possible and far easier to communicate with a horse with a ray of thought than most people appreciate. The voice and the thought together are a very strong influence, but the rider's thought applied with belief and concentration can be extremely powerful on its own, whereas the voice often reinforces and adds finesse to the co-ordination of the rider's physical aids even more than to the mental-bond of communication with his horse.

ESP and telepathy are two subjects which are gaining in substance and recognition, and much exciting research is being made into supersonic bio-rhythms and other similar fields which could well prove to be of great value to the training and the riding of horses as well as in the realms of health and of healing treatments.

The horse's senses

Technically speaking, there are the five faculties by which sensation is received through special bodily organs – they are: sight; hearing; touch; taste and smell. Then there is the sixth sense which enables the horse to receive and transmit ESP, telepathy and other intangible forces. Finally there is the inborn sense of balance which incorporates co-ordination and the proprioceptive sense.

Sight – it is very important that every person working with horses appreciates how dissimilar the horse's vision and sight is to his own. A surprising number of riders and trainers are unaware of these differences and fail to make fair allowances for them.

Whereas the retina in the human's eye has a regular or symmetrical concave shape, the horse's retina is 'ramped', i.e. it is irregularly concave. This is an excellent arrangement when the horse is nearly stationary, grazing, or quietly roaming. He has to regulate his vision in order that the light falls on to the best

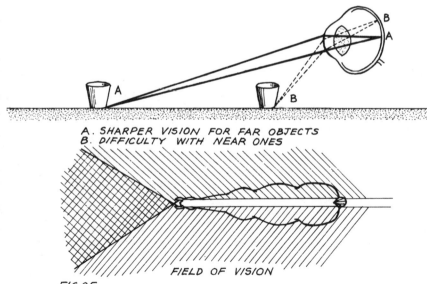

A. SHARPER VISION FOR FAR OBJECTS
B. DIFFICULTY WITH NEAR ONES

FIELD OF VISION

FIG.85

223

part of the retina for the focus required. In order to do this he has to raise, lower or angle his head, rather like an angle-poise reading light, his natural instinct acts as both a built-in light meter and a regulator. This is why the horse must have sufficient freedom of his head to have free vision range when he is carrying his rider over fences or across rough terrain, especially if he is being asked to do so at speed.

The eyes are specially positioned in the horse's head to enable him to see forwards, sideways and even behind him – 'all the better to be aware of predators'. This is a preservation safeguard dating back to when horses were creatures of the plains and the prey of wolves, bears and other hunting carnivores. Native breeds or those with native blood in their ancestry have wider vision than highly bred thoroughbreds who are bred to race *forwards*!

Most veterinary experts seem to feel that horses see only in black and white, that they are colour-blind, but many of our horses have done their best to prove this theory to be incorrect, e.g. when they have spied a rider exercising a horse in the middle or far distance, wearing a bright red anorak the immediate reaction of our horses is one of excitement, 'Can't you see? Hounds are over there – wake *up*!' they seem to say. No other coloured jersey or jacket has the same effect. I remember well show-jumping in the enormous indoor school in Lüneburg when a comparatively small and innocuous yellow wall in the middle of the course eliminated half of the competitors. I wonder what is the scientific answer to practical arguments of that nature.

There are two other important major differences between the workings of the horse's eye and that of the human. Horses' eyes take longer to focus accurately and with sharp distinction, and, once focused on a specific object their vision of their surroundings is dimmed. The horse is unable to see an object on the ground or a fence, after he is within a range of 1·40 metre from it – his close vision is more restricted if he has the added obstruction of a thickly padded sheepskin noseband which was so popular a few years ago. If the horse wishes to look well at something which is within this radius he will have to tilt his head, thereby adjusting his light-meter and regulator and moving his muzzle to the side so that it does not impede his view.

Riders must remember these facts, especially when they are jumping, hence the rule, 'the last three strides belong to the horse.'

Hearing – the horse's sense of hearing is far more acute than man's. He also has far greater mobility of his ears! The horse's thoughts, his sight and his hearing are closely related and co-operate together. His ears can be directed to pick up distant sounds which are too tiny or too high or too low pitched for a human to detect. A secondary advantage to this mobility of the horse's ears is almost more helpful to the human than to the horse, for by watching their movement and positioning the trainer and rider can read much of the horse's thoughts and emotions.

The horse's sense of hearing is better than man's in two other respects; he can distinguish individual sounds, e.g. footsteps, voices, motor-engines with far sharper perception, and he can tell exactly from whence they come. Human ears are especially weak in locating sounds as any instructor will know who has tried to call a pupil at a horse show, only to see them look in every other direction but his!

Mr R. H. Smythe, an Examiner in Surgery to the Royal College of Veterinary Surgeons, 1937–1959, volunteers the possibility that the large air cavities in the horse's skull may amplify sounds which are indiscernible to the human ear, as well as any vibrations which have travelled up the limb bones from the horse's foot on the ground. This made the horse of yore even more aware of his foes and added to the efficiency of his early warning system. The Red Indians used to tune in to these vibration signals when they put an ear to the ground, and the rival tribe bound their horses' hooves with skins to diminish the tell tale concussions. Indeed, in the more subtle ways horses have a superior brand of communication to Man's and they are amazingly good-natured too.

Horses are not particularly fussy about the actual words being used or in which language they are pronounced, but they do understand a great deal from the tone in which the words are spoken; they are extremely receptive and perceptive to the meaning behind the words – in the main, they love being talked to.

Being highly sensitive creatures, horses abhor loud noises, until they are trained to withstand them, for example, the horses of mounted bands, and police horses. By nature they are quiet animals. In the herd the mother calls her foal with a low, comforting whicker, and although the stallion may bellow and shout as he asserts his possession or protection over his herd, this rampaging usually makes the foals dash to their mothers for safety!

Touch – that horses are extremely sensitive in their reactions to being touched is not always recognized, especially by beginner-riders when they are mounted on fat, lazy horses! A wild, untouched pony, straight off the moors will soon prove his acute sensitivity to any disbeliever, who can then be told that the apparent numbness of tamed horses is invariably due to human behaviour. Bad, uneducated riding is the most usual cause of insensitivity, or incorrect training with riders constantly banging the horse's sides with their lower legs, or horses may be spoilt by lack of fair discipline.

A small fly, a midge or even a strand of gossamer can drive a thin-skinned horse almost to desperation, and yet the same horse can also 'switch-off' his sense of feel when he panics with fear or temper. This latter reaction is more of a psychological than a physical happening, caused by rough or tactless human handling.

The sense of touch and of feel amongst equines is acute and has many facets. It is natural for a horse to enjoy being touched in a friendly manner, for from his early foal-days his mother has nuzzled, pushed, rebuffed or nudged him, and when running free he is always delighted to find a partner for a mutual back-scratching session. Thus a firm but soft touch is an important quality for any trainer to possess, for it will convey gentleness, calm and confidence to the young horse.

The contact of his rider's or trainer's hand on his neck or shoulder always has a marvellously soothing effect on a frightened horse, and his understanding of a rewarding pat in the same area has already been discussed. When first making acquaintance with a horse this is the ideal, 'How do you do?' area; if the horse is a stranger, or is shy or wild then a soothing rubbing with the tips of the fingers on his neck, shoulders or central ribs will be accepted as friendly communication and will soon be enjoyed.

225

Human contact and touch on a horse can be a wonderful form of communication providing that it is made with sufficient thought and judgment, well measured and mixed with the less tangible sort of feeling – one that conveys meaning, a bond of sympathy, patient understanding, calm and confidence or a *giving* sensation. The quality and sincerity of the touch is translated immediately and very accurately by the horse; he will use it as a barometer of his handler's character and his mood, as well as receiving kind, moral support from him, if it is given.

Taste – this sense is highly developed in the equine species; in his former wild state its effectiveness was a matter of life or death to the horse, for he relied on its information as to whether food was good, poor, stale or dangerously poisonous. All horse-owners will know how extremely efficient are the horse's taste-buds when they have gone to a great length to disguise medicines for the horse's benefit, only to have the first mouthful of the painstakingly prepared feed scattered around in frenzied spitting and the remainder of the meal ignored. Most horses will avoid eating ragwort but for some unaccountable reason they do not seem to receive the same warning from yew-trees – perhaps the yew family has gained in subtlety over the centuries. Whatever the cause all poisonous plants should be treated as obnoxious enemies; they should be destroyed by pulling them up by the roots and burning them in an incinerator.

Smell – the sense of smell is closely related to that of taste in horses, as it is in man. We lose our ability to taste when we suffer from a severe head-cold which blocks our noses so that we can neither smell nor taste, and often we lose our appetite in consequence.

The horse has a comparatively wide range by which to gauge smells and scents, particularly those of food, water, friend or foe, or fear in other living beings. The horse's muzzle is generous and his nostrils can be extended and flared ... 'all the better to smell with' – the long nasal chambers contain innumerable, highly sensitive smell-buds, and they are also an important part of the horse's respiratory system.

This system of warning and discernment by a sense of smell was an essential herd-survival factor, many centuries ago. It remains as acute and sensitive today and human beings must be extremely careful not to upset or injure any part of its workings with too strong medicaments.

The last two senses are:

'The sixth sense', as it has been referred to with belief or disbelief over the centuries. The sixth sense refers to extra sensory perception or ESP, telepathy and other strong but subtle forces still being explored in the world of radionics. Although for many years the acceptance of a sixth sense was strongly resisted, much progress has been made and its importance as well as its existence is now appreciated as far as modern experts have been able to research and prove to date.

Balance – the horse's sense of balance is instinctive but it is given many additional tests, trials and difficulties when the horse is burdened by the weight of the rider. For this reason the rider must ride at all times with thought and consideration; he must be a helpfully leading partner, and never an awkward, restrictive or unbalancing burden.

The horse's balance-system is an extremely and marvellously intricate part of the horse's nervous system, and it works in co-operation with the closely allied sense of co-ordination and the proprioceptive sense.

From the rider's point of view he must realize that the often repeated phrase, 'the horse uses his head and neck as a balancing pole' is absolutely true and that it is only a part of the whole intricate picture.

The governing cells of the horse's balance are situated in the rear portion of his brain. Certain cells (the cristae) record the movement of the head and others (the maculae) record the position of the head. They combine with gravity-power to fire the neuropitheleal cells which are surprisingly slow to adapt. Any tilting or restriction on the horse's head changes the firing pattern of these cells. This is a scientific fact and gives a sound reason for allowing young horses to have freedom of their heads and necks, especially when they are learning to balance themselves in new work on the lunge and under the rider's weight, both on the flat and over fences.

The proprioceptive sense might be said to put the finishing touch to co-ordination. Just as it enables humans to go up and downstairs without looking at or counting the steps, so it makes it possible for the horse to manoeuvre his hind feet even though he cannot actually see at the time what they are having to negotiate, for he is already busily working things out which are well ahead of himself. The horse's hind limbs are cleverly and accurately organized by all the relative muscles and nerves as a direct result of instant messages from the proprioceptive senses which are received and transmitted through the horse's brain. Safe co-ordination depends on this vital and delicate mechanism.

The proprioceptive sense's control centre is housed in the horse's inner ear, just within the bony structure of the skull – a good enough practical reason, if such were required, to condemn striking a horse about the head, or putting a twitch on to his ear.

The myriad living parts which combine to form the horse's balance can only function with 100 per cent of efficiency if:

There is no impeding excess tension in the horse's mind or body.

There is no restriction to his need to use his head and neck freely (in this respect, he will need more freedom of movement in the early stages of his training than in the later stages when he has learned to carry himself and his rider with gymnastic poise).

The rider is well educated, sits with ease in a correct and balanced position, leads his partner into new directions and movements with his thought and weight aids and rides thoughtfully being constantly aware of being in complete harmony with his horse.

The horse is given plenty of time to realize there is going to be a change of gait or direction and to reorganize himself accordingly. The bigger, younger and less trained he is, the longer this time-lag will have to be.

Riders must *think* and feel, and *feel* and think.

The horse's sign-language

Instructors should be especially aware of helpful voluntary demonstrations of the signals by means of which the horse reveals his feelings, moods and intentions. These will be given freely by the horses involved in lectures on stable management, riding and training, and instructors should point them out, and teach their meanings to their pupils.

Although the basic sign-language of horses is simple, there are many variations of each part which can only be fully analysed, and appreciated after considerable experience in working with horses. However, if pupils are not taught the basic good and bad tempered signals in their early lessons and lectures the instructor will have failed in his duty to teach them important rules of safety, and many opportunities for observing and translating these signals will have been wasted.

The most obvious signals are those given by the horse's voice and his breathing, his eyes, his ears, his legs, his tail, and his general attitude. The latter will also often reveal his state of health – whether he is feeling well or off-colour.

If the instructor offers a small token prize such as a rosette and an extra lesson for the best written paper on the horse's sign-language this will spur pupils on into making keen and detailed observations, and the best paper will provide an interesting lecture.

The subject is most easily started with a mare and foal lecture as the foal will usually provide many vivid and varied signals, from the tooth-showing pre-suckling foal-face made with a head outstretched, subservient posture as if to say, 'I am only very little, please may I be your friend?' to clear signs of *joie de vivre* which involve his whole being from his bright eyes and his whiskery muzzle to his twinkling hooves and his fuzzy mane and twizzling tail!

The horse uses the whole of his body to express his thoughts, moods and emotions to his human and equine friends, and also to those he dislikes or distrusts – his enemies or rivals. His whole physical attitude reflects his mental attitude and his facial features reveal his emotions.

The horse's eyes will mirror his thoughts, feelings and opinions.

When he is resting, at peace with the world – his eyes are not fully wide open and they may appear to be a little misty.

When he is hungry and food is around – his eyes are extra-bright and very wide open.

When he is scared or afraid – he will often show the whites of his eyes; if he is very afraid they will convey blind panic.

When he is angry or jealous – he will look 'real mean', probably showing the whites of his eyes.

NOTE Some horses' eyes are so shaped that they look as if they are rolling their eyes viciously, showing the whites of their eyes, due to nervousness or temper, when in fact, this is the eye's normal appearance – it is made that way. A horse may be born with a 'white ring' showing in one or in both eyes, this is a matter of conformation and not of temperament.

The above are a few easy signs which may be read; the horse's eye may portray nervousness, perplexity, or contrary thoughts and many others besides.

The horse's ears point to where he is listening; to where he is thinking or communicating, and they give away his thoughts:

When he is expectant of something pleasant – his ears are pricked forward.

When he is relaxed or happy in his work – his ears will be quietly in 'neutral'

228

FEAR

HATE

FIG. 86

HAPPY & FRIENDLY

nearly forward and nearly back, if there is no constraint and he is working under his rider, the horse will seem to add 'I am aware; I am happy and I do hope I am pleasing you'.

When the horse is nervous, confused or perplexed – his ears will be more tense in their mobility, turning forwards and backwards individually; he may be concentrating on demanding work or this may indicate that he needs reassurance and sympathy.

Panic and flight – are very close when the horse's ears appear to have an electric tension forwards – his attentiveness to his rider will decrease rapidly unless the panic is parried.

Discomfort, distrust, resentment – are shown by the ears being slanted backwards.

Dislike, anger and jealousy – are all indicated by the ears being flattened back against the horse's neck. In extreme cases it can be dangerous for the handler to show the slightest sign himself of hesitancy or fear.

The horse's muzzle, his *nostrils*, *mouth* and *chin*, can be very expressive. When he is curious, the rootlings of a horse's top lip seem to develop the strength and mobility of an underdeveloped elephant's trunk! Horses will always greet each other nose to nose, and this means of calming and communicating with young and frightened horses has been used by man for many, many years. Those who were near to Nature such as the Red Indians and the Romany gypsies often used the taming method of breathing into the nostrils of a wild or 'rogue' horse, thereby striking up a strong rapport and gaining his trust. Horse-whisperers they were called, and fascinating they were to watch. When I was a small child I never could make out what worked the Romany spell, the strong tobacco chewed first, the breathing or the kind but very strong will. .... 'How do you do?' 'Who are you and what is that?'

Worry, anxiety, annoyance or excess tension – when the horse is worked this may be shown by a grinding of his teeth. The instructor and the rider must find out which is the true cause; if a worried or anxious horse is reprimanded it will only magnify the fault. It is best ignored, then as his confidence improves, the habit will disappear.

The horse's tail – hangs down, relaxed when he is peacefully at rest in the stable. If it hangs down when he is being ridden the horse is not yet moving in balance and with sufficient impulsion – he should carry himself, his rider and his tail. The horse will usually carry his tail when he is aroused, and when he is in excessively high spirits he will carry it *very* high as he prances and passages around – showing off! If he is about to buck he will usually tuck his tail down strongly and hump his back. In the stable a twitching or swishing tail will often indicate stomach-pain and colic. If he is being ridden it may be a warning for a kick, or it could be a sign of discomfort.

The horse's legs and feet – will amplify several of the horse's feelings:

If he is comfortable and contented – he will be quiet and still; he may rest one of his hindlegs, very occasionally he may also rest the diagonally opposite foreleg, pointing it lightly a short way in front of him.

If he is ill-at-ease or leg weary – he will be restless, constantly shifting his weight from one foot to another.

If he is angry – he will readjust his equilibrium and the weight on his feet as a pre-warning that he has freed a foot ready for a defensive, or an attacking kick.

The horse's foreleg – can be a painfully powerful weapon or dangerous form of play. Pupils must be warned of this and also told never to bend down with their head in front of a horse's knee or, if the horse picks up his front foot he will accomplish a knock-out, for the force behind an uplifted foreleg is considerable, even though the blow is quite unintentional.

The language of the horse's *hindleg* can be taught in stable management lectures. For instance, the following movements and 'translations' can usually be demonstrated:

Hindlegs standing square, supporting the horse's weight or in the resting position:

lifted slowly, 'Do you want to pick out my foot?' or 'Why should you feel my leg?' or 'I might – just might KICK.'

lifted quickly, 'Damn that fly', or other irritant – 'Get off my leg!' or 'Get out! – and stay out!'

held just above the resting position – 'Ouch! poor me, that heel, foot, joint or back tendon is sore.' – or 'My back hurts.'

in resting position, 'Peace – at last!' 'I'm relaxed – you're a friend.'

From one or two examples such as these, and the ear-signals already mentioned on p. 227, pupils will quickly progress to noticing and translating the horse's sign-language for themselves which will add considerably to their efficiency and their enjoyment of all their work with horses.

An example of an emotion which is easily read, because the whole horse's being is united in chorus to proclaim the message, is:

FEAR – when the horse is frightened his eyes and ears will be straining, the former as though popping out of his head and the latter as if trying to meet at the tips. His nostrils will be flared, possibly showing the pink lining within them, and his breathing will be heavier and much more accentuated than usual as he tries to catch and interpret the scent of that which has aroused his fear. The whole horse is involved from his outermost hairs to his innermost spirit and he appears to grow in stature as he tenses up ready for fight or flight.

Fear is one of the most obvious emotions to discern, it is rather like one short sentence at the bottom of a picture-page of a human toddler's 'Easy reading book'. Pupils must be encouraged to study the horse in depth so that they can understand his language even during his most complex conversations. Thoughtful, patient and sympathetic concentration on how the horse ticks physiologically and psychologically and on self-correction – 'Can he understand me?', 'Am I sitting in the best poise and balance for him to be able to carry me with ease?' 'Are my aids soft and smooth, kind, helpful and non-disturbing?' 'Is his contentment, health and performance improving as he works with me?'

These are some of the thoughts which should be foremost and constant in every horseman's mind and actions; he should train himself to think of others before himself. Surely this is why riding is the finest sport for developing a nation's character?

In conclusion, while it is not suggested that any one lecture should contain all the facts given in this chapter, they should be 'fed' to pupils in small but regular doses. By knowing and understanding these important but often unconsidered aspects of the horse's nature and psychology, the members of the audience and of the school will be encouraged to treat, care for and work their horses with a greater understanding. Thus in turn, they will reap rich moral and economic rewards.

Most schools have an equine personality who has become a trusted and valuable member of the establishment's family because formerly he was 'untrainable', 'unrideable', a criminal or a lunatic. If this character is used for the final scene this will make the best possible impact on the audience for if he is seen to work willingly and well to a high standard he will prove all the points which have been taught and will justify the lectures more impressively than any concluding speech could hope to do.

19 Basic physiological studies

Most novice riders, and indeed many student-instructors, tend to think of a horse as a mobile pram with four legs replacing the four wheels, and unless they are taught about the physiology of the horse there would be no reason for them to think any differently. Unfortunately many instructors shy off this subject themselves, thinking it to be a specialist topic, the mystiques of which only a veterinary surgeon can explain – and veterinary surgeons are very important personages and far too busy to be expected to lecture to groups of young riders, or even to budding instructors too often.

In a way, this viewpoint is justified. The expert is not needed for the introductory work; it is far better if the instructor teaches this to his pupils in as practical a manner as possible. Unless the pupil is a classical scholar too many of the formally correct names of bones, tendons, muscles and so on, repeated in quick succession, will cause a mental 'nap' in most riding pupils' minds, and they will be turned off the subject for ever more.

As with all teaching, the chief instructor must learn the subject himself, making sure that his own knowledge is correct. He must understand it thoroughly so that he can translate the facts into everyday language and then deal them out with his instructors to students and pupils, little by little, awakening their interest and their curiosity, and encouraging their researches.

The dictionary defines physiology as 'the science of the normal functions and phenomena of living things'; – it further defines a phenomena as – 'a wonder' – and surely that is a very apt description of the physiology of the horse?

There are countless, beautifully illustrated books which describe the various systems which enable a horse to eat, breathe, and move, but all of them will mean very little to a student or pupil unless the instructors lead the way. This is a fascinating subject – where to start?

In early lessons, when pupils are watching a horse or pony while he eats, the instructor can tell them that a horse has forty teeth (unless the horse is a mare when she only has thirty-six – which sounds like an Irish story, smacking of sex discrimination!). They should be shown the horse's teeth together with the safe areas for human fingers, within the horse's mouth. As they look at the teeth the instructor can warn them never to take liberties with the front end of strange horses. Pupils should be shown how delicate are the bars of the mouth which is why they must never exert rough or excessive pressure on the bit, and must be particularly kind and careful when taking off the bridle. They can be told that later they will learn how to age a horse by checking the appearance of his teeth.

This is just one example of how the subject of physiology can be introduced with the earliest lessons. Instructors should be encouraged to think up other similar short practical lectures which will bring about further advancement to the pupils' studies of horsemastership as well as those of equitation.

Teaching an eye for and an understanding of a horse's form when it is correct and he is on the bit, should be introduced little by little as soon as the pupils are capable of sitting well and in balance on their horses, at all three basic gaits both in the school and out in undulating country. Providing that the pupils are also proficient and smooth in the application of their aids for school figures and progressive transitions the time has come for their instructors to lead them to observing, assessing, thinking about and feeling *how* their horses move – their manner of moving.

This is a vital step in a horseman's education; it is also one which, probably due to its obscurity and the difficulty of explaining feelings, is often postponed until too late or it is even omitted altogether.

The chief instructor should designate a time and date for a lecture-demonstration on this subject, which he himself will give, with compulsory attendance for staff and pupils. This provides an excellent opportunity for strengthening the school's team spirit and ensuring unity of doctrine and understanding.

For demonstration purposes, the chief instructor should select four to six horses of similar size but of varying conformation with regard to their backs, e.g. a well-muscled back, and one which is muscularly weak, with a prominent back-bone; a short back, a long back and a dipped or sway back.

Most of the equestrian experts through the ages have likened a horse's back to a bridge; this simile can be further developed by imagining three different bridge designs and relating them to horses:

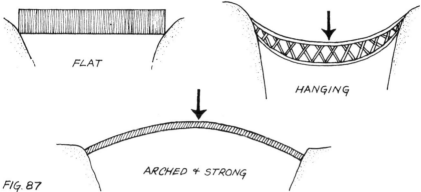

~ THE MECHANICS OF THE HORSE'S BACK

FLAT

HANGING

ARCHED & STRONG

FIG. 87

   i A flat bridge – a horse walking on his own across a field, or when ridden on loose reins with a light rider on his back.

   ii An unstable, hanging rope bridge – a horse who has a dipped or sway back due to his having had too heavy a weight on his back for his size, age and fitness, or as a result of incorrect training and bad riding, i.e. 'All hands and no seat and legs' – restricting the horse's natural movements, and changing his shape to a shortened top line and a hollowed back.

   iii A suspension bridge – a miracle of man's engineering skill – a well-trained horse whose musculature has been developed and strengthened by correct training, so that he has a long, strong and rounded top line.

The chief instructor should demonstrate how the rider's horsemanship (or lack of it!) will affect the way the horse carries himself and moves, and eventually, how his conformation will be affected and considerable changes wrought. Photographs taken 'before' and 'after' provide excellent substantiating evidence for this part of the lecture.

It should then be explained that the pupils have reached a most important stage in their education. Henceforth they will be using their rein-aids thoughtfully, smoothly and softly to support their other aids, and they will learn to ride their horses between leg and hand, 'on the bit'.

At this point the chief instructor can call out one of his instructing team to explain to the audience exactly what is meant by the term 'On the bit' – see page 139. This gives the audience a refreshing change of voice, and ensures that his team has learned the work and is on the bit!

It must then be explained that it is not possible for riders to execute half-halts or even the easiest school-movements, e.g. turns on the forehand or leg-yielding as correctly ridden gymnastic exercises for the horse unless they know something of the horse's mental and physical make-up. They must have at least a basic understanding of how he moves, and how he can be helped to move in better balance and activity, and yet economically with regard to expended effort, and with an increasingly majestic presence.

This knowledge must be offered in as attractive a manner as possible.

Three of the best ways for an equestrian lecturer to capture his audience are:

1 To give his lecture in story-form.

2 To use an attractive horse for his demonstration.

3 To produce proven facts to back up his theories.

All pupils enjoy being involved in making new discoveries – as did the explorers of ancient times, but equally readily will they turn away from a monotonously dry, 'bookish' list of Latin names. Before embarking on a string of high-faluting names for deep-seated muscles, I would like to recount a chain of events which has occurred over the years at Talland, providing us with a fascinating saga which can be amply illustrated on any available horse. In the simplest yet most effective way possible, the horse will prove the story and the conclusions to be drawn from it before the pupil-audience's very eyes. The student-instructors and pupils will then be anxious to search for further knowledge for themselves and all that remains is for the instructor to advise them with regard to the best technical books for their study.

Our story began in 1962 when Major Boltenstern came to run his first Official Dressage Course for the British Horse Society at Talland. To our uninitiated eyes he seemed to do several strange exercises with our horses, and he showed politely veiled disapproval of many of our long-established methods. However, there is no point in going on a course unless the participant is prepared to listen to the expert – especially if that expert has proved himself as an instructor of world renown in all the equestrian disciplines, by his performance-record at the Olympic Games and other international competitions, and by being acclaimed as an outstanding horseman by judges and rival competitors alike. Clearly there was nothing to be gained by closing one's eyes and registering disapproval to that which was new – better, by far, to open both eyes and ears wide, to write notes and draw diagrams, to give all the new work a chance. Positive thinking always reaps great rewards.

One of the exercises which seemed at first to be very peculiar was one where Major B., as he has since become 'labelled', worked the horse quietly in hand in a kind of mobile turn on the forehand, with a few steps of leg-yielding added at intervals, both movements being used to complement each other to remove any constraint and to loosen the horse, rather as a runner jogs, aimlessly-for-a-purpose in a tracksuit to warm up before the work-out or the race.

Briefly the aids for this work are:

1 Thought – of course. Working kindly with the horse's mind, so that he would never be asked too much or too hard but that he was quietly encouraged to have confidence to do good steps compliantly, just as his trainer wished.

2 Forward-driving aids – the trainer's thought, presence and movement urging the horse forward, with an occasional tongue-click added if necessary, but only arousing enough impulsion to make the horse accomplish the exercise, for surplus impulsion would necessitate the use of unnecessary restraint. The whip was also forward-driving in its influence (see 4 below). At all times the trainer moved well with the horse.

3 Restraining aids – the trainer's hand on the inner rein was always

234

extremely tactful, being light, soft and smooth in its action. His voice was often used to slow the horse, to reassure him, and to praise good work.

4 The schooling whip – the butt-end of the whip was applied with a soft or a firm pressure, exactly as required, on the horse's side just in front of the girth and approximately 20 cm above his elbow. On sensitive horses the butt end of the whip was practically hidden inside the trainer's hand, for the pressure of his knuckles had a softer feel which was sufficient for the purpose.

Occasionally the whip-hand was turned and the tip of the whip was used with a quick, light tap just behind the horse's stifle-joint, to encourage the horse to use his hocks more actively.

The effect of the whip used in this way was to move the horse both forwards and sideways, and it was supported by all the other aids.

5 The rein-aids – these were partially supporting to the whip-hand's aid and partially guiding, with a fractional degree of restraint when required. On the small circle the trainer's hand would lead the horse forward and downward without exerting any pressure. To increase the circle with a few steps laterally, the hand was moved smoothly in that direction under an imaginary vertical line from the horse's poll, down, below his lower jaw.

I had to admit that the result to be seen, and to feel when riding the horse afterwards was always one of remarkable improvement, and all the horses working with the trainer made a lovely picture to watch, but why on earth it worked with such a fantastic loosening effect I just could not figure out. Therefore I did not manage to carry it out very well in my early attempts. This in itself provided a challenge for me – I *should* be able to do this seemingly simple work – I resolved that I must find out why and how it worked and wherein lay its magic.

It was subsequent research into what was the full meaning of a horse having a good 'form', why the turn on the forehand and leg-yielding exercises when executed correctly did have the excellent effects which were claimed for them that I began to understand the true value of what our family nicknamed, 'Uncle Gosta's little folk-dance'. It worked and developed the horse's mind and his musculature in the correct way, it helped him to move himself in an even better way, without the impediment of the rider-burden on his back; it improved his top-line, slowly but very surely. All our horses became living proofs of the success of the work. It was particularly beneficial to those whom Nature had not endowed with the best of necks, loins or haunches – all these weaknesses were overcome and the horses turned from ugly geese into much more beautiful swans. (Apologies to Hans Christian Andersen!)

At about this time I met Mr MacTimoney, the famous British chiropractic who was as successful with animals as he was with humans. Talland became a centre for his clinics and I found the work fascinating. He also ran a 'box' for cases whose vertebrae he could not reach to treat manually, and here again he had considerable successes. Working with Mr MacTimoney made me want to increase my knowledge of the horse's anatomy so that I did not rely merely on touch, instinct and feel, but most of all I was urged on by the challenge of a vacuum of knowledge about 'Major B.'s exercises'.

It was then that I realized that the generally accepted standard of education concerning the horse's psychology and physiology was very sparse, and that wider horizons in this sphere could do nothing but good to instructors, riders and to the horses themselves. I searched the military and civilian manuals and hand-books in vain. They contained admirable drawings of horses accurately labelled, to teach the reader the external points of the horse, and defined bones, tendons, ligaments and muscles. Easily read veterinary books written for the layman horse-owner did much the same, with additional plates of ghastly diseases, deformities, ailments and injuries, some of which were nearly enough

FIG. 88   THE MAGIC SPOT! — AND ITS EFFECTS

to put the reader right off buying a horse – ever! It was not until I was kindly lent some technical textbooks by a young, practising veterinary surgeon that I found out more about the *why* and the *how* that I wanted so desperately to solve.

From these veterinary textbooks I sketched some diagrams for my own use. I did not realize then how much interest they would arouse amongst instructors and riders at home at Talland and when teaching abroad.

To return to the physiological saga – the next chapter started with an accident, when a bossy horse delivered a mighty kick backwards on to the knee of a top-class thoroughbred 4 year old. He must have been caught unawares grazing in the field when 'all his elastics were loose', and he was as relaxed as he

236

could be without actually falling down (minimum tension). As well as suffering a very sore, stiff and swollen knee, when viewed from behind he looked like a fishing boat in a sandy Cornish harbour at low-tide – he had a distinct list to starboard – his pelvis was well and truly *out*.

Twice another chiropractic and his assistant did their best to readjust the bones and set the horse right. They nearly succeeded, but not quite, and there is seemed that the matter (and the bones) would have to rest.

Then on a memorable day, we all went to Badminton 'to ride for the Queen' in the special horseman's celebration of Her Majesty's Silver Jubilee. We had ridden past the Duke of Beaufort, the Queen's Master of the Horse, in front of that house so full of wonderful, ancient and live memories – hounds and horses and horsemen and women of every walk of life had come to pay tribute – the band played, the horses bucked and all were full of festive spirit; some saddles were emptied and quickly refilled; the turf felt and smelt glorious and the park looked serenely magnificent. We all felt our privilege at having been invited to participate and then, quite soon at the end of a thrilling afternoon, it was time to cool off and go home.

As I was grazing my young horse, prior to putting him up in the horse box, I heard someone tell my husband that he was just back from Hickstead where he had been attending to horses' backs for one of the visiting foreign teams. I immediately pricked up my ears and, wanting to hear more, I asked Pammy to hold my horse while I investigated further. 'How do you do backs?' I asked. 'In my plimsoles.' 'Oh, yes' I said, hoping that my astonishment was not too obvious. I gathered that he had been a very successful steeplechase jockey, and he further explained that he had come from a long line of bone-setters. He had found that he was able to help horses as well as humans, especially those with bad backs. 'Are you able to replace a horse's pelvis?' I asked. 'Oh, yes,' he said with a nice mixture of optimism and humble confidence. Whereupon we agreed that I should telephone him to fix an appointment for him to come to Talland during the following week.

Sure enough, when he walked into the yard, Mr Taffy Jenkin's feet were clad in plimsoles. When he climbed up on to and along the rafters inside the stable, above the young horse my heart was in my mouth for his safety. 'He *is* only four and he is a very sensitive thoroughbred, you will be careful, won't you?'

After weighing up the horse's problem from a bird's-eye view, he waited until the young horse had accepted his presence and was standing in exactly the right position before he sprang lightly and very deftly on to his back and with footwork and choreography worthy of any ballet-star he used the play of the horse's muscles and his own weight to realign the horse's pelvic girdle. It was fascinating to watch.

As luck would have it, Major Boltenstern had just arrived to start a 2-week course-cum-holiday with us and was watching these manoeuvres and manipulations with great interest. We took the young horse outside the stable, to check the result at walk and trot and at the halt. All seemed absolutely straight and level, then Mr Jenkins asked me to put my hand on top of the horse's loins as he stood still, to check his reactions. He then poked the horse quite firmly in the very spot where Major B. pressed with the butt-end of the whip or his knuckles for his 'folk-dancing' exercise. Certainly I could feel the reaction – every time Mr Jenkins poked the horse above his elbow, his loins sprang up. It was *most* intriguing and I asked Mr Jenkins why there was this marked reaction. He explained that the horse has a very superficial nerve just where he was pressing, and that it could spark off a spontaneous signal to the muscles under the lumbar vertebrae so that they arched and stretched those above the spine. 'There is also another connection with the muscles, which bring the hind leg on the same side forward,' he added. This was a most exciting discovery – rather like finding three of the last six pieces of a perplexing jigsaw puzzle.

Shortly after Major B.'s course had finished, I went to give a course-cum-holiday myself in one of my favourite spots, the lovely island of Bermuda. After 3 days of pure holiday, my first pupil, at 8.30 a.m. was Mr Paddy Heslop, a veterinary surgeon with a lovely thoroughbred horse called 'Pal'. 'Paddy, while you are quitting and crossing your stirrups, will you please tell me if there is a nerve just in front of the girth which is sensitive, which affects the muscles in the lumbar region and also those of the hindleg on the same side?' 'Oh, yes, the intercostal nerve does just that for it is very near to the surface about a foot above the elbow and it will effect immediate reactions, just as you described.' This confirmed what Mr Jenkins had told me and added one more piece to the puzzle – the name.

I confirmed all these facts with Mr Stuart Hastie MRCVS when he gave an interesting and highly informative talk to owners of British Horse Society Riding Schools at the National Equestrian Centre, later that year, and he added one more puzzle-piece as there is yet another muscle which has a spontaneous reaction from the main intercostal nerve, the obliquus abdominis externus, or external abdominal muscle, which together with the abdominal tunic plays a most important role in raising the horse's rib-cage – lifting up his middle.

On the stage with Mr Hastie at that time was a skeleton of a horse – how frail it looked without its furbishings of muscles, tissues and skin – no wonder the horse often finds man an unwieldy burden when he sits askew or bangs about on his back. The skeleton was standing facing the audience, and at that angle the shoulders look quite unattached, for the horse has no collar-bone, only muscles bind the shoulders in place. I was reminded of Major Boltenstern's oft-repeated instruction that riders should attach far more importance to loosening their horse's shoulders to give the horses room to move freely with the desired impulsion from behind, and that there was no point in creating impulsion if there was no where for it to go! I resolved then to add to my sketches to illustrate the main points of the horse's complex anatomical features, which I could use to show young instructors how the rider can effect and improve the horse's physique and movement. See Figs. 89–90. There are a few Latin names but only the most important ones which are relevant to their present interest in this work. If student-instructors learn these major structures then they will only need a small nudge to do further research in more detailed veterinary textbooks to increase the depth of knowledge for themselves.

Although we had been using half-halts, turns on the forehand and leg-yielding for many years, we did so mainly because we were told they were good exercises. That half-halts rebalanced our horses we did understand, and that the two latter exercises made our horses obedient to the leg was undeniable. So far so good, but several critics will say, 'Why does the FEI claim that those

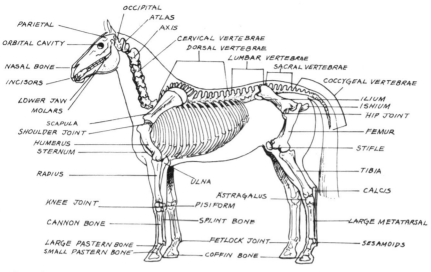

PARIETAL
ORBITAL CAVITY
NASAL BONE
INCISORS
LOWER JAW
MOLARS
SCAPULA
SHOULDER JOINT
HUMERUS
STERNUM
RADIUS
KNEE JOINT
CANNON BONE
LARGE PASTERN BONE
SMALL PASTERN BONE

OCCIPITAL
ATLAS
AXIS
CERVICAL VERTEBRAE
DORSAL VERTEBRAE
LUMBAR VERTEBRAE
SACRAL VERTEBRAE
COCCYGEAL VERTEBRAE
ILIUM
ISHIUM
HIP JOINT
FEMUR
STIFLE
TIBIA
CALCIS
ASTRAGALUS
PISIFORM
SPLINT BONE
LARGE METATARSAL
ULNA
FETLOCK JOINT
SESAMOIDS
COFFIN BONE

FIG. 89   ~   THE HORSE'S SKELETON   ~

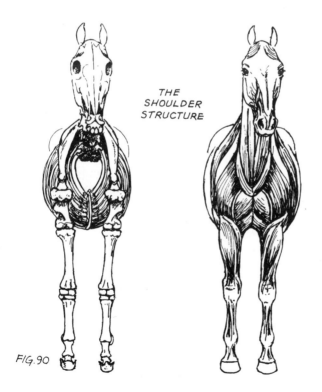

THE
SHOULDER
STRUCTURE

FIG. 90

239

exercises 'remove constraint'? Again, undeniably constraint is removed – and these exercises work miraculously in this respect for all high-mettled horses of whatever standard their training may be; they are calmed down by them and their gaits improve – but *Why?* and *How?*

To the more discerning instructors and riders it becomes quite obvious that horses have to arch their backs in order to cross the inside hind leg over in front of the outside hind leg. That these exercises involve much deeper and extensive muscle-work is not at all obvious until the veterinary experts are consulted and their textbooks studied, then, and only then, does the last piece of the jig-saw puzzle slip into place with almost maddening clarity.

The reasoned answer is twofold. First, as the exercises are so simple and easy they are usually well executed which makes the rider calm and contented, and his partner the horse, feels happy that his rider is so pleased with him. Secondly, although the exercises are simple they utilize all the main muscles throughout the horse's whole body; these muscles are all stretched, suppled and worked so that a sense of well-being pervades his whole being. Thus it is plain for all to see and to understand that mental and physical constraint is removed, easily and effectively by these basic school movements.

The fact that the important gymnastic working of the deeper muscles of the horse's shoulders, back, lower line and the hindleg on the same side can be 'triggered off' by a certain pressure on the intercostal nerve provides the reasons for the success of several actions which hitherto we have either taken for granted, misunderstood or ignored.

M. de la Gueriniere directed that the rider's lower leg should be on the girth with his spurs touching the horse's sides a hand's breadth, no more, behind the girth. It seemed strange, to the point of contradiction, that M. de la Gueriniere, who wore long necked spurs and trained horses up to high school work, should use his legs comparatively so far forward. Yet all his horses showed true collection of a very advanced standard, and he was most insistent that aids must be invisible, which makes it unlikely that he would countenance riders swinging their legs back and forth. He must have had a feeling for the intercostal nerve even if he did not know its name or its exact whereabouts.

Discovering the significance of the intercostal nerve also justifies the Swedish cavalry directive, 'The rider's lower legs should be used on the girth, just behind it, or sometimes in front of the girth to improve the quality of the strides.' Certainly the girth area is far more sensitive and deeply effective to the musculature of the horse's shoulders, middle-part and haunches than that farther back on the ribs where the nerves are well protected and concealed by layers of flesh and muscle, and where there are no major muscle 'terminals' as there are in the girth area.

Since making all these discoveries I have been able to teach riders and horses how to carry out half-halts, turns on the forehand and leg-yielding with utmost conviction and therefore with better effect than ever before because I have resolved the why and how of this work from the psychological and the physiological viewpoint. This has clarified comprehension and put the seal on perfecting the work, so that even the most difficult and 'dangerous' problem horses have been corrected with astonishing ease and a miraculous transformation to their demeanour and to their conformation.

Pupils can get a feel for the work and can carry it out for themselves at a

M. de Pluvinel.

"Behold ~ the Magic Spot !"

Louis XIII aged 16 years, and his courtiers.

91.

(With apologies to M. Crispian de Passe.) P.I.S.

comparatively early stage of their riding career, providing that their instructors know enough themselves to be able to explain and demonstrate the mechanics of the work and its effects.

The sketches shown as Figs. 88–90 can be used to clarify the instructor's explanation either in book-form, as they are, or as the central part of a lecture where they may be enlarged and shown on a screen by means of an epidiascope.

It was when I was browsing through M. Antoine Pluvinel's book, 'Le Maneige Royal', written in 1623 as a dialogue between Louis XIII of France and himself, that I came across a plate which seemed heaven-sent as a *pièce de résistance* with which to finish my 'Physiological Saga'. In this scene M. Pluvinel is depicted teaching the King the very same 'magic spot' which Major Boltenstern has been emphasizing to us for so many years. The plate's caption could well read:

'Behold the intercostal nerve – use this knowledge to good effect!'

20 Mounting and dismounting

Instructors will find it best to use one horse to each pair of pupils, for all of them should be taught how to assist a rider when he mounts, as well as learning how to mount and to dismount.

241

To assist a rider to mount requires a courteous approach as well as an efficient technique, and both aspects must be carefully taught. Pupils should be prompt to offer to help each other and anyone else who is about to mount a horse. Too often assistants seem neglectful, walking off without a backward glance as soon as they have handed the horse's reins to the prospective rider; this is usually due to lack of education rather than to lack of co-operation or good manners.

When assisting, pupils should be taught how to check that the saddle is well placed, behind the horse's shoulder-blade, how to pull each foreleg forward, to stretch out any wrinkles which might have formed under the girth, thereby avoiding the risk of girth-galls. They should be shown how to help with all the preparations until the rider is ready to mount, whereupon the assistant takes up a position on the far side of the horse and facing the point of his shoulder, and sets the stirrup iron so that it stays at a right angle with the horse's body. The assistant then holds the rein firmly yet with a soft feel with the hand nearest to the horse's head, approximately 10 cm from the bit. He should gently mobilize the bit in the horse's mouth to retain his attention, deflecting it from the mounting operation, and keeping the horse still. He grasps the top half of the stirrup leather with his left hand, placing his hand under the leather and supporting its grip with the outside of his hand and wrist against the saddle flap, while the rider springs up on to the saddle. Then the assistant quickly removes his hand from the stirrup leather and uses it to hold the stirrup iron ready to receive the rider's foot. He continues to control the horse until the rider has made all necessary adjustments, takes command and is ready to move forward.

There are five alternative methods of mounting, all of which have their respective merits; there are also four ways of dismounting from a horse, two of which are acceptable whilst the other two are very dangerous and pupils should be warned never to try them and why.

Although these descriptions seem lengthy as they contain much detail, the manoeuvre of mounting should be swift, and accomplished with 'promptness', agility and grace.

A brief description of each of the five methods of mounting follows. All are directed as for the left or near side of the horse, for clarity, as this is the most usual side from which riders mount; however, mounting should be practised from both sides. It should be carried out as one continuous, smooth and graceful movement.

In all cases the instructor must ensure that the pupil is taught to check the fitting of the bridle and saddle and that the girths are suitably tight. This presents an excellent opportunity to acquaint the pupil with the existence of the horse's INTERCOSTAL nerve – its superficiality in the girth area; providing the reason why the girths should never be tightened too much, or suddenly, and why a horse should not be asked to turn about in a restricted area after he has been girthed up. At the same time he will absorb a vital fact regarding his leg-aids, their placing and effect resulting from the horse's extraordinary sensitivity in the girth area.

Before mounting the rider should make an approximate assessment of the required length of his stirrup leathers, by holding the bottom of the stirrup iron in his left hand, stretching the length of his right arm up the length of the

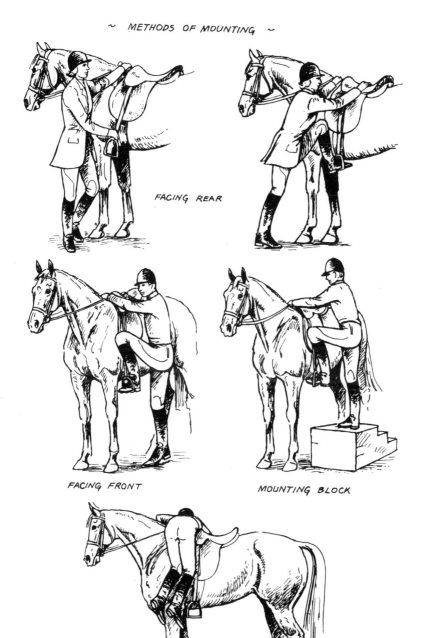

~ METHODS OF MOUNTING ~

FACING REAR

FACING FRONT

MOUNTING BLOCK

VAULTING

FIG. 92

243

stirrup leather so that his fingertips touch the top of the buckle and the bottom of the stirrup iron reaches his armpit.

Both stirrup irons should be lowered quietly by lifting the top of the stirrup out, away from the saddle and easing it down the leather. It should not be scraped down noisily. The stirrups should be compared from a view in front of the horse, that they are of an equal length. The right stirrup should be 'set' with an outward twist to the stirrup leather immediately above the stirrup iron so that it is positioned ready to receive the rider's foot when he has mounted.

To mount, from the ground, facing the rear – traditional British style

The rider stands close to and facing the horse's left shoulder. He takes up the straightened reins, suitably adjusted, into his left hand, where he also places the whip, point down, and keeps it close to the horse's left shoulder. He rests his left hand across the top of the horse's neck, approximately 10 to 20 cm in front of the withers. He must be cautioned that although he may apply a light grip over the neck, he must not grasp or pull out the mane. He drops the spare end of the reins down the far side, to lie down the horse's right shoulder. If the right rein is kept very slightly shorter than the left rein, it will ensure that if the horse moves, he will bring his middle-part and hindquarters towards the rider rather than swinging his haunches outwards, away from him. However, the horse *should* stand still!

The rider then turns to face the horse's left hip, keeping his left shoulder close to the horse's left shoulder, while he lifts up his left leg, with a bent knee, and with assistance from his right hand which holds the rear side of the stirrup iron, he places his foot in the stirrup, pressing the toe of the boot well down so that as he turns quickly round on his right foot to face the horse, his left toe remains down, on or under the girth, and does not dig into the horse's side. This thoughtless digging fault is a common cause of a horse becoming restless to mount – hardly surprisingly!

The rider should press his left knee on to the saddle-flap, near to the front, gather himself together and spring up resolutely from the right foot, straightening his left leg and taking a light support on the waist at the far side of the saddle with his right hand, he straightens himself from the top of his head to his heels, the latter being close together. He then swings his upper body forward in order to facilitate the swinging of his straightened right leg clearly over the back arch of the saddle, being particularly careful to clear both it and the horse's hindquarters. At the same time he moves his right hand forward to the right side of the front arch and lowers himself gently into the saddle – as if on to a nest of eggs. Finally the rider sits up straight, quietly manoeuvres his right foot into the right stirrup without touching it with his hand or looking down, he then takes up and adjusts his reins and whip as required.

The main advantage of this method lies in the fact that if the horse moves he will move forwards towards the rider who is caught in a position from which it is relatively easy for him to swing up into the saddle as the horse comes underneath him. There is however a danger of a twisting pull on the saddle and the horse's back, and fairly energetic riders are liable to flop into the saddle with a resounding bump, from the sheer relief at having made it! They must be warned against these faults.

To mount from the ground, facing the front – traditional American style (possibly because it is impossible to mount using the firmly positioned stirrups of a western saddle facing any other way). After preparing the saddle, girths and stirrups, the rider should take up his reins in the right hand, they should be carefully adjusted so that each rein has a level contact with the horse's mouth. The whip should be held in the right hand, pointing down the horse's right shoulder. The rider then places his right hand firmly on the front arch of the saddle, and facing the front, takes the left stirrup in his left hand, and places his left foot in it keeping the knee close to the saddle and the toe well clear of the horse's side. He moves the left hand on to the horse's neck just in front of the withers, before gathering himself together and springing up neatly, straightening the left leg. The rider then leans forward and transfers a fair proportion of his weight on to his hands and swings his straightened right leg carefully over the back of the saddle and the horse's hindquarters. He lowers himself softly into the saddle and takes the right stirrup and his reins, adjusting the latter as required.

The advantages of this method are:

It is easier to spring up, and to come into the saddle softly. There is less risk of the rider digging his left toe into the horse's side in one of the horse's most sensitive spots, just above and behind the elbow.

Riders are less likely to haul themselves up by means of the saddle, thus it is better for the horse's back, for the saddle (especially if it has a spring tree), and for the rider's back.

All these advantages are apparent as long as the horse remains stationary when being mounted, and all well-trained horses should do this.

The disadvantage is that if the horse moves forward and if the rider is unready, is caught off-balance and forgets to hold on with his right hand he could fall backwards and might injure himself. However, before castigating this method for this one disadvantage, it should be remembered that cowboys mount facing the front safely and efficiently at the trot, canter and gallop!

To mount by means of a mounting-block

The horse should be positioned alongside the mounting-block so that his body is parallel to it and within easy reach for the rider to mount. After the preliminary preparations have been made, as in (a) and (b) the rider steps quietly on to the mounting-block; he makes his acquaintance with the horse, and proceeds to mount using a compromise of the two previous methods. He takes up and adjusts the reins in his left hand which he then places on the horse's neck, just in front of the withers. The whip is also carried in the left hand, the tip pointing downwards close to the rider's left thigh. He slips his left foot into the left stirrup, with the toe facing the front and keeps his left knee close to the saddle. The rider then places his right hand firmly on the front arch of the saddle and leans his shoulders forward while swinging his straightened right leg over the horse's back prior to lowering himself gently into the saddle. He sits upright, places his right foot in the right stirrup and adjusts the reins in both hands.

Many stable-yards are equipped with a mounting-block and there are some aged and stalwart specimens still standing outside country churches. Besides the obvious advantage for short or less agile riders, this method is the best for the horse's back and the saddle, besides being less arduous for the rider, neither his back nor his breeches are exposed to undue strain!

If a custom-built mounting-block is not at hand, it is often possible to improvise using other suitable stabilized objects, e.g. the edge of the kicking boards, the front bumper of a Land-Rover, the lowered horsebox ramp or even an ant hill – every little helps!

To mount by being given a leg-up.

For this method to be carried out efficiently and with ease and elegance, both the donor and the receiver of the leg-up must be carefully taught.

Until the horse and the two participants are accomplished at this form of mounting, an assistant should hold the horse as described on p. 242.

The pupil giving the leg-up should help with all the preliminaries and then stand attentively behind the rider's left shoulder as he faces the horse's left shoulder. The rider should agree a timing system with the assistant, e.g. 'One, two, THREE', or 'One, two, three, *UP*', as the success of the manoeuvre depends on an exact synchronization of actions.

The rider takes his reins and whip in his left hand and rests it over the horse's neck 10–20 cm in front of the withers, he drops the ends of the reins down the horse's far shoulder. When having a leg-up, the whip should be on the far side, pointing downwards towards the ground, in order that it does not give the donor a poke in the eye. The rider takes up his position, fairly close to and facing the front half of the saddle-flap; he places his right hand on the far side of the saddle's waist or its front arch, and raises his left foot backwards up to knee level.

Meanwhile the legging-up pupil bends down and grasps the rider's left leg from behind and slightly to the left, placing his left hand under the rider's left knee and his right hand under the ankle-joint. As his left leg is grasped, the rider starts to count aloud and on the prearranged signal he springs up from his right foot, keeping his back straight and his shoulders square with the horse's spine.

The pupil giving the leg-up should lift the rider straight upwards, mainly with his left hand, his right hand supporting the action and keeping the rider's left knee bent. He should move in towards the horse to give his lifting-power a well-placed support base, i.e. directly under the load to minimize the strain on the assistant's back. He should aim to place the rider's left knee on to the right spot on the saddle flap. In this way surprisingly heavy loads can be lifted!

As soon as the rider senses that he has been raised up sufficiently, he transfers his weight forward on to his hands, swings his straightened right leg cleanly over the rear arch of the saddle and the horse's hindquarters and lowers his seat gently into the saddle. He then takes up his reins and his stirrups. The pupil should hold the left stirrup and help the rider to place his foot in it when he is ready; the assistant should help with the right stirrup. Naturally, the rider should thank both helpers before he moves forward.

To mount from the ground, without stirrups, vaulting *into the saddle*

As before, the assistant stands on the far side of the horse, influencing him to stand stock still and holding the stirrup leather to support the saddle.

246

The rider takes and adjusts his reins fairly short, in his left hand, and places his whip in it with the point down and close to the horse's left shoulder, before putting his left hand over the horse's crest with a firm hold, the ends of the reins being dropped down the far side of the horse's neck. He grasps the far side of the saddle, with his right hand either at the waist or on the front arch.

The rider prepares by gathering himself together, mentally and physically (determination and spring), bends his knees and springs up to lie briefly across the horse withers, he may use his right elbow for extra pulling power. He then swings his right leg cleanly over the back arch of the saddle and the horse's hindquarters, straightens his arms and settles himself gently into the saddle prior to taking up his reins, whip, stirrups and his position.

This is a very quick and efficient way of mounting, it is favoured by most jockeys as it causes least disturbance to the horse. It does however, test the agility of the rider.

When riders vault on without a saddle they must be warned to be extremely careful that their right elbow is cushioned on muscle on the far side of the withers. If they are careless and 'hook on' with their elbow into the ridge of the horse's spinal-processes they could easily damage a horse's back – putting it 'out' in exactly the same way that a chiropractic puts it 'in'. For the same reason the horse's back should always be protected by one or several layers of blanket or similar material when he is ridden bareback, or the rider's seat-bones can bruise or damage the horse's spine.

NOTE *Vaulting* is a gymnastic exercise whereby a mounted rider dismounts and remounts while the horse is on the move, (usually trotting or cantering).

Dismounting without stirrups (The safest and most usual method)

The rider removes both feet from the stirrup irons, he takes the reins and the whip in his left hand and places both hands on either side of the front arch of the saddle, or just in front of it, backs uppermost. Alternatively the left hand may be placed on the horse's neck just in front of the withers. The rider then swings the weight of his body forwards on to his hands and vaults off the saddle, being very careful to swing his straightened right leg high enough to clear the rear arch of the saddle, and the horse's hindquarters. He should land lightly on his toes with bending knees and ankles, facing the horse's shoulder but not too close to it, or to the forefeet. He then steps forward quietly to face the front, releasing the reins from his left hand retaking them firmly but lightly about 20 cm from the bit, in his right hand.

The rider's last moves will depend on the purpose for his dismounting. If it is only for a temporary pause in his riding, to reward, for a short rest, or to wait for the instructor or judge to ride his horse, then they will be as described above. If the dismounting is of a more lengthy nature, then, after he has made much of his horse the rider should slide the buckle-ends of the reins quietly up the horse's neck before lifting them carefully over the ears, and hooking them over his left arm so that they lie in the crook of his elbow, and he tucks his whip out of the way, under his arm-pit pointing down to the ground behind him, and then puts up his stirrup irons or crosses them over in front of the saddle, out of harm's way, and loosens the girths a hole or two. If the horse is hot the rider should lift the saddle for a few seconds to refresh the horse's back, and replace the saddle 3–5 cm farther back.

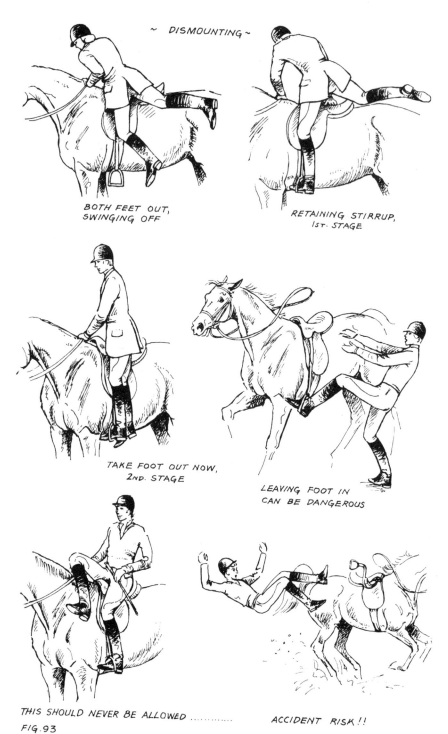

~ DISMOUNTING ~

BOTH FEET OUT,
SWINGING OFF

RETAINING STIRRUP,
1st. STAGE

TAKE FOOT OUT NOW,
2ND. STAGE

LEAVING FOOT IN
CAN BE DANGEROUS

THIS SHOULD NEVER BE ALLOWED ....
FIG. 93

ACCIDENT RISK !!

He then unhooks the reins from his left arm and sorts them out quickly so that they run straight, in order, without any twists, through his right hand which holds them approximately 20 cm below the bit. He turns to face the front and takes the ends of the reins and the whip, point down and to the rear, into his left hand. The rider now has maximum control over his horse to stand still for any length of time, or to lead him away to the stables, horsebox or to any other place.

Novice riders must be taught the reasons for all these actions. For instance if they learn what may happen if they do not put up their stirrups they will be particular about this for the rest of their lives, e.g. if the stirrups are left hanging down the following accidents may occur:

i The stirrups may bang against the horse's sides and frighten him.

ii If the horse turns his head to frighten away a fly irritating him on his ribs or girth area by biting at it, he may get the incisors of the lower jaw caught through the hanging stirrup iron.

iii If the horse cow-kicks at a fly he may get his shoe caught in the stirrup.

iv If the horse slips up, the stirrup iron could cause a serious injury.

I have witnessed no's (ii), (iii) and (iv) myself, and in all these instances the injuries to mouth, hocks and side were horribly severe; in fact the horse who fell on to the stirrup did so in a brick stable-yard, the stirrup broke two ribs which pierced her left lung and she died of pneumonia four days later.

Dismounting, retaining support from the stirrup for the first stage

The rider takes the reins and whip in his left hand. He grasps the front arch of the saddle with his right hand and places the left hand on the horse's neck just in front of the withers, and removes his right foot from the right stirrup iron. The rider then tips his upper body forward on to his hands and at the same time swings his straightened right leg clearly over the rear arch of the saddle, moving his right hand back to the waist of the saddle. His hands remain as the main support to his weight as he slightly straightens his body and brings his right foot level with his left one. He should be nicely poised and balanced directly over the horse's withers. At this moment the rider slips his left foot out of the stirrup and then springs lightly down to the ground with bending knees and ankles, allowing the reins to slide out through his hand as he does so. After he has 'touched down' the concluding moves should follow as was described on p. 247 for dismounting without stirrups.

This method of dismounting is easier for riders who are more stiff and less agile due to age or injury, it is comfortable for both the rider and his horse and it is *safe*.

Dismounting, retaining and using the stirrup throughout

Although this method is still taught occasionally, it is not to be recommended as it presents too great an accident risk. The rider does not remove his left foot from the stirrup until he is standing with his right foot on the ground. The horse has then only to move forward one step and the rider either has to hop about, or he may be pulled off balance on to the back of his head. This method was taught universally in cavalry schools for it enabled the rider to step carefully off his horse without damaging his sword or other military equipment.

Dismounting, swinging the right leg forward over the horse's neck is extremely dangerous and should be forbidden. If the horse moves his head upwards the rider's right heel can easily be checked in its swing whereupon the rider will lose his balance and fall off, breaking a limb or injuring his back or head.

NOTES

1 Instructors must remember to teach their pupils to dismount from both sides, and to practise both equally.

2 No instructor should ever teach either of the last two methods.

21 The rider's position in the saddle

There are three factors which must be given priority in a new rider's early lessons:

i The pupil must be put into a correct position on the saddle, the instructor actually placing his seat, legs, upper body, head and arms where he wishes them to be, to give the rider the correct feel. The instructor however must never be over forceful as any discomfort always causes unwanted stiffness in the pupil.

Details of the correct position are given in Chapter 13; the main points should be taught initially and the finer details introduced when the pupil is ready to receive them.

ii The length of the stirrup leathers – must be checked meticulously both when the pupil first mounts, and again when he is on the move.

The rider must be able to sit in a position which allows him to align his ear, shoulder, hip and the back of his heel as near to a vertical line as is comfortable for him.

He must be able to remain in balance with his horse.

He must be able to move if and as he wishes, without being cramped or stiff in any way; particularly his lower legs must be unhindered.

The stirrup leathers should hold the stirrups at a level height from the ground, unless the rider has one leg shorter than the other; this is a fairly common problem, but also there are pupils who like to think one leg is shorter because they have a habit of sitting crookedly over to one side on the saddle. The instructor must always compare that their stirrups are level – and if not – find out why not!

Faults of the rider's position – which instructors must correct diligently with short demonstrations and explanations whenever they occur in every lesson, at all standards.

The horse cannot give his best performance unless the rider sits in a correct position and applies his aids with educated tact and harmony.

First the instructor must check that the stirrup leathers are adjusted to a suitable length, and that the rider's seat is in the centre of the saddle, when viewed from the side, and from the rear, as many grave faults are caused by too long, too short or unlevel stirrup leathers.

The four major faults are first:

1 A fork seat – the weight of the rider's body rests on the crutch and the inside of the thighs. Often caused by trying to ride with too long stirrup

leathers, or an over-correction. This fault causes the lower legs to go too far back, and makes the rider and his aids unstable.

2 A chair seat – the weight of the rider's body rests on the back of the lower edge of the pelvis, the seat is too far back on the saddle, the tail-bone is tucked underneath and the rider's back is rounded. Often caused by too short stirrup leathers. The rider is too far removed from the horse's centre of gravity, co-ordination can be difficult and aids become rough – the rider is a more awkward (and tiring) burden for the horse to carry.

3 A hollow (or sway) back – the weight of the rider's body rests on the front of the lower edge of the pelvis. The pelvis and hips are fixed to a lesser or greater degree, which blocks the essential suppleness of the rider's hips and loins, for if they are not supple they cannot be directed and used by the rider as the first and most important of all the physical aids – the weight-aids.

4 Excess tension – a very common fault in beginners and in over-zealous or ambitious pupils. The instructor must appreciate that this *is* a major fault but he can only correct it with tact and understanding.

5 Poor posture of the upper body – slouching, head, shoulders and hands not carried.

6 Looking down – may be due to poor posture or lack of confidence, and general shyness.

7 Habitual, unnecessary gripping – clutching knees and calves, and rising heels, bringing the rider up out of the saddle and impeding feel and influences.

8 Crookedness – this may be of two kinds, either the rider may have formed a habit of sitting to one side, or he may slide out on either or both reins when the horse moves on a curved line. The instructor must be guided by the position of the rider's seat bones for a few riders do have odd legs, in that one is shorter than the other.

9 Fear – to be conquered by being replaced by confidence, but never to be despised.

A word of warning to all instructors – Whenever a major or minor position-fault is spotted, be sure to ask if the pupil has any physical problem. For example, he may have to ride with one stirrup leather 10 cm shorter because due to an accident that leg has been shortened, or maddeningly rising heels may be the result of a hideous accident with a field mower, or polio may leave distortions which in turn may be helped by riding.

22 How to hold and adjust the reins

These details are described in Chapter 13, p. 115 and should be taught very carefully from the first and practised frequently, so that correct procedures become subconscious habits waiting on super-quick, inconspicuous, natural reactions.

How to adjust the girths and stirrup leathers
In all these lessons pupils should be warned against shifting their seats about in the saddle; they must be careful not to disturb the horse's mind, his back or his balance.

ADJUSTING GIRTH

FIG. 94

ADJUSTING STIRRUP

To adjust the girths

As a general practice it is best to tighten the girths on the off-side before mounting, and to tighten them on the near side after the rider is in the saddle, as young, fit or highly strung competition horses are usually more approachable from the left should assistance be required, and the surcingle should also be adjusted from the near side.

To check or adjust the girths when mounted, the rider should lift his left leg forward so that the knee and lower leg hang down the horse's shoulder, in front of the saddle. He should keep the weight of his body quietly and evenly balanced on his two seat bones. He then takes the reins in his right hand and lifts the saddle-flap up outside his left thigh so that he can pull up the buckle guard and feel for the girth straps with his left hand. Without looking down he should carefully grasp the free end of the front strap from above, with his thumb and first finger close to the girth buckle. The rider should make a quick test with a smooth upward pull. If the girth is loose, the tongue of the girth buckle will become disengaged, in which case the rider should guide it deftly into the hole above with his first finger. He should make a similar adjustment to the other one or two girth buckles. He should ensure that all the buckles are securely fastened before he replaces the buckle-guard so that it lies flat over the girth buckles, lowers the saddle-flap into its normal position, replaces his left leg on the saddle and takes up the reins.

To adjust the stirrup leathers

The first reaction of most beginners who wish to lengthen or shorten their stirrup leathers is to remove the foot from the stirrup itself; the instructor should be on the alert to prevent this mistake or a dangerous habit will form. The instructor should explain the two main reasons for retaining both stirrups.

252

i That if the horse were to be alarmed and jump or make a sudden move when the rider has one foot out of a stirrup he could lose his balance, have a nasty fall and even break several bones.

ii The rider should use his foot to expedite the adjustment to the stirrup leather by lifting or pressing, as required.

If the rider wishes to adjust his left stirrup leather when he is mounted, he takes the reins in the right hand. He keeps his left foot in the stirrup and slightly eases the pressure on the tread and his knee from the saddle as he grasps the spare end of the stirrup leather in his left hand, from above, with his first finger and thumb close to the buckle. He gives a small pull, just enough to disengage the tongue of the buckle from its present hole and controls the tongue with the tip of his first finger.

If the rider wishes to lengthen the stirrup leather, he presses down on the stirrup iron to pull some extra leather through the buckle re-engaging the buckle-tongue in the required hole.

If he wishes to shorten the stirrup leather, the rider lifts his foot a little more and pulls an extra length of the stirrup leather through the buckle before re-engaging the buckle-tongue.

In both cases, the rider must then change his grip on to that part of the stirrup leather which is next to the saddle, pulling it down firmly until the buckle is lodged as high as possible, next to the stirrup bar on the saddle. He should check that all parts of the leather are flat, that the clip at the end of the stirrup bar is flat and not pushed up; that the skirt of the saddle lies flat under the rider's thigh and that the spare end is replaced in the desired position, i.e. either turned back under the stirrup leather, lying snuggly just below the buckle, or diagonally down and through the keeper on the saddle-flap. The spare end should not be pushed down through the bottom half of the buckle as this renders quick adjustment impossible, especially if the horse is moving at trot or canter, and it will make an uncomfortable lump under the rider's thigh.

23 The rider's influence – The Aids – and their effects

Pupils should be taught the code of signals they should use to communicate with the horses they ride and which the horses have been taught to understand and obey:

1 The rider's thought, mind and will.

2 The weight-aids – combined with feeling the horse's movement beneath his seat.

3 The leg-aids (without spurs.)

4 The rein-aids – minimal at this stage.

5 The voice – often of great value in early riding lessons, as its use cultivates a true and natural sympathy between the rider and his horse, it harmonizes the timing, the aids, and its tone invariably reveals much to the instructor.

6 FEEL – the helpful co-ordination of all the aids. The three main effects which these aids may have on the horses are:

(a) forward-driving,
(b) sideways-moving,
(c) restraining.

Also the aids may have the secondary effects of:
(d) supporting,
(e) regulating.

These aids and the rider's influence on his horse are described in detail in Chapter 14 and must be fully explained and demonstrated, especially with regard to exactly how the aids are applied and coordinated and the various effects they have on the horse. The pupils must try and feel these aids for themselves, at the halt, before they have the added complication of the horse moving underneath them.

Before the class start thinking and feeling, and feeling and thinking, with their horses on the move, the instructor can give them a mental comparison to help them to understand a little of the harmony of the aids. He can relate a rider making a transition with his horse to a driver of a motor car or a bicycle-rider changing gear. To make a smooth and speedy gear-change the driver has to make a finely adjusted play with and between the brake, accelerator, clutch and gear-lever; so also the good rider will make a similar use of the subsidiary aids to support and regulate the main aid effects – he will never isolate one aid, and use it entirely on its own. The class should be shown and made to feel for themselves the heaviness of an incorrectly given guiding rein-aid with the elbow and the heel of the hand lifted up and out to the side; then to contrast this with the lightness of a correct, smooth turning of the forearm and thumb-part of the hand, made whilst keeping the upper arm and elbow close to the body. See Fig. 58. Pupils should also feel the effects of different inclinations of their heads upon the seat bones below. All these seeds of *thought* and *feel* must be sown both early and correctly.

The instructor should explain and demonstrate the following simple movements fully and clearly, ensuring that all details are fully understood:
(a) How to walk forward from a halt – and later, to trot from a walk.
(b) How to halt.
(c) How to circle or turn on the move.

The turning or circle points and the school figures themselves must be selected and explained with care, so that it is easy for the pupil to understand and to carry out the chosen exercise smoothly and accurately.

The aids to walk straight forward from the halt

The rider *thinks* and makes a plan, with regard to direction and destination. He corrects his own position and then calls the horse to attention with all the aids gently co-ordinated.

Next the rider employs his forward-driving aids applying pressure with both legs, on the girth; this pressure may be light, stronger and more vibrant, or applied with the strongest determination – dependent on the horse's response.

In early lessons the pupil should be encouraged to use his voice with a simple, clear command, 'Walk on.' This will provide a natural key, co-ordinating the rider's aids as well as helping to establish a rapport between the rider and his horse.

Simultaneously, as the rider applies his forward-driving aids, he must ease his hands forward. He then retains a feather-light contact with the horse's mouth, the rider's hands following the oscillations of the horse's head and neck smoothly and with constant sensitivity. As soon as the horse walks forward the rider must follow the movement well with a supple seat and should regulate his aids so that the horse maintains a purposeful, forward-going, balanced and regular walk.

The instructor should remind his pupils frequently that there is a horse's mouth at the other end of the reins; this is by far the best way to impress riders that they must *never* hang on to or by the reins. Later, similar aids may be used *to trot forward from the walk*, in which case the words, 'Trot on' will be substituted. As they progress riders must diminish the use of their voice-aids, and come to rely solely on the aids of thought, weight, legs and reins. Pupils should then be taught to measure and balance their forward-driving and restraining aids to maintain the horse's impulsion and form at the required gait, tempo and speed.

The aids – to halt the horse

The rider must think, he should plan the distance, approach and destination for the halt.

He should correct his own position.

He should call the horse to attention by a tactful co-ordination of all his aids.

He should think, 'Steady, Whoa!' (Halt) – in the early lessons he should voice these thoughts aloud. He should be taught to use his voice, thought and weight-aids principally to obtain a downward transition; he should *not* be taught to exert a backwards pull on the reins.

Later, when the pupil has progressed sufficiently to ride his horse forward, on the bit, the instructor should explain and demonstrate further details, e.g. the differences between correct and incorrect halts and methods of riding them in a more educated manner. How the rider should retain sufficient forward-driving influences to keep his horse straight and on the bit, then 'grow tall ears', and press softly on the stirrups, whilst moving his fingers to give subtle restraining aids within still hands to bring the horse quietly, compliantly and smoothly to a balanced and still halt. As the horse halts the rider should ease his weight, leg and rein aids, keeping them in readiness in case they should be required.

He must ensure that the horse stands absolutely still, by being very still yet unconstrained himself in mind and body.

As the rider progresses he can be taught further requirements such as:

i The use of a preparatory half-halt.

ii To ride for a square halt – riding forward and making a new halt when he is not successful.

iii The dangers of fiddling about, ruining the immobility of the horse's halt.

iv The resentment and resistance which may be caused by too-strong rein aids, the rider's hands restricting, or even worse, pulling backwards.

Further notes

Pupils must be taught responsibility for their horses' behaviour, even when they are resting with long reins.

It is very important that riders are *never* taught to pull on their reins in order to bring their horses to a halt. Regrettably this does happen, and a bad habit is formed which is extremely difficult to erase later.

Even in the first lesson beginner-riders must be taught to influence their horses mainly with their thought and weight-aids, with their leg-aids 'in attendance', and that the rein-aids should restrain only a minimal amount.

Riders' hands should never pull backwards.

Beginner-riders should be encouraged to say 'Steady – whoa!' to aid mental and physical sympathy and co-ordination. ('Steady' is the very first step towards a half-halt).

Later, similar aids are used *for all downward transitions*, the aids carefully co-ordinating to attain and maintain the desired gait, tempo and speed.

Downward transitions must be made smoothly – with minimal rein-aids.

The halting-places should be selected with care; they may be between two barrels or poles, but should seldom be on the outer track because of the wall and its interfering influences.

The instructor must remind his pupils frequently to retain an upright position, pressing down lightly on the stirrups and growing tall above his waist to allow the horse the necessary freedom of his back muscles so that he may engage his haunches before and as he halts.

If the rider leans back the horse's back and hindquarters will be overloaded and their action impeded. If the rider leans forward he can no longer influence the horse's haunches, and the hindlegs will remain straight instead of bending in all their joints and the horse's weight will be on his forehand, which will put undue strain on his forelegs. The horse's hindlegs are constructed to produce braking power; his forelegs are not.

The instructor must avoid asking for direct transitions to halt before riders (and horses) are ready, nor must he cause abrupt halts by too sharp or staccato a command. It is important that beginners (and riders on young horses) are asked to make progressive halts so that the slowing down is made through the intervening paces to avoid straining the horse's legs and so that the rider may use minimal rein-aids.

The better the horse is ridden and trained the more elegant will be the halt, from invisible aids, and with an ease and poise due to the overall elasticity of the horse, from bending hind legs to a light acceptance of the bit. The horse should come to a smooth well-balanced halt, standing still, squarely on all four legs, in good form, tranquilly awaiting the next signal from his rider.

To circle or turn the horse (turns on a single track, on the move).

NOTE A turn in these early riding lessons refers to a turn on one track, whereby a quarter of a circle rounds out the angle between two straight lines which are at right angles to each other; the larger the circle diameter, the easier the turn. The instructor must first explain that horses were not constructed or put into this world to carry man, this happened to be one of man's better ideas! In fact, the horse is *not* custom-built either to jump fences, or to carry a man on his back, thus it is up to the rider to make the business of carrying a man as easy as possible for the horse. If the instructor shows his class of beginners a horse's pedal bone during one of the early lessons, it will impress the delicacy of the horse's mechanism and of his balance upon their minds.

If the rider wishes his horse to deviate from the track which lies straight ahead, he must make it easy for the horse to understand his rider's wish and to carry the rider in the new direction.

The rider must work out a ground-plan which is of a suitable size and shape for a large, four-legged animal to follow with ease. The horse's hindfeet must follow within the tracks of his forefeet and his central line must match the line of the circle track, his head and neck must not be bent inwards any more than the rest of his body.

The aids: to circle or turn to the left

First the rider must *think*.

He must then correct his position.

At least two horses' lengths before reaching the prearranged circle point, the rider smoothly shortens his left (inner) rein, without putting any increase of pressure on it. (In the earliest lessons this should be more of an abstract gesture, to form a good habit, rather than an actual preparation for the giving of a soft, guiding rein-aid.)

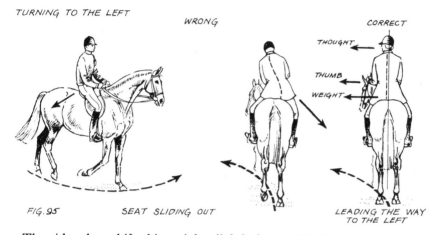

TURNING TO THE LEFT   WRONG   CORRECT

THOUGHT

THUMB

WEIGHT

FIG. 95   SEAT SLIDING OUT   LEADING THE WAY TO THE LEFT

The rider then shifts his weight slightly but positively to the left. This weight adjustment must be made sufficiently early to allow the horse enough time to feel it and to adjust his own equilibrium so that he may carry his rider in the new direction with ease. In order to perfect his weight-aid, the rider must also keep his left hip (joint) or groin, well forward to allow the horse to move his left hind leg well forward under him. This preparatory alignment of his hips will place the rider's legs naturally in the best position for giving the forward-driving aids necessary through the circle or turn for maintaining the horse's form and the rhythm of the gait while asking for correct amounts of bend and of impulsion, i.e. the left leg is on the girth and the right leg is very slightly farther back.

When riding a whole circle the rider may need to move his outside leg a little farther forward on the several occasions when its forward-driving influence is required by the girth. (The hindquarters of a horse who is moving *forward* well do not swing out!)'

Approximately half a horse's length before the circle point the rider smoothly turns his left forearm so that the thumb-part of the hand 'leads the way' inwards, towards the centre of the circle; at the same moment, he eases his right hand forward sufficiently to allow the horse to bend and turn in the direction so clearly indicated to him. The little finger part of the right hand

257

moves forwards towards the horse's mouth with a smooth give allowing the horse to stretch his outer side. The rider brings his outer shoulder forward so that the axis of his shoulders is facing the next circle point or is at right angles to the new track.

In early riding lessons and when training young horses the guiding-effect of the inside rein should be clear, to the point of exaggeration, the rider retaining a light contact as he moves his inner hand even as much as 30 cm away from the horse's withers. As the education standards improve so the guiding rein-aid can be refined until it is just a feeling between the rider and his horse.

As soon as the circle, half- or quarter-circle is completed, the rider straightens himself, sits centrally in the saddle and rides his horse straight forward with both legs by the girth.

Further notes

This section has been explained at length and in depth as the basic principle of riding circles or turns by means of, 'Thought, weight and thumb' is of the utmost importance. Pupils must be taught these aids in their first riding lessons and be reminded to apply them as often as may be necessary until they become subconscious, never-to-be-forgotten laws, for on these correct foundations will the rider's future development and attainment depend.

These aids should be applied, as above, for circles and turns on a single track at all paces, and of all sizes down to a 5 metre volte.

In the first lessons on turns, when the pupil is led by an assistant on foot, and also when he follows a lead-horse, he should be discouraged from using his rein-aids. It is very important that the rider learns to apply and to rely on his thought, weight, leg and forward-driving aids, and to move his inner hand as described, so that these actions become well-established as a natural habit, after which the rein-aids may be added as a delicate luxury when the rider is sufficiently experienced to start to understand about the horse's form.

While the pupils practice simple turns and transitions the instructor should watch weight adjustments from the rear, checking that they are made sufficiently, that there is no awkwardness and that the hips are correctly aligned, the inner seat bone being slightly forward, and never back. The rein-aids should be checked both from the rear (shoulders, upper arms and elbows) and from in front of the ride (shoulders, elbows, wrists, hands and reins), as well as from the side.

The instructor must be extremely patient, imaginative and painstaking throughout these lessons and ensure that they are thoroughly assimilated and consolidated before proceeding over any new ground.

24 The gaits

The following short chapters are but precis of the basic facts, given as simply as possible to provide a quick reference for the instructor and for ease of understanding for beginner-riders. The instructor must remember all the work he himself has already learned, but above all he must keep the work *simple* and *natural*.

The walk lessons

The walk is the gait which is used exclusively for all the early riding lessons.

The instructor has already taught his pupils how to move their horses forward to the walk and how they should sit on the horse's back, upright, with a good posture, yet supple and unconstrained. He has taught them how to halt and how to change direction. The instructor must consolidate all these lessons *at the walk*. He must not be impatient nor lazy-minded, relying on the greater activity and excitement of a faster gait to supply the rider's need for interest to stimulate his enthusiasm and application.

Providing that the instructor has a sincere desire to produce good riders, he will not require any extraordinary talent or imagination in order to compose an endless supply of work-outs, instructional games, musical rides and tests, all of which can be carried out at the walk. He must use these to confirm his teaching, to build up his pupils' confidence, feel and understanding, and to keep his novice riders safe and happy, as they learn and improve – at the walk.

Many instructors pay far too little attention to the rider's and the horse's performance at the walk, with the result that both partners show a deterioration of the gait rather than an improvement, as the months (and years) go by.

Beginners should be led, and told to ride with loose reins until they have an independent, balanced seat and are absolutely confident. They should *never* be asked to ride collected walk – nothing is more damaging to the horse's gaits.

The following subjects should be taught, first when led by an assistant; secondly when taken out on a leading rein, or as a member of a ride working in single file, and eventually individually. Pupils must be encouraged to think and to feel as they practise, and they must be carefully supervised both with regard to correct methods, to safety, and to their enjoyment.

1 Position and aids:
   A. To walk forward from the halt.
   B. To halt from the walk.
   C. To ride large circles and wide turns – at the walk.
2 Rein adjustments.
3 Carrying a short whip, and changing it quickly yet smoothly from hand to hand, or to reverse it, as directed.
4 Riding without stirrups for short periods at first.
5 Suitable, easy balance and suppling exercises may be introduced.
6 Later, school figures may be ridden at the walk.

The instructor must impress upon the riders and the leaders alike the need for clear planning, thought and application of the aids in order that the pupils learn to ride accurate ground-plans for circles and turns and other basic school figures, Teaching the school figures at the walk, comparatively early in the rider's curriculum adds interest and incentive to the work at the walk which otherwise could be rather slow, almost boringly so. At the walk the rider has plenty of time to practise applying his aids, feeling the results, and of having his endeavours corrected and improved, and he will have gained an insight and education into a vitally important equestrian subject which is often delayed far too long. The later a rider learns about school-work the more difficult and confusing he will find it.

7 Walking out of doors, on warm days, is an essential part of walk lessons as it is of the later trot and canter lessons. Mentally it is more enjoyable and it is good for the riders to feel and to learn to adapt themselves physically to the many changes caused by the horse's movement as he picks his way over uneven or undulating ground. The horse must be led at first – and be very quiet and reliable.

8 A large variety of simple, safe and educational games to be ridden at the walk may be made up by any instructor who has some imagination; these enliven children's lessons.

THE TRAIN GAME

FIG 96

'The Train' is a great favourite and is outlined below as an example: the riders are formed up as a ride in single-file. The leading file is the driver and the rear-file is the guard who issues the orders, 'Stop!' 'Go!' The remainder of the ride are passengers one in each carriage. A station may be constructed at X, using two pairs of barrels and one row of straw bales to form a platform along one side of the E–B line and three pairs of poles for railway lines on the B side of it. Dismounted pupils can be standing on the platform, waiting to board the train, and two can be the signal-man and the points-operator respectively. The instructor is the station master and gives the orders re: signals, direction and movement, and when the train is brought to a halt in the station he gives the guard a list of disembarking and embarking passengers and they help each other to mount and dismount. Further pairs of barrels to ride between add purpose to the trains route and some may be designated as tunnels – all passengers leaning forward when passing under the imaginary roof!

9 The beginner-rider should be taught the sequence of the footfall at the walk, and to feel and name the tread of the hindfeet. Gradually pupils should be taught to watch and feel how the horse starts to walk forward, and how he uses his head and neck and his whole body at the walk, how his hindfeet over-step the imprint of the forefeet, and how to differentiate between good and bad walks.

The pupil must be encouraged to move his hands quietly and rhythmically forward with each stride, inviting the horse to stretch and use his head and neck and to move forward freely over the ground. It is very wrong to teach beginners to have still hands at the walk, unless they are nervous, in which case they may hold the front arch of the saddle, with loose reins, while they are led. At all other times they must move their hands forward freely and fluently from their shoulders, through supple shoulder, elbow and wrist joints.

The pupils must be taught that although their upper body (above the hips) must remain poised and unmoved, this is made possible only if their seat-bones and hip joints move freely with the horse's movement under them, and their loins are supple too, acting as a shock absorber, transferring the movement below into a stillness above.

10 Gradually, when they are ready, pupils should be shown how to use their forward-driving aids to ask their horses to find and retain a good form when they are on the move. This lesson should be firmly implanted at the walk.

The instructor can illustrate the requirements of a correct outline, or a rounded top-line, if he likens the horse's back to a bridge.

'The right sort' is like a well-built suspension bridge, and gives a splendid feeling of safety and security to the user.

'The wrong sort' is like a native bridge, weak, sagging and swaying over a chasm below – not a bridge one would like to cross after hunting, at night!

So it is with a horse's back – he can carry the rider more easily and with less wear and tear to his frame if he is trained to move in a correct form (like the suspension bridge) when he is ridden. Thus any rider or trainer who causes the shape of the horse's back to be hollowed by his work is abusing his responsibility.

Pupils should be shown how faulty riding can spoil the quality of the horse's walk.

1 Rigidity in the rider's back, or in his pelvic girdle will shorten the steps of the horse's hindlegs and prevent the movement from going through his back. The fault will be magnified if the rider's back is hollowed, thus putting the weight on to the front of the seat bones.

2 If the rider's lower legs hang stiffly still or are held, sprung away from the horse's sides, below gripping knees, or if they continuously bang together on his sides, without feel, rhythm or meaning – any of these rider faults can spoil the horse's walk and damage his training.

3 If there is any deficiency of feel, rhythm and elasticity in the rider's bones, joints and sinews which combine to give the rein-aids, or if there is a lack of sensitivity, the hands being still, heavy or hanging, they will over-restrain, or restrict the horse's movement, and will deaden his mouth.

As with all lessons of this sort, the instructor should show the correct method and several further changes from the bad to the good to make quite sure that the whole class have understood its content. He should be mounted on a well-trained horse who has a good walk, so that he can demonstrate clearly the improvement in the horse's activity and the length of his strides when the rider invites the movement to come from the two hind-heels and through the horse's back, by moving his seat bones forward softly with each step forward of the horse's hind legs.

The instructor should demonstrate the correct placing, timing and use of the lower legs to ask the horse to move forward in a good form and at a regular and active gait. The lower legs should remain close to the horse's sides at the girth and should nudge the horse up and forward with alternate legs, just as the hind leg is moving the horse's trunk forward over the ground. This timing is an easy one for the rider because the horse's movement prescribes it if the rider will just accept the prescription.

Finally the instructor should confirm that his pupils understand how to 'ride their horses forward with their hands', keeping the lightest possible contact to feel the surge of the horse's movement coming forward into the fingers of each hand as the horse walks on long reins, retaining a correct form.

JOCKEY RIDING THE HORSE FORWARD
WITH THE HANDS

FIG. 97

The pupils should be encouraged to consider their equine partners, to understand their horse's or pony's way of thinking and of moving and his natural reactions, at all times.

In the lecture-room they should be taught the basic rules for riding in the school and out of doors, and they should copy down and label diagrams depicting the school figures. See Chapter 11, p. 64, to help them to learn their respective ground-plans as this will widen the scope and interest of all their future lessons at the walk, and later at trot and canter. During early walk lessons pupils should be led quietly over mildly undulating ground. They can learn how to help to open and close gates correctly, and may be led over poles on the ground at the walk.

Too often the walk is thought of merely as a pace of rest and relaxation for the rider. It should be afforded much more careful consideration. Instructors and riders must *think*.

As the training standards of riders and horses rise so they must improve their execution of movements at the walk, and the instructor must continue to assess this work through all lessons, at every standard.

To finish on a final note for beginners' lessons, I will add two cautions:

i The instructor must be patient and ensure that the walk lessons have been assimilated and are established and that the pupils are thoroughly confident before they are asked, expected or allowed to trot.

ii Each pupil's nerve is a very individual factor, dependent on his imagination and previous experience as well as his temperament. No pupil must be 'pushed' to trot before he is ready, nor must a whole class be kept back for one nervous individual; he must have special, individual attention to encourage him patiently 'over the hump'.

25 Mounted leading-rein lessons

Lessons given by a mounted instructor to a pupil on a leading-rein have numerous advantages, many of which are not always immediately apparent:

1 The instruction can be given in a happily informal atmosphere, with a

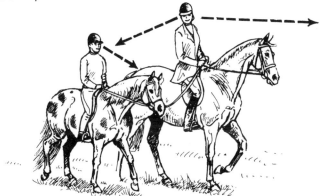

~ LEADING REIN LESSONS ~

CORRECT COMMUNICATION & CARING

FIG. 98

HOW *NOT* TO GIVE A LEADING REIN LESSON

closeness of communication which makes this form of lesson particularly good for nervous or highly strung pupils.

2 Demonstrations are continuous; they are easily imitated and assimilated.

3 Explanations can be given exactly when required – although they should also allow comfortable intervals during which the pupil has time to himself to take in, concentrate and try out the various sensations of feel, actions and reactions. Silence can be golden sometimes.

4 Nature, the ways and the lore of the countryside can be taught during a led instructional hack which will stimulate the pupil's interest and make riding out in the country all the more agreeable. At the same time he will learn the correct code of behaviour and courtesy towards farmers and landowners.

5 Pupils can be taught the practical aspects of the Highway Code, and learn the horseman's responsibilities when riding on the road in the safest possible manner.

6 Lessons can be educationally progressive, particularly in the acquiring of knowledge and feel, as the terrain and the horse's gaits change. Confidence will grow and self-consciousness disappear in a most natural way.

7 Pupils are given the opportunity to practice the work and the corrections taught in the enclosed manège.

8 Lessons will be safe, stimulating and fun, for, as the pupil's horse is under the instructor's control, new horizons and territories can be explored, e.g. riding across fields or moors and through woodland, areas where the beginner-riders could not ride unless they were led, as the risk of their horses getting out of control is too great.

9 Horses and ponies benefit mentally and physically, for they prefer to work out of doors. It helps to keep them sweet and fresh. The instructor must see that they are not over-fresh; this may be a real hazard if ever school horses are 'cooped-up' indoors for too long; neither should they be over-fed, too fit nor fully clipped, without a blanket in the winter.

As with all early riding lessons, those given on a leading rein should always be taught by an instructor who is both trained and experienced and who is enthusiastic and yet 'keeps his cool' in a confidence-giving way.

The leaders should be well trained and naturally able to establish an effective rapport with the horse as well as with the pupil. They should know the correct procedures when leading horses so that the instructor can rely on them to keep their horses moving forward well, shoulder to shoulder when they are leading on foot, and with the back of the horse's head level with the leader's knee when he is mounted. They must always see that their pupil's horse is moving regularly and well – they should never make the led horse jog – they should regulate their own horse's speed.

Young instructors must remember that adventure should never be sought from speed, and that to a novice, walking up or down a slope or over uneven ground can produce quite sufficient novelty and excitement and thrill.

The pupils' horses must possess all the qualities required in a beginner's horse. They must be of a suitable size (height and width); they must have equable temperaments and good, comfortable gaits. They must be well-trained, being willing and ready to move forward or to stand stock still at the slightest indication from the person leading them. They must lead well from either side whether the leader is on foot or mounted on another horse. They must show no inclination to bite or kick, even when provoked; they must be traffic and bombproof. The leader's horse or pony should possess similar qualities, being utterly reliable and well-mannered under all circumstances.

Method

The preliminary preparations are important and must not be skimped.

Both the horses involved (the leader and the led) must be acquainted and get on well together. They must accept the leading-rein routine from either side, and be accustomed to it by two experienced riders, before entrusting the led horse with a novice rider. These preparations must be made with all school horses who may be used in a leading-rein lesson.

The pupil should be prepared through three logical stages, all of which should be practised on both sides equally to avoid horses or riders becoming in the least one-sided.

i He should be taught how to lead his horse on foot, to either hand, so that he understands how easy it is to control the horse, and how well the horse responds.

ii He should be led when he is mounted; the instructor will lead and teach him on foot. If the instructor is teaching a group of riders in a class then he must be sure that his leaders are well trained, and that they strike up the necessary rapport with the novice rider and his horse. In an enclosed manège the leader should lead the horse on the side furthest from the surrounding wall or fence, and on a public road they should always be on the traffic side.

iii The pupil is then prepared, confident and ready to be led from another horse. Any sign of apprehension may be quickly dispelled by adding a dismounted leader on the far side for a short time, until the beginner rider signals that he feels safe and happy to be led by the mounted leader alone.

A beginner should never be put straight on to an instructional hack, led from a horse, without a preliminary introduction as outlined above, it is asking him to cope with too much at once, and if any mishap were to occur it could prove to be the last straw, and put him off riding, ever again.

The leading-rein itself, should be between 3 and 5 metres in length, and be made of leather or cotton webbing – the former is best, though more expensive; the latter is light but is unreliable as it rots with age and weathering and then breaks. Usually the fastener is a leather strap and buckle, or a spring clip – either must be in good working order.

The rein should be neatly coiled and held in the hand nearest to the led horse; that hand may be given additional stability by being placed firmly on the inner edge of the top of the leader's knee for extra purchase if this is needed.

Providing that the horse is quiet, responsive and easy to control, the leading-rein should be attached to the back of the cavasson noseband. This is the best attachment as there is absolutely no risk of damaging the horse's mouth and the leading-rein can be changed from one side to the other, sliding it carefully yet easily under the horse's chin.

If the leader wishes to exert a little more control (small leader, large horse) or similar problem, he may fasten the leading-rein both to the noseband and the snaffle ring nearest to him. Although the leader then has a direct influence on the bit the noseband will prevent any undue disturbance to the led horse's mouth. Changing sides is not so easy, the horses must be brought to a halt while the leader unfastens the leading-rein and refastens it on the other side. He may well have to dismount to do this unless both horses are exceptionally steady.

Occasionally an experienced instructor may find he has cause to exert even more authority over his pupil's mount, e.g. taking a good child rider out in company or out hunting on an impetuous young pony. In this case, he should have a leading-rein with a double fastening, so that it can be attached to the bit and noseband on both sides of the pony's head. This extra refinement combines good control with a quick and easy changeover.

There is one method of attachment which should not be used, i.e. when the leading-rein is passed through the nearest snaffle ring and fastened on to the ring on the far side with a free and direct pull through, under the horse's chin. In this way the horse's lower jaw is encompassed by an ever-tightening band, of metal on the top and leather underneath, added to which the nut-cracker action of a jointed bit will be intensified, as will the pressure on the horse's tongue if the bit is unjointed.

If the led horse becomes unwilling and hangs back, the leader must never try to pull him forward by the reins like a form of 'haulage contractor'; he must use a forward-driving aid of some sort. As timing is an all-important factor in the giving of a long-lasting but not too drastic effect, it is wiser not to rely on the beginner rider to give this aid. Certainly he may experiment under his instructor's guidance but if he is not successful, and if the instructor is adept at using his schooling whip, he will find that a quickly delivered and appropriately sharp tap on the horse's far flank will produce a good result without startling the horse – in fact, he will rarely guess who has delivered the awakening tap!

If the led horse pulls forward, urged on by some excitement, the leader should give a little before restraining him in order to regain control tactfully. If he merely exerts an immediate and harsh pull, the horse will fight back and the leader may even be pulled out of the saddle – with dire results in all directions! If the led horse shows signs of excitability the leader should shorten the leading-rein smoothly and immediately.

If a group of novice riders is being escorted on an instructional hack, each pupil should be led by an experienced rider who can help them with their positions, discuss all their 'discoveries' of feel and observation, and answer their questions. This is an excellent opportunity for student-instructors to learn to communicate clearly, to pass on what they have been taught and to reap the rewards of seeing their pupils' positions, confidence, ability and enjoyment improve and grow – they may even learn something from their pupils, certainly they must always be ready to do so.

Whenever instructional hacks proceed along public roads the Highway Code must be strictly observed. The ride must be well-organized into groups of not more than four pairs with an instructor as the outside rider of the leading pair, and another experienced rider on the outside (traffic side) of the rear pair; these two riders will control the ride, be responsible for its dressing and discipline, and for signalling acknowledgements or warnings to approaching and oncoming traffic. Before embarking on such a hack, the instructor should explain the rules of the road and encourage his pupils to study the British Horse Society's Road Safety Manual and be courteous to drivers and pedestrians, farmers, country workers and landowners alike.

That horsemen may ride in their national countryside is not a feudal right; it is an honour, a precious gift, the continuance of which is dependent on the goodwill of the state or of the individual landowner or their tenants, and the care and courtesy of the nation's riders. Each and every rider is responsible for retaining this happy relationship.

26 The trot lessons

It is imperative that beginners are introduced to work at trot most carefully; not only is the gait itself new for them but also it is a completely new and strange sensation. Thus it is helpful if they can be acquainted with the look and the basic mechanics of the trot before they are asked to ride it.

The instructor should explain that the horse trots in a two time rhythm fitting his four feet into two diagonal pairs. That these are named from the fore leg; i.e.

The left diagnonal = left fore and right hind together
The right diagonal = right fore and left hind together

with a period of suspension, spring or bounce between each beat. The instructor should explain that a horse at trot will feel much more 'springy' to sit on than he has at the walk, and that he covers the ground more quickly, i.e. there is an increase of speed.

The instructor should then show his pupils horses working quietly at trot; he could lunge a horse he knows well to show the trot and the walk, and the transitions between the two gaits. They should also see more experienced riders working at sitting trot.

The aids to trot – should be taught simply and carefully,
The rider should ensure he is sitting correctly,
He thinks, 'Trot',
He applies both lower legs a little more firmly on the horse's sides by the girth,
He eases both reins very slightly. (In early lessons this should be a small, giving gesture for his reins will be long; later, pupils should give enough to allow the forward movement, without losing the contact).
He adjusts his aids as soon as the horse complies, feeling for the swing of the horse's back, the rhythm and the forward impulsion with each step.
The instructor should remind his pupils of:

The aids to walk from trot – (closely resembling those from walk to halt).
He corrects his position,
He thinks 'Steady – *walk*' (and says it).
He keeps both lower legs by the girth, straightens his spine with a feeling of 'growing tall ears' and pressing softly on his stirrups.
He keeps his hands still, remembering that rein-aids come from the back of the shoulder-girdle, the back and the seat. (Later, when considered to be sufficiently proficient to ride with a rein contact, the rider will move his fingers within his hands to give smooth restraints, if necessary).
As the horse obeys, the rider rewards him with a word of praise or a quiet yet meaningful pat.

267

He adjusts his aids as required for the walk.

NOTE Beginners should ride these transitions on long reins so that they develop belief, reliance and confidence in the efficiency of their *thought* and *weight* aids -- this will then stand them in good stead for the rest of their riding lives.

The instructor should explain that there are two ways of riding a horse when he is trotting – the rider may sit in the saddle continuously, smoothly following the oscillations of the horse's back, or he may rise, or post on alternate diagonals, to the trot. It is thought that the rising, posting or English trot originated from the olden days of post, stage or state coaches when riders were added to each pair of horses to enable more horses to pull greater loads with a maximum of control and safety to all parties (or parcels) concerned.

In former years the rising trot was often taught before the sitting trot, in order to get riders trotting as soon as possible, avoiding the discomfort of 'the bumping trot' as the sitting trot was then, descriptively called. This encouraged novice riders to categorize the sitting trot as the '*un*comfortable method', and they used it as little as possible, which was just as well for their horses' backs as they rode it very badly! For many of these riders the sitting trot remained an anathema to them always.

Thus, the sitting trot should be taught first, so that riders learn to sit comfortably with their horses at trot in a soft, fluent and easy way from the start.

During the early trot lessons pupils should be led, riding with long reins. They should be told to take a light hold on the front arch of the saddle for their first attempts at sitting trot and at any time thereafter if they are in danger of losing their balance, or if they start to stiffen up and bump on their horse's backs. They should only be asked to trot for five to ten strides at first.

It is essential to keep the lessons safe and enjoyable. The instructor must make haste slowly, adding simple and appropriate facts, exercises and tests to maintain interest and to build confidence. It is far better for pupils to learn to do a little sitting trot correctly, than that they trot for too long, become a little tired, bump on the saddle and then faults start to arise like a row of seedlings after a shower of rain. Patience must overrule ambition; the latter may be that of the parents, the instructor, the leader or the pupil.

As in earlier lessons, the instructor must again use tact and discretion in achieving correct positions at trot; although he must continually encourage his pupils to sit well, as near to the classical ideal as their conformation will allow, there must be no force, stiffening or constraint. Even plump legs will mould to a better shape and allow their owners to sit deeper into the saddle providing that the instructor shows the pupil how to move back and place the rounded muscle on the inside of thighs, so that it stays behind the thigh bone, and that the pupil works conscientiously enough thereafter.

As the pupils gain in experience, confidence and proficiency, short periods of sitting trot without stirrups will be found to be most beneficial to pupils' positions, balance and co-ordination, and they will not form the bad habit of treading too much on the outside stirrup for support when riding through corners or on a circle.

Later, when he considers his pupils are ready, the instructor will allow his pupils to take up their reins and to ride with a light, steady contact. However he must impress what a cardinal sin it would be if any of them were ever to use the reins as a means of support, to help them to stay in the saddle or to regain lost balance – the riders' seats must always be entirely independent of the reins.

The rising trot – This should not be taught until the pupils can ride well at sitting trot, i.e. maintaining correct positions and balance during the transitions as well as at the actual trot. The timing of the introduction of the rising trot can have a long-lasting or wrong effect. The pupils should be allowed plenty of time to become thoroughly accustomed to the sitting trot first, until their seats stay quietly and softly in the saddle with supple hips and a good posture born of practice and confidence. Not until the rider has achieved a comfortable ease at sitting trot should he be taught the rising or posting trot.

When he considers that his pupils are ready, the instructor should explain the rising trot, its method and advantages, e.g. it is less fatiguing for horse and rider when long distances have to be covered at trot; that it is useful for horses with weak backs, for unfit or young horses; and that it is a helpful means of checking and improving the rider's feel for the horse's rhythm and movement.

The instructor should explain and demonstrate the difference between the sitting and the rising trot, and how to rise to the trot. That the rider uses the horse's movement rather than making an obvious effort himself, although he also uses an extra support from his knees and the stirrups, with supple knees and ankles.

Before his pupils attempt rising trot, the instructor should test each pupil individually, that they can synchronize their counting with the timing of their horse's trot, for this is by no means an automatic or fairy-godmother's gift to all would-be horsemen. This timing can be acquired by training and must be established before the rising trot can be learned.

The instructor should explain that the rider must first obtain a good sitting trot, before accentuating the rhythm in his own head and then allowing himself to be lifted slightly as the horse raises one of the diagonal pairs of legs from the ground, The rider remains over the saddle with a slight forward inclination of his upper body and supple knees and ankles during the next step, and then sinks down again, softly as the original diagonal pair of legs comes to the ground. He is then ready to receive the upward impetus once more and the rhythmical cycle is repeated.

The rider should re-establish a good sitting trot before asking the horse for a smooth downward transition, or later, before making a smooth upward transition to canter.

To impress upon his pupils the need for a soft, supple and careful return to the saddle, the instructor can give his class a simple yet effective demonstration, using a set of kitchen scales and a kilo bag of salt. He can show them the comparative effects on the weight registered at the moment of impact, first when he gently lowers the bag of salt on to the scales, and then when he drops it down – in the latter case the scales may record a momentary doubling of the true weight. Thus the gentle lowering illustrates how the rider should return to the saddle in the rising trot, and the second shows how he should not!

Before they try the rising trot themselves, the class should be told to take a gentle hold of the horse's mane or a neck strap, 10–20 cm in front of the withers to give them an added stabilizer which should be psychological rather than actual, for they should not be taught to rely on a secure hold with their hands.

Initially the rising trot should be taught to each pupil individually, the instructor or an experienced assistant running or riding alongside and calling, '*Down* – up', in rhythm with the pupil's horse's forelegs. If the instructor is mounted he should ride at sitting trot to avoid confusing the pupil. He should be careful to emphasize the word, 'Down', rather than 'Up' to help the pupil to catch the horse's movement. Children may even find the words, 'Bump – up; bump – up' more relaxing and easier to grasp.

As soon as the pupils have become accomplished at the rising trot they should be taught how to select and change the diagonal. For this work, as well as for the first few introductory lessons on the rising trot, novice riders should be allowed to glance down to watch the movement of the horse's shoulder-blades. They should be told to see and name which one comes back as they sit down in the saddle, and that if they sit as the left shoulder-blade comes back they are riding on the left diagonal and vice versa.

To change the diagonal, the rider should sit for one extra beat. Occasionally even experienced riders may be observed staying up off the saddle for an extra beat to change to the other diagonal, this is an indication of lack of thought or of feel, or of bad teaching originally. As soon as possible the instructor must lead his pupils to discipline themselves to feel for the desired diagonal or to change the diagonal without looking down, just feeling and analysing their horses' movement through their seat-bones.

Pupils must be taught that they should change diagonals quite frequently, working on both diagonals equally, so that neither they nor their horses get one-sided, and to ensure that the horses' backs are evenly muscled up and that all four legs share an equal work-load. They should also be taught that as a general rule they should ride on the left diagonal when trotting on the right rein and vice versa, in order that their weight is in the saddle when the horse's inside hindfoot is on the ground to facilitate the horse's balance and the rider's influence on that leg.

Hacking out, under instruction, led by or from a quiet horse, along quiet lanes, through woods or across downs, common land or fields with permission is an excellent means of gaining experience, consolidating all the foregoing lessons, and of improving the rider's position, feel and proficiency at walk, and at sitting and rising trot. It is much more natural and enjoyable than being confined to an indoor school or by a lunge-line.

Common faults in rising trot

1 Rider in front of the movement – upper body inclined too far forward – sometimes combined with resting weight on hands, and lower legs displaced to rear, heels rising into the horse's sides.

2 Rider behind the movement – both in position and in timing. Upper body too upright for the rider's standard of training, often combined with a pulling up from the hands (and reins) and lower legs which are stiffly straight, forward and away from the horse's sides.

3 Poor timing – to an obviously marked or to an almost imperceptible degree.

4 A hollow back – seat left out behind, rigid pelvis and back.

5 A rounded back – usually sitting down heavily on to the horse's back.

6 A loose back – having a wobble rather than the desired poise and controlled suppleness.

7 Looking down – with all its bad effects and consequences.

8 An exaggerated rising movement – the rider rising abruptly and too far out of the saddle and hitting it each time with a hard bump, which is injurious to the horse's back and to his gait.

This is often due to being taught the rising trot too soon: the rider has formed the habit of rising too precipitously, preceding the horse's timing, lifting himself from the saddle too energetically and too soon in order to avoid the unaccustomed and uncomfortable bouncing from the horse's back under the saddle, instead of allowing the rising to originate from the upward thrust of the horse's movement.

9 Too indefinite a rising movement – which may even appear as a double bump.

10 Unsteadiness – particularly of the hands which should never be affected by the rider's rising, and of the legs which should remain steadily on the horse's sides by the girth.

11 Stiffness – caused by excess tension in the rider's mind and body, and results in a loss of suppleness, fluency and harmony.

12 A false pulling up with the shoulders, upper arms and elbows – rather than allowing the horse's movement to push the rider up for the rising trot.

13 Crookedness – the rider's shoulder and hip axis not being straight, level and central when riding on straight lines nor positioned slightly to the inside and parallel with the horse's shoulder and hips axis when rising on a curved line. Alternatively a rider may use the support of one knee and stirrup more than the other ones, in which case he will rise crookedly and may even twist the saddle causing the horse to have a sore back.

14 Abrupt or careless transitions – to or from sitting trot and then to the gait above or below.

27 The turn on the forehand

It is very important that the instructors understand the merits and the aims of this movement themselves, before they teach it to their pupils, for only if they understand the exercise fully will they be able to teach it with sincerity.

The turn on the forehand is a very valuable exercise in the education of the riders and of their horses, and yet it is a movement which is rarely understood fully, and therefore is not used as often as it could, or should be.

Originally, and up to a decade ago, British adult dressage tests of novice standard and those for Pony Club members contained turns on the forehand, as do the novice tests of all other countries foremost in equitation to this day. Alas, the turns were often poorly executed – even judges were taught that the horse should pivot or screw round on his inner front foot – and consequently the turns themselves were castigated, removed from the tests, and their use was actually shunned by some riders. One or two instructors even jumped to hasty, wrong conclusions based on half-truths and misconceptions which resulted in confusion amongst their pupils.

271

The three most common mis-statements were:

i 'The horse's inner foreleg should swivel round, remaining stuck to the ground.' *Untrue;* this is a very bad fault, and should be marked down severely by the dressage judge.

ii 'The turn on the forehand is an unnatural movement' – *Untrue;* young colts will turn on the forehand when snorting suspiciously at a strange object lying on the ground in their paddock.

iii 'The turn on the forehand makes the horse put all his weight on to his forehand and is therefore a thoroughly bad exercise' (the adjective, 'dangerous' has even been applied!). *Untrue;* unless it is taught incorrectly. If there were any truth in this last false statement, one would wonder why Sweden, Germany, France all include turns on the forehand in the early dressage tests for their young horses, as does the Spanish Riding School of Vienna whose horses are required to develop more sustained collection than the horses of nations whose riders also like to jump and ride across country.

However, a little healthy opposition is always good; it produces a challenge which encourages an extensive search, and research; study, trial and proof – and then, better understanding, and . . . better tuition, which in turn brings rewards to riders and horses alike, as their performances improve with positive results.

As there has been controversy and confusion over this subject, it is imperative that this lesson should be well and thoroughly taught, preferably by the chief instructor. He should cover the following aspects:

1 The turn on the forehand – what it is, and how the horse does it.

2 The educational aims of the turn on the forehand.

3 How the rider asks his horse to turn on the forehand – the aids.

4 The most common faults to be avoided.

5 The practical uses of this exercise, e.g. when opening and shutting gates while mounted, and in the training of riders and horses, and in their retraining.

1 *The turn on the forehand – what it is, and how the horse does it.*

A turn on the forehand is a turn-about, on the spot, with the inside forefoot as the pivot of the turn. The horse moves round on two tracks in a half-circle, the radius of which is his own length. In the introductory stages for riders and horses it is better ridden at the walk, *nearly* on the spot, after a half-halt, and only for a quarter of a turn.

The turn is named 'left' or 'right' depending upon the direction in which the forehand (the head) turns.

The forelegs 'mark time', the outer foreleg moving around the inner foreleg, which returns to the same spot each time it comes to the ground. The two hindlegs move in an arc around the forehand, the inside hindleg crossing well over in front of the outside hindleg – the horse rounding his back in order to do this.

The horse should be on the bit and maintain a good form before, during and after the turn, this is most important. He should turn smoothly round, step by step, the rhythm and the sequence of the walk being maintained exactly, throughout. The horse should be straight, except for an almost imperceptible bend at the poll in the direction of the turn – i.e. in a turn on the forehand to the left, the rider should just be able to see the horse's left eyebrow and nostril.

Experienced riders may ask for a slight bend at the poll away from the direction of the turn, when preparing horses for more collected work, e.g. half-pass, travers and renvers. Instructors may use this form of the turn on the forehand to teach his pupils how to use their diagonal aids, for being a simple, slow-moving exercise it is relatively easy for the pupils to understand and to *feel* the work.

It is very important that the horse maintains his forward impulsion during the turn on the forehand. He should never move backwards in the slightest degree; he should not even think backwards, and if he does so, the turn should be stopped forthwith and the horse pushed forward by the rider's outside leg, or both legs, into a lively trot, before the turn is tried again. Neither must the horse be allowed to deviate sideways with his forehand; invariably this fault will occur if the turn is ridden too near to the outer track, i.e. within magnetic range of the wall. This 'sideways wander' is a favourite fault of novice riders and is quickly cured if the instructor withdraws the offender for three or four minutes to 'Watch to see how it is done'. Thus he will curse himself and then cure himself, and the remainder of the class will ride well to avoid a similar fate!

On completion of the turn on the forehand the first steps of the subsequent gait should commence immediately, clearly, and with a lively impulsion. The quality of the ensuing gait should be good, from the first step onwards; in fact, it should be even better as a result of the turn on the forehand, followed immediately by vigorous use of the rider's outside leg on the girth, or even just in front of it. (Nearer to the intercostal nerve.)

2 *The aims of the turn on the forehand*

(a) To further the rider's education; to improve his feel for a correct form as he learns to influence the horse to lift up his middle-part; to introduce him to a feel for lateral work, and to teach him thoughtfully to co-ordinate his forward-driving, restraining and sideways-moving aids, tactfully, smoothly and effectively. All this by means of a slow-moving exercise, which allows him to think and feel, and to feel and think, and to appreciate the value of the work.

(b) To improve the horse's obedience to the rider's co-operative aids, especially those of the inside leg and its supporting rein aid on the same side.

(c) To remove mental and physical constraint from the horse.

(d) To develop the horse's physique, especially the muscles of his back and loins, of his shoulder-girdle and haunches, loosening, stretching and suppling them, and strengthening his external abdominal muscles.

(e) To improve the quality of the ensuing gaits – the walk, trot and the canter.

(f) To prepare the horse for lateral work, i.e. leg-yielding, and later on for shoulder-in. Also, with diagonal aids, preparing him for half-pass and travers.

(g) To prepare the horse for the rein-back.

(h) To retrain spoiled horses, particularly those who are nervous, who do not accept the bit, and are not forward thinking, who are stiff in their backs, or whose basic gaits are faulty.

(i) To freshen up horses, who are sluggish or disobedient to the forward-driving aids; the rider uses his inside leg for the turn – then his outside leg strongly to move the horse *forward* into the required gait.

3 *The aids for the turn on the forehand*

(a) The rider must first select a suitable place, well ahead of where he is riding. He should not be close to a wall, fence or other horse which might cause an unwanted influence, or an impediment or interruption to his own horse's turn or to the work of other riders.

N.B. If he is working on a circle, the rider should always move the horse's hindquarters over *inside* the circle track; he should not teach his horse to swing his hindquarters outwards.

~ RIGHT TURN ON THE FOREHAND ~

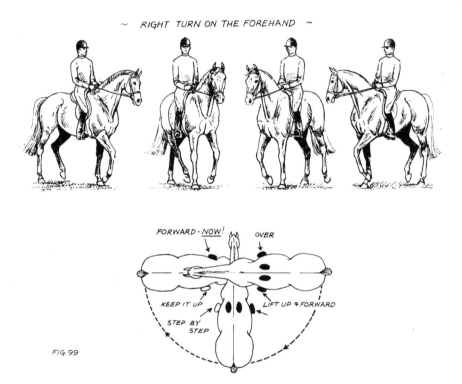

FIG. 99

(b) The horse must be on the bit, and prepared by a rebalancing half-halt, if necessary.

(c) The turn on the forehand may be ridden directly from the walk after a half-halt, or it may be preceded by a halt – in the latter case the halt must be square and not over long.

(e) The turn on the forehand is carried out mainly by pressure from the rider's inside leg (i.e. the left leg for a left turn).

(f) The rider's outside leg contains the horse's impulsion and his form, and regulates the movement so that the horse moves step by step, and ceases moving over to the side when the turn is completed.

The rider's outside leg is then used on the girth to drive the horse forward into the new gait. It is important that the rider does not miss the moment here, or he will lose much of the benefit of the turn for the gait itself.

(g) Both legs keep the forward impulsion during the turn and prevent the horse from even thinking backwards or taking the slightest step in that direction.

(h) The inside rein supports the inside leg as necessary; it indicates the direction of the turn, and bends the horse very slightly at the poll, to the left for a left turn.

(i) The outside rein regulates the bend, keeping the horse straight, except for an almost imperceptible bend at the poll.

(j) Both reins have a smooth restraining influence, preventing the horse from going forward during the turn.

N.B. It is of the utmost importance that the turn on the forehand is executed by pressure of the rider's inside leg and as little as possible with his inside hand.

4 *The most common faults*

(a) The rider fails to select a suitable place in which to make the turn on the forehand.

(b) He does not *think* carefully enough before he acts – before, during or after the turn.

(c) Lack of tact, co-ordination and co-operation between his aids.

(d) Mental or physical constraint causing the rider's seat and aids to contradict each other'or the horse's movement. The horse will show resentment and resistance, he will lose his form and will side-step with his hindlegs, as he will be unable to arch his back as required in order to cross the inside hindleg forward and over in front of the outside one.

The rider's mistakes are revealed by the horse's faulty performance, as follows:

i The horse comes off the bit, and loses his form.

ii He does not lift his outer hindleg forward underneath his body nor move his inner hindleg freely forward to cross it over in front of the outer hindleg.

iii The horse runs away from the rider's inside leg with quick side-steps.

iv The horse deviates sideways with his forehand.

v He is bent too much; the impulsion escapes due to his shoulder 'falling out'.

vi The horse loses his forward impulsion, he misses a beat of the walk, or even steps backwards.

vii The steps themselves, the regularity, tempo and fluency of the movement are inconsistent.

viii The horse walks forward, losing the turn.

5 *The practical uses of the turn on the forehand*

(a) Opening and shutting gates. All pupils should be taught the correct procedures, i.e. the rider should ride up to the hinge end of the gate, in order to turn his horse so that he stands alongside the gate, with his neck by the latch. The rider takes the reins and whip in the hand farthest from the gate and then unfastens the latch with his free hand. The horse must be kept still and pressed close to the gate with the rider's co-ordinating aids, particularly the leg which is farthest from the gate. The nearer the horse is to the gate the easier it is for the rider to lift it should this be necessary, to free the latch.

If the gate opens towards the horse, the rider grasps its latch-end and pulls it quietly towards him. If he is riding in company, he keeps his horse alongside

FIG. 100   PRACTICAL USE OF TURNING ON THE FOREHAND

the gate as he opens it, as this makes it easy for him to control the gate and his horse, especially the latter's hindquarters and his heels. When all the other riders have filed through (quietly and acknowledging the gate-opener's help), the rider then turns his horse on his forehand round the latch-end of the gate until he is alongside the far side of the gate with the other side of his neck close to the latch. The rider exchanges the reins into his other hand in order to close the gate carefully and refasten it securely.

If the gate opens away from the horse, the rider lines his horse up as above and keeps his horse close to the gate, moving forward as it opens. If the gate is reluctant to open the rider can get his horse to help by pushing his shoulder against the latch-end of the gate to ease it with extra persuasive-power! When the gate is open sufficiently he then turns his horse around on his forehand, keeping the horse's head as close as possible to the latch-end. The rider deftly exchanges hand-duties at the most convenient time and holds the gate open with his horse realigned with the far side of it. When closing the gate the rider moves his horse over with it, using a few steps of leg-yielding, and presses the horse against the gate with the leg which is farthest from the gate while he fastens it exactly as he found it.

The instructor should emphasize the following points:

i The above procedures ensure quick and efficient gate-opening.

ii The riders should observe, remember and practice correct equitation principles throughout. Careless riding, especially rough or over-strong hands should be severely reprimanded.

iii Courtesy – must prevail, especially amongst all other riders for whom the gate is being opened. Not only should they be sure to express their thanks cheerfully but also they should ride through and time their halt beyond the gate with awareness and consideration, i.e. if they halt too near to the gateway they may leave insufficient room for the remainder of the ride; if they halt after riding too far into the field, the following horses may not realize that they are going to halt, they may get excited as they feel they are being left behind and may make exuberant endeavours to buck off their restraining riders – they might even succeed!

276

iv Consideration for the owner of the gate – gates are increasingly expensive, the stock and the land which they safeguard rise in value, while labour for repairs is almost non-existent – for all these reasons gates must be opened and closed with care. They should never be allowed to slam shut or allowed to swing free. They should be re-fastened exactly as they were latched, tied or secured originally.

v Children should be taught to take a pride in being an expert gate-opener, as each time they have an opportunity to practice it will improve their horsemanship, their ponies' schooling and the manners of both.

(b) There are many other occasions when a few steps of a turn on the forehand will prove to have a practical use, particularly when placing a young horse's hindquarters into a hedge or other form of protective barrier between other horses travelling fast, approaching hounds, or similar unusual sights against which they might work up an attacking defence.

Additional notes for instructors

The turn on the forehand is a simple, loosening movement, it should be included in riders' early lessons as an exercise to practice the application of their aids and to give the pupils a slow-moving and therefore easily assessed feel of their effects and of the horse's movement under them.

As with all lessons, the instructor must explain and demonstrate the turn on the forehand carefully before he asks the class to carry out the exercise individually. He should keep the remainder of the class involved by inviting them to offer observations and comments at the end of each performance.

The first lessons on the turn on the forehand must be carefully carried out in order that the pupils have the time to assimilate the new work. The instructor must teach enthusiastically himself in order that his pupils are inspired and do not become in the least bored. The more his pupils are encouraged to think and to feel, the greater will be their appreciation and enjoyment.

As soon as the pupils are each able to make reasonable turns on the forehand to the left and right, they may be worked together as a ride, preferably on 20 metre circles, or 'cog-wheels'. Working together, as a team, will help them to ride with a natural co-ordination of their thoughts and physical aids, and will develop their feel for the work as a whole.

The value of the turn on the forehand when carried out correctly will be further confirmed in pupils' hearts and minds when, at a later stage, they ride young horses and have older, spoiled horses to retrain, when it will work like a magical key.

Whereas the novice pupil will accept his instructor's teaching that the turn on the forehand is an excellent loosening exercise for the horse, and that more than any other exercise, it removes mental and physical constraint, the more experienced pupil with an enquiring mind will wish to know, 'Why? How does the turn on the forehand do all this?'

Requests for a deeper understanding should be answered by a lecture demonstrations of two important sections described earlier:

i All that is meant by the term. 'On the bit'. See p. 139.

ii The intercostal nerve at the magic spot – its location and effect on the nervous system and musculature of the whole horse. See Fig. 88, p. 236.

The more experienced riders should be encouraged to work their horses in hand at turning on the forehand on the move to enable them to get a better understanding of this work and also for all subsequent lateral work where the same principles apply – especially in the preliminary exercise of leg-yielding. Regular, supervised practice of this exercise will ensure that the school's horses retain their standard of training and that their form does not deteriorate under more novice riders. See p. 234.

28 The canter lessons

By the time pupils are ready to learn to ride at canter they will have seen horses cantering and the keen pupils will say they 'know all about it' and be anxious to try it for themselves. However, the instructor must remember the rule, 'never assume knowledge'. He must show the class his horse working at canter for short periods on the lunge, or when he is loose-schooling him so that they can see the horse moving at canter unimpeded by a rider and can watch and work out the three-time rhythm and the sequence of legs, as well as the transitions to and from the canter. The instructor should point out further interesting points for the pupils to note: the horse leading with the fore- and hindlegs on the same side in a correct canter:

that it is easier for a horse to canter with the inside legs leading;

how awkward the horse looks when the canter is disunited;

when working loose in the school, how it is customary, being most natural, for the horse to strike off with the outside legs leading if he starts cantering at the beginning of a long side. This seed of equestrian knowledge can be referred to usefully in later lessons on counter-canter and for introducing a flying-change;

how canter work can be quite tiring for the horse, and that it should not be prolonged.

The instructor should always be alert to draw the class's attention to any unprogrammed happenings or reactions which the horse may offer as an extra bonus.

The instructor should then explain and demonstrate the rider's seat at the canter, pointing out its similarity to that for the sitting trot, the rider remaining quietly down in the centre of the saddle due to the controlled suppleness of his loins and hips. The rider should try to remember and maintain the correct upright position he has been practising during all the previous lessons; he must preserve the posture of the upper body, especially of the shoulder-girdle, and the suppleness of his hips, when the horse moves at the new, slightly faster gait. The class must be warned not to bump in the saddle and not to canter too far – 'Little and good' should always be their motto.

As the aids for the canter-depart or strike-off should be invisible, the instructor must select the most advantageous ground plan and explain and demonstrate exactly as and where he will ask the class to ride the transition and the new gait for themselves. He should demonstrate on a 20 metre circle at one end of the school as the riding of this particular track will automatically invite the rider and the horse respectively to ask for and produce a canter with the inside leg leading. The rider's weight will already have been shifted slightly to the inside with the inner hip forward to ride the circle and this is how he should be positioned for the canter-depart. The rider should check that his own position at sitting trot is correct, and that the horse's gait is well balanced, after which he only has to think, 'Canter' and look up momentarily, to the outside to put extra weight on to the inside seat-bone, and a willing horse will canter as if by magic! A less sensitive horse may need a more definite signal from the rider's inside leg on the girth and the outside leg supporting, only fractionally farther back. The rider's hands must ease just sufficiently to allow the horse to move forward into the canter, after which all the aids must be regulated to maintain the gait.

The aids should be applied when the horse is on the open side of the circle, immediately after passing over the centre line; as he is approaching the wall and the enclosed side of the circle, this will invite the horse to canter with the inside legs leading, and both rider and horse will feel comfortable, balanced and at ease.

The class should carry out the exercise, two to four riders to each 20 metre circle, each rider cantering individually from the prescribed place for about half of the circle.

The instructor should tell the riders if they are cantering on the wrong leg; this is unlikely but it might happen if the rider loses his position. He should *never* allow his pupils to look down hopefully to see if the inside front leg is coming forward as this disrupts all his aids. The instructor must be quick to *help*, this attitude of mind is essential in order that the pupil is given a positive correction to assess and feel and is not merely made to regard himself as an outstanding idiot for having made a mistake.

When giving early lessons at canter the instructor should remember the following:

1 He must not assume courage or sangfroid – he must remember how the pupil will feel, being carried away by a large unwieldy animal, faster than he has been on him before, over the ground – and rather far from it! This can be a frightening experience, especially if it is protracted by being expected to canter too far.

2 Nervous tension, breath-holding, stiffening up, loss of balance; any one of these can spell 'trouble', joined together they can lead to a disaster; these all must be guarded against and avoided.

3 The pupils must canter one at a time, each one being helped individually; later two may canter at the same time in very open order, for a short distance. The riders must be safe, happy and reasonably experienced before several riders are asked to canter their horses at the same time.

4 In the first lessons, pupils should be told to take a light hold on the front arch of the saddle to make them feel more secure for the few canter strides. As in the sitting trot lesson, this support should be psychological more than physical.

5 The site of first lessons at canter must be selected with care for due to increases in speed, rider-apprehension, horse-excitement and in the distance covered before a decrease in pace is effected, the accident-risk escalates.

The site for a class-lesson should be no larger than 40 × 40 metres, slightly smaller is better, but not less than 20 × 20 metres. It should have good, level footing and safe surrounding fences. It should be cleared of obstructions as these might create difficulties, especially if the horse decides to go on one side

279

of the hazard while the rider selects the other side. All fences, cavalletti and poles should be removed (and carefully stacked), so that there is no risk of an accident, due to an over enthusiastic horse unexpectedly jumping over any of them during the lesson.

The site of the first canter when the pupil is on a leading-rein, must also be carefully chosen. The instructor should select a wide, smooth track which is fenced on the led horse's side. It should be quiet and peaceful, with good footing; a slight uphill slope is pleasant but not necessary. It should be straight for at least 40 metres, and the pupil and the horses should be well-acquainted with the track and its surroundings at the slower gaits of walk and trot before they try out a few strides at canter along the same track.

6 Before a pupil or class tries the canter the instructor must assure them that to reduce the pace from a canter to a trot and then to a walk is a very simple matter. He must explain and demonstrate the upward and the downward transitions clearly and establish that the pupils understand and that they feel confident and happy to try it for themselves. Any sign of nervousness or diffidence should be respected. There is always another day.

The aids to trot from canter, are very similar to those from trot to walk:
The rider plans the downward transition well in advance,
He corrects his position, particularly that his legs are close to his horse's sides by the girth (as if lifting up his horse's middle part),
He thinks, and quietly says, 'Steady – trot.'
He straightens his shoulders (growing tall), and rides one further canter stride to make a smooth but forward-going transition to trot.
Even in early lessons, pupils should be encouraged to keep their horses *straight* and to appreciate the feel of good transitions and gaits.

Later the class should be taught the sequence of the horse's footfalls at the canter and his movement in greater detail so that they can perfect the timing of their transitions.

The instructor must be very careful not to overcorrect faults or to cause any excess tension or stiffness, instead he must do all in his power to foster a feel for rhythm amongst his pupils and to produce riders who can sit correctly, in balance and with elegant ease. Their seats must stay quietly in the saddle, and their backs must be supple enough to allow their hips to move in perfect harmony with their horses' canter, and during the transitions to and from the gait.

Perhaps this sounds an over-ambitious ideal for the average school –? Certainly it is both practical and possible, providing the instructor is sufficiently knowledgeable and conscientious, and it is a MUST if the pupils are to become riders and if the school's horses are to remain happy in their work and retain the purity of their gaits.

29 Physical education exercises

This is another important area of riding instruction which is seldom considered in sufficient depth. The more obvious objects of mounted physical exercises are to develop and improve:
1 A position in the saddle which is as near to the ideal as the rider's

conformation and present training standard will allow; a seat which follows the horse's movement exactly and with ease.

2 Confidence, and thereby the removal of constraint.

3 Physical fitness, muscular development and thoughtful control – (all are important to the rider's influence on his horse as well as to his security).

4 Good posture (both on and off the horse).

5 Balance.

6 Suppleness.

7 Feel.

8 A closer understanding of the horse's ways, his gaits and his reactions.

9 Co-ordination – the rider's own, feeling for and in harmony with his horse's co-ordination.

10 The fine adjustments necessary to lead the horse's manner of moving, as well as the direction he should take – blending the rider-burden to become one with his horse, mentally and physically.

11 Effective, yet soft and invisible aids.

12 A spirit of elation and fun – last, but never least!

Physical education exercises may be given as a class lesson or as a lunge lesson. The advantages of the former method are that more pupils may benefit during the same period of time and that it is easier to obtain a good spirit of fun and team-work, combined with one which is mildly competitive, and each individual may concentrate in an easy way, without feeling he is the sole target of his instructor's critical eye!

The instructor must be careful not to ask for any exercise in which his pupils work their outside limbs as the walls or perimeter fence will present a danger which can be avoided in a lunge lesson but not when the horses are working in a class, especially if they are on long reins. As with all work, both riders and their horses must be worked equally to either hand.

Class lessons

The instructor must lead his pupils to think as they work and to feel for the control, co-ordination and reactive effects of moving and working one part of his body, and the counter-measure required so that no unwanted, involuntary movements occur. The demand of the exercises can be raised gradually, not necessarily by an increase in the speed at which they are carried out, but the challenge should be that of *concentration*, through relaxation, made possible by a strengthening self-discipline. The rider will assume a good posture, and become more aware of his effectiveness, all with a natural and easy mental and physical poise.

To be truly beneficial this work must be directed by a senior instructor who by virtue of his trained eye and expertise will know exactly which exercise is needed, for how long the riders should be worked, and all the other relevant details. However, once he has established a thoughtful observation and a sound working knowledge of the exercises, student instructors and the more experienced pupils can achieve constructive results if they work in pairs, one mounted and working while the partner directs and corrects, and exchanging roles at suitable intervals.

As with all physical exercises, maximum benefit is achieved by regular and thorough work and daily practice.

Safety is always a vital factor. Physical exercises should always be given in an enclosed area with a good enclosing fence and footing. The horses must be quiet and well-mannered, yet forward-going, with reasonably good, free movement and they should be well ridden-in before work without stirrups is begun.

The spice of variety is an essential ingredient of this work, instructors must constantly apply their initiative as well as imagination and humour in its planning in order to make it interesting, corrective and challenging as well as being enjoyable.

Initially the ride should work uniformly as a team to the instructor's command, later as a variation, and to promote extra practice the instructor may set specific exercises to help each pupil individually. They will continue to 'do their own thing' until the instructor commands them to finish.

Riders should never be overtaxed by being worked for too long, at too fast a gait, or by the use of too difficult an exercise, or by the work being directed too strenuously.

WORKING THE RIDER WITHOUT STIRRUPS

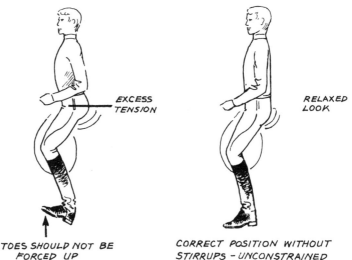

EXCESS TENSION

RELAXED LOOK

TOES SHOULD NOT BE FORCED UP

CORRECT POSITION WITHOUT STIRRUPS – UNCONSTRAINED

FIG. 101

As soon as riders feel confident at walk on long reins, they should be halted, to 'quit and cross' their stirrups for further work. It is best to remove the stirrups and leathers from the saddles, but if this is not practical then the instructor must be sure that all his pupils know how to pull the stirrup leather buckles away from the stirrup-bar for about 7 to 10 cm, and to make the leathers absolutely flat before crossing the irons over in front of the saddle (the right one first to facilitate quick remounting should it be necessary).

The introduction, explaining the purpose and method of the work, and the exercises themselves, should always be given at the halt: this allows for an easy assimilation of the explanations and demonstrations. Only when they have grasped the new exercise fully, at the halt, should the ride carry it out on the move.

The instructor must appreciate that nervousness is the greatest cause of excess mental or physical tension, and that great harm can be done to a rider's nerve if he is overfaced in any way.

When executing physical exercises on the move, the pupils should be directed to ride at walk on long reins on a circle track of 18–20 metres, this being an easily consistent track to ride with thought and weight-aids alone. Up to four or even six riders may be worked together on one circle. A greater number can be accommodated by enlarging the circle, or by increasing the number to two, or even three adjoining or conjoining circles ('cog-wheels'). This is the best formation for preserving the school horses' gaits and their training, and of testing the correctness of the riders' position, balance and influence.

The ride should be halted at regular intervals for interrogation, explanations and discussions as well as to provide well-earned rest periods for both riders and horses.

Beginners should be mounted on horses with shorter, softer strides, and more advanced riders should be given horses with stronger movement – providing that they can sit softly to it and do not bump in the saddle.

At all times the riders' hands must be watched for any unsteady or disturbing movements. Although, from the first, pupils must be cautioned that their bridle hands must retain a correct position and stay steady, the instructor must be aware that a slight degree of excess tension in a rider's position will cause his bridle hand to jostle and will disrupt the rider's aids and the horse's movements. The rider's hands provide a first-class gauge against which to measure his constraint or suppleness; for hands will only stay still if the rider is supple in his seat (hips), in his back, his shoulders, elbows and wrists. If the instructor sees any discordant hand movement he should immediately direct a slower pace, and form the ride up to the halt while he explains and demonstrates the wrong and then the right way of doing the particular exercise. After repeating the exercise at the halt, the ride should try it once again, on the move, while the instructor gives extra help and encouragement to the weaker members of the class.

Similarly, during all exercises, the remainder of the riders' positions must be under continuous surveillance for any involuntary contraction or unwanted movement, e.g. the positions of the seat and legs should remain constant during an arm-swinging exercise. Not even an eyebrow should be moved without intention!

As a pupil tires so his ambition and physical ability to maintain a correct position will wane, thus no exercise must be prolonged, especially if it is energetic or ridden at a faster pace.

Although work without reins, and exercises at trot and canter are beneficial to more experienced riders, the instructor must use great discretion and keep the work on a low key – slow and leisurely rather than over-active, or contraction and constraint will result and more harm than good will be done.

The chief instructor must impress upon his instructors that it is very important that neither they nor their pupils ever allow this work to degenerate into mechanical, thoughtless gymnastics – using the horse purely for their convenience, and conveyance – they must always retain a keen regard for the horses' feelings, movement and reactions.

Exercises should always be carefully selected to suit the standard and the corrections required by the class; some useful examples are listed below:

1 *Leg positioning – from the hips, out and down*

Special objectives – To open the hips and to enable the rider to acquire a deeper seat in the saddle. A 'broad base', rather than a narrow tense seat, perched up on top of the saddle.

~ *EXERCISES* ~

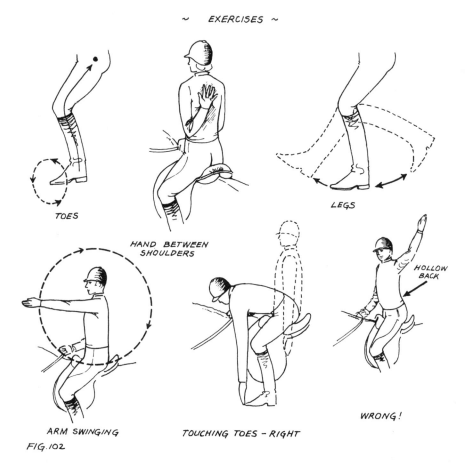

TOES

HAND BETWEEN SHOULDERS

LEGS

ARM SWINGING

TOUCHING TOES – RIGHT

HOLLOW BACK

WRONG!

FIG. 102

Method – At the halt, initially, and most often. The rider should nearly straighten each leg in turn and lift it out and back, away from the saddle. The rider should lower the thigh on to the saddle flap with the knee well lowered, pressing back the muscles which run down the inside of the thigh bone so that they are pushed back and the thigh can lie flat on the saddle. More experienced riders may exercise both legs simultaneously.

Caution – This exercise should never be done strenuously, nor at a faster gait than the walk, or the hip-joints might be strained or damaged.

2 *Ankle and hip turning*

Special objectives – To supple the ankle joints and to help to deepen the rider's seat by opening the hips. An additional, practical use – this exercise will also improve the rider's ability to retake a 'lost' stirrup iron quickly.

Method – The riders are directed to turn their toes up, IN, down and out, in a smooth, imaginary circle, with extra emphasis on the second count.

Caution – The instructor must guard against forced, stiff, or jerky movements, or unco-ordinated movements in other parts of the rider's body.

3 *Lower leg swinging*

Special objectives – to make the lower legs quite independent; to supple the knee joints; to improve the strength and the quickness of action of the rider's lower legs.

Method – Each rider raises his toes very slightly before swinging his lower legs alternately forwards and backwards rhythmically, while retaining a low, still knee position on the saddle. The toes and feet should be relaxed on completion of the exercise.

Caution – The instructor must warn his pupils to keep their lower legs quite free from their horses' sides while carrying out the exercise, in order that the swing is unimpeded and so that the horse is not disturbed by any unexpected and unwarranted buffeting.

4 *Head and neck exercises*

Special objectives – To improve posture, muscle control and co-ordination, and to remove excess tension especially in the neck where constraint usually arises.

Methods –

(a) *Head turning* – slowly, to left and right, to the fullest extent,

(b) *Head rolling* – slowly, forward on to chest, upright; as far back as it will go without strain, and upright again.

(c) *Nose signalling infinity* – the rider rotates his head on the top of the spinal column, as if his nose is writing the sign for infinity ∞, or a figure of eight lying on its side, in the air in front of him. (This is one of Major Boltenstern's exercises.)

5 *Shoulder exercises*

Special objectives – To improve posture, particularly rounded shoulders and depressed chest and rib cage; to develop control of the shoulder-girdle and awareness of its effect on the rider's back, his balance, and all his influences on his horse.

Methods –

(a) *Shoulder shrugging* – the rider raises the points of his shoulders up to his ears and holds them up there before slowly stretching them down and back as far as they will go and retaining this last position – while he *feels* all the effects. The instructor should advise his pupils to practise holding this position as often as possible, at all times during the day.

(b) *Rounding and straightening the shoulders* – a self-explanatory exercise. Both extremes of position should be attained slowly and then held for the few seconds necessary to feel and consider the relative effects of the bad and the good positions on all other parts of the rider's body. The correct position should be held for an appreciable period at the end of this exercise, while the rider is encouraged to reflect on what he has felt, and to resolve to improve his posture.

(c) *Self-improvement* All riders take their reins and whips in their inside hands and place their free hands behind their backs, as far up the shoulder-girdle as they can reach with the back of the hand and the outstretched fingers pressed against the shoulder-blades, testing the latter's flatness. The instructor must check that his pupils keep these hands high enough, that their weight does not slide out and that they keep their inner hips forward.

This exercise may be ridden at all gaits and during transitions. It has many beneficial side-effects for the horses which can best be felt by the riders when they work their horses on long reins, outside, on undulating ground, e.g. in ridged and furrowed water meadows.

6 *Chest expansion and deep breathing*
Special objectives – to improve posture, control and breathing efficiency.

Method – again this exercise explains itself. When the instructor conducts this exercise he should point out its importance, to help blood circulation, brain and muscle power, control and relaxation, as well as the more obvious lung-development, and the forming of a positive, good natural habit.

Unfortunately the usual natural instinctive reaction is to hold the breath in times of stress – riders must be taught the importance of *exhaling.*

7 *Arm swinging*
Special objectives – Posture, to straighten, relax and supple the shoulders, to improve the independence of the rider's seat and the rider's feel for rhythm, control and concentration – moving one limb without disturbing any other part of the rider.

Method – *With the reins and whip in the outside hand*, the rider allows the inside hand to hang down loosely by his side. He then swings the free arm rhythmically forwards, backwards, forwards, up, over (close to his ear) and repeats the exercise. His hand should be held in a lightly closed position, the thumb being uppermost in the forward position. The arm should be relatively straight, softly, not stiffly so – any excess tension will cause a similar, and serious fault in the rider's seat.

8 *Wrist circling*
Special objectives – control, especially of shoulder girdle and upper arms, to supple wrists and to instil a correct movement for the guiding rein-aid.

Method – The rider takes the *reins and whip in the outside hand*, and holds the inside hand in a correctly carried position. He rotates the forearm, wrist, and hand with the thumb leading the way, up, *out and round*, moving his hand out, away from the horse's withers about 35 cm, during three or four *rotations*, after which he moves it in front of him and recommences the exercise.

9 *Bending down to touch the toes*

Special objectives – suppling the rider's waist and hips; improving control, agility, confidence and balance and strengthening the seat – preparing for a quick recovery after a horse has made a mistake, when going across country, or jumping.

Method – This exercise is best commanded as follows: If the ride is on the left rein – 'Take your reins and whip in your right hand, your left hand hanging down. Bending down to touch your left toe – Down, one, two, *up*.' The exercise should be repeated several times, slowly on the down beat and quickly up.

Caution – The instructor must warn the riders not to rest their rein hands on their horses' necks as by so doing they rob the exercise of much of its value. They must check that the riders' seats and leg positions remain unmoved. They should never start the exercise from a raised arm position as this movement tends to hollow the small of the back, tightening the loin muscles which then pull the back of the pelvis forward and the seat out of the saddle when the rider leans down to touch his toes.

10 *Body bending forward and backward*

Special objectives – as for the toe touching exercise.

Method – The riders should be taught to lean their upper body forward from the hips, to return smoothly to the upright position, to lean backwards until their shoulders touch the horses' croups (or as far back as modern saddles will allow), and then return to the upright position, prior to repeating the exercise. The instructor should command the exercise as follows: 'The ends of your reins and your whip in your right hand, control your horse with the left hand. Body bending forwards and backwards – Forwards, one; upright, two; back, three, and upright four.'

The riders should look up between their horses' ears on all four counts; they must slip the reins out through their left hands on the third count and pull them through again on the fourth count. This rein-adjustment gives the exercise an additional side-benefit, for the riders gain the feel for slipping their reins which will stand them in good stead in later demands, i.e. riding young horses or jumping.

Caution – The instructor must see that the horses' mouths are not disturbed, nor the riders' seats, particularly that their knees do not rise.

Most of these exercises and those for lunge-lessons, described in the next chapter are suitable and should be used for additional homework dismounted. Riders should be encouraged to work together, drilling each other at these and other suppling exercises, possibly against a background of unobtrusive yet 'swingy' music. Dismounted Yoga or more simple yet *thinking* 'keep fit' classes are extremely beneficial to all riders. If he is to ride well the rider must be dedicated, thoughtful, supple and fit, conversely he starts with a great disadvantage and will never make a good rider if he is lazy, stiff or fat.

It is always most helpful and acceptable if friendly discipline and example are applied to any overweight pupils by the fellow-members of the class.

30 Early lunge lessons for novice pupils

That a rider's position may be corrected, practised and improved during a series of lunge lessons is an undeniable fact but there is considerably more scope, variety and depth to this subject than is usually accorded by instructors. Both student instructors and pupils should be taught this work with careful attention to detail, enthusiasm and skill.

In his introductory lesson, the instructor should first explain the main advantages and disadvantages of lunge-lessons:

ADVANTAGES

1 Being near to the instructor, the pupil is helped by a direct and close contact and communication; he can understand and implement the explanations and instruction most readily.

2 He has the instructor's sole and undivided attention.

3 The instruction can be concentrated – much of value can be taught in a short time.

4 Because the instructor controls the horse, the pupil can give his undivided attention to the improvement of his position.

DISADVANTAGES

1 *For the school's horses*

Only if the instructor is sufficiently skilled will he be able to avoid lunge lessons degenerating into a low-grade, soul and gait-destroying occupation for the lunge-horse. Too often horses can be seen jogging round and round resembling a tread mill machine, or an old-fashioned horse-powered elevator.

2 *For the pupil*

There are several artificial aspects which can obliterate a rider's natural balance and feel if he receives too many lunge lessons within too short a period of time. One or two short sessions on the lunge per week are quite sufficient for any novice rider.

The continuous circling intensifies the centrifugal force and riders build up a subconscious defence against it, which tends to become more established with each lunge lesson. Unless they are watched from outside the circle by an instructor who is not doing the lungeing, the pupils can form bad habits of crookedness or of gripping. Alternatively if they get too set with their weight slightly to the inside, pupils can lose the natural, instinctive ability to shift their weight to lead the way in changes of direction.

Learning from demonstration

From the earliest stages of their training students must be encouraged to watch horses and riders of all standards being worked on the lunge. For their part they must be alertly perceptive watching the instructor's, the horse's and the pupil's thoughts, actions, realizations, reactions and discoveries. This is the finest way to learn how a horse moves, how the rider's position and his influence on his horse may be improved by tactful correction and suggestion from the instructor, and the wonders that a good and close rapport can work in a remarkably short time.

Student-instructors should be told that they will be taught how to lunge a quiet, trained horse or pony, and how to help in the giving of a lunge-lesson to a beginner rider. At the same time they must be warned that this is but the beginning and that although proficiency at these preliminary stages will provide an excellent foundation in no way will it qualify them to train young horses or to give more advanced lessons to experienced riders. They will require much experience and further tuition before they should contemplate executing these lessons themselves. However, students should be encouraged to watch and help whenever young horses or more advanced riders and horses are being taught on a lunge by a senior instructor.

PRELIMINARY PRACTICAL LESSONS FOR STUDENT-INSTRUCTORS

Preparations

Before an assistant instructor can be expected to help during a lunge lesson he must learn how to lunge a horse who is already trained to the work. He should not be expected to lunge untrained or awkward horses until later when he is both confident and competent.

The instructor must teach his students to pay meticulous attention to every little detail concerning all phases of a lunge lesson.

Student-instructors must learn how to get the lunge horse ready so that they, in turn, may teach the pupil how to do this, quickly, efficiently and comfortably for the horse. The last is not always considered sufficiently. Students must be taught how to handle and use the equipment correctly. They should practise coiling the line or rein into even loops which are of a suitable length for the lunger (between 40 and 50 cm from top to bottom is usually best). They should learn the knack of giving each coil a small twist so that it lies flat against its fellow loops in and from the lunger's hand – and they should practise until they can pay out the line or take it up, as required, both quickly and smoothly, the left hand helping the right hand and vice versa. Students should practise correct handling of the line, working in pairs together until they have developed a reliable dexterity which should be tested by the instructor before he allows them to work with a horse. The left hand is the rein hand when the horse works on the left rein and vice versa.

Similarly students should practise the correct way to use the lungeing-whip. They should use an inanimate object such as a saddle-horse with a rug over it, until the instructor is satisfied with their accuracy, and they can use the whip to touch the rug exactly how and where they wish. The right hand is the whip hand when the horse works on the left rein and vice versa.

Handling the lunge-line or rein – in detail

To fasten, coil and hold. From the first introduction, students must be taught how to coil and hold a lunge-line in a correct, efficient yet fluent manner, each loop containing approximately 1m of line, all loops hanging flat and being of even lengths. If the lunger is about to work the horse on the left rein, he holds the line at or near the buckle in his right hand and with quick but unobtrusive arm-stretching movements with his left hand he measures out just over 1m of line into the right hand and repeats this, untwisting the line as he goes, until the whole line is neatly coiled in the right hand, he then transfers the coil into his left hand so that the buckle-end of the rope is now nearest to the horse and it can be released smoothly and freely as required. The procedure is reversed in order to prepare the line for work on the right rein, i.e. the left hand holds the cavesson-end of the line whilst the right hand measures, gathers and feeds the coils into the left hand, before finally taking the coiled rope. If the lunger's index finger divides the first loop of the line, running in a straight line to the cavesson, from the remainder of the coils, the cross-over within the hand gives an extra purchase.

It is extremely important that the loops are kept exactly even and of the correct length; one over-long loop can trip up the lunger and just one loop which is short and wound round the hand can break that same hand if the horse plays up.

As a rule the lunger's rein-hand should be held with the thumb uppermost and the knuckles facing towards the horse. The rein-hand should be held fairly close to the body, on a level with the horse's muzzle and should keep an elastic contact or be ready to follow or to allow a rewarding give if deserved.

To shorten, little by little: the hand holding the whip in the 'at rest' position, takes a hold on the line in front of the other hand and smoothly shortens the line. The lunger must be careful not to disturb the horse in any way. He may need to reverse the whip.

To shorten a considerable amount, quickly: the hand holding the whip 'at rest' is stretched forward, up to 1m, along the lunge-line, in front of the rein-hand. The whip hand grasps the line, and with a smooth but firm pull, supported by a very firm stance, the horse is brought in towards the lunger, who then takes the extra coil of rope into his rein hand, leaving the whip hand free once more. This can be repeated as required. If the horse is at all whip-shy the lunger should first reverse the whip and then take it up again when he has adjusted the rein.

To lengthen the lunge-line: the grip of the hand holding the lunge line is released to allow sufficient line to run out, and if necessary the other hand may assist in paying out the necessary number of loops. The grip is tightened smoothly as soon as the rein is the required length.

Contact and communication – As with the reins when riding, there should be a suitable and smooth contact between the horse's head and the trainer's hand.

This does not mean that the line should always form a dead straight line between the lunger's hand and the horse, for that would indicate a contact which is too strong and heavy. At no time should the line hang down in festoons on the ground, as this clearly signifies lack of control. Instead the tension should be alive to the need of the moment.

Action of the lunge-line

(a) *Leading* – when leading the horse in hand, the leader keeps the horse well forward 'shoulder to shoulder' and holds the line with the thumb away from the horse and the finger nails downwards, his hand moving forward in the direction of the horse's movement.

(b) *Giving* – when the lunger moves his rein-hand towards the horse's head.

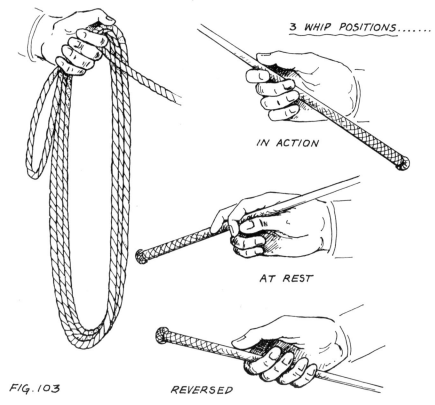

FIG. 103   REVERSED

(c) *Restraining* – the lunger turns his hand over with the fingernails upwards and moves it smoothly against the horse's movement.

(d) *Holding* – controlling – the lunger moves his rein-hand in towards his body in this way he can bring the horse in towards him.

Handling the lunge whip (in detail)

The whip should be carried in the opposite hand from the rein on which the horse is working, or with which he is being led.

It may be carried and used with the thong and lash furled, twined down the stock, or open, hanging free.

The four basic whip-positions are:

i 'Attentive' – held with the point uppermost and towards the horse; the most usual position.

ii 'At rest' – without changing his hold on the whip-stock the lunger moves the point back, away from the horse and the whip lies along the top of the forearm with the point and thong behind him.

iii 'Reversed' – the whip itself is reversed and held upside-down with the point behind the lunger and pointing towards the ground, virtually 'out of sight' from the horse.

291

iv 'Furled and reversed' – and at the ready to lead the horse in hand, or to walk up to him.

If the lunger wishes to approach the horse from the centre of the lungeing area, or requires the use of both hands to give reward or to adjust tack, he should furl the whip and then tuck it high up under his arm, with the point down behind him, he should not leave the whip on the ground where horses might tread on it and break it.

The lunge whip should always be handled with thoughtful and controlled movements, it should never be waved about with meaningless gesticulations – it must be used with the utmost tact, skill and care.

The instructor must teach the two methods for using the lunge whip as a forward driving aid:

In the first method the lunger stands in the centre with the whip pointing towards the horse's hindquarters, and the lash free, trailing on the ground, he may then make a supple circling movement with his whip, hand and arm 'up, forwards, down and back' so that the lash is set into a forwards circling motion towards the horse's hindquarters and then more subtlely at the girth. With the majority of trained horses this method is a strong enough forward-driving influence.

The second method is stronger and may be necessary for more sluggish horses – the lunger surreptitiously decreases the circle and then changes the movement of the whip hand and arm, so that after moving up and forwards it is suddenly arrested, the hand is stretched and the whip is aimed at a certain spot on the horse's hindquarters, middle, or at the girth. When the lash contacts the horse with a sharp flip, or sting-hit, the arm, whip and thong should all be in a straight line. The circle is then increased to allow the horse to go forward freely with reinforced respect and energy. Student-instructors should be taught this stronger aid but they must be warned against using it except under dire need and never when the rider is in the saddle.

The whip should be used with discretion, the minimum amount so that the horse always pays attention to its actions. 'Familiarity breeds contempt', and just as the horse can become numb-sided as he learns to ignore his rider's constantly banging legs, so a lunge horse can become oblivious to a whip which is always pointing at his hindquarters. Every gesture made with the whip should convey purpose and meaning, for this reason it is a mistake to hold the bulk of the lunge-line and in the whip-hand as this method tends to make the hand's movements clumsy and thereby interrupts the whip's messages, added to which, this method does not provide the strongest control.

Every student instructor should be taught the correct procedure of holding a horse who plays up and tries to escape the lunger's control:

To strengthen the lunger's control over an obstreperous horse, if the horse is working on the left rein, the lunger immediately strengthens his purchase between the ground and the lunge-rein and improves his control as follows:

He moves his right side forward, bending his left knee slightly as he places his right foot firmly between the horse and himself to form a supporting strut. Simultaneously he places his left hand, the rein-hand, firmly on his left hip, between point and joint so that his left hand is anchored securely behind his body-weight. Within the same instant he reverses the whip and uses the

FIG. 104   *LUNGER STRENGTHENING CONTROL*

whip-hand to help to hold the rope and to re-establish a 'feel' with the horse on the rein in a similar manner to a deep-sea fisherman.

He must be light, quick and firm on his feet in order to retain the essential alignment with the horse's shoulder. The strength and anchorage given to the lunger by the adoption of this stance is quite remarkable; it enables comparatively small lungers to control proportionately huge horses.

GENERAL PROCEDURE

Much of the following is applicable to all lunge lessons, therefore it is described and should be taught in detail.

First the aim of the lunge lesson should be resolved:

A. *To improve the rider*

Here the instructor controls the horse, thus the rider's responsibility and efforts can be concentrated fully on the improvement and appreciation of his own riding. The main objectives are:

1 Safety, security and thus CONFIDENCE.

2 FEEL – from the earliest lessons the instructor should encourage the rider to understand the horse's mental and physical reactions and movements.

3 The correct riding position in the saddle at the halt and during the three basic gaits – a lunge lesson will help a pupil to gain an understanding for sitting deeper down in the centre of the saddle.

4 Balance, controlled relaxation, suppleness and togetherness with the horse's mind and movement.

5 Close-quarter advice and supervision, producing a strong rapport between the pupil, the horse and the instructor, to the mutual benefit of all three.

6 Using exercises to their best advantages to improve the rider's position,

and the smooth effectiveness of his aids by eliminating, impeding stiffness or lack of harmony.

7 Improvement of the rider's thought, his education and understanding and his application of the aids.

8 Through the instructor the pupil will learn to think about and analyse 'How is my horse going?' step-by-step.

9 The instructor may help the rider in the schooling of his horse; the instructor using his lungeing aids to help the rider to achieve and to feel improvement in the gaits and in the transitions.

B. *To improve student-instructors*

Giving a lunge lesson is an excellent training project for riders who are learning to instruct, once they have been taught the basic requirements of lungeing the trained horse and of teaching the correct position in the saddle. Simple, supervised practice will:

1 Develop confidence – for teaching one pupil at the end of a lunge-line is far less awe-inspiring then being expected to instruct a class in the wide expanse of an indoor or outdoor manège.

2 Help the students to develop and improve an 'eye' for assessing the horse's form and the good and bad points in a rider's position, and in the way he sits on his horse at the different gaits and transitions.

3 To practise and develop the use of the voice to command, control, to express views with clarity, to give simple explanations and corrections in a readily acceptable and encouraging manner.

4 By working together, lungeing and correcting each other, it is easy for them to understand the faults and relevant difficulties and how these may best be overcome.

C. *To improve the horse–rider partnership*

This aspect should be mentioned in the introductory lecture-demonstration.

Here the proportion of control and influence on the horse may be varied to suit the circumstances. Initially, the instructor must lunge the horse without the rider in order to make a full and free assessment of the horse, and to enable him to form a controlling rapport with his lungeing-aids, with a horse who may be a stranger to him. Once the instructor has achieved these two objectives he may put up the rider and will then work them together on the lunge, with a gradual transfer of influence from instructor to rider, as the latter's position and ability improve.

The greatest advantage in this form of lesson lies in the ease, speed and closeness of the rapport between the horse, the pupil and the instructor, thus making the best possible use of the latter's expertise.

Warning! Lungeing can be a harmful exercise if:

(a) The surface is poor – ruts, stones, hard, sloping or slippery going may all cause injury to the horse's joints or tendons, which may be serious or even permanent.

(b) The lunger is inexperienced.

(c) The horse is lunged on too small a circle – causing mental and physical strain.

(d) If the equipment is incorrectly adjusted – especially side-reins, which if used, may be too low, not level, or even too tight and restrictive, or too loose and swinging heavily.

(e) The speed of the gait is too fast – causing strain and deterioration of the gaits themselves – and fatigue or fright to the rider.

Requirements

1 The instructor – the more knowlegeable the instructor, obviously the greater will be the value of the lunge lesson. Chief instructors should make sure that all his instructors are well-versed in this method of teaching.

2 The lunge ground or area – should be quiet and enclosed with safe, though not necessarily permanent fencing. It must have a good, resilient surface underfoot. In size it should be approximately 20 metres square to work on circles of up to 20 metres, as an average of 17 metres is most useful for lungeing riders; or of 20 × 40 metres to accommodate two 17 metres circles as well as work up and down the centre-line. The surrounding fence may be of a temporary nature such as rails or ropes between upstanding barrels, straw bales or jump-uprights.

Although it is quite possible to give a satisfactory lunge lesson in an open field, enclosing fences are an aid to its accuracy and add a sense of security, which is of great psychological value to a beginner or nervous rider and, later, when training or re-training inexperienced or fractious horses.

3 The lunge horse must be reliable, well-trained and used to the work. He should be over 5 years old, or the constant circling with a rider on his back may cause permanent injury to his joints. He should have three good basic gaits and be comfortable to sit on, being neither too wide nor too narrow. He should be mentally and physically fit for the work he will be expected to do. However good he may be at it, no horse should be restricted solely to working on the lunge for it is monotonous and arduous work and will soon sicken the most willing horse. Beginners, children or nervous riders must only be lunged on very quiet horses.

4 The bridle – the horse should wear his normal snaffle-bridle; the noseband should be removed for the duration of the lesson and replaced immediately afterwards.

5 The lungeing cavesson – should fit well, its noseband may be of a pattern which is designed to go above the bit, under the bit's cheek-pieces, or below the bit, as a drop-noseband. The former is usually padded all round, whereas the nose-strap of the latter style is shorter and the rear-strap is longer and is not padded. If the cavesson-noseband type of lunge cavesson is used it often has a front strap; this should support in theory only, for if it is adjusted tightly enough to do so in practice and the horse plays up, this front-strap can pull the head-piece forward over the horse's ears with the utmost ease and dexterity!

6 The lunge-line – should be light yet strong, and approximately 9–10 metres in length. Lunge lines are usually made of rope or doubled webbing; the former is less cumbersome and bulky to hold in the hand, and webbing makes more disturbance on the cavesson when it untwists itself or when being used out of doors, where it has more wind-resistance than has rope. The lunge-line should have a spring-clip at one end to fasten on to the cavesson's centre ring, and usually has a loop at the other, but the lunger's hand should never be placed through this, as it could prove dangerous if the horse were to panic and bolt.

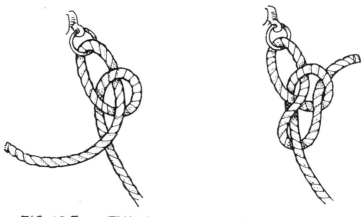

FIG·105   TYING ON A LUNGE-LINE

7 The saddle – a dressage saddle which has a good central dip in its seat and which fits the horse and the rider. The seat should not be too short, or the rider's seat bones and hips are too restricted, 42 cm is a good average saddle seat length for an adult, neither should the front of the saddle-flaps be too straight. The seat should be comfortable to sit on – new saddles are invariably too hard for comfort, for a lunge-lesson. The saddle must be put on correctly, well behind the shoulder-blade. It should not have too much stuffing in the front, but should be well stuffed at the rear, so that the rider can retain a central position in it without having to fight a continual battle 'up hill', forward from the rear arch. The saddle should be securely girthed, and the girth itself should be short enough that its buckles do not interfere with the position of the rider's legs, particularly that they are not up under his thighs.

8 The side-reins (if required) – should be lightweight so that they do not cause needless movement on the bit and they must never be adjusted so that they restrict the horse's movement. They should be a pair, be easily adjustable, non-elastic, and should have spring clips to clip on to the rings of the cavesson or of the snaffle bit. They should be fitted underneath the front girth-strap and fastened on the middle or back girth strap so that they are held up securely at a level height measured from the ground. They should only be used for trot and canter work; they should *never* be used with too much contact at the walk as the horse must have freedom to move his head and neck at this gait. Their purpose is solely to assist the lunger to control the horse's behaviour and his pace and to retain his form. The horse should work forward to the outside rein. Normally the side reins should be of the same length, but the instructor should not be dogmatic over this point, as some horses work with a correct form and bend which corresponds exactly with the circle line only if the inner side rein is a hole or two shorter than the outer rein.

9 Reward – rewarding tit-bits are just as important for this form of lunge-work as they are in the more obvious case of training the young horse.

10 The whip – should be long enough to be effective – light and slim to handle and it should have an easy balance. Modern whips with a fibreglass shaft fulfil all these requirements well.

11 Grass reins – must be fitted on all ponies being lunged on a grass surface.

12 Boots or bandages – If a horse moves close in front or behind, he should wear protective covering on his legs; the forelegs usually need protection more than the hindlegs. The instructor must ensure that they are correctly applied, for a bandage with uneven pressure, or grit between the boot and the horse's leg can cause serious injury, also too much bandaging can be weakening to the horse's legs.

13 Dress – The instructor, his assistant and his pupil should wear clothes which are neat, comfortable and safe. As a well-cut riding jacket can hide a multitude of sins, pupils should wear a plain, tailored shirt or a whole-coloured jersey or sweater, in order that the positioning of the seat, the back, the upper body, and the play or tension of the various muscles involved are in no way concealed. Whereas gloves must be worn by all parties to protect their hands, spurs should be removed – the rider's spurs may upset the horse; the lunger's spurs may upset the lunger!

The aids or signals which the lunger uses to communicate with the lunge horse are:

1 The lunger's thoughts – the most important aids (as always!). Positive thinking which must be projected with premeditated plan and purpose, and with quick judgement for the measuring and co-ordinating of the other aids.

2 The lunger's voice – he must be consistent with his commands, speak them clearly and endorse their message with well-defined meaning in the tone and manner of delivery. Although the lunger should maintain a constant communication with the horse he is lungeing, this should be one of quiet understanding, rather than a flow of meaningless chatter.

The usual commands for upward transitions are:
'Walk-on'; 'Trot-on' or 'TR-ot', and 'Canter'. All spoken rather crisply and at times with a sense of urgency.

The commands for downward transitions are:
'Steady', meaning 'Balance yourself, we are going to change down' – i.e. a form of half-halt – and then, 'Trot' or 'Walk' – spoken in a slow, soothing, drawn out tone.

Words of praise – 'Good' or 'Good boy or girl' must be given to the horse spontaneously and sincerely, exactly when deserved.

3 The lunger's body (and limbs) – by placing, positioning, or moving himself, the lunger can exert a strong influence on the horse. He must never forget himself and make false or sudden movements, or he may upset a sensitive horse – and the pupil too. He should keep the line of his shoulders just behind that of his horse; his feet should be mobile but steady and his hand and arm movements should be soft, supple and unobtrusive.

4 Tongue-clicking – a forceful aid which must be used with tact and discretion as its effect can be stronger than intended, or it may disturb other horses being worked in the vicinity.

5 The lunge-whip – may be thought of as an extension of the lunger's arm, its use is to reinforce or replace the rider's leg-aids, in their simplest form. The lunge-whip may indicate direction or intention, or it may be used to urge the horse forward with a slight or more vigorous flourish, a crack of the lash or with a small sting-hit. The whip is used to encourage the horse or to emphasize a command. It should never be flapped meaninglessly (like an unlikely

fisherman), or dragged on the floor, or used aggressively – and *never* used in temper. Students must be taught that under no circumstances will they ever use a lunge-whip to punish a horse.

The effects of these aids used when lungeing a horse are
  (a) *The forward-driving aids*
  i The lunger's thoughts – the major influence.
  ii His voice – used with clear distinction of tone.
  iii The positioning or movement of his body – towards the horse (but not within kicking range).
  iv Tongue-clicking – an occasional click will produce an immediate result unless the horse's response is deadened by continuous and monotonous clicking.
  v The whip – to back up the main forward aids.
The forward-driving aids are used to keep the horse happily thinking forward, to move him forward and to maintain a correct form. They should not be used too strongly; the horse must not be hurried out of his own rhythm in walk, trot or canter.

  (b) *The restraining aids*
  i The lunger's thoughts – again the most important.
  ii His voice – used to call to attention, to make a small half-halt with the word 'steady', to slow down, or to make a downward transition. Clarity of meaning by intonation and command is essential.
  iii The positioning or movement of the lunger himself – by increasing the distance between the horse and himself, by paying out a little of the lunge-line rather than by stepping backwards. By making a definite side step – to the left if the horse is working on the left rein and vice versa and then, perhaps by freeing the left hand and raising it in a pedestrian 'stop' sign.
  iv The lunge-line may be given one or two definite shakes. As a last resort the horse may be headed quietly into the wall.
  NOTE. The horse must stand still, and straight on the circle line, whenever he is halted.

  (c) *The sideways moving aids*
  i Thought – 'Forward and over, in good form' should be the main theme.
  ii Positioning or movement of the lunger himself – towards the horse's body where the intercostal ganglion is positioned, just in front of the girth. This target area and the aim at it will ensure that the horse moves well in a correct form, which in turn enables the rider to obtain a correct *feel*.
  iii The whip – using the butt end, or the tip, usually with the whip furled down the stock.
  iv The voice – to clarify the thought and co-ordinate it with the movement – 'Forward and over' – aided by tongue-clicking to improve impulsion, if required.
  Providing that the horse is well-trained and he is being lunged by an instructor, basic, easy lateral work may be introduced into the lunge lesson programme to the benefit of horse and rider.

298

Learning from practice

As soon as the instructor is satisfied with his students' proficiency at handling the equipment he should organize and supervise lungeing sessions during which students work in pairs and practise lungeing each other on horses they know. These sessions should be presented as extra opportunities to learn, and to think and to feel, and feel and think – they should not be allowed to deteriorate into a double circus act. Voltige is a separate and specialized subject. The instructor must teach his students the basic rules:

1 Method. When lungeing a horse the lunger envisages a triangle of which he is the apex and the horse is the base, the lunge-rein forms the line from the apex to the front of the horse and the whip forms the line from the apex to the back of the horse. When working on a circle the lunger should preserve a good posture and move on the spot in the centre of the circle; he should urge the horse forward on a large circle track round him. If he is lungeing to the left he should keep his right shoulder, hip and foot moving forward with the horse.

The lunger must adapt these basic patterns to suit the various requirements, they must not be regarded as over-restrictive disciplines or the lunger's mind and body could be rendered too stiff for him to get the best results from the horse and the rider he is lungeing.

The lunger must remain 'tuned-in' to both the horse and the rider during all the time that they are working together. He must keep the horse working willingly, calmly and well with a quiet co-ordination of his forward-driving and restraining aids while he works with the rider and encourages him to improve his feeling for, appreciation of, co-ordination with, and influence on *the horse*.

To move the horse forward, to start the lungeing, the lunger should keep the horse on a short rein so that communication is close and control is absolute. 'The quieter the better' is the rule for this stage, for it is a vital time for the horse and the lunger to get acquainted with each other's signals. A horse who rushes off when lungeing commences gives the game away, for such behaviour is a sure indication of bad handling and training – past and present. The only allowable excuse is an outside influence such as a sudden noise, another horse playing up, or a gust of cold wind.

2 The size of the circle. Ideally for the horse, the circle should be 16 to 20 metres in diameter. Smaller circles put an undue strain on all the horse's joints, particularly his hocks, lower limbs and feet. The only exceptions when this rule may be eased are for naughty, small ponies or nervous beginners, but in these cases the lunger should shorten the lunge-line and walk on a small circle inside the track on which the horse or pony is working. Sometimes this pattern may be used for work carried out at the walk, especially if the horse has a sleepy disposition.

3 Other tracks may be used as riders become more proficient, e.g. two straight lines between two half-circles; a square of 15 × 15 metres, a small rectangle of approximately 10 × 20 metres. Whatever track is being used it must be well-defined, and the lunger must move well on his feet.

4 To change the rein – The instructor should train his pupil to change direction by changing the rein within the circle. See Fig. 31 on p. 83. This provides an additional opportunity for the pupil to feel the effects of changing

299

his aids of thought, weight and thumb as he rides the second part of the first half-circle.

5 To halt – The horse must be brought forward to a smooth *still* halt, and he should stand straight, square (or nearly so), and attentive on whichever track is being ridden at the time.

6 The gait at which the horse works during a lunge lesson is a prime factor. The instructor must choose and consider which gait will be most helpful for his pupil, that the quality does not dwindle, and that work at the faster gaits is not prolonged.

As a general rule the instructor should give his explanations, introduce new thoughts, adjustments and exercises, and allow his pupil to try out these new ideas at the halt. Furthermore, the instructor should watch his pupil's work patiently and with great interest; he should give encouraging corrections, and praise whenever it is deserved, whilst he is *halted.* Then, and only then, should he expect his pupil to continue with improvements and exercises on the move, at the walk. Pupils must have time to think and feel, and feel and think. Eventually, at his request, the pupil may try the work at the trot.

Being lunged at the trot can contain a thrill of excitement for the more adventurous beginners, and many children take to it like ducklings to a duck-pond; however, in early lessons it should be used sparingly and with caution. The instructor must look out for any sign of fear, loss of balance, fatigue or stiffness; if any is evident he must make the horse walk immediately and see to it that his pupil's mental and physical equilibrium are regained, and that he is enjoying himself once more.

Most of the exercises for beginners should be carried out thoughtfully and slowly and at a slow and easy gait. In later, more advanced lunge lessons experienced riders will be worked mostly at working trot, and sometimes at canter and the tempo of the exercises will be varied – slowly, to improve the stretch and the posture and to allow time for thought and feel; and more actively, to test the rider's balance and reactions, the independence of his seat and his physical tone, suppleness and agility.

Frequent halts should be made during all lunge-lessons to provide sufficient practice for the riding of downward transitions with minimal rein-aids (if any!), and so that the halt itself may be used for rest and discussion.

The instructor must emphasise to his students that a lunge lesson is very concentrated work and that mental and physical fatigue will cause the rider to tense up or to adopt a faulty position to avoid strain or pain, any of which would render the lesson harmful rather than beneficial.

Lunge lessons for the rider may be divided into four different categories:
  i The beginner or inexperienced rider.
  ii Children
  iii The very nervous rider who has almost lost his nerve.
  iv The experienced, more advanced rider.
All these categories share four common goals:
  Safety – nurturing confidence.
  Comprehension – fostering interest.
  Improvement – progressing towards perfection.
  Enjoyment – arising from an increase of comfort, ability and mental stimulation.

The introductory stage is very important. It should be brief and not boring, and be thoughtful and not superficial. The instructor must establish a friendly rapport from the first few minutes. Tactfully he should discover as many relevant facts as possible, with regard to his pupil's previous riding experience, any problems he may have had and his aims and ambitions for the future.

After the pupil has helped to get the lunge horse ready and has led him under supervision to the lungeing area, the instructor should put the pupil in charge of the reward bag and ask him to watch the horse while he is being lunged. He should encourage his pupil to assess and discuss the horse, his form and movement.

If the horse is well-trained he should be lunged without side-reins. If they are required, e.g. when working on grass, they should be fitted carefully to give a light contact but not to restrict. They should be attached and the horse worked for a few minutes to the right and to the left before the side-reins are unclipped and the rider is invited to mount. Whenever the horse is halted, is being mouthed or led, is being worked at walk and when the rider dismounts the side-reins should be unclipped from the bit and fastened back on to the D's on the front arch of the saddle. Side reins should only be used if they are necessary for safety, or the horse's natural forward urge, willingness, and gaits may be impaired.

The lesson programme

1 The pupil mounts and takes up his stirrups and reins, the latter loosely adjusted.

In principle pupils should always be allowed to have both stirrups and reins at the beginning of every lunge lesson, in order that they may feel safe, confident, in balance and in control, and may thus get together with the horse and the instructor as quickly as possible. Remember, fear breeds excess tension and stiffness.

2 The rider should be encouraged to feel and assess the horse's walk first on one rein and then on the other. This thinking of his horse will enable the pupil to ride naturally without constraint. Riding continuously on a circle is a strange, awkward, uncomfortable and unsafe sensation to most riders when they first experience it.

3 When halted, before changing the rein, the instructor will suggest dispensing with the stirrups and/or reins as he thinks fit. In the case of beginners, children or nervous riders he should encourage the request for this to come from the pupil rather than enforcing a demand for which their nerve may not yet be ready. It is up to the instructor to 'throw down the glove', as a subtle challenge and then await the pupil's move to 'pick it up'.

(The same principle applies to starting to trot, to riding outside, to coming off the leading rein and to teaching the canter or jumping.)

4 The next stage comprises the major portion of the lunge-lesson and has five main aims:

i To teach the rider to *think* and to awaken and develop his awareness and feel.

ii To help the rider to sit in equilibrium, so that his centre of balance is adjusted to suit the horse's pace and the circle on which he is working.

iii To promote suppleness – controlled relaxation throughout; his seat and back absorbing movement, not being stiffened by it.

iv To perfect as nearly an ideal classical position as conformation and present standard will permit; these are both very important qualifying factors for a correct position cannot and must not be forced.

v To raise the pupils' standard of physical fitness.

The instructor will make systematic use of suppling, balancing and corrective exercises to promote these aims. He should start with the rider's seat, his middle part, and then work from his feet (emphasizing their effect on the hips, or vice versa), upwards to the head and hands. This order may have to be rearranged if the pupil has one outstanding fault which impedes the balance, suppleness and harmony of his whole position.

The instructor must make a quick assessment of the pupil's riding faults at the beginning of the lesson; he should be discreet about his discoveries for if he divulges them too soon the pupil will cease to ride as naturally which immediately makes the corrections more complex.

All the physical education exercises described in Chapter 29, provide excellent material for lunge lessons. There are additional exercises to be added to the repertoire which were not included in the earlier list because they are best practised on the lunge when the lunger controls the horse and the rider can be worked safely without reins.

The reins should be put out of harm's way, either by making a simple knot in them at the length they would normally be held, or by twisting them once round the horse's neck and then catching up one rein by the throatlash after the reins have been given an extra twist round each other, by the bit. See Fig. 106. Tying a knot is simple but it does cause an uneven pressure on the bit; the twisting method is best; it is more complex but it is one which once learned will be used on many other occasions during a career with horses, e.g. lungeing a horse for exercise, loose jumping, etc.

FIG. 106   SECURING REINS

Whatever exercises he uses the instructor must encourage the rider to *think* what he is doing, particularly what muscles he is using or what part of his body he is moving, to the exclusion of other muscles, e.g. if the rider moves his head, his shoulders or one or both arms, he must remain balanced on his correctly placed seat-bones with erect yet supple hips and his legs must maintain their position. Perfect control without constraint, will allow the rider to feel and to have a correct influence on his horse with invisible aids.

6 The length and substance of the lunge lesson should be dependent on the pupil's requirement. Fortunately endurance or exhaustion and legs rubbed raw are no longer regarded as essential proof of a good lunge lesson. On the contrary the ill-effects of strain and pain are widely appreciated.

There is an obvious danger to extending a lunge lesson too far. This fault may be due to the instructor's zeal being greater than his experience, or to non-horsey staff or parents who are determined that the pupil shall 'have his money's worth'.

It is a well-known fact that an average maximum limit for concentration in human beings is 40 minutes; a lunge lesson can be one of the most taxing riding sessions a pupil may have. Put these two facts together and it is easy to conclude that the full 45 minutes of a normal lesson period is too long a time for a pupil to be lunged without a break. Once appreciated, the problem is easily overcome in any one of the following ways:

(a) The pupils may be paired; one pupil rides while the other one watches for 5–10 minutes, after which they exchange roles, and so on, through the lesson. This does not mean that the dismounted pupil is left standing in a corner or is parked on a bench and ignored. Both pupils must be included in the teaching all the time.

There are several ways in which the dismounted pupil may be involved. If the horse is very reliable, the pupil may be invited into the centre of the circle to hold the reward bag and to stand or walk immediately behind the lunge line, close to the instructor, just where the lungeing assistant would be when he carries the whip for the trainer. Or the dismounted pupil may be seated in the gallery by one of the circle points where he may be questioned or asked to report on the horse or the rider, e.g. if the cavesson has slipped too close to the horse's outer eye, whether the horse is over-tracking, if his hindfeet are following the forefeet, or whether the rider's outside leg is stiff, clamped, or sticking out – and so on. This provides an observation lesson as well as an extra challenge for the rider – he will have his chance to reciprocate in a few minutes!

(b) The pupil can have a break every 5–10 minutes, while he is led on his horse about the manège, or walks him on his own if he is sufficiently accomplished to do so safely. He can practise changes of direction by means of his thought and weight aids, before returning for a further session on the lunge.

(c) The lunge lesson can be halved; the other half of the lesson period can be spent having a short instructional hack, or learning practical stable management.

Every lunge lesson should be highly educational, short and sweet – a well-sugared pill!

The success of these exercises will depend to a great extent on the rapport the instructor achieves between himself and his pupil.

Special objects – to improve the rider's co-ordination, to improve his balance and the suppleness and independence of his seat, being aware of the weight resting on, and the placing of, the two seat bones; improving confidence, control, posture and freedom of arm movements; to enliven enthusiasm and imagination.

1 Patting the horse all over, down to the front leg and back on the haunches. This is especially good for stiff hips; the seat bones *must* stay in place.

2 Putting the imaginary shot – aim and 'fire', outside the circle (not at the instructor!).

3 Juggling imaginary ping-pong balls – The pupil should look where he is juggling them. The instructor can suggest changes of height of the throwing, changes of tempo, and of the number of ping-pong balls being juggled.

4 Throwing an imaginary beach or tennis ball – this exercise explains itself. It may also be used to bring in and involve riders or students who are spectating or waiting their turn if the instructor names individuals to 'catch' and return the ball.

5 Climbing an imaginary rope – slowly, little by little, as high as possible and then sliding down, letting go of the rope, and repeating the exercise.

6 Threading an imaginary needle and sewing the fingers together. This exercise should be carried out by each rider ambidextrously (left and right handedly).

FIG. 107   FUN, ACTIVITY EXERCISES

7 Shortening and lengthening imaginary or actual reins. The instructor should be very particular that the hands are carried correctly during this exercise and that rein adjustments are carefully and smoothly made.

8 Alternate arms raised to the side and bent – left up, right up, and both together, up – and hold.

The upper arms should be raised to shoulder height with the elbows bent so that the forearm forms a right angle, and the hands should face each other with soft fingers (ballet style, not at all military!). See Fig. 107. This is a good exercise to do to music. It helps to give riders a feel for developing soft arm movements, and control from the back of the shoulder-girdle.

Some exercises to supple the waist and improve the rider's position

As with all physical exercises, these must be introduced in an easy way. Some riders may be surprisingly stiff at first. The instructor must be patient and be satisfied with only a slight turning from some pupils. He must not force the riders in any way, but must allow the exercises themselves to improve the rider's suppleness, and make a gradual increase in the demands.

9 Trunk turning

(a) with hands on hips and a lifted diaphragm, the rider turns his head and upper body round slowly to the left, gives an extra little push and holds the position for a few seconds; he then turns his upper body to the right, pushes and holds. This is repeated only a few times before the rider is told to rest.

(b) With arms raised and bent – as in exercise No. 8. This is a much more natural position for a rider's arms during the trunk turning exercise than if they are outstretched at shoulder height. The rider should think of turning the little finger part of his hand so that it is towards his head and his thumb is farther away, as this will also confirm a correct rein-aid movement.

(c) With arms outstretched and lowered to touch the horses neck and loins. The extra, physical contact with the horse can help to increase confidence and eliminate constraint.

10 Trunk bending, laterally – to supple the waist and free the rib-cage. This exercise may be executed with the hands hanging down loosely or with the hands on the hips. In either form it should be carried out slowly with care to preserve correct alignment (e.g. the trunk must be bent directly to the side without disturbance to the seat and legs). The hand or elbow must slide down an imaginary vertical line, the axis of the shoulders must follow smoothly and the head must remain at right angles to it. The instructor must see that the rider's head neither leads the way nor is left behind, as either fault is indicative of a lack of co-ordination and harmony and the rider will not obtain full benefit from the exercise.

11 Correcting upper body posture

There are two halves to this exercise, both of which are aimed at improving the rider's feel for the ability to correct his own posture.

(a) Retaining an upright position with the pelvis, the rider bends his upper body back as far as it will go. From this extreme position he slowly and thoughtfully straightens himself to a correct, upright position, so that he can feel the easy balance and poise as he thinks and looks ahead.

(b) The rider slowly collapses forward from the waist to the top of his head. He rolls his trunk up into as small a ball as possible, and holds it whilst fully

305

realizing the discomfort, before slowly and thoughtfully unrolling into a correct, upright position.

These exercises and their variations can have a great effect on the pupil's own endeavours providing that the novelty is preserved and is not diminished by over-use. Both of the last two thought-provoking and position-correcting exercises have maximum value when they are carried out at the halt or at the walk; nothing is gained by trying them at a faster gait.

Obviously all the material contained in this chapter cannot be covered in one lecture-demonstration. The chief instructor should give the first main lecture to all his instructors, students and pupils. No two lectures on this subject need ever sound too alike, for there are so many possibilities of approach and of content. Thereafter, the instructors should lead their rides into developing this work, which can culminate with a competition for the best fifteen minute work outs, in one or all three of the following sections:

1 A dismounted PE class.
2 A group of riders.
3 A lunge lesson.

The physical education exercises described in Chapter 29, may also be incorporated into lunge lessons.

31 The half-halt

This lesson subject should be taught both carefully and gradually, not because it is complicated or advanced, but because it is so very important. If the thought and feel of half-halts is omitted from pupils' early lessons, they will learn to do without them, and this will make it comparatively difficult for them later to use half-halts instinctively at the best time and in the right proportion to suit exactly the horse, the movement and the moment.

If pupils are taught to think of correcting their own positions, of re-balancing their horses or ponies whenever they might need that little bit of help, half-halts become a natural part of their riding, which is just what they should be. It is true, some half-halts are plainly obvious, especially those of competing riders on colder-blooded horses but by far the greatest number are more subtle and remain a close and invisible secret between the rider and his horse.

As instructors should always be at least one jump ahead of their pupils, the chief instructor must make sure that his team of instructors understand this work thoroughly and are thus able to teach it correctly. They should all know the FEI's definition of the half-halt: 'The half-halt is a hardly visible, almost simultaneous, co-ordinated action of the seat, the legs and the hands of the rider, with the object of increasing the attention and balance of the horse before the execution of several movements or transitions to lesser and higher paces (gaits). In shifting slightly more weight on to the horse's hindquarters, the engagement of the hindlegs and the balance on the haunches are facilitated for the benefit of the lightness of the forehand and the horse's balance as a whole.'

This should be the basis for their learning and for supporting their training and teaching, in discussion and in arguments. Despite all the acknowledged masters of equitation's descriptions of the half-halt and its intrinsic value to the whole of the horse's training, there are a few trainers who have a hang-up on this subject or who have not yet 'seen the light'. This fact helps to put young instructors on their mettle, but they must be given logical facts and sure ground on which to base their defence.

The seeds of half-halts can and should be sown in early riding lessons, when pupils are riding at walk without stirrups and with long reins. It is best to teach the first feelings for a half-halt within the confines of an indoor school where there are no interfering distractions. Pupils should be given a brief explanation and demonstration of half-halts before being set the task of riding the movement at specific and sensible places in the school, thinking of improving their horses' balance, for example, when crossing the centre line or when rejoining the outer track.

If the instructor tells his pupils to think and even to say, 'Steady,' with a simultaneous straightening of his shoulders, down and back, this exercise and riding action will also give the pupils a feel for applying smooth restraining aids, when they are allowed to ride with a rein-contact. At the same time they will be introduced to the correct way to brace their backs, for if they start this important action by tightening the muscles across the lower part of the shoulder-girdle, this will become a subconscious habit and very little extra thought will be required to bring in the support of the deeper back muscles. This approach will ensure that pupils do not brace their backs in the wrong way, i.e. with a rounding of the back which can be a thoroughly harmful action. If the rider tenses his back in the wrong way, the small of his back and his pelvis become rigid so that the latter no longer swings with and allows the horse's movement, but instead it blocks the action of the horse's back muscles.

There are a few instructors who do not believe in half-halts, nor in teaching them to their pupils, this must be incorrect and lacking in responsibility. This movement, which plays such an invaluable part in maintaining the balance and harmony of the rider and his horse must start from small beginnings and be developed to have a deeper meaning as their education escalates.

Colonel Nyblæus has an impressive little true story about half-halts which he related to an assembled gathering of senior dressage judges at the British National Equestrian Centre in the spring of 1978. At the European Dressage Championships in St Gallen, he was sitting with Mr Fritz Widmer, the Secretary General of the FEI during the final prize-giving, when they started to discuss half-halts. Several of the competitors had neglected to use even hardly visible half-halts to increase the attention and balance of their horses before transitions from one gait or movement to another. Then Mr Widmer told Colonel Nyblæus that he had just asked one 'Bereiter' at the Spanish Riding School how many half-halts he thought he made when working his horse daily for about three-quarters of an hour. The answer was: 'I must say, I never thought about it, but I think it must be somewhere between 300 and 400.'

However, to return to the novice pupil, I am convinced that whether they are children or adults, they should be taught to include half-halts in their riding at a comparatively early stage. The lesson should be kept simple:

'The half-halt consists of two equally important parts:

i The rider corrects his position on his horse.

ii He re-balances his horse – "Steady", and "Ready".

Think it, and say it – but do very little and you will *feel* it.' The correct riding and feel for half-halts is of paramount importance in every rider's career whichever ladder he is thinking of climbing – half-halts should never be restrictive and hindering – but there are many, many times when they can be most helpful to the performance of both mount and man and will add the vital safety factor to daring and courageous riding.

32 Ground-poles and cavalletti

Ground-poles and cavalletti are essential items of equipment in all riding schools. It must be realized however, that they will never supersede the value of the trials provided by natural trails. Instructional hacks along bridleways, over moorland or through forests will always prove to be more inspiring and improving than lessons which are restricted to the confines of the indoor school – both types of lesson should be used to complement each other, in fact it is said that the Italians invented cavalletti in order to bring gnarled roots and fallen branches of the woodland paths into their enclosed manèges.

The real value of ground-poles and cavalletti lies in the fact that they provide a most convenient means for introducing and teaching the techniques of a new range of subjects. They are easy to set out, to move or to remove, but as with all equipment, the principles and methods of using them must be carefully taught so that they are not abused – misuse and accidents often go hand in hand.

Working riders and horses over ground-poles and cavalletti has several good points, some more obvious than others.

For riders – the work
Opens new fields in the experience of FEEL.

Encourages, tests and confirms their adjustments of balance and co-ordination – particularly that riders go *forward* with their horses' movement.

Improves the fine play between the forward-driving aids and the restraining aids.

Provides an excellent means of introducing and practising the variations of the balanced seat, and to develop a fluency of control and adaptation before the pupil rides over small fences. (For details of the seat-adaptations, please see Chapter 35, Early jumping lessons.)

Teaches pupils to practise and to remember to check their horses' girths and to shorten their stirrup leathers a hole or two as may be necessary, *for themselves*, so that these essential preparations become instinctive precautionary reactions.

Emphasizes the importance of riding their horses *straight* forward, and provides plenty of practice in this respect.

By increasing the challenge, a spirit of adventure and fun is fostered, and yet the work is well within their reach and it is safe.

Extends riders' technical knowledge and control, and strengthens their confidence and general ability.

Widens the riders' knowledge of how the horses move – by feel from the horses they are riding and by observing each others' horses.

Provides the riders with excellent practice to which they can apply their thoughts and analyse the effects that their riding has on their horses.

Strengthens the riders' seats, as a preparation for jumping lessons.

Provides an excellent preliminary school for learning the nine phases of the jump, so that the basics are established before the rider is asked to jump a fence.

They should also be taught the correct drill for holding on to the mane half way up his neck, or the neckstrap, under not over the rein hand, where the reins are held in one hand, or with two fingers on the mane side of the neck when the reins are in both hands, so that this too is a natural reaction.

For the horses, the work has many advantages about which much has been written already. Variety, and gait restoration are the two most important factors for school horses.

General considerations

Ground-poles and cavalletti should be 2–3 metres in length and stout both in appearance and in construction.

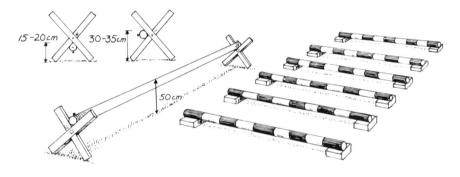

FIG. 108   CAVALETTI & GROUND POLES

Light-weight poles and cavalletti are dangerous as they roll over too freely. If a horse treads on a light ground-pole he may twist or bruise a joint or strain a tendon. If poles or cavalletti are easily knocked out of place, this displacement can prove dangerous, and replacing them will cause unnecessary interruptions within the lesson.

Ground-poles should be considerably thicker than those used for show-jumping. Rustic poles which have not been stripped of their bark and which are not quite straight are best, for they settle on to the ground and are not easily dislodged. If thinner poles are the only material available they should have cupped blocks fixed on to both ends so that they are slightly raised, and the horses can see them, they then have to make a more definite step over them, and the poles cannot roll about. Ground-poles are the most economical form of gymnastic equipment; they are easy to carry, to transport, to store and can be utilized as fillers to schooling fences.

Well constructed cavalletti are the ideal equipment for they can be set at low, medium or full height, thus they give more variety and they are of greater value later, in the training of the horse, when symmetry and accuracy are essential to the regularity of the horse's gaits. Obviously cavalletti are more expensive and are more difficult to handle and to store.

The greatest disadvantage of cavalletti lies in the risk of abuse due to lack of training in their use. Horses' legs can so easily be injured from knocking against the projecting end cross-pieces, their hocks can be strained from being walked or trotted over cavalletti which are set too high for those gaits, and cavalletti are positively dangerous if they are stacked on top of each other in an endeavour to build a fence.

Cavalletti should never be wider than 3 metres or they will be too heavy and cumbersome to be used or moved as often as they should be. It is also much more inviting for riders and horses to go *straight* over the centre of a row of cavalletti if they are not too wide.

Every riding school should possess sets of at least six ground-poles and six cavalletti for each manège as, correctly used, they are invaluable props in the training of riders and horses.

Every exercise that the instructor sets for his class must be planned to have a layout which is suitable for him to teach his pupils to learn, consider and practice the nine phases of the jump. His pupils must be well taught in this respect so that they remember this discipline and apply it instinctively for the rest of their riding careers.

The nine phases of the jump are:

1 The track – before, over and beyond the fence or throughout a course of fences.
2 The turn before the fence.
3 The approach.
4 The last three strides.
5 The take off.
6 The leap.
7 The landing.
8 The stride after landing. The get-away.
9 The turn after the fence.

All horses with sparse manes should be fitted with shorter-than-usual neck-straps round the middle of their necks. Pupils should be taught that by taking a quick, light hold of the horse's mane or the neckstrap they will prevent the horses' mouth from being disturbed. They should never regard either of them as a safety handle to hold on to in order to stay in the saddle or they will spoil the position and security of their balanced seats. The instructor should point out that he will never regard a steadying of the hands as a sign of a rider's lack of nerve or ability, but rather as welcome evidence of a thoughtful rider's wish to safeguard his horse's mouth.

This is no new or personal teaching foible, for this method of saving the horse's mouth or mind from injury or shock was written into the instructor's Manual of Horsemanship of the leading cavalry schools, including the Italian school at Tor di Quinto following Caprilli's teaching, and before that Xenophon taught:

'You must wash the hairs of the mane and tail if you want the hair to be long and healthy – the hairs of the mane are a most useful thing to hang on by.' and 'When jumping through a gap and when going up hill it is a good thing to get hold of the mane so that the horse does not have the double problem of dealing with the jump and with the interference of the bit.'

Methods and measurements

To keep the text as short and simple as possible only cavalletti will be referred to in the following notes; the same rules apply for ground-poles, any exceptions will receive special mentions.

1 Cavalletti should be treated with care. They are expensive items of equipment, and should not be dropped on to the ground, nor should they be dragged along nor stacked in the jump-store in a haphazard way. Unless students and pupils are taught this they will rarely think of it for themselves unless they have done a course in carpentry. Prevention is better than replacement.

2 Cavalletti must be laid out to a prepared plan, to fulfil a special purpose.

3 Work over cavalletti will disturb or wear the footing, therefore they must be moved frequently and the footing levelled.

4 The introductory stage must be easy to perform well – e.g. one low cavalletti; the demand should be increased gradually and logically – little by little.

5 Cavalletti should be set parallel with the short or the long side of the school, so that the rider can ride a straight track over them which is exactly at right-angles with them, and he can align his own axis of head, shoulders and hips, and those of his horse with the wall he is facing. There is no real advantage to setting them out on a diagonal line.

Alternatively cavalletti may be set out with the outer edges on the circle line and the poles directed to the centre of the circle, like a cart-wheel. Cavalletti laid out on a circle track must have correct and regular distances to be fair to the horse; irregular distances are very difficult for him to prejudge on a curved track. Riding over cavalletti set out on a circle is not work for novice riders, however it is an excellent test of the more experienced rider's ability to control and co-ordinate his balance and his weight. Another advantage to this pattern is that the length of the horse's steps can be varied without having to rearrange the cavalletti, merely by riding on the inner or the outer circle.

6 Low cavalletti may be employed to present several different problems:
(a) Spaced out singly on the outer track they will teach the rider to leave the horse undisturbed to make his own arrangements, and to have confidence in his ability to do so.

Riders should be taught to treat these poles as a challenge not a nuisance; they score a point for every pole negotiated smoothly as if it was not there, and the pole scores a point every time a horse hits it!
(b) Set out in line at correct and regular intervals they will help the rider to feel the regularity of the gait and of the movement through the horse's back with extra emphasis.
(c) Set out at less regular intervals the cavalletti will make the horse more footsure, he will have to measure and alter the length of his steps and the rider will learn to stay with the horse as he does so. This is an excellent preparation for riding across country – for 'God will not have measured out the distances between the roots in a woodland path'. (Boltenstern.)

7 As with jumps, cavalletti must always be set out with the due regard for the track through the turns before and after the cavalletti – the lay-out must leave room for and encourage good riding of these turns.

8 Similarly the instructor must insist that riders always ride a straight

approach, pass over the centre of the cavalletti and ride their horses straight forward afterwards.

9 Although a horse can be walked over a ground-pole with absolute safety this is not the case with a low cavalletti for there is not quite enough impetus in the walk to overcome a last minute lack of nerve. If the horse stops and tries to retract his foot his heel may catch under the cavalletti which will then be pulled underneath the horse, probably knocking at least one of his other legs and giving both the rider and the horse a frightening experience. Thus riders and horses must be thoroughly confident and steady walking over ground-poles or trotting over low cavalletti, before they are asked to walk over low cavalletti.

10 As horses come in all sizes and shapes, the height, type and action of each individual horse must be considered carefully when cavalletti are being set up and before the horses are worked over them.

11 All cavalletti work should follow a simple, gradual and logical progression. Even if the eventual aim is to work over a series or grid of cavalletti the lesson must always start with single ground-poles or one cavalletti.

12 The next stage is to insert the fourth cavalletti. After the first and fourth cavalletti have been ridden over several times, in both directions, the second and third cavalletti may be added in to their accurately measured spaces. Finally the fifth and sixth cavalletti may be added at correct distances, if required.

NOTE If the first, third and fifth cavalletti are set out in the middle stage, although theoretically this will seem a good plan, in practice it will prove to encourage an irregularity in the trot, as the horse has to make an extra effort with the same diagonal pair of legs all the way down the line.

13 At canter three or four cavalletti are quite sufficient. A larger number of cavalletti cover a greater expanse of ground which creates problems for the rider, the horse and the instructor. For the latter, discipline and control becomes more difficult, as can the teaching of techniques and style, especially as the horses naturally become more excited and are inclined to rush down a long series of canter cavalletti.

14 When cavalletti are used for canter work they should be made to look as inviting and solid as possible. This can easily be achieved by using two cavalletti, side by side, close together, or by adding a sloping ground pole to each side of every cavalletti, or pair of cavalletti.

15 Cavalletti work should not be too concentrated nor prolonged. Twenty minutes, two or three times a week is usually quite sufficient.

16 The variety of education and enjoyment which may be provided by correct work over ground-poles and cavalletti in the training of riders and horses is limitless, providing that the instructor has been well-trained in their use. This is a subject which must be carefully taught to student instructors and supervised, to ensure that pitfalls, injuries and accidents are avoided.

Measurements

The ideal vital statistics for a cavalletti are shown in Fig. 108:

They should be bolted, plated and screwed together – nails and wire are unstable and then become dangerous as they work loose.

The distances at which cavalletti should be set out for the three gaits should be taught both theoretically and practically to students and riders alike. Pupils should be taught to measure and practice steps of half or one metre in length so that they can use their own steps to reproduce measurements quickly and accurately.

It is worth pointing out that a single human step does not require the same stretch as a series of continuous steps as the length of the stationary foot is included in the former measurement whereas continuous steps cover the ground from toe to toe.

The following table relates to cavalletti for horses of 16 hands high. Smaller horses and ponies will need a shorter spacing, and ground-poles, being slightly lower than low cavalletti, may require slightly shorter spacing.

Cavallettii distances: At the lowest setting, ridden at a working gait.

Walk 0·07–1·10 metres

Trot 1·20–1·50 metres

Canter 3·00–3·30 metres   On middle height, with double or treble spacing at first

N.B.

1 The instructor must be watchful and diligent in suiting the distances exactly to the horses' gaits.

2 All cavalletti in a series must be precisely spaced to be fair to the horse and to give him confidence.

3 Cavalletti must be opened out or closed-in both gradually and uniformly.

4 The horses must be kept in good form throughout all cavalletti work, whether they are ridden on long reins or on the bit.

5 The rhythm of the gait must be suitable for each horse, and regular.

6 Reward for work well done must be spontaneous and generous.

EARLY LESSONS OVER GROUND-POLES AND CAVALLETTI

Introduction

As has already been mentioned, all beginners should have been accustomed to walking over ground-poles on very quiet horses, in their earliest lessons, before they even learned to trot; after which they will have ridden at trot over single ground-poles. In this way they will have accomplished the first cavalletti lesson without really realizing it. This important stage must never be omitted and should be repeated at the beginning of every cavalletti lesson for novice riders to tune them in for the work.

All lessons which include cavalletti-work must be well-planned and organized if the pupils are to make maximum progress and the horses' training is to be retained.

Whenever they teach this work instructors must remember the following rules:

1 The balanced seat – this will be improved by exercises involving cavalletti, it must be adapted as necessary. When pupils have lengthened their stirrups for work on the flat, they may be allowed to shorten them one to three holes (depending on the leather-holes and the legs!) before riding over cavalletti, in order to give their seats more stability when the horses' movements are increased.

Whether the rider adopts an upright position, inclines his upper body

313

forward from the hips, or sits or rises to the trot, his seat should stay softly in the saddle, or return quietly to it, in order that he can *feel* the horse's back muscles, whether he is tense or relaxed, and how he is moving under the rider, as he passes over the ground-pole or cavalletti. The rider must not stiffen, bump or bear down on the saddle, for any awkwardness will hamper the action of the horse's back.

The rider's shoulders must remain straight all the time whether the upper body is upright or inclined while his hands and arms move freely, going with the horse, and inviting him to stretch along his top line. Although the upper arms should be kept close to the rider's sides, all the arms' joints – shoulders, elbows, wrists and hands must be 'well-oiled' and supple. The hand on the mane side of the neck should be ready to grasp the mane 20–30 cm in front of the withers in case the horse might make an unexpected leap.

The rider should look ahead without stiffness, whether he is upright or in a more forward position, and must give his horse confidence, while thinking of riding the ground-plan in the best way for his equine partner. He must give careful consideration to the turn before the line of the cavalletti, the track approaching, over the centre, and beyond the cavalletti and of the turn afterwards.

The rider's legs should remain in a correct position, in close, supple contact with his horse's sides, urging him forward, keeping him straight, and retaining his form as they may be needed.

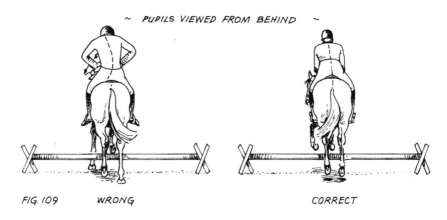

~ *PUPILS VIEWED FROM BEHIND* ~

FIG. 109   WRONG   CORRECT

When viewed from behind, the rider should look tidily parcelled – no elbows sticking out, and no lateral wobbles or weaknesses, he should be straight, yet supple, with an easy poise. From all views the whole picture of the horse and rider should look happy, well-balanced, neatly efficient and both in harmony with each other.

2 The horse – novice riders must be mounted on quiet, well-trained horses who are used to and happy in the work, and who can be relied on to walk or trot steadily and rhythmically over ground-poles and cavalletti so that the riders are given a good feel from the start.

3 Togetherness – the riders must be with their horses, in mind as well as in body; they must not disturb nor oppose their horses' thoughts or actions.

To ensure that his pupils are ready, even for an unexpected movement, the instructor should teach his pupils to incline their body forward slightly and to grasp their horses' manes, half-way up the necks, for a few seconds as they pass over any pole or cavalletti for the first time. Only when the horses are confident and steady should the riders adapt an upright position, over low cavalletti, and then this trot work is excellent for suppling the rider's pelvis and back, the hips moving well with the horse, allowing the seat-bones to remain softly in the saddle and the horse's back to move freely underneath the rider.

4 Position correction – quite often old, and some new, faults will rise to the fore again when riders are worked over cavalletti. The instructor must be sure to pinpoint the basic fault, to explain it and how to correct it, and then to give his pupils plenty of opportunity to correct their difficulties with his guidance before he increases the demand of the work in any way.

5 Control – as the pupils' confidence and co-ordination progress so can the exercises be used by the instructor to improve their ability and control. Cavalletti, ground-poles, and the other riders and their horses, can all contribute to the education, stimulation and enjoyment factors of working as members of a ride. The instructor must bear these three important factors in his mind whenever he is planning his cavalletti lesson.

6 Cavalletti exercises – to provide continuous practice for the whole ride. All instructors should know at least three ground-plans for setting out a lesson with ground-poles or cavalletti and how to command the ride through each of the exercises.

7 Use cavalletti, do not store them!

In cavalletti work, as in all other phases of a horseman's education, the chief instructor should never assume knowledge, not even amongst his own instructors, as any lack of knowledge or forgetfulness will lessen the value of this important work.

As soon as pupils can ride well over series of cavalletti at walk, trot and eventually at canter too, they are ready to progress to jumping small fences and riding over more varied terrain.

Exercise to introduce and practice variations of the balanced seat

If the pupils have been working without stirrups and have let down their stirrups a hole or two, they should shorten them a similar amount for this work. So also should those pupils who are riding with reasonably long leathers due to having well-shaped riding legs or because they have had more lessons and have applied themselves.

The instructor should explain and demonstrate:

(a) How the horse uses his head and neck and his back in order to negotiate a ground-pole. The instructor should use a young horse for he will show this more obviously than a more experienced horse who may be rather blasély effortless.

(b) How the rider must allow the horse freedom of his head, neck and back – first with an upright seat and then a moderately light seat.

(c) At the halt, he should show the class how to swing forward from the hips, keeping their leg-position constant, their backs and shoulders flat, their heads well carried and eyes looking straight ahead – considering the horse and the track. Their hands should ease forward towards the horse's mouth.

315

FIG. 110   ALLOWING HORSE FREEDOM OF HEAD, NECK & BACK

(d) The class should practise this swing, forward and upright, so that it is easy, smooth and fluent, before they try it on the move.

Make haste slowly! to develop confidence and style.

The class will then carry out simple school-figures, at the walk, over strategically-placed ground-poles, e.g. at A, X and C of a short arena, for work on large circles, and then at the circle side-points as well; or three ground-poles across the centre line at 8–10 metre intervals, for work down the centre line. Pupils should be told to swing forward moderately and smoothly as their horses move over the ground-poles and to resume an upright position at all other times. This easy exercise will start the pupils thinking and feeling for timing and fluency. Once established at the walk on long reins this may be ridden at trot, rising at first and then sitting.

Later, more experienced pupils may be given a similar exercise in order to practise and establish the light or forward seat – when they are sufficiently confident and competent over small fences, riding with a moderately light seat. The lesson should be based on the above format but using cavalletti rather than ground-poles, to increase the horses' movements and to make the exercise more real.

More experienced pupils should be told to hold the light or forward position for several strides on the flat, then over a series of ground-poles, before they are asked to ride down a series of cavalletti in the forward position.

Pupils must be sufficiently experienced, confident, supple, balanced and *fit* before they are expected to hold the forward position for this length of time or they will lose their natural fluency and effectiveness, and they will probably bump about, disturbing their horses' backs, mouths, balance and footwork – and spoil their confidence, willingness and training.

33 Leg-yielding

Leg-yielding is the important preliminary lateral movement. It is both the simplest and the most basic and is therefore the essential foundation-stone upon which all the more advanced lateral work is built.

316

As neither collection nor bend are required qualities of leg-yielding, its demand is straightforward and easy, and thus it provides an excellent, clearly understood introduction for both riders and horses to the more difficult lateral movements which will be developed at a later stage of their training. Shoulder-in, half-pass, travers and renvers are much more demanding movements, requiring both collection and a uniform bend throughout the horse; for this reason they are beyond the capabilities of inexperienced riders and of young, novice horses. In fact, it could be dangerous to the horse's training if these advanced lateral movements were taught without the sure foundation provided by leg-yielding. If difficult lateral movements are asked for too soon, inexperienced riders will then resort to pulling their horses into a restricted shape and movement rather than being able to develop collection from a loosening of the shoulders and a naturally growing musculature and engagement of the haunches which is provided by the preliminary exercise of leg-yielding, and its fore-runner, the turn on the forehand.

That leg-yielding has met with opposition in some quarters in England is probably due to two main reasons; first, a national distaste for something which is 'new', and second, insufficient research and understanding. This opposition has been unfortunate for some riders and horses, but it has also encouraged thought, question and solution which is always highly beneficial.

The answer to the first reaction is that it is not new. Horsemen have been leg-yielding for centuries, in fact William Cavendish, the Duke of Newcastle, our own undisputed classical equitation expert, described leg-yielding in detail and advocated its use with great enthusiasm in his famous book 'A General System of Horsemanship', written in the eighteenth century.

It is true that in more recent times, Colonel Podhajsky did not advise the use of leg-yielding, other than for one or two lessons and then only at the walk. There are two good reasons for this. First, in the years when Colonel Podhajsky began his career, as a young lieutenant, there existed an old German military form of leg-yielding, in which the horse was made to bend considerably as he moved away from the rider's leg. As it was more of a military manoeuvre than an equestrian movement, nobody minded if the horse's shoulder 'fell out' as long as he yielded to the rider's leg. Colonel Händler subsequently confirmed to me that this bent form of leg-yielding was the version which was disliked at the Spanish Riding School – quite understandably! Now the FEI have restored the shape of leg-yielding and its value as a schooling movement by decreeing that the horse must be *straight*, that former disadvantage has been abolished.

The differences, particularly in conformation and movement between Colonel Podhajsky's horses and those of the outside world could well provide the second reason for his opinion, for the Lipizzaner horses with whom he worked are built and move very differently from thoroughbred or half-bred horses. In conformation they are comparatively 'square', stout and sturdy, their centre of gravity is moved backwards relatively easily, they have shorter, rounder strides and are naturally very loose in their shoulders. Thoroughbred horses are bred to race – to go forward as fast as possible in a straight or almost straight line, their centre of gravity is moved forward easily and backwards not so easily; although their forelegs can sweep forward there is often an inbred tightness in their shoulders which restricts their sideways movement and the

317

freedom of their gaits. From these facts it is easy to conclude that thoroughbred horses have a greater *need* for gymnastic exercises to develop their athletic range and to improve the quality of their gaits, just as they also need rebalancing by means of half-halts to enable them to move in equilibrium with a better engagement of their haunches. Instructors have a great responsibility to teach their riders how to work their horses systematically to a steady improvement; little by little, leaving out no rungs of the training ladder.

As this is new work to many instructors, as well as to their pupils, it will be described in detail.

The ancient Masters of Equitation did not give leg-yielding a separate title from the more advanced parent movement, used at a later stage of training – shoulder-in. However, to introduce shoulder-in to riders and horses it was advocated that they should first move forwards and sideways at the walk, fluently and well balanced (but not yet in collection) and with the horse only very slightly bent away from the movement. In other words leg-yielding at the walk. When ready, the same movement was developed at the trot. Eventually, as collection and bending improved through these early stages, shoulder-in grew out of it as a plant produces a perfect flower.

The main misconception in England was that, 'Leg-yielding spoils a horse's half-pass because it teaches him to look the wrong way.' This argument was truly a revelation that the complainants had not considered the subject in depth or with reasoning. These same objectors had no such complaint against shoulder-in, where the horse is also bent in the opposite direction from a half-pass, and they would teach it quite happily to horses and riders who were not *nearly* ready for such an advanced movement. The simple truth is that leg-yielding is the introductory stage of shoulder-in; in both of these lateral movements the horse looks away from the direction of the movement. On the other side of the 'lateral fence', the half-pass at an easy angle, as in Medium level tests, is the introductory stage of the more advanced travers, renvers or the half-pass at Grand Prix level where the angle of the tracks is very acute. In all of this second group of lateral movements the horse looks towards the direction of the movement.

It is interesting to note that although the writings of the Duke of Newcastle and of our cavalry manuals of the nineteenth century contained correct conceptions of shoulder-in, during the years between the two world wars our writers went haywire and caused much confusion between themselves and their readers, to say nothing of their horses! E.g. Shoulder-in became a kind of, 'Half-pass, tail to boards.' It was not until we started watching, listening, competing and learning on the Continent that we realized that our rules and textbooks were teaching our riders much that was incorrect – even our 'figures and curlicues' were wrong.

Due to these earlier muddles being only partially corrected, and to the pressure of modern life leaving too little time for thorough research and training, too-quick methods were being used in an endeavour to reach a quick result.

In 1969 Colonel Gustaf Nyblæus came to the British National Equestrian Centre and ran a most interesting and inspiring course for dressage judges in which he explained that several horses were showing very good leg-yielding instead of shoulder-in or instead of a half-pass, due to a general lack of collection and of bend, or even a wrong bend in the latter case – in fact, we were nearly 'in a lateral mess'!

In 1973 the Dressage Committee of the Bureau of the FEI decided to offer guidance to the world's dressage judges, instructors, trainers and riders, asking them to revive the ancient proverb 'Slow but sure wins the race', and to reward horses which showed, 'Suppleness, looseness, flexibility, compliance and obedience – the horse being on the bit with a maintained impulsion, and – little by little-increased collection.' As a more positive measure the FEI introduced leg-yielding as a required movement with their dressage-tests for junior riders and thus gave it their official blessing, and, in a subtle way ensured that all instructors, trainers and riders would learn more about it – and *use* it. The success of this venture has certainly been proved by the riding of the juniors of those days, who are now competing amongst the top-flight in senior international competitions, executing the most demanding lateral work with expertise, ease and elegance.

An introduction to leg-yielding can best be concluded by quoting from Colonel Nyblæus' 'sermon' – which he reiterated in 1977 and again in 1978 to British instructors, trainers, dressage judges and riders.

First, three quotations from 'Ecole de Cavalerie', written in 1733 by Francoise de la Gueriniere:

i 'To our disgrace we must admit that the desire for the beautiful in this fine art has decreased a great deal in our time. Instead of, as was formerly the case, striving to gain with patient understanding the most difficult movements which constitute the grace of the manège and shed lustre on reviews and ceremonies, one nowadays contents oneself with a too careless practice.'

Colonel Nyblæus fears that Gueriniere must be turning in his grave as he sees that his words still apply after over 250 years.

ii 'A horse which is not absolutely supple, loose and flexible cannot conform to the will of man with ease and carriage.'

iii 'Shoulder-in is at the same time the most difficult and the most useful movement to make a horse supple, loose and flexible.'

Colonel Nyblæus suggests that perhaps even Gueriniere sometimes had to crawl before he could walk, i.e. 'that he reduced the difficulties when he began to teach his horses to yield to his legs (before they were able to lower their quarters), that he did not try to have them "uniformly bent from the poll to the tail" (as they should be in shoulder-in), but had them much more straight at first in order to reach the first aim of all lateral work, namely to teach the horse to yield to the inside leg in an easy way.'

However, to return to the riding school, as there has been a certain amount of controversy and confusion on the subject, leg-yielding must be taught with care and belief, combined with a sincere desire that all the pupils shall learn and understand the work. Young instructors should be encouraged to delve much deeper than those who produced the early, superficial criticisms. Constructive study, correct teaching and resolute practice of leg-yielding, so that it is well established before the invaluable but advanced shoulder-in, could lead to a remarkable breakthrough and major improvement in the general standard of British equitation.

The plan for the lesson should resemble that outlined for the turn on the forehand.

1 *Leg-yielding – what it is, and how the horse does it*

Leg-yielding is the introductory lateral movement. It is the easiest for both the rider and the horse; it is related to the shoulder-in.

Leg-yielding may be executed at an early training level, before the horse is mentally or physically ready for collected work, and the more advanced demands of shoulder-in, or the other lateral movements, e.g. half-pass, renvers and travers.

FIG. III

LEG YIELDING

During the leg-yielding the horse remains on the bit as he moves forwards and sideways at a well-balanced yet lively gait. His body should be straight. There should be an almost imperceptible bend at the poll away from the direction of the movement; his ears should be level and the rider should just be able to see the outer edges of the superciliary arch (or eye-brow) and of the nostril on the side away from which he is moving.

The horse's inside fore and hindlegs cross over and pass in front of the outside fore and hindlegs, fluently and with ease.

The strides should be uniform in length and spring, and the gait must retain its regularity, tempo and impulsion.

Leg-yielding is the forerunner of the more advanced shoulder-in, requiring none of the latter's bend and collection. In both movements the horse looks away from the direction in which he is moving.

2 *The aims of leg-yielding*

(a) To further the rider's education, particularly his feel for lateral work. Improving his confidence by the practical experience of an easy introduction, so that his forward-driving, restraining and sideways-moving aids are well co-ordinated and as effective yet invisible as possible. The rider learns to feel for the movement coming through the horse's back, with a definite lifting of the horse's middle-part.

(b) To remove mental and physical constraint – from the rider and from the horse.

(c) To improve the horse's obedience to the rider's aids, especially to the co-ordinating aids of the inside leg and rein.

(d) To supple the whole horse, and to 'loosen' him, particularly his shoulders, thereby improving his gaits.

(e) To develop the horse's physique, especially the muscles of his back and loins. The stretching and suppling of the deep muscles of the shoulder-girdle and of the haunches enables the horse to move with more freedom and cadence, and the strengthening of the external abdominal muscles and of the loins which will facilitate elevation – a necessary quality for collection.

(f) To 'open the way' for young riders and young horses, etc. to understand how to apply and to obey the aids used in lateral movements, thus preparing them for the more advanced movements, i.e. shoulder-in, and half-pass.

(g) To retrain spoiled horses, helping to overcome and eradicate their worries, confusions and resistances – replacing these with a calm understanding, confidence and willing ease.

3 The aids for leg-yielding

(a) First the rider must make out a suitable ground-plan for himself and his horse, so that it is easy if not encouraging for his horse – e.g. towards rather than away from the outer track in the manège, so that the wall's magnetism may be used to good effect; or measuring out the angle to a distinguishing 'marker' such as a patch of clover or cocksfoot in a field, or crossing to the other side of a green woodland or moorland track.

(b) With the horse on the bit and moving at a lively gait, in a good form, the rider should make a suitable half-halt to improve his balance and to shorten his steps and his form slightly, keeping the latter well rounded. Both rider and horse must be particularly well-balanced mentally and physically before they commence any leg-yielding.

(c) The rider then applies the main leg-yielding aid, *his inside leg*. He applies the pressure of his inside leg either just behind the girth if he wishes to influence the horse's hindquarters, or farther forward if he wishes to influence the horse's forehand.

(d) The inside rein supports the influence of the rider's inside leg, when required, and bends the horse slightly, at the poll, so that the rider can just catch a glimpse of the horse's eyebrow and nostril on his inner side. The rider moves his inside hand softly and smoothly towards his inside hip, only as much as is necessary.

(e) The outside leg regulates the movement and, together with the outside rein, prevents the horse from bending or moving sideways too much, or from running away from the rider's inside leg. The outside leg is usually applied by the girth, or it may be used slightly farther back to regulate or control the hindquarters.

(f) The outside rein leads the forehand in its forwards–sideways track, and regulates the bend, safeguarding the straightness in the horse's body. The rider's forearm, wrist and hand should be turned out softly with the thumb 'leading the way.'

(g) Both legs, especially the outside leg, maintain the impulsion.

(h) The rider's weight should remain in the centre of the saddle. As he gains in experience he will learn to give a small push with his inner seat bone. His upper body should be poised well with the movement, there being no sign of constraint.

(i) The movement should be ridden thoughtfully, step by step. Quality rather than quantity should be the aim.

(j) The rider should drive his horse straight forward at a lively gait by an energetic use of his outside leg, after the horse has completed a few good steps of leg-yielding.

'Little by little' and 'little and often' are two mottoes which are very applicable to this work.

4 *The most common faults*

(a) The rider fails to make a suitable plan, early enough for the horse to have time to organize himself, i.e. he asks an unfair question.

(b) He forgets the preliminary half-halt, and commences the movement before the horse is prepared and well-balanced, or when the tempo is too fast for him to manage the movement and his footwork with ease.

(c) The rider bends the horse too much with too strong an influence of the inside rein (hanging on the rein). He blocks the movement by bringing the inner hand across to the withers – or even, over them.

(d) The rider's outside rein is restrictive, held against the withers with the back of the hand uppermost, instead of guiding the forehand with a slightly open rein, the rider's thumb 'leading the way' (as if thumbing a lift), while his elbow remains close to his hip and the rein-aid is soft and smooth.

(e) He does not regulate the bend sufficiently with his outside leg and rein – the hindquarters must be aligned with the forehand.

(f) The rider may concentrate too much on the horse's hindquarters, using his inside leg behind the girth for too prolonged a time.

(g) He loses the feel and thus the influence for the qualities of the horse's form and his gait, so that there is a deterioration rather than an improvement of these qualities during and as a result of the leg-yielding. This is a major fault and must be guarded against most meticulously in all lessons.

The first lessons

The instructor should give his pupils an introductory, practical lecture, using several different horses to illustrate how the horse looks and moves when he is carrying out the exercise, exactly how the rider applies his aids, and most important, the effect of the work on the horse's form and gaits. He should encourage his pupils to take notes, which he should check as students' rough notes can be notoriously ambiguous and inaccurate! He should encourage questions and be prepared to answer them with further explanatory demonstrations if necessary – until he is satisfied that his pupils do understand the aims and aids of leg-yielding.

The pupils should then be mounted, and the lesson should follow the usual format.

(a) It is simplest, easiest and therefore best if the instructor tells his pupils to think only of loosening the horse's shoulders at first.

(b) He then explains the basic aids for this first stage of leg-yielding.

From left to right (the left is the inner side): Firstly the rider must sit as correctly as possible, without constraint. He must shorten the reins and make sure that his hands are carried correctly. He feels for a good gait and thinks where he is going. He makes a half-halt and then he uses his left leg actively on the girth to move the horse over, assisted, if necessary, by the left rein, smoothly towards the left hip; the right rein guides, the right hand being turned over, fingernails uppermost and thumb-part of the hand leading. At this first stage, these are the three most important rider-actions. The other aids are present, but only play a very minor supporting role.

(c) The instructor demonstrates, first at the halt and then at the walk and at the trot, exaggerating his aids slightly so that they are clearly seen and understood, and the pupils can also see that even though the instructor is using visible aids for their benefit, his horse responds willingly and remains calm and unconstrained.

(d) The instructor answers any questions put to him, demonstrating again if necessary.

(e) He shows the class exactly how he wishes them to carry out the first simple exercise as follows:

Increasing the circle on two tracks –

As long as the pupils already know how to ride a 20 metre circle correctly and how to decrease its size to an inner 10 metre circle, on a single track, they will find it very easy to move their horses out to the 20 metre circle again on two tracks by using their inner, sideways-pushing leg, actively on the girth. The exercise is ridden first at walk, and then at trot. This is one of the best methods of developing leg-yielding for both riders and horses. Several riders can work together on the same circle, in fact they will help each other by so doing. If, after decreasing the circle on a single track and increasing it on two tracks

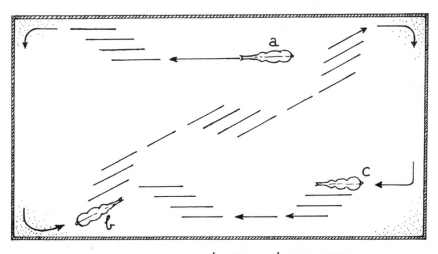

FIG.112   STAIRCASE OR 'SKATING' EXERCISES

several times, the instructor then puts the riders on to two diamonds, they can feel the benefit of the loosening work as they change the rein out of the diamonds with lengthened strides on the diagonally ridden changing line, before repeating the decreasing and increasing of the circle on the other rein.

Alternate shoulder-loosening, staircase, or 'skating' exercises – free from the wall. All excellent means of improving riders and horses.

Here the instructor explains and demonstrates a variety of patterns which his rider may use, all of which have the same objective – to loosen the horses' shoulders and to remove all constraint from every part of their being. See Fig. 112.

Additional notes for instructors

Although leg-yielding is a relatively simple movement it is also an important one. It must be taught in careful detail so that pupils get a clear idea of this basic lateral movement, and where and how to ride it, so that they acquire a correct knowledge and feel which will stand them in good stead as a foundation-stone for all lateral work and for all their equestrian endeavours in the future.

The early lessons should never be too ambitious. Leg-yielding should be well established at the walk, before pupils are asked to try it at trot.

As the pupils progress, the instructor should explain the benefits of carrying the schooling-whip in the *outside* hand. He should demonstrate the correct timing and show the effect the whip has on the horse's whole form when it is used in a carefully controlled and tactful manner to support the influence of the rider's outside leg. It encourages the horse to bring his outside hind leg forward underneath him as well as slightly to the side, which in turn ensures that the inside hindleg reaches forward well in order to cross over in front of the forward reaching outside hindleg. Thus the hindlegs are active, the haunches are engaged and the work goes through the horse's back; at the same time the shoulders are stretching laterally and the horse uses himself like a true athlete.

The rider should be encouraged to think and feel, and feel and think, by being directed to ride prescribed ground-plans and transitions, using downward transitions immediately before some steps of the leg-yielding so that the previous faster gait will help to maintain the impulsion during the leg-yielding, and the leg-yielding will help to improve the transition up to the next gait, as well as the quality of the gait itself.

Leg-yielding, together with the turn on the forehand are two of the most useful and beneficial exercises which an instructor has in his handbook for educating and re-educating riders and horses of all standards.

34 The rein back

This is an unfortunate name for a good exercise, for its title presupposes an unseemly emphasis on the use of the reins. In fact, far too many riders do force their horses backwards by pulling on the reins, and using little or no forward driving aids, whereas the proportionate use of their influences should be reversed. In my humble opinion the title would be improved simply and effectively by omitting the word 'rein'. However, when teaching, instructors must conform to the FEI leadership, books and tests, so 'rein back' the title remains. *Pro tem.*

This lesson is included at the end of early riding lessons for four good reasons and with four provisos.

To list the four aims first:

1 The movement develops the pupils' feel and tests their equestrian tact, especially that their forward-driving and restraining aids co-operate together with careful balance.

2 It improves riders' thoughtfulness, control, confidence and ability.

3 Practically, when out hacking or hunting, it is often necessary to be able to move the horse backwards when there is no room to turn around, and when opening and shutting gates. It is essential that pupils are taught how to ask their horses to move backwards correctly. If this movement is not taught at this juncture, horses will suffer, for the untrained beginners' method is to pull and keep pulling until the horse is forced backwards, away from the pain in his mouth.

4 It is an excellent physical exercise for the horse, developing the muscles of his top line, his neck, back, loins and haunches, and also those at the base of the shoulder-girdle and under his rib-cage, all of which are involved in the lightening of the horse's forehand. Pupils should be taught to think of the movement in this way, for only thus will they be able to assess its correct qualities.

The four provisos are:

1 The horses used to teach the pupils must be well-trained in order to give the pupils a correct feel. The movement could spoil both the training and the physique of a half-trained horse if it is badly ridden; his forward-thinking, his mouth, back and hocks could all be damaged by bad riding. Only good and experienced riders should be allowed to teach this movement to young or half-trained horses – and then they should be carefully supervised.

2 The riding of this movement should never be overdone, by riding it too often, by the use of force, or by asking for too many steps backwards.

3 The pupils must be sufficiently educated, i.e. they must have good, supple seats and correct influences, and be capable of riding circles and turns and transitions smoothly and with a nice harmony. They should be able to execute and assess good halts fluently from walk and trot, with invisible aids (or very nearly so!), before they are taught how to move their horses backwards.

4 The horses' halts must be preserved. Good, still halts should be practised frequently so that the horses realize that they are the major requirement, while they may be asked to step backwards afterwards sometimes as a special exercise.

INTRODUCTION

Explanation and observation. The instructor should explain the movement to the class, demonstrating the various points. He should outline the FEI's definition of the rein-back, that the horse moves straight backwards, the feet being clearly raised and set down almost simultaneously in diagonal pairs.

As every intelligent human being enjoys an argument, it will interest student-instructors and pupils to know that the word 'almost' is a fairly recent addition to the official wording and that its insertion caused some controversy. For many decades experts have been describing the rein-back as a two time gait, until the diagonal aspect became the be-all and end-all. However, Colonel

Nyblæus observed with his discerning eye and recorded for all time in the FEI rule book that horses move backwards not in exact diagonal pairs as was hitherto thought to be the case, but that 'almost simultaneously' is more precisely correct and this is now accepted as the official practical requirement.

It is to be hoped that the addition of 'almost' will deflect instructors, trainers – yes, and dressage judges too – from concentrating exclusively on the exact synchronization of the legs moving in diagonal pairs. They should after all, be much more concerned about the important factors of whether the horse is calm, straight, on the bit and maintaining a good form, while picking up his feet cleanly over the ground as he moves backwards with distinct and regular steps. The pupils can hear and see for themselves that when a horse reins back on a hard surface, four hoof-beats are clearly heard. The steps are not widely and evenly spaced – one – two – three – four – but the diagonals are sometimes very slightly off-beat – 'almost in two-time'.

The instructor should emphasize that all the transitions must be smooth, and that during the transition to the halt, the halt itself, and during the steps back and into the upward transition afterwards, the horse should retain his form, being well balanced, on the bit and maintaining his desire to move forward throughout. His hind feet should remain in line with his forefeet, and he should be absolutely straight in his body as well as his steps.

As he completes the last step backwards the horse should comply willingly with his rider's wish to move forward. He should enter the required gait of walk, trot or canter with clearly defined steps and a lively impulsion at the first forward step.

The aids to move the horse backwards

First the rider must bring the horse smoothly to a good, well-balanced halt, knowing in his own mind exactly how many backward steps he is going to ask his horse to make. One, two or three steps are quite sufficient for these early lessons.

The rider must be very careful not to lose the horse's form as he stands at the halt – the suspension bridge (his back) must remain 'suspended'. The forward-driving aids must be kept in attendance, the lower legs remaining close by the girth as if lifting up the horse's middle part. The horse must remain between leg and hand.

The instructor must emphasize that the forward-driving aids are, as usual, the most important aids when riding the rein-back. His pupils may look bewildered or disbelieving, in which case he can use a mental picture of the sea to help to illustrate the feeling he wishes them to have. The sea surges forward to the sea-wall, from whence it surges backwards. The rider's legs cause the horse to surge forward, his rein aids restrain and the horse moves back.

The rider's forward-driving aids ask the horse to move forwards, particularly with both lower legs by the girth. As the horse commences the forward movement and picks up a hindleg the rein-aids restrain evenly and softly while the legs maintain their influence, sustaining the necessary impulsion and preventing the hindquarters from deviating to either side. The reins aids should give slightly as each step is made; they must also be ready to support the leg aids should the horse think of moving his hindlegs out to one side or the other.

326

The rider's upper body should remain upright and supple, and he should feel and analyse the movement of the horse's legs and back under his seat bones. The rider must count the steps, giving very slightly as each one is made, and he must think and ride the horse forward at the prearranged gait as the horse completes the last step.

Throughout the whole series of movements the rider must ensure that his forward-driving aids are predominant and that the restraining aids are soft, smooth and minimal.

Lesson procedure

The ride should be introduced to this lesson individually. The class should be halted on the C or A circle line, facing X.

~ THE REIN-BACK ~

FIG. 113   BAD   GOOD

The instructor should explain that he wishes each rider in succession to ride their horse forward at trot on to the centre line between X and D (or G). The rider will halt his horse smoothly and briefly at D before riding a quarter turn on the forehand and while his horse's middle-part is lifted he will ask for one or two steps backwards. He should then ride his horse forward at a lively trot and re-take his place in the ride, or the instructor may tell him to repeat the exercise if the first attempt was not very successful.

The instructor must be sensitively observant as he works painstakingly but unobtrusively with each rider. He should watch and take note but he must not interrupt the communication and co-operation between the rider and his horse as they carry out the quarter turn on the forehand, rein back and move forward.

The rider should make a smooth halt and stand square and still while he listens to his instructor's appraisal and advice for improvement, before riding forward and repeating the whole exercise once more.

After following this procedure for several lessons, providing the riders understand the work correctly and can carry it out with smooth co-ordination and not a vestige of pulling with their hands, the turn on the forehand may be omitted. However, pupils should be practised at the original format at regular intervals so that they remember it well when they train young or spoiled horses, later in their careers.

327

The most common rider faults

1 A rough, abrupt or unbalanced halt, making the rein back even more difficult for the horse.

2 Poor preparation – reins too long, and lower legs sprung away from the horse's sides, so that the horse is not on the bit even before he is asked to move backwards.

3 Excessive or forceful rein-aids. The rider's hands being held and used heavily – hanging hands pulling on the reins – a very bad and physically damaging fault.

4 Insufficient forward-driving and 'uplifting' influences. This is a very common fault, it is also one which the instructor must understand for to an inexperienced rider it does seem to be a contradiction of terms to ride forwards in order to move backwards.

5 Stiffness or excess tension in the rider's mind or body will make it difficult for the horse to 'get the message'; his confusion is often mistranslated as obstinacy by the rider – which is an unfair assumption for which he is sometimes abused. The instructor must remember that stiffness is often caused by the rider trying too hard.

6 The rider may think backwards, forgetting to preserve the horse's forward impulsion with alert forward-driving aids; in which case the horse will antici-pate his rider's request and move backwards of his own volition, becoming 'behind the bit'.

In conclusion

Although the horses should be obedient and well-trained, to give the pupils a correct feel for this work, occasionally a pupil may have a genuine problem in moving his horse backwards; he may have made a false thought or move, or the horse may feel a little unco-operative.

If the instructor tells the pupil to close his lower legs as if he is trying to make his feet meet under the horse's girth, the horse will invariably move back willingly and correctly, much to the rider's surprise and delight.

In a more difficult case, the instructor should tell the pupil to walk his horse forward to the centre or the three-quarter line, to make a quarter or a half turn on the forehand and while the horse's back is round and resilient to ask him to move backwards for one or two good steps. The rider should reward his horse with praise and patting as he steps back – later is too late.

The instructor must constantly remind his pupils that the rider and the horse must think forwards although they are moving backwards.

35 Early jumping lessons

Before instructors, or assistant-instructors under supervision, teach this subject they should revise the doctrine set out in Chapter 16, 'Riding over fences' so that they can teach it clearly and simply to their pupils.

The foundation work for jumping lessons is of great importance. It can be subdivided as follows:

1 Lecture.

2 Practical demonstrations.

3 Preparatory work.
Details of the preparations above, together with suggested content:

1 *Lecture*

The theory of the basic principles must be taught first, in the lecture room where the pupils can concentrate without the distraction of sitting on their horses, and where they can take notes for future study, reference and discussion.

Pupils should be taught the main points of the following subjects:

(a) Descriptive jumping terms, and their meanings. See pp. 177–80.
(b) The nine phases of the jump. See pp. 180–81.
(c) Equipment and safety precautions. See pp. 181–4.
(d) How the horse jumps the fence. See pp. 186–7.
(e) How the rider adapts his position and rides his horse over a fence. See pp. 187–98.
(f) Riding faults and their corrections. See pp. 198–202.
(g) Reward and discipline – including the right way to correct refusals.

These subjects must be well taught in a thorough and interesting manner, with audience-involvement and the support of visual aids. Photographs, blackboard drawings, a frieze of sketches or a loop of slow-motion film may be used, or even the instructor emulating the horse's actions with appropriate gesticulations will make a better impact than nothing but the bare theoretical facts.

2 *Practical demonstrations*

Pupils must be given the chance to understand and watch the theories they have learned being put into practice without interruption to their thinking and deliberations.

By being taken to watch more experienced riders' jumping lessons, or competitions, pupils can assimilate the facts which they have been taught in the lecture room and watch them being applied, as they spectate, quietly guided by their own instructor's mini-gesticulations and carefully rationed, whispered comments.

Ideally there should be no surplus movement or word from the gallery which might cause an interrupting influence to the class or its instructor, or to the competition where they are spectating. All comments or criticisms must be made very discreetly and tactfully or a wrong spirit could be engendered.

Novice pupils should be given opportunities to observe more experienced riders jumping before they embark on this themselves, and again later, at regular intervals during their subsequent training. At a school, the instructors' ride, loosening up their young horses over low fences in the indoor school, will provide ideal demonstrations, as here the pace will be slow and jumping should appear easy, interesting and problem-free.

The instructor should encourage his class to note:

(a) How the horse negotiates the fence, the anatomical mechanics, his footwork, actions and movement, especially the use of his head and neck, and of the hindquarters and back – and his overall co-ordination.

N.B. Here is the instructor's opportunity to instil and emphasize how important it is that the rider stays *with* and allows the horse to use himself freely, without any interference, restriction or disruption while he jumps.

(b) The horse's eye-sight, and how it affects his jumping – particularly the lack of clear and accurate vision for near-objects or obstacles. How the horse sizes up each fence as he approaches it – this is usually very clearly demonstrated by young horses jumping from a trot.

(c) The fluent variations of the rider's position and his smooth and unobtrusive influence throughout all the phases of the jump or course of jumps, as he remains in quiet control of the partnership.

(d) The improvement of the quality of the horse's gaits on the flat due to the loosening effect, and the improved forward impulsion provided by the fun and gymnastics of the jumping.

(e) The riding of the track between fences – at the instructor's discretion. This may well include transitions or easy loosening exercises taking advantage of the horses' extra impulsion and eager willingness.

(f) The ease with which the riders ride in company, looking and planning well ahead, causing neither impediment nor obstruction to each other, but instead co-operating and working as a congenial team. (Hopefully this is just how it *will* happen!)

(g) How the horses, working together, improve in confidence, steadiness and forward impulsion due to the team-spirit emanating from their riders.

(h) How the jumping part of the lesson is finished on a high note, after a comparatively short time, before there is any risk of deterioration of elation due to horses or riders being over-taxed – or bored by unnecessary, dull repetition.

The chief instructor should always bear in mind that whereas his instructors' lessons do provide excellent demonstrations for the less-experienced students and pupils, he must moderate the tone and format of his lesson to suit the audience. He must gear his explanations, instructions and question-times to suit and involve the audience. However he must never degrade himself by playing to the gallery at the expense of his instructors; he must be particularly tactful in correcting them in front of their pupils, thus he may need to reserve frank corrections for later, more private moments; the culprit will probably have read his instructor's private criticisms anyway, for often a silence can be more meaningful than a verbose comment! He should never ask new or more taxing demands in lessons which are opened to an audience; loyalty to his instructors is a most important factor.

3 *Preparatory work*

In earlier lessons over ground-poles and cavalletti, and before riding outside over undulating terrain, pupils will already have learned to check their girths and to shorten their stirrup leathers one or two holes for themselves.

They will know how to hold the mane or the short neck-strap whenever there is a chance that the horse might make an unexpected or prodigious leap, to save the horse's mouth from being pulled or 'jobbed'.

Pupils will have learned also how to make well timed and fluent adjustments to their positions as their horses negotiate the poles and natural hazards.

As soon as a pupil's confidence, balance, co-ordination and ability have been developed sufficiently, and he has control over himself and his horse, the pupil is ready to receive instruction in riding over fences.

Progression to the first jumping lesson should be so well prepared that it is hardly noticed as such by the pupils, and in this way unnecessary tension is avoided.

General considerations

Early jumping lectures, demonstrations and lessons must be kept simple. Jumping must be introduced as an easy and enjoyable exercise for both the rider and his horse, as well as one which improves the former's horsemanship and the latter's basic gaits, agility and manner of going. Jumping is also a fine gymnastic exercise, it develops co-ordination within both members of the partnership – and it is *fun*!

FIG.114   HAPPINESS   OVERFACED

In all early jumping lessons the fences must be low and inviting rather than high and alarming. The instructor should *never* risk over-facing any pupil or horse; there is no need for fences to exceed 70 cm in early jumping lessons. The chief instructor must teach his team that any instructor who raises the fences above that limit at this stage is merely revealing his own lack of training, feel and skill as an instructor.

Junior instructors or those with less experience must be supervised that they do not increase the demands unnecessarily, when they may tip the scales the wrong way with frightening ease and speed

from	to
Safe	Danger
Progress	Accident
Improvement in	Injury to horse or
riders' and horses'	rider
style	Refusals
	Loss of nerve.

Make haste slowly

The aim of early jumping lessons must be to teach the correct methods and techniques, to provide practise and correction and thus to develop confidence, natural talent, style, and ability.

As the fences will be low throughout the early jumping lessons, the variations of the balanced seat will not need to be marked or exaggerated;

smoothness and harmony must be the aims, combined with the main aim, that of jumping the fence.

If the pupils have been riding in an upright position with longer stirrup leathers, the instructor should tell them to shorten their leathers a hole or two to increase the angles of their hip-, knee- and ankle-joints and thus increase the stability, suppleness and elasticity of their positions. He should not try to teach an exaggerated forward position in these early lessons.

If novice riders are put into an entirely new position with leathers shortened suddenly six to eight holes, this places their seats farther back on their saddles and they have to make considerable compensatory movements when the horse jumps over a fence. They feel awkward, tense and unsafe, and all too often they *are* unsafe. If his horse refuses, the novice rider may well jump the fence without the horse and, his lower legs being cramped, are rendered ineffective if he has too short stirrup leathers at this stage of the game. Another serious disadvantage to the practice of teaching novice riders to jump with very short stirrup leathers before they have attained a natural feel for the work is that invariably their seats slide out when turning or following curved lines, and their hips develop a faulty twist whereby the inner hip is brought back instead of forwards. These two mistakes combine to make a really serious riding fault, and like all bad habits, once established they are very difficult to eradicate. The gravity of this fault lies in the disruptive effect it has on the rider's influence on his horse. He can no longer lead the way with his weight aids, and his sliding out upsets the horse's balance and makes the rider a very difficult burden for him to carry on the course and over the fences.

Most novice horses and riders of novice standard and later, at medium standard, will gain more from class than private lessons as the former are less concentrated on the individual and are therefore more relaxing; pupils learn to look about them naturally, they have good opportunities to learn through observing and hearing their companions' corrections as well as their own, and often a slightly competitive element is useful.

Inexperienced pupils should not be expected to ride 'hot', sticky or awkward jumpers during the early stages of their jumping careers. Balance, smoothness and harmony are essential aims for early lessons – these can only be acquired with confidence that the lessons will be SAFE and FUN.

Most novice riders, almost without exception, view the impending approach of a jumping lesson with apprehension, some are better at concealing their apprehension than others. Instructors must never think a mocking thought or show the slightest scorn over this very natural nervousness, instead they must resolve to help their pupils to overcome it. They must build up their pupils' nerve, enjoyment and ambition and foster a spirit of adventure, courage and daring which is based on and never overrides their feeling and consideration for their horses.

The military form of a drilled jumping lesson, with the class lined up by the side of the fence, has some advantages in that it provides a safe routine for controlling an unruly mob of riders or horses; it allows ample opportunity for observation and helpful criticism, and for rest in hot climates or weather, or when the riders and/or horses are not very fit. It also provides an excellent and simple means of introducing the nine phases of the jump to beginners. However, it is generally far better for the horses to be kept on the move so that they

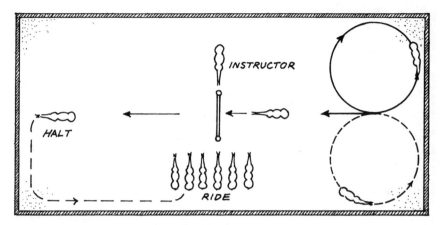

FIG.115 AN UP-DATED, FLUENT FORM OF DRILLED JUMPING LESSON

do not stiffen up, standing still, awaiting their turn in the ride, and so that neither riders nor horses lose their forward urge.

Provided that the fences are set up with forethought and planning and the instructor possesses a fund of suitable exercises, small fences can be included in the lesson in much the same way that pupils were worked over ground-poles and cavalletti.

The fences should always be set low, with a good track which is untrammelled by hazards. In a manège they should stand free from the outer track and the centre line. Preferably small fences should be built to be jumped from either side. They should have clear ground-lines, be safe and look inviting, and in early lessons they should have helpful wings to encourage the riders and the horses to go over the centre of the fence. Later, all related fences must be carefully measured to suit all the horses.

Personally I think that the practice of putting a whole class of pupils over a fence as a ride, one behind the other in quick succession is extremely dangerous. The risk of accident and injury is far too great as novice riders do not possess the quickness of thought and action to prevent their forward-going horses from stepping on to a fallen rider.

Although in the first few lessons it is best to work the class individually over one or two fences with intervening barrels or stationary members of the ride to pass on the left or right to improve their thought of the track and control between the fences, as soon as it is deemed safe it is more advantageous to work two or three pupils at the same time, on the same rein, so that they learn to think of other riders and to look up, for themselves.

If riders are left behind or in front of the horse's movement

This may be due to fear or some form of over-anxiety, causing stiffness and lack of rhythm.

They should be taken back to easier lessons – e.g.

Practising position changes as a ride, to command, and individually, when riding over ground poles at walk, trot, then canter.

333

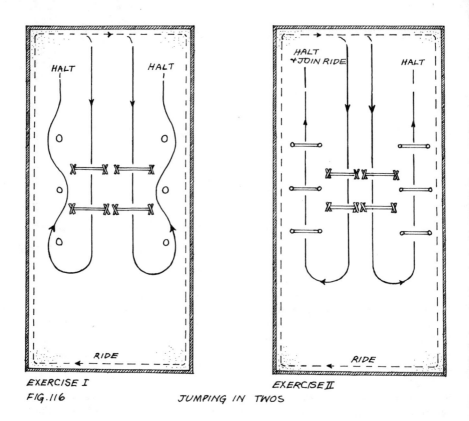

EXERCISE I

FIG.116   JUMPING IN TWOS   EXERCISE II

Practising maintaining the moderately light position as a ride, in open order, through simple serpentines at trot and on large circles and half circles at canter, to strengthen their muscles and improve the control of their position, so that it is easier for them to adjust or sustain the more forward position.

When jumping fences the pupils should be told to imagine they are jumping into a low barn or into a wood with low, overhanging branches.

They should be told to say, 'Trot' or 'Canter' out aloud, with every stride – throughout their individual rounds.

The instructor must guard against reprimanding the pupils for riding faults which are due to lack of co-ordination and harmony; they must encourage for improvement, remembering that confidence, enjoyment and ease are essential ingredients for a fluent performance – 'doing what comes naturally'.

All further faults will be seen in Part B (Doctrine).

Epilogue

36 The Rope Ladder of Responsibility

Gradually, during their course, students will have been taught the school's 'code of conduct'. They will have learned the safety rules which must be observed and adhered to all day and every day when the students are working with horses and where members of the public are accepted into the school's premises to visit or school their own horse kept at livery, to help look after them or to ride them or to have a lesson with a school horse.

By accepting these people into its premises the school automatically accepts responsibility to take reasonable care for their safety. This is quite a frightening aspect of the law, but that is how it stands and the stark reality must be faced. All staff and students must be made aware of the risks involved, and taught to keep their eyes wide open at all times for the safety and well-being of the school's horses and all its property, as well as its clients. Obviously young, temperamental or badly trained horses are a higher risk, and novice riders and children are more prone to accidents.

Instructors and students must be warned to be very guarded in their speech, if by some misfortune there is an accident. In the last few years there has been a sharp rise in the number of insurance claims and quite innocent remarks made spontaneously at the time of the accident can be picked up and used out of context to boost a claim based on a school's negligence, where no negligence occurred. Because of this, nowadays, when a school takes out an insurance cover, the principals of the school agree that no statement admitting negligence shall be made until the insurance company has been notified of the accident and the full facts thereof. As they sign this declaration on behalf of the school they must be sure that all members of that school know about it and abide by it.

EXAMINATION DAY

Examinations for students share more than one aim in common with dressage tests for horses. They both provide an assessment of practical ability. They require a substantial amount of self-confidence to allay a state of 'nerves' especially as there is always a fair chance that programmes and plans may not go completely as scheduled.

335

Both the human and the equine 'candidates' should already be working well above the standard required for the examination or test for which they are entered.

Correct and thorough training will always show through on the day.

Preparations

As well as the obvious preparatory training which the school gives to its students and at which the students have to work to their utmost for all national examinations, a special pre-examination routine should be followed by the whole school.

The examination dates should be fixed well in advance and they should be listed in the school's diary, day-book and leaflets, and on the office wall-chart. On the pre-arranged dates, the examination, the examiners and the candidates must receive top-priority treatment. There should be no counter activity within the school and even outside lessons should be reduced to a minimum for the day so that all instructors, students and pupils can concentrate on doing their best to make the day run smoothly, efficiently and happily.

All horses should look especially well-trimmed, and their shoes and saddlery should have been carefully checked. Ideally, each candidate should plait up one of the horses being used in the examination.

All areas throughout the school should look neat and tidy, clean and well cared for. Yards, tack and feed rooms, toilet facilities, the indoor school and lecture rooms must all be set fair.

Outside facilities must be organized so that all paddocks to be used are free from stock, jumping fences are unwired and enclosing fences are safe.

The 'props' required for the practical stable management and all the other sections must be put ready, also ground-poles, cavalletti and any jumps which may be needed in the school.

Detailed programmes including those for all sections of the examination should be thought out and typed. The candidates should be grouped according to their weights and measures' statistics so that they can be mounted on suitably sized horses. One programme should be affixed to the school's notice-board the day before the examination, while the others are given to senior instructors, with some programmes kept in reserve for the examiners.

For the examiners' comfort, chairs, cushions and rugs should be set out and refreshments must be provided.

Instructors and students must be reminded to look after every external candidate on the examination day. They should be looked for and welcomed immediately on arrival in the yard and should be tucked under the school's wing to help them to feel at home without delay.

External candidates who are abandoned and ignored on arrival can suffer from paralysing nervousness before they meet the examiners; it is the school's responsibility to see that this does not happen.

At least one senior instructor should be detailed to oversee the organization of the whole examination on the day, so that it runs smoothly, efficiently and calmly from all aspects – thus the main aim of assessing the candidates' merits and standard by the national examiners may be achieved.

On completion of their first career course, students should be capable of doing a good job as an *assistant instructor* or an *assistant stable manager*. They should have a reasonable amount of competence, based on good training and backed up by plenty of practical experience and developing common sense.

End of course examiners and future employers will be looking for a person who displays the following:

1 Evidence of a good grounding in equitation, horsemastership, and basic veterinary subjects, i.e. minor common ailments and injuries, when to call in the veterinary surgeon and how to collate information for him.

2 The ability to act in a supporting role in running a stable yard, and personnel management; in the taking and giving of information and messages; in taking charge of and instructing small groups of novice pupils correctly in a cheerful manner and with good control; in setting up the facilities necessary for lecture demonstrations, and in running informal, internal lectures for junior students and novice pupils. A friendly welcome and a genuine interest in all persons visiting the school, and a lively support for all the school's activities.

3 Standard of horsemanship which is good enough at least to retain the present standards of the horses he rides and which presents the right image of riding, of turnout and of conduct to his pupils.

4 Sound principles and techniques in his riding and lungeing lessons and recognition of and a seeking for and the preservation of correct form, basic gaits, a suitable tempo and balance, in all the horses he works with his pupils.

5 A knowledge of safety precautions and accident procedures in the stable-yard and when riding in or out of doors. How to conduct instructional hacks and games and to teach his pupils the Highway and Country Codes as well as pertinent rules of first aid.

6 A well-developed horse-sense enabling him to handle reasonable horses of all ages with authority and tact and consequent safety to all concerned.

7 A quick-thinking and workmanlike approach to all his duties. He should be adept, efficient and careful in the handling and use of the equipment, be it for mucking-out, grooming, clipping, travelling, hunting, jumping or showing, for simple office work, or for riding, driving or lungeing.

Before the course draws to a conclusion, the instructors should discuss the students' future with them. They should encourage them to widen their equestrian horizon to gain experience by working in racing, showing, dealing yards, a stud, a veterinary practice and so on, and to offer to teach at riding club and pony club functions. Although this list implies variety, continuity is also a vital quality to the career they have chosen. For this reason their first position must be selected with care, after which they should stick at it and do the job well; they should not hop about like a sparrow in a grainstore. Temporary application does not suit horses nor horse-owners. If it is economically viable, it is often to the student's advantage to take a post where the salary is smaller but the standard, and examination and competition results are good, especially if there is a real opportunity for sound tuition and personal advancement.

337

Students should be advised to keep their loose-leaf note books up to date when they leave the school, adding all new work covered, and to keep a personal log-book in which recommendations can be entered by their employers, and which, together with national certificates gained, will provide them with a very valuable record of their careers.

When the course finishes and the student emerges from the cocoon with the required certificate in his hand, the chief instructor should assure him of a warm welcome if ever he has the opportunity and the wish to return to the school for a fleeting visit, a refresher course, or a further long-term career – advancement course; also that he may ask for advice at any time should a problem arise.

Finally, a word for employers. *An assistant must never be expected to be more than an assistant.* Many employers imagine that wise old heads sit on inexperienced young shoulders and they make unfair demands of work and responsibilty, of capability and of control.

By passing the first, basic examination the student puts his foot on the first rung of three ladders, those of riding, of stable management and of instructing. All three ladders may be climbed separately in the years ahead, but a great deal of supervised study, tuition and practical application is necessary before the next rung on any ladder can be attained, or more responsibility and expertise may be expected from the assistant instructor or the assistant stable manager.

Every employer should welcome an employee's wish to better himself and should help him further his studies whenever opportunities arise, for there is much more ground to be covered before that assistant will be ready to sit for the next examination and thus climb up any further ladder-rungs.

Although the ex-student employee will have to be corrected in his work during his first and subsequent posts, employers must be careful to do so constructively. They have a life's career in their hands. Constant carping can extinguish a young equestrienne's flame with devastating speed and finality, whereas encouragement and praise for work well done will have a heartening and stimulating effect. The reward of going to competitions, as a respectful friend – not as a 'dog's body' – or even occasionally as a rider, will increase keenness and ability far more than a pay rise, as a rule. Horse-owners must be aware of their responsibilities. The quality of horses is improving impressively all over the world and more and more people are yearning to know how to ride properly; but well-trained, dedicated instructors are rare birds – we cannot afford to lose one of them.

This first book has only covered the basic beginnings. When it was suggested that I should make a book based on my loose-leaf file 'Talland Notebook' I thought that to transpose my working notes would be a simple matter – 'but would there be enough material to fill a book?' I wondered. I soon realized that if I tried to put everything into one book the result would be too much to digest. In a way, this was providential, for *correct beginnings* are absolutely essential and yet they are often glossed over or even omitted altogether, so I am glad I have had to limit my subject matter and hope that the reader will gain more from dealing with this vast subject in a thorough and progressive way. Once the correct foundations are laid and consolidated more advanced education can be given. Subjects such as further training of instructors and riders, competitive riding, training young horses and retraining spoilt horses – all these exciting horizons lie ahead and can be explored in due course. First, riders must learn how to ride horses naturally and well, and must be led to find the thrill of working with invisible aids, with a strong bond of love and understanding between themselves and their horses. A simple goal – but, just as 'Rome was not built in a day', learning to ride a horse takes a great deal of time, energy and effort, of *feel* and of THOUGHT.